T0385984

HABSBURGS ON THE RIO GRANDE

Habsburgs

ON THE

Rio Grande

The Rise and Fall of the

SECOND MEXICAN EMPIRE

Raymond Jonas

HARVARD UNIVERSITY PRESS
Cambridge, Massachusetts
London, England
2024

LIBRARY OF CONGRESS CATALOGING-IN-PUBLICATION DATA

Names: Jonas, Raymond, 1954– author.
Title: Habsburgs on the Rio Grande : the rise and fall of the second
Mexican Empire / Raymond Jonas.
Other titles: Second Mexican Empire, Europe, and the United States
Description: Cambridge, Massachusetts ; London, England :
Harvard University Press, 2024. | Includes bibliographical
references and index.
Identifiers: LCCN 2023034763 | ISBN 9780674258570 (hardcover)
Subjects: LCSH: Mexico—History—European intervention, 1861–1867. |
United States—History—Civil War, 1861–1865—Influence. | Mexico—
Politics and government—1861–1867.
Classification: LCC F1233 .J66 2024 | DDC 972/.07—dc23/eng/20230814
LC record available at https://lccn.loc.gov/2023034763

For Scarlett

Contents

CONTENTS

HABSBURGS ON THE RIO GRANDE

UNITE

• Chihuahua

Piedra

• Guaymas

Gulf of California

• Parral

MEXICO

Parras

• Durango

Mazatlán   San Sebastian

Zacat

Aguascaliente

• La Paz

PACIFIC OCEAN

San Blas

Lagos de Moreno

León

• Guadalajara

C

Puerto Vallarta

La Piedad

More

• Colima

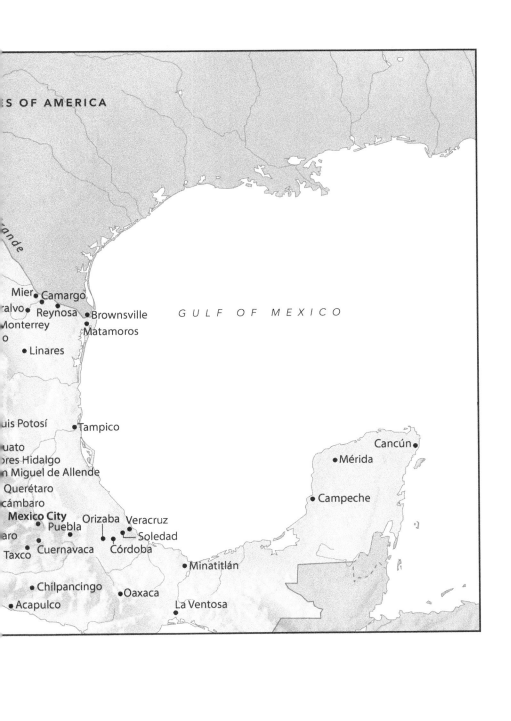

ES OF AMERICA

rande

GULF OF MEXICO

Mier • Camargo
ralvo •
• Reynosa • Brownsville
Monterrey • Matamoros
o
• Linares

uis Potosí • Tampico

uato
res Hidalgo
n Miguel de Allende
Querétaro
cámbaro
Mexico City Orizaba Veracruz
aro • Puebla
Taxco • Cuernavaca Córdoba — Soledad

• Minatitlán

• Chilpancingo • Oaxaca
• Acapulco La Ventosa

Cancún •
• Mérida

• Campeche

Prologue

AN ANTI-IMPERIALIST EMPIRE

IF THERE IS A SINGLE FIGURE who captures the contradictions of the Second Mexican Empire, it may well be Matthew Fontaine Maury. Today he is best remembered as one of the founders of modern oceanography, but in 1861 Maury chose secession. Four years later, following the collapse of the Confederate States of America, Maury, like other prominent Southerners, was coming to terms with the consequences of having served the rebellion.

As an officer in the Confederate navy, Maury had developed naval mines and electric torpedoes credited with wreaking havoc on vessels of the US Navy, but he also played a prominent role abroad, putting his name and reputation to work as a lobbyist for the Confederacy. He was in London in 1865 when the Confederate capital of Richmond fell and Robert E. Lee surrendered. In early May he left London for Havana, hoping to make his way to Galveston, Texas, to join Confederate forces still in rebellion, but by the time he reached Havana that option seemed closed. Rather than return to the United States and face an uncertain future, he chose exile. On May 24 he boarded the *Atrato,* a vessel that would carry him from Havana to Veracruz, Mexico.[1]

In choosing Mexico, Maury was following a well-trodden path. At the beginning of the Civil War many wealthy Confederate families had sought safety and comfort in Europe.[2] For those not quite so well off, migration to Mexico offered a more immediate option. When New Orleans fell in 1862, some displaced Southerners settled in Veracruz, establishing one of

Matthew Maury. *LC-USZ6-635, Prints and Photographs Division, Library of Congress.*

the earliest Confederate refugee enclaves in Mexico.[3] After Lee's surrender at Appomattox, Confederates unreconciled with defeat looked to the Trans-Mississippi West—notably Texas and the US-Mexico borderlands— as a haven from which to continue resistance. Jefferson Davis, president of the former Confederacy, attempted to join them but was apprehended on his way there. After Juneteenth and the gradual closing off of the US Southwest as a base of resistance, Confederate refugees looked beyond Texas for yet another refuge—Imperial Mexico. Created by Europeans in concert with Conservative Mexicans while the United States was distracted by its Civil War, Imperial Mexico beckoned as a final option for a base of operations, as a more durable refuge from federal power, or as a new homeland for the Southern way of life.

Upon arrival in Mexico City in June 1865, Maury took a room at the Hotel Iturbide. From there he composed an ambitious plan for the colonization of Mexico by Confederate refugees. He then sent letters—one to a prominent contact in the French navy, the other to Maximilian, the emperor of Mexico—laying out his plan for Confederate resettlement in Mexico. In his letters he lamented the collapse of the South and explained the frame of mind of his fellow Southerners. "Our cause is lost," he wrote, articulating a sentiment with a long future.

Confederate alienation was complete. He predicted a mass migration southward. "All those who can leave the country will leave," he vowed. They would build a future elsewhere: "We have had enough of republics."[4] Maury's advantage was that he was known to Mexico's emperor. Maximilian was a Habsburg archduke who, prior to accepting the throne of Imperial Mexico, had learned of Maury's oceanographic work when he served as an officer in the Austrian navy.[5] By late June Maury was meeting Maximilian and his wife, Empress Charlotte, at Chapultepec Palace, their residence on the outskirts of Mexico City. A few weeks later, obviously on familiar terms with the imperial couple, Maury wrote to friends that "Max" was an enthusiastic supporter of Maury's idea of bringing Southerners to Mexico as settlers.

As Maury's relationship with Maximilian grew, his status evolved from Confederate refugee to friend of the empire to imperial administrator. He renounced his American citizenship on September 23, 1865, committing himself fully to a new life in Mexico. Four days later Maximilian appointed Maury the imperial commissioner of colonization with a princely salary of five thousand dollars a year and a budget for office furniture, official correspondence, and a clerk.[6] By November Maury had set up the Office of Colonization in Mexico City at 13 Calle de San Juan de Letran.[7]

Maury's mission as a salaried employee of the empire was to establish Mexico as a new home for Confederates who, like Maury, could not abide the thought of living under federal rule. Maury claimed that there were two hundred thousand families across the South ready to leave, a number that implied a mass exodus, including families, households, and formerly enslaved laborers.[8] As the descendant of the great migration of persecuted Huguenots that had also brought DuPonts, Bowdoins, and Faneuils to America, Maury was convinced that Confederate migration would transform Mexico. Even before his arrival in Mexico, he had written to a sympathetic friend, "If 'Max' is wise and will encourage [my] schemes, these people will establish his empire and make him great."[9] Maury was a Virginian, so he called his planned community "New Virginia," and he set himself the task of transferring Southern households and the Southern plantation economy to Imperial Mexico.[10]

Maury offers us the perfect introduction to the Mexican Empire, because his role and advocacy as head of settler recruitment underscores the complex and sometimes contradictory ideas—anti-Yankee, anticolonial, anti-republican—that underpinned the Empire of Mexico. European promoters of the empire drew upon recent examples of Yankee continental expansion, long-standing European hostility to republics, as well as the opportunity afforded by the distraction of the US Civil War, to offer a vision of a resolute, independent Mexico prospering under the stewardship of a European ruling family. Defending Mexico against a predatory American republic may seem implausible today (or maybe it doesn't), but at the moment of its conception it surely was not. Mexico had lost half of its territory to the American republic in 1848, in the aftermath of defeat in the Mexican-American War. For Mexican Conservatives the American republic was *"la ladrona República"*—the Robber Republic—a fair summation of recent history and a view that Maximilian and Charlotte heartily embraced.[11] Resistance to Yankee aggression was not only a defining value of the Confederacy, it was one of the founding principles of the Mexican Empire.[12] Maury and Maximilian carried on a lengthy correspondence in which they had discussed the possibility of clawing back territory Mexico had lost to the United States, an ambition dear to Maximilian.[13] This convergence of shared values was part of what made Imperial Mexico a congenial environment for Confederate refugees like Maury, especially as the empire showed itself to be flexible when it came to defining race and labor. The Civil War may have settled the slavery question in North America, but part of what made Mexico an attractive resettlement option for Southern plantation owners was imperial flexibility when it came to slavery's successors—"Black peonage" and "coolie" labor.

The Mexican Empire was imbued with racial ideas from the beginning, long before the arrival of disgruntled Confederates. The "Mexican Intervention" was plotted in Parisian drawing rooms and cafés but above all at the court of French emperor Louis-Napoléon and Empress Eugénie. Mexican exiles, including José María Gutiérrez de Estrada and José Manuel Hidalgo y Esnaurrizar, lobbied the French imperial couple relentlessly, fostering the illusion of a Mexican people seething under an inept

Mexican republic and ready to greet Maximilian and the Europeans as liberators. They were supported by Michel Chevalier, a public intellectual who articulated a vision of a specifically *Latin* America. Today we use the term "Latin America" reflexively, but in 1860 it was a neologism that invoked a racially and religiously defined community—Catholic and Latin—beset by a Protestant and Anglo-Saxon aggressor, the Yankee.

The Second Mexican Empire has often been dismissed as an amusing anomaly. Seen from the United States, it was a bungled attempt to undermine the Monroe Doctrine. For many Mexicans it was "the French Intervention"—a convenient expression designed to set up the empire as a transitory regime imposed by outsiders, a parenthesis in the history of Mexico but otherwise alien to it.[14] In Europe, but also in Mexico and the United States, the empire's central figure, the Habsburg archduke Ferdinand Maximilian, was dismissed as an airhead, the inept puppet of Napoléon III.

These caricatures have had the unfortunate effect of discounting insights of enduring value. Maximilian's vision of nation building as a noble enterprise had dupery built in, to be sure, but it was durable and adaptable, ready to be repurposed long after the empire was gone whenever power needed a high-minded companion. Likewise, treating the empire as an anomaly, or as the setting of an epic struggle between democracy and autocracy, misses other useful perspectives the empire afforded. In *Habsburgs on the Rio Grande* I argue that the Second Mexican Empire offers a unique position from which to understand the globally destabilizing effect of US encroachment under the guise of Manifest Destiny.

The story of the Mexican Empire is rooted in Mexican dismay and European astonishment at unrelenting US expansion. The American republic doubled in size with the Louisiana Purchase, but what set off alarms in Europe were the annexation of Texas in 1845 and the pretext it gave the following year for an American war of aggression against Mexico. Mexico lost nearly half of its territory in 1848 under the Treaty of Guadalupe Hidalgo. Among American contemporaries, the US war against Mexico—a war of conquest led by one republic against another—put into stark relief the decay of the values of the American republic since its founding. Ethan Allen Hitchcock, an officer in Zachary Taylor's invasion force, regarded the war against Mexico as a turning point in the moral history of the American nation: "I see, the United States of America, as a people, are undergoing changes in character, and the real status and principles for which our forefathers fought are fast being lost sight of."[15] Years later another officer, Ulysses Grant, confessed, "I do not think there was ever a more wicked war than that waged by the United States on Mexico." He lamented that "as a youngster . . . I had not moral courage enough to resign."

Not only did the furious pace of US expansion seem to reveal an imperial demon gnawing at the heart of the republic, it also gave the lie to the apparently benevolent intent of the Monroe Doctrine. What had appeared, in the 1820s, to be a generous commitment to defend weak, newly independent sister states in the Americas against rapacious European monarchies was beginning to look like its opposite—the declaration of an American hinterland jealously cordoned off.[16] Europeans competed with one another in their denunciations of the insolent and "arrogant" American republic.[17] Even the cautious Otto von Bismarck would eventually chime in, dismissing the Monroe Doctrine as "a piece of international impertinence."[18] But the American challenge remained.

The discovery of gold on the American River in 1848 led to statehood for California within two years of its annexation, thus anchoring a fully continental vision of the still-young American republic. In those very same years the dream of European republicanism known as "the Springtime of the Peoples" had blossomed from Paris to Bucharest and from Warsaw to Palermo. Almost as swiftly it had been brutally suppressed by European monarchies, in what seemed like the definitive triumph of the dynastic old regime over the republican idea in Europe. Yet by the 1850s a United States confident of its destiny and continental in its reach dwarfed European states once regarded as "great," just as it espoused political ideas corrosive to dynastic rule. It embodied an aggressive republicanism Europe thought it had laid to rest.

From the perspective of Europe, in the space of two generations the American republic had transformed itself from a postcolonial backwater—distant and easily ignored—into an insolent continental powerhouse and an existential threat to Europe and European hegemony.[19] In 1815, at the end of the revolutionary and Napoleonic wars, Europe could confidently pretend to reestablish the international world order. By the 1850s this pretense was shockingly out-of-date.[20] The outbreak of the American Civil War created an opportunity to challenge and weaken the impertinent American republic, eliciting an almost reflexive sympathy—albeit private and unofficial—for the Confederacy. As the German émigré Carl Schurz recalled it, European sympathy for "the slave-holders' insurrection" was strictly pragmatic. It "sprang only from a wish . . . that this great Republic should be disrupted." The "ruling class in Great Britain," he noted, "disliked and feared the American Republic as a democracy and a rival power."[21]

Europe did not hesitate to seize the opportunity of Confederate rebellion. At the start of the Civil War, in 1861, Britain, France, and Spain claimed Mexico's nonpayment of European loans as a justification to invade Mexico; on closer inspection, this looks more like pretext than motive. Napoléon III, who took the lead in the matter as French head of state, speculated on the possibility of close cooperation between the Second Mexican Empire and the Confederate States of America in the event of Confederate victory. Indeed, within months of the allied landing in Mexico, President Lincoln and Secretary of State Seward had considered the possibility that the conquest of Mexico was only the first step in a campaign whose true aim was to turn on the United States with the support of the Confederacy.[22] At a minimum, the success of the Mexican Empire hinged on Confederate success and a United States permanently riven and weak.

Racial ideas were at the founding of the Mexican Empire. The Mexican Empire justified itself in part as the defender of a racial borderland, a strategic bulwark defending all of Latin America against a predatory Yankee power.[23] The image of embattled Latinity was the brainchild of Michel Chevalier, France's leading public intellectual of the day. His vision of a specifically *Latin* America provided the ideological underpinnings for the "Mexican Intervention"—a military invasion seconded by Mexican exiles in Europe, including José María Gutiérrez de Estrada and José Manuel Hidalgo y Esnaurrizar.

The future of this vision depended on the imperial couple whom France would sponsor to defend it—Maximilian, a Habsburg prince, and his spouse Charlotte, a cousin to Queen Victoria and sister to the notorious Leopold II of Belgium.[24] Not only did Maximilian and Charlotte readily embrace their role as defenders against Yankee aggression—including their role as champion of Indigenous tribes and peoples—they justified their place in Mexico in dynastic terms. Mexico had been under Spanish Habsburg rule when it was known as New Spain. Who better to defend Mexico against encroachments from the Yankee north than a Mexicanized Habsburg monarch, above faction and dissent? Maximilian and Charlotte imagined themselves at the head of a political *Reconquista,* uniting a Mexico beset by internal divisions and restoring it to its former glory. And what better way to revive a faltering Habsburg dynasty than to transplant it to a New World?[25] In recurring fits of romantic reverie, Maximilian imagined Habsburg Mexico surpassing Habsburg Vienna.

Such visions were cultivated by members of the Mexican exile community in Europe, who eagerly fed Maximilian's imperial vanity. Mexicans of European descent—*criollo* (creoles) in Mexican parlance—felt their authority threatened by the Mexican republic, which founded its support on a population that was overwhelmingly Indigenous and mestizo. Men of European descent—and their partners in the Catholic hierarchy—had dominated Mexico when it was New Spain. They had tried to turn Mexico's territorial loss after the US invasion to political advantage; they blamed the republic for Mexico's weakness and defeat. In their appeals to Maximilian, Gutiérrez and Hidalgo cast him in the role of savior, the embodiment of the monarchical and Catholic values that alone could secure Mexico's integrity in the face of US aggression.

They were ably seconded by leaders of the Mexican Catholic hierarchy, also in European exile. The most important among them was Monsignor Pelagio Antonio de Labastida y Dávalos, bishop of Puebla and Tlaxcala, who had left Mexico for exile in Rome in protest over the Reform Laws of the Mexican republic. The Reform had nationalized and sold Church lands in an effort to broaden land ownership, to revitalize the Mexican economy, and, not incidentally, to break the power of the Catholic Church.[26] From his European exile, Labastida kept alive the hope that the wealth and power of the Catholic Church in Mexico might be restored. To that end he played a key role in persuading Maximilian and Charlotte to accept the imperial throne. Labastida would also play a role in bringing about the collapse of the empire. Once Maximilian and Charlotte were in Mexico and it became clear that they would not undo the nationalizations of the republic, Labastida and the Church turned on the empire, fatally weakening it.

The Second Mexican Empire began in 1861 with an invasion led by France, Britain, and Spain. By the time these forces reached Mexico, the Austrian and Belgian monarchies were laying the groundwork for volunteer forces that would support their respective ruling families in the New World. Across Europe, young men were drawn by the offer of pay, transport to the Americas, and farmland in Mexico. At its height, the empire of Maximilian and Charlotte was supported by troops drawn from Austria, Baden, Basilicata, Belgium, Bohemia, Calabria, Catalonia, Croatia, France, Hungary, Poland, Portugal, Prussia, Saxony, Serbia, Silesia, Slovakia, Slovenia, Spain, Ukraine, Venezia, Wallachia, Westphalia, and Württemberg, as well as Mexico itself. When the army of the empire capitulated, Mexicans could claim, with some justice, that they had "defeated all of Europe."

Partisans of the empire justified their actions as having been undertaken *on behalf of* Mexico. Though they came as conquerors, they claimed the role of liberators. In doing so, they borrowed from the French Revolution, whose armies invaded the Low Countries, the Rhineland, and Italy, claiming to set them free. This was what empire in a democratic age would mean: it would have to justify itself in terms consistent with national sovereignty, to recast domination as liberation. The Mexican Empire added a wrinkle. Not only did it claim to liberate Mexico and Mexicans from the tyranny, corruption, and ineptitude of the Mexican republic; it claimed to do so as an exercise in what the twentieth century would call nation building. That is, it claimed for itself no higher object than to serve the people of Mexico by rescuing them from an unacceptable fate.

Maximilian inhabited the role of savior with absolute conviction. Men in European dynastic families are born to rule. They are raised within a culture in which the exercise of power is a noble obligation, and they are prepared for it minutely from childhood. But when Maximilian came of age, he was frustrated by the inadequacy of the available outlets for his talent and ambition. Learned and sophisticated in ways his older brother, Franz Joseph, was not, mere birth order meant that Maximilian's patently superior abilities would be wasted. Thrones in Greece and Poland offered only meager consolation. Instead, egged on by Mexican émigrés, Maximilian and Charlotte crafted a vision of Mexico as the site of Habsburg revival. Prior to their departure for Mexico, they planned to decorate their home near Trieste with scenes depicting their grandiose vision, commissioning frescos of Maximilian in dynastic triumph. So enthralled were they that they brushed aside warnings that their dreams were based on a false premise—there simply was no monarchist majority in Mexico seething in resentment under republican rule and eager to welcome them. This was painfully evident in 1862 after Mexico's victory at Puebla on May 5—chastened French officials in Mexico said as much—but proponents of the empire revived the fantasy by asserting that the problem was the absence of a monarch. Mexico's monarchist majority would manifest itself confidently only in the presence of the monarchs themselves—but the monarchs were still in Europe. Maximilian and Charlotte, utterly captivated by their vision of a revived Habsburg Mexico, were only too eager to be deceived. Once in Mexico, even as their preferred narrative succumbed to reality, they grasped at quick fixes—a concordat, an embrace of Indigenous Mexicans, an infusion of Confederate settlers, a rapprochement with Juárez. None sufficed. None could.

Imperial Mexico was opportunistic; it could only have taken place against the background of the American Civil War, which distracted an otherwise vigilant nation. Moreover, support for the invasion traded on deepening European alarm at the rapid growth and outsize scale of the American republic, which posed a threat to the European old regime on both ideological and geopolitical grounds. In *Habsburgs on the Rio Grande* I offer a new, global perspective on Manifest Destiny. By viewing events from a position of triangulation above conventional national histories, we can witness the globally destabilizing effects of American continental expansion, especially in the eyes of Europeans who were increasingly seduced by a racial understanding of the world. According to an emerging racial geopolitics, US expansion raised the specter of Europe being trapped between the "Anglo-Saxon" American colossus and Slavic Russia, the sleeping giant, whose population and resources would, in due course, surely allow it to tower over Europe.[27] If the future belonged to power organized on a continental scale, Europeans would have to reassess their options. France might position itself as the champion of Latinity. For lesser European powers, remaining relevant might mean following the example of Britain—gaining scale by pursuing empire beyond Europe.[28] Or it might mean organizing a preemptive strike for hegemonic power in Europe, the kind of move made by Imperial Germany in 1914.[29] By the end of the century, the academy was being colonized by racial geopolitics.[30] In his inaugural lecture in political economy at the University of Freiburg, Max Weber warned of an encroaching "Slavic race" advancing by way of Poland—a racial borderland where Germanic peoples were losing "an unfolding process of selection."[31] In *Habsburgs on the Rio Grande* I shed new light on two key subsequent events—the global scramble for empire, and the Great War—by exposing how US expansion radically shifted perceptions of the scale of power well beyond its borders.

I

Rescuing the Latin Race

JOSÉ MARÍA GUTIÉRREZ DE ESTRADA was born Mexican, but his
soul was European. It was a paradox that fit his heritage, for Gutiérrez
Estrada, although born in Campeche and educated in Mexico City, was
of European descent and he embodied the reflexive *criollo* preference for
things European. This accumulated cultural capital, embraced as heritage and deployed as social snobbery, marked Mexicans of Spanish descent, setting them apart from the Indigenous majority of Mexico.[1] Because
heritage mapped easily to the new scientific concept of race and the hierarchy race sustained, heritage was worth defending.

Gutiérrez was barely twenty-eight years old in 1828 when President
Guadalupe Victoria sent him to Europe to cultivate relations there. Europe
in the 1820s was recovering from the traumas of the French Revolution
of 1789, brought to a close in 1815 by the defeat of Napoléon Bonaparte.[2]
During those years, revolutionary France had portrayed its expansion
from Madrid to Moscow as a war of liberation that would free the peoples
of Europe from the despotism of kings. Aggressive republicanism toppled
monarchs and seized church property. Even the pope was forced into exile,
prodded by French bayonets.

The allied monarchs who had defeated France resolved to combat any
attempt to revive republican ideals. In a joint statement, the kings of Austria, Prussia, and Russia announced a Holy Alliance in 1815, by which they
affirmed themselves rulers of "three branches" of a single "Christian
nation." In their declared culture war, they defined Europe in terms of
Christian nationalism and as a haven for monarchical ideas. In the
1820s these principles were put to work combatting liberalism in Spain

José María Gutiérrez de Estrada. *ÖNB/Wien PORT_00011186_01.*

and driving Islam and the Ottomans from Greece. For Latin America, the Holy Alliance carried the threat of the return of Spanish rule under the restored Bourbon Ferdinand VII.[3]

None of this was objectionable to Gutiérrez, who was "fanatical" in his Catholicism and "reactionary . . . to the depths of his being." When he returned to Mexico from Europe in 1832, he arrived as a confirmed Europhile. He brought wealth to wealth when he married into a prominent *criollo* family from Mexico City.[4]

Gutiérrez returned just in time to witness the coming apart of Mexico, initiated by Anglo settlers in Texas who chafed under Mexican rule. Mexico had encouraged Anglo settlement in Texas, on the assumption that a large settler population would bring economic growth and stability.[5]

For Mexico, the main conditions for settlers were that they become citizens of Mexico and abide by Mexican law, including laws against slavery.[6] But at very high levels within the US government, settlement was already seen as prelude to secession and annexation. In 1825 the US minister to Mexico, Joel Poinsett, wrote to Henry Clay of the importance of establishing "a hardy race of white settlers" in Texas, with a clear view to establishing facts on the ground.[7] As for the Anglo settlers themselves, they wanted to use cheap Texas land to get rich growing cotton, following the examples of Mississippi, Alabama, and Louisiana. The catch was that, apart from a few farms producing cotton with free labor, cultivating cotton on that wealth-producing scale implied the use of enslaved labor. When, in 1828, the government of Mexico sent General Manuel de Mier y Terán on an inspection tour of what was then called Tejas, he found ample evidence of the use of enslaved labor.[8] His report prompted the Mexican congress to adopt a law in 1830 aimed at reasserting authority in Texas. At the urging of Lucas Alamán, a close associate of Terán, the Mexican legislature passed a law forbidding new American settlements. To no avail. As Stephen Austin noted two years later, settlers in Texas wanted "negros to make cotton to buy more negros"—a dynamic that scorned Mexican law and undermined Mexican sovereignty. Terán drew the inevitable conclusion: Mexico would lose Texas not to "armies, battles, or invasions" but to the steady accumulation of facts on the ground—the relentless, piecemeal annexations of settlers.[9] In July 1832, in a moment of deep despair, he took his own life.

Terán's despair proved prescient. In October 1835 Texas seceded from Mexico, a move that eerily prefigured the secession of the slave states of the southern United States twenty-five years later.[10] The Texas declaration of independence of March 1836 duly echoed the language of 1776, defending "life, liberty, and property" and professing hatred of tyranny. But when work began on a constitution for the Republic of Texas, a more complex picture emerged. The new constitution, with its specific provisions for "free white persons" and its exclusions of "Africans, the descendants of Africans, and Indians," made it clear that the Republic of Texas would be a white man's republic.[11]

Equal alarm greeted the possibility that an independent Texas would be drawn into the United States, which only exacerbated fears that nothing could halt the westward drive of the American republic.[12] Both Britain and France cultivated relations with the independent Republic of Texas in order to prevent US annexation. Their geopolitical vision was convergent with economic interest. The processing of cotton in places like Manchester (England), Rouen and Roubaix (France), and Ghent (Belgium) had driven industrialization in Europe.[13] Cotton textiles had been a motor of wealth in Europe for two generations, but by midcentury the source of raw materials was dangerously concentrated. As much as 90 percent of European cotton came from the American South.[14] Textile mills on either side of the Channel would welcome cotton from independent Texas, which would reduce their dependence on US supply. Britain had a particular interest in such an outcome. British import of raw cotton from the southern US stood in glaring contradiction with Britain's moral leadership in the fight against slavery. Some British diplomats persuaded themselves, against all odds, that the young Texas republic would abolish slavery. Such an improbable move might even spark an emancipation movement that would roll across the US South, yielding a source of free-labor cotton for British mills.[15]

France, meanwhile, tended to see itself in competition with Britain in cultivating relations with the Texan republic. France's representative, Alphonse Dubois de Saligny, urged Paris to help stabilize independent Texas by offering recognition. Such a move would both prevent Mexico from taking Texas back and stymie US annexation.[16] Both Britain and France had profound geopolitical concerns that extended well beyond Texas.[17] "Texas," noted William Kennedy, British consul at Galveston, "is the Key to Mexico"—a view Saligny independently endorsed.[18]

In the end, both Britain and France failed. The United States annexed Texas in 1845. Short of war, which they were unwilling to countenance, Britain and France were powerless to prevent this new extension of the American republic. What was more ominous for the future, Texas had perfected a model of imperial expansion seemingly compatible with the democratic values of the age. Under this form of democratic colonialism, the rhetorical arsenal of freedom and independence provided the moral underpinnings for a modular, "hands-off" territorial expansion. Settlers established "facts on the ground" in the form of farms and ranches, then used their numbers to pursue independence, annexation, and statehood. This was imperial expansion accomplished by unimpeachably democratic means.

Texas was a catastrophic loss for all Mexican patriots.[19] For someone like Gutiérrez, it was a political weapon to be used to expose the supposed weaknesses of the Republic of Mexico. In 1840 Gutiérrez produced an incendiary document—effectively an open letter to President Anastasio

Bustamente—in which he expressed a fundamentally disenchanted out-look, blaming the republic for the misfortunes of Mexico since independence, including the loss of Texas.[20] He warned that unless something was done, the American Stars and Stripes would fly over Mexico City and Protestant services would be offered in the national cathedral.[21] Gutiérrez insisted on seeing the world for what it was, not as one might wish it to be, and argued that Mexico simply lacked the men of quality needed for republican self-rule. His critique implicitly criticized Mexico's Indigenous peoples, who were the vast majority of the population.[22] It followed from Gutiérrez's remarks that republican politics were the politics of illusion. The politics of monarchy were the politics of realism.[23]

Critical response was swift.[24] General José María Tornel, pretending to speak for an important constituency—the military—asked whether Gutiérrez had a "monarchist protuberance" in his brain.[25] More ominously, Gabriel Valencia, another critic, invoked a law that penalized speech or writings calling into question the independence of Mexico. Punishment included the death penalty.[26] Gutiérrez understood that his pamphlet was effectively his valedictory; he left Mexico for Europe, never to return.[27]

Leaving didn't mean that Gutiérrez stopped thinking about Mexico. On the contrary, Mexico became a place in the imagination, a place for Gutiérrez to reflect, using contemporary European politics as a compass and citing European ideologues as authorities. Given his Europhile convictions, for him Europe represented the apex of civilization; Europe charted the path of ascent that others would follow. Gutiérrez masked his hostility to republics behind a quote from the French royalist author and diplomat François-René Chateaubriand to the effect that while republics represented the future of the world, for Europe their time "had yet to arrive." If Europe wasn't ready for a republic, how could Mexico be? Behind this deference to some future republican moment lay a deeper, intransigent assertion: only monarchy was consonant with Mexico's past and its present. To be sure, Mexico's political culture, even after independence, bore the imprint of its colonial past, but Gutiérrez was espousing a kind of originalism of national political culture in which the colonial past was an inescapable deadweight. Even after independence, Mexico's institutions, culture, and habits of mind argued in favor of monarchy.[28]

Subsequent events only deepened Gutiérrez's convictions. John Quincy Adams had warned that the annexation of Texas would "entangle the United States in a needless war with Mexico."[29] Indeed, the needless war

Adams feared was easily engineered. Mexico regarded Texas as a lost province, its secession illegal, and its annexation by the US illegitimate, although Mexico was in no position to contest any of it. The Nueces River had been the Texas border when it was a province of Mexico, but the US insisted on the Rio Grande, 150 miles to the south, as the limit of the newly annexed state and thus the new boundary between the two countries.[30] President Polk forced the point. He ordered General Zachary Taylor to lead his forces across the Nueces River, to seek confrontation with Mexican forces near the Rio Grande, while a squadron of ten US Navy vessels cruised coastal waters between Galveston and Veracruz.[31] Just one year after annexation, the US provoked war with Mexico.

Mexican defeat in the war of 1846–1848 led to catastrophic losses. Arizona, California, Nevada, New Mexico, and Utah became US possessions; in all, Mexico lost nearly half of its territory to the American republic. It might have been worse.[32] The possibility that the US might absorb all of Mexico was rejected not out of an awakened respect for Mexican sovereignty but owing to US doubts about its ability to absorb the Mexican population.[33] The Polk administration drew back, pinned in place by anti-Catholic prejudice. Religion and the density of Mexico's Indigenous populations were poison pills that would prevent the successful absorption of Mexico. Only prudence grounded in religious and racial bigotry saved the rump of Mexico from annexation.[34]

Gutiérrez followed these events from Europe, where he had established himself in the papal city of Rome. He had suffered the loss of his wife but had since remarried. His new European bride brought with her a considerable fortune, which included the splendid Palazzo Maffei Marescotti on the Via della Pigna. The newlyweds made the palazzo their home.[35] An ordinary person might have decided to suffer self-exile in idle splendor, but Gutiérrez was not ordinary. Instead he used his prominent position in Roman society to court the ruling families of Europe and to seek out partners to support his scheme to establish a Mexican monarchy.[36] He didn't have to look far.

In 1850 Gutiérrez connected with José Manuel Hidalgo y Esnaurrizar.[37] They formed an enduring partnership based upon their *criollo* heritage—Hidalgo was descended from Andalusian nobility—and their shared vision of a monarchist future for Mexico.[38] Hidalgo had been posted to London after the war with the United States. He made his way to Rome as part of the delegation representing Mexico to the Holy See, arriving in the Eternal City in 1848, just as a liberal revolutionary tide was sweeping across Europe. For the first time since 1798, the world was presented with the humiliating spectacle of a pope driven from the capital of the papacy. A revolutionary Roman Republic had come to power, forcing Pope Pius IX to flee to Gaeta, where he enjoyed the protection of Ferdinand II, King of Naples. Hidalgo joined the traumatized pope in Gaeta, along with other diplomatic representatives who had followed him into exile.[39]

The counterrevolutionary rebound to 1848 was profound; it created an environment much more congenial to the ideas of men like Gutiérrez and Hidalgo. The reputation of Pope Pius prior to 1848 was that of a "liberal" pope, but the shock of revolution changed that. Although the Roman Republic was put down by armed force and papal authority was restored, Pius and the papal entourage drew the most reactionary conclusions from the revolutions of 1848—specifically, that the Revolution of 1789, the rebellion against God and King, remained a threat.[40] It seemed to echo the events from the New World, where aggressive Yankee republicanism had pushed Mexico to the brink. This was the world Gutiérrez and Hidalgo now inhabited, a world where only the constant vigilance of the defenders of religion and monarchy would keep revolution at bay.

Gutiérrez and Hidalgo also encountered new ideas—racial ideas—that reinforced their thinking about religion, Mexico, and monarchy. Already by the 1840s Michel Chevalier was setting out the work that would make his reputation as one of the leading public intellectuals of the day. Chevalier's 1851 book, simply titled *Mexico* (*Le Mexique*) stated its ambition confidently on the first page: Mexico is "comfortably inhabitable by the white race." He proceeded to lay out the geological, strategic, and hydrological features that made Mexico an attractive destination for white settlement and thus an attractive target for US expansion.[41] Chevalier's vision for Mexico built upon insights elaborated during a lengthy stay in the United States in the 1830s, by which time he already imagined—with dread—a United States stretching "from sea to sea."[42]

By laying out the promise of Mexico for white settlers, Chevalier was not promoting US expansion at Mexico's expense.[43] On the contrary, he was sounding the alarm about the ease with which US westward expansion—having reached the practical limit of the Pacific—could turn the corner and continue southward. Alexis de Tocqueville had offered such a perspective nearly two decades earlier in his *Democracy in America* (1835), in which he noted that "the Spaniards and the Anglo-Americans are . . . the only two races which divide the possession of the New World."

Michel Chevalier, carte de visite. *Reproduction © National Portrait Gallery.*

Though the boundary separating them was clearly drawn, "I do not doubt that [the Anglo-Americans] will shortly infringe this arrangement."[44]

Tocqueville's words had been prophetic. The northeast Mexican state of Texas seceded from Mexico the year *Democracy in America* went to press. Ten years later Texas was annexed to the United States.[45] The modularity of the American republic—territories are settled, populated, and annexed—could be repeated infinitely and made it possible for the republic to grow, if not exactly by stealth, then at least without overt military conquest.[46] Certainly, settlement involved violence, but it need not rise to the level of state-to-state violence. State-to-state violence remained an option, however, as President Polk's use of a border dispute in the newly annexed Texas had shown. There seemed to be no limit to America's territorial ambition.[47]

Chevalier's critique identified what he saw as a specious parallelism between the United States and Mexico in which these two former European colonies would, having secured their independence, prosper alongside one another as sister republics.[48] Instead, the story of the two newly independent countries sharply diverged. Why? Chevalier set forth an argument based upon a racial theory whereby Mexico, inhabited by a people "of Latin origin" and "essentially Catholic," faced a trajectory different from that of Americans, a people "of Germanic origin and of protestant religion." Chevalier argued that it was foolish to expect peoples of such profound difference to thrive under the same political system. Politics needed to be understood through the lens of race. While the republican idea had served the expansion of American power, he argued, it had only brought weakness to Mexico, thus providing a perfect example of the racial maladaptation of a political system. Unless something could be done, Mexico's fate seemed clear: left at the mercy of the United States, Mexico would undergo "an enslavement" of the kind already experienced by Indians and those of mixed heritage who were dominated by whites.[49]

Chevalier was articulating the view that political forms, in order to thrive, must be grounded in race. He was also formulating a racial geopolitics. We tend to think of geopolitics—the role of geography in calculations of politics and power—as a late nineteenth-century formulation. The concept is associated with the turn-of-the-century work of Alfred Thayer Mahan, but sometimes a concept can exist for years before a term is coined to express it.[50] The word itself did not appear until the twentieth century, and even then it entered the world as a hybrid, as *geo-politics*—a neologism whose hyphenation betrayed its complicated birth.

In fact, Chevalier's worries for the future of Mexico and "the Latin race" were the mirror image of racially informed expansionist ideas in circulation in the United States at the time of Chevalier's sojourn. By the time of the Texas secession from Mexico, racial geopolitics were assuming the form of an idea taken as given, if not quite yet as common sense. In the aftermath of the secession of Texas from Mexico, James Pinckney Henderson, the diplomatic representative for the new Republic of Texas, had sought to woo British Prime Minister Lord Palmerston—and with him, Britain—in Texas's favor. Henderson cast the Texas secession as an inevitable step in the extension of "Anglo Saxon Blood" at the expense of a "weak, ignorant, and degraded" race.[51] By the time of the Mexican-American War, Sam Houston was expressing an expansive vision of the destiny of the "Anglo Saxon race"—a vision that encompassed the entire hemisphere.[52] The presence of the Sabine River in Texas lent itself to crude references to Roman antiquity, the rape of the Sabines, and sexual conquest. With a wink and a leer, Houston invited an audience of men in New York City to ponder the "annexation" of "señoritas."[53] So while Chevalier's views on race were not particularly new, at least from an American perspective, he certainly served as a relay and a warning for ideas that were becoming commonplace in the United States as American eyes turned westward and southward.

American triumph in the war with Mexico did nothing to quell such visions—or nightmares. Mexican Liberal Manuel Crescencio Rejón warned that Anglo-Americans "will inundate us."[54] John Forsyth, US minister to Mexico, could write about the United States and Mexico with an air of inevitability. In a letter he wrote to US secretary of state Lewis Cass while stationed in Mexico City, Forsyth proclaimed in candid terms the irresistible power of the white race. "I believe in the teachings of experience and history," he wrote, "and that our race, I hope our institutions—are to spread over this continent and that the hybrid races of the West, must succumb to, and fade away before the superior energies of the white man."[55]

Chevalier did not dispute such racial visions of history, or even this vision of hybridity as a source of debility rather than strength; he merely questioned the confident outcome predicted by the likes of Forsyth. Several contemporaries agreed with Chevalier. The answer was not to succumb to an imagined inevitable outcome; the answer was to resist. As Chevalier was completing his manuscript, Hippolyte du Pasquier de Dommartin was in northern Mexico, seeking to implement a plan of defense. Pasquier wanted territorial concessions in Chihuahua and Sonora. For what purpose? To construct a border wall to protect Mexico against an "American invasion."[56]

What was to be done? The answer was obvious. Alone, Mexico was helpless to defend itself. France had a key role to play. France, Chevalier wrote, is "at the head of the Latin group; she is its protectress."[57] Chevalier was charging France with a heavy burden—that of being the defender of the Latin race. But for all the bold talk about defending Mexico and the Latin race, such rhetoric passed over an obvious point. Mexico was "Latin" in only the very narrowest sense. Only if one took *criollo* Spanish-heritage figures like Gutiérrez as the paragon of Mexican-ness would such a concept hold true. An aggressive defense of Latin Mexico ignored most of Mexico's population, its Indigenous and mestizo peoples. Yet the core idea remained—France had a role, a duty, to protect Latin peoples against Anglo-Saxon aggression.

Thus it was that the dream of a monarchy for Mexico traveled by way of Europe.[58] Conservative refugees from the Mexican republic, like Gutiérrez, welcomed the support of Michel Chevalier. Not only did Chevalier recognize the threat of the American republic to Mexico, he gave this struggle a sophisticated theoretical veneer that made monarchy organically "Latin" and made "Latin" synonymous with the historical complexity of Mexico.[59] In time, Emperor Maximilian would embrace this paradoxical vision, somehow imagining himself *both* as guardian of Mexico's Indigenous *and* as the defender of the Latin race—an idea he professed would be "engraved in gold letters in the pages of history."[60]

Chevalier articulated an increasingly pervasive view of the United States of America as an existential threat to the European old regime on both ideological and geopolitical grounds.[61] Westward expansion of the American republic under the guise of Manifest Destiny mirrored the aggressive expansion of the French republic a generation earlier, when it menaced monarchies from Madrid to Moscow. After the Treaty of Guadalupe Hidalgo annexed half of Mexico to the United States, the Imperial Republic threatened not just the monarchical ideal, but the very scale of power. From the perspective of Old Europe, the Imperial Republic across the Atlantic was the harbinger of an era of sovereignty on a continental scale. Alexis de Tocqueville had already noted in 1835 that the "Anglo-American republic" had grown "as rapidly as a man passing from birth and infancy to maturity in the course of thirty years." This growth put the United States on a footing equaled globally only by Russia. "Both grew in obscurity, and while humanity's gaze was focused elsewhere, they abruptly vaulted to the first rank among nations," he noted. From their dominant positions, each was now destined "some day to sway the destinies of half the globe."[62]

In German-speaking Europe, political economist Friedrich List was one of the earliest proponents of such geopolitical thinking. As he urged the unity of German-speaking peoples in Central Europe—a vision fully realized only in 1870—he warned of Europe being crushed between two continental giants, Russia and the United States.[63] When Russia sought to push southward against the Ottoman Empire, Britain and France acted in unison to block Russian aggression, waging war in Crimea between 1853 and 1856, handing Russia a serious rebuke. Was it now time to stage a similar intervention against the American colossus?[64]

Chevalier's radical vision of the world divided—of competitive border-lands at once racial and cultural—was a grand vision.[65] It would eventually attract the admiration of the French poet Alphonse de Lamartine, who called this vision "sublime" as he denounced the Monroe Doctrine. Chevalier's dark vision of American hegemony was ready-made to be exploited by Mexican Conservatives who recognized a strategic alignment between European anxieties about the American republic and their own deep opposition to the Republic of Mexico. Mexico was the principal victim of "the Robber Republic"—the United States. Chevalier wed the image of Mexican victimhood to a vision of a specifically *Latin* America beset by a nimble aggressor, the Protestant and Anglo-Saxon Yankee.[66]

It turned out to be a compelling vision for Napoléon III and Eugénie, the emperor and empress of France, who eagerly embraced the role of champions of a besieged Latinity and resolved to rally Europe against an American republic that, if left unchecked, threatened European hegemony.[67] "Europe must form a league against the United States," urged Eugénie.[68] Together they sought an opportunity to intervene to block the Yankee republic.

That opportunity presented itself in 1860 when a convergence of events in Mexico and the United States created an opening. In December 1860, following the election of Abraham Lincoln as US president, South Carolina voted to secede. It was soon followed by the secession of other Southern US states. The year 1860 was decisive for Mexico, too, when its own civil war—the War of Reform—entered its final stage. The US invasion of Mexico in 1846, followed by Mexico's defeat and the devastating territorial loss in the 1848 Treaty of Guadalupe Hidalgo, had had a profoundly destabilizing effect, inviting mutual recrimination among Mexicans and eventually civil war. In the febrile state induced by defeat and humiliation, Mexican Conservatives argued that Mexico's mistake had been to ape the United States in adopting republican institutions— "[throwing] ourselves into the arms of the United States, to imitate servilely its institutions"—when monarchy better suited Mexico's history, culture, and religion.[69] Political differences weren't so much a matter of degree as of fundamental forms, of republic versus monarchy. General Antonio López de Santa Anna, who had been a central figure in post-independence Mexico, returned to power in 1853 as president and as an ally of the Catholic Church, patron of a Conservative vision of Mexico. He gave his personal backing to Gutiérrez, already a longtime resident of Europe, to visit courts of Paris, London, and Vienna to pursue his vision of establishing a monarchy in Mexico with a European ruling family at its head. The initiative came to an end when Liberal forces rallied, entered Mexico City, and forced López de Santa Anna from power in 1855.

Mexican Liberals began to implement a progressive vision for Mexico, one that required coming to terms with Mexico's colonial past. This involved breaking the power of the Catholic Church, starting with its cultural power (by instituting a public alternative to Catholic schools) and its control over the great moments of life (by requiring civil registration of birth and marriage), and culminating in the nationalization of Church properties, in order to break the Church's stranglehold on national wealth in land. The Constitution of 1857 and the Reform Laws incarnated these values but ignited the War of Reform, a renewed civil war with rival governments and armies.[70] Liberals rallied around Benito Juárez, who became president in 1858 according to the laws of succession when the president of the Mexican republic resigned.

Benito Juárez. *Palacio Nacional, Mexico City*. Photo: *R. Jonas*.

Mexican Conservatives rallied around Miguel Miramón, a general. At the level of symbols, it was a perfect matchup: Juárez, the Zapotec Indian, representing a progressive, inclusive vision of Mexico against Miramón, a *criollo* (with French and Spanish ancestors) who incarnated the coalition of Church and army.[71] Starved for cash, Miramón made two desperate moves. In what has to be a record for predatory lending, a Swiss banking house advanced Miramón some one million dollars in exchange for fifteen million dollars in new debt.[72] Then, in December 1860, Miramón ordered a break-in at the British Legation at 11 Calle de Capuchinas in Mexico City.

Jésus Corral, *Miguel Miramón, 1859. Museo Nacional de Historia, Castillo de Chapultepec. Photo: R. Jonas.*

It was a bold move, to say the least, but the prospect of free money was too much to resist. The British Legation was holding more than six hundred thousand dollars in Mexican customs revenue earmarked for British investors. Claiming that the money rightly belonged to the Mexican state, Miramón sent an armed contingent to the British Legation. The money was behind a door that was locked and sealed, so Miramón sent along a carpenter and a locksmith. If the room could be opened but the door left intact, it could be claimed that the funds had been retrieved without breaking the seal.[73] The larger problem, of course, was that the break-in violated diplomatic norms. It also demolished the argument that Conservatives were the best guardians of property and good order in Mexico.

Meanwhile, President Juárez was facing money problems, too. For most of 1859 his minister of foreign affairs, Melchor Ocampo, had been negotiating a treaty with the United States that would have transferred transit rights and other benefits to the United States in exchange for four million dollars.[74] Although the US Senate ultimately failed to ratify the treaty, the willingness of the Juárez government to sell off national assets was used to buttress the claims of his enemies that only monarchy, not the republic, could defend Mexico against a predatory Yankee republic bent on expansion.[75]

Forces loyal to Miramón drove Juárez and his government out of the capital and to refuge in Veracruz—a republican citadel and a source of customs revenue. In March 1860, forces commanded by Miramón were again taking the fight to Juárez. They moved against Veracruz, hoping to drive Juárez and his government into the sea. Miramón's forces were repulsed, and by the end of the year the tables had turned—supporters of the republic were advancing on Mexico City. In December 1860 Juárist general Jesús González Ortega defeated Miramón at Calpulalpan, northeast of the capital.[76] Soon Miramón was a fugitive on horseback, making his way to the coast, at one point escaping pursuers only by tumbling—horse and rider—down a steep ravine.[77] He had managed to slip away at Veracruz, apparently with the connivance of the French; he boarded the French vessel *Mercure* in the company of a French diplomat.[78] Miramón's defeat and departure closed out the War of Reform, but it didn't bring peace. Soon Miramón was in Madrid, lobbying for European intervention. His defeat had meant only the closing of one chapter of the civil war in Mexico and the opening of another.

2

The Vicar of Cranborne

MEXICAN CONSERVATIVES WEREN'T the only ones to argue that the future of Mexico was monarchical. By the 1860s, global investors were increasingly impatient with the declining value of their Mexican investments. They began to lobby for political change.

Mexico had issued its first bonds in 1824, three years after securing its independence.[1] European investor interest was keen. During the Napoleonic wars, bond investors had grown accustomed to bonds with a return of 5 percent. As the Napoleonic wars ended, British state borrowing requirements fell, taking with them the 5 percent returns investors had come to expect. As British bonds trended toward 3 percent after Waterloo, overseas bonds yielding 5 and 6 percent seemed compelling, especially for men and women looking for reliable income to support them in retirement. Investors large and small lined up to invest in newly independent states in the Americas, the "emerging markets" of the mid-nineteenth century. Mexico, with its legendary silver mines, seemed especially safe and attractive. Mary Robertson of Folkestone became a bondholder at £800. Richard Cowan of Bathwick Priory was good for £1,500. Mary Catchpole and Mary Legrey of Piccadilly each scraped together £200.[2]

In the years to follow, reality set in. It turned out that a 5 percent yield on Mexican bonds was not the same as 5 percent British, especially when dividend payments became irregular or stopped altogether. In February 1861, Reverend John Hemery Carnegie, the vicar of Cranborne, took up his pen in frustration. Reverend Carnegie explained to British foreign secretary Lord John Russell that he had agreed to a reduction of interest on his Mexican bonds in exchange for a promise that dividends would resume, yet they had not. Meanwhile, his legal costs were mounting.[3]

Investors like Mary Catchpole and the vicar of Cranborne depended on income from bond earnings to make ends meet. Now they no longer had that stream of earnings; worse, they began to doubt that they would ever even see their principal returned to them. As taxpayers, they argued, they were entitled to the assistance of the British government. They banded together to form The Committee of Mexican Bondholders, aiming to serve as lobbyists in support of their own cause. They saw a solution. Customs duties, notably those imposed at Veracruz, were the main source of revenue for the government of Mexico. One way to reassure investors would be to dedicate a portion of that revenue stream to the payment of dividends. It was an effective strategy, if it could be enforced. When General Anastasio Bustamente became president in 1830, his government sought to reassure investors by promising to dedicate one-eighth of customs revenues (12.5 percent) to the repayment of bondholders. When Antonio López de Santa Anna launched his rebellion against Bustamente two years later, he began, notably, by seizing Veracruz, where most revenues were collected. Once installed in power, Santa Anna's government reduced the allocation of customs revenue to investors to a mere 6 percent.[4]

In addition to customs revenues, land figured large in Mexican attempts to appease British investors. Cash was scarce in Mexico; land was not. Mexico encouraged British bondholders to accept compensation in land—even better, to emigrate to occupy it and thus assume a role in Mexico's strategic defense. The lands in question were in the US-Mexico borderlands, so the threat of US aggression played a role in Mexican calculations. The United States might ignore Mexican sovereignty or, worse, mistreat Mexicans, but it couldn't invade if it meant running roughshod over British subject settlers, who in effect would become a tripwire in the event of Yankee aggression.[5] An alternative to the settlement idea was to sell off bits of Mexico to the United States and use the proceeds to pay British investors. The Gadsden Purchase of 1853, which transferred land south of the Gila River to the United States in exchange for ten million dollars, raised the hopes of British investors, who elbowed their way to the head of the line for compensation from the funds.[6] US compensation—some fifteen million dollars—paid to Mexico at the conclusion of the Mexican-American War of 1846–1848 was an earlier example. Both led to disappointment.

As British bondholders became increasingly pessimistic about the stability of Mexico (and the safety of their capital), they became advocates of foreign intervention. Some, prizing stability above all else, joined the many voices in the United States calling for the outright annexation of Mexico. Others saw in US annexation the realization of a greater fear. Haunted by the thought that a wobbling Mexican republic would fall into the hands of the American colossus, they came to see the answer in strong government—a monarchy for Mexico.

Bond investors were not alone. The threat of civil war in the United States brought home to European textile manufacturers the great fragility of the global cotton supply. The American South was crowding out other producers as a source of abundant, cheap cotton. In a manner similar to the later global dependence on oil producers in the Middle East during the heyday of OPEC, European textile manufacturers risked finding themselves at the mercy of American cotton.[7] By the 1830s Britain was looking to its own empire and the East Indies for alternatives—and US Southerners increasingly suspected British abolitionists of ulterior economic motives—but Mexico opened up new perspectives. Mexico, under the right conditions, might become a major cotton producer and thus provide an alternative to a looming US stranglehold. It followed that US designs on Mexico threatened to concentrate supply in a few (American) hands. Even without the threat of civil war, by 1860 there was an acute awareness that cotton, from an economic point of view, had become a strategic commodity and that Europe was increasingly at the mercy of the United States. Mexican independence became not simply a desirable thing in the abstract, in the sense that all nations are entitled to sovereignty; it was a formidable alternative in a struggle to avoid utter dependence on US supply.[8]

Charles Lemprière, a British conservative, visited Mexico in 1861 and 1862. His sketches of Mexican provinces and their resources read like prospectuses, compelling only to the deeply invested. He was not the first to note a superficial similarity between Italy and parts of Mexico—when he visited Orizaba, it brought to mind Tivoli—but unlike other commentators and their obsession with precious metals in Mexico, Lemprière was keenly drawn to the production and processing of cotton.[9]

On the matter of cotton, Lemprière didn't bother to hide the fact that abolitionism could also be good business. Fighting slavery, "even more than the immense interest of opening up a new channel for the supply of Manchester and Rouen," should "rouse the peoples of France and England to the value of Mexico as an independent and flourishing country." With the US "Southern States" eyeing Mexico for "a fresh supply of land," two things were obvious: continued US expansion into Mexico would mean not only "the wholesale importations of negro slaves" but also the enslavement of "four millions of wretched Indians." In effect, human rights and European business interests converged in Mexico. To drive the point home, Lemprière held up a horrific vision of the future of Mexico absent French and British intervention: "Mexico . . . in the hands of the Southern States" transformed into "a gigantic slave State."[10] Intervention was a moral obligation.

European concerns were brought to a head on July 17, 1861, when the Mexican legislature voted to suspend payments on foreign loans for two years.[11] President Juárez signed the bill, handing interventionists the pretext they needed. The *Times of London* and the *Manchester Guardian* printed articles expressing exasperation with Mexico, but also satisfaction that both Britain and France had broken diplomatic relations with Mexico.

At the same time that they condemned the American republic as aggressive and militaristic, they characterized the Mexican republic as feeble. All parties agreed that a strong Mexico was necessary, but they disagreed on what form it should take and how to bring it about. The French asserted that the will of the Mexican people should prevail as to the type of regime, though they hastened to embrace the claim that Mexico yearned for a monarch. In that case, Napoléon III professed agnosticism when it came to dynasties, although he preferred the Habsburg archduke Maximilian, and he took comfort from the idea that the interests of a strong and secure Mexico would inevitably align France and the world against the United States.

British interests, at least as articulated by diplomatic representative Charles Wyke, could accommodate a government composed of moderates, perhaps under a British protectorate.[12] In some ways Wyke was more aggressive than the French, willing for Britain to act alone in order to put British investors at the head of the line for reimbursement for their losses.[13] He was removed once it became clear that his views diverged sharply from those of Lord Palmerston.[14]

Spain claimed the right to avenge an affront to its honor. Spain's ambassador to Mexico, Joaquín Francisco Pacheco, made little effort to conceal his sympathy for the forces of reaction in Mexico, the enemies of reform. President Juárez ordered Pacheco expelled in January 1861.[15] Upon his return to Madrid, Pacheco insisted that something must be done in the face of such an insult and criticized the Spanish monarchy for its weakness.

He lobbied aggressively for intervention, insisting that Spain must place itself "at the head of the Spanish race in America"—an argument that clothed nostalgia for lost colonies in the lofty and fashionable language of race. Even discounting his extreme views, Spain saw that Pacheco's abrupt expulsion provided a pretext and, still nursing a grudge for having lost Mexico to independence, opined that "historical traditions and ties" united Spain and Mexico; Spain gently nudged into the open the candidacy of a prince of the Spanish Bourbon dynasty.[16] Spain would rarely miss an opportunity to invoke the memory of Hernán Cortés and the story of how "a handful of heroes" had planted "the banner of Castile" in New Spain on behalf of "a Catholic queen"—a reference to both Isabella of the era of the *conquista* and to her namesake, Isabella II, the reigning queen of Spain.[17]

The allied plan of action took the form of the Convention of London of 1861. The Convention (or Treaty) was cast as a mechanism for pursuing the claims of interested parties in Britain, France, and Spain—jilted investors like the vicar of Cranborne and dishonored diplomats like Joaquín Pacheco. The opening paragraph demands of Mexican authorities "a more efficacious protection of persons and property" in the name of the monarchs of Britain, Spain, and France.[18] They agree to send naval and land forces to seize and occupy positions on the coast of Mexico. Once there, commanders may act as they see fit to fulfill their mission, especially with regard to the security of foreigners in Mexico. At the same time, they denied any attempt to acquire territory or to influence the internal affairs of Mexico, including the form of government. This last point denies the fundamental purpose of the agreement—namely, to provide tripartite diplomatic cover for a scheme to dominate Mexico through a European monarch.

All parties were eager not to alarm the United States. True, the United States was in no position to intervene. The Convention was hashed out amid the Secession Crisis and signed in October 1861, just six months after the Confederate attack on Fort Sumter, a mere three months after the Battle of Bull Run, but they were taking no chances. To head off any US opposition, the Convention directly addressed the United States, acknowledged that the United States had grievances against the Republic of Mexico, and invited the United States to join them. It was an empty invitation but it served to support allied claims that the invasion was neither directed against the United States nor launched in secret. The United States was welcome to join the Europeans as an ally. In a reply almost as long as the Convention itself, the United States declined; and in the pages of the *New York Daily Tribune,* Karl Marx condemned the "contemplated intervention in Mexico" by England, France, and Spain.[19]

The Convention of London was the road map for the European invasion of Mexico, but it was also a veil that concealed divergent intentions. For the British, the main point of the Intervention was to collect debt. To that end, a successful landing and occupation of Veracruz and other ports on the coast of Mexico would suffice.[20] Spain still nurtured dreams of reconquering Mexico and restoring Spain's status as head of the Spanish race.[21] France's aims were at least as ambitious—to conquer Mexico and establish a friendly government there, to check Yankee ambitions, and to secure France's role as defender of the Latin race. Spanish and French ambitions mirrored one another in certain respects, but as there could be only one dominant power in Mexico, they soon were at odds.

Differences emerged over where the allied forces would rendezvous. The British proposed that the fleets meet in neutral waters west of Cuba before moving together on Veracruz. Spain proposed Havana, which it controlled, for the rendezvous.[22] France, eager to avoid conflict, suggested that its forces would join Spain at Havana before proceeding together to meet the British.[23]

But Spain's best hope lay in acting quickly to secure an early advantage. For a time it looked as though historic ties with Mexico would give it an edge. In March 1861 Spain had recaptured control of Santo Domingo, using a Dominican general to topple the Dominican Republic. Was this scenario repeatable? Might Spain retake its empire piecemeal, using internal *criollo* allies to draw former colonies back into the imperial fold? Most urgently, might a similar scenario play out in Mexico? While Santo Domingo was returning to Spanish rule, defeated Mexican Conservative general Miguel Miramón, fresh from defeat in the War of Reform, was seeking refuge and succor in Madrid. Miramón soon became a presence at court. A plan began to take shape. In September, Isabel ordered Spanish forces in Cuba to mobilize for action against Veracruz and Tampico, with the aim of restoring the authority of the Spanish monarchy in Mexico.[24] In October a story in the conservative Spanish newspaper *Correspondencia de España* announced that Miramón would return to Mexico as a Spanish general.[25] Would an alliance between Mexican Conservatives and the Spanish crown bring about the restoration of Spanish rule? Was *criollo* discontent the secret to restoring the Spanish Empire in the Americas?

On December 2, Spanish admiral Rubalcoaba left Cuba with a flotilla of vessels carrying sixty-three hundred men under the command of General

Manuel Gasset. Among the vessels were the evocatively named *Pizarro*, *Guadalquivir, Francisco de Asís*, and *La Cubana*, whereas Admiral Rubalcoaba's flagship, the *Isabel la Católica*, honored the monarch, both past and present.[26] Nine days later they began to arrive at Veracruz. On December 14 Spain demanded and received the surrender of Veracruz.[27] President Juárez had told the governor not to offer resistance. Veracruz had been shelled for four days during the Mexican-American War; when the city surrendered, eyewitnesses described shattered buildings and counted five hundred civilians dead.[28] Juárez and the republican leadership were eager not to repeat the experience, having already decided on a defensive strategy of guerrilla warfare. Spain took possession of Veracruz "in the name of Her Catholic Majesty" without a fight.[29]

But the Spanish mission foundered on Mexican realities. Veracruz was republican in its politics—Juárez had used it as a base of operations during the War of Reform—and the arrival of the Spanish military did nothing to change that; in fact, their presence only revived anticolonial sentiment. In the face of Mexican hostility, the size of the Spanish landing force was inadequate to anything so grand as the restoration of Spanish rule. During the Mexican-American War, US general Winfield Scott had commanded eighty-five hundred men on his successful campaign from Veracruz to Mexico City. Spain in 1861 had only two-thirds that number.[30] So while on December 22 Senator Pacheco was giving a speech in Madrid urging Spain to put itself "at the head of the Spanish race in America"—apparently in anticipation of good news from Mexico—in Veracruz it was already clear that this grand vision had failed.[31]

On January 9, 1862, French forces under Admiral Jurien de la Gravière and British forces under Admiral Milnes arrived at Veracruz. Together, Spanish, British, and French leaders agreed to move inland, to La Tejeria, to relieve congestion in Veracruz but above all to minimize the impact of yellow fever. They began work on a joint statement explaining the purpose of their mission, but almost immediately sharp differences emerged, the first of them occasioned by the arrival of General Miguel Miramón. A mere two months earlier, when Miramón was president of the republic and about to be defeated militarily and chased from Mexico, he had broken into the British Legation in Mexico City and made off with more than six hundred thousand dollars in customs revenue stored there. He managed to escape Mexico, boarding a French vessel at Veracruz under an assumed name and wearing a French naval uniform.[32]

Having succeeded in such a daring stunt, Miramón was now returning under a new (false) identity, bearing a passport issued by Spain. He arrived in the company of a sizable group of Mexican Conservatives, including Father Francisco Javier Miranda and a clutch of Mexican officers, so maybe he thought that in such a crowd his arrival would go unnoticed. In any event, the British were not fooled. They announced that they planned to haul Miramón back to London in irons, to be tried as a thief in British courts. General Juan Prim, the Spanish representative, defended Miramón by pointing out that he had recently been received in Madrid at Isabel's court. The French representative Saligny protested that Miramón likewise had recently been received in Paris at the court of Napoléon III.[33] In the end the British representative settled for deportation. Miramón was shuttled off to Cuba.

Matters turned quite serious for the European forces, and not merely because war is a serious thing. As the French convoy settled at anchor at Veracruz in the ominously named Bay of Sacrifices (*Sacrificios*), French admiral Jurien de la Gravière visited each vessel in turn. Veracruz was unable to accommodate the vessels and their crews, so they were obliged to stay at anchor for two days in order not to overwhelm the port and the city. As Jurien made his rounds, it immediately became clear that all on board were at risk from yellow fever—the mosquito-borne disease casually known as *vómito negro* after one of the disease's more convulsive symptoms.

François-Charles du Barail, a general who had traveled on board the *Aube,* reported several sick on board from yellow fever and one dead within days of arrival. Back on his flagship *Normandie,* Admiral Jurien found most of his crew sick. Three days after the *Normandie* dropped anchor, the ship's physician died. The good doctor was buried alongside many others on the Island of Sacrifices, which the survivors dubbed, in a bit of black humor, the *jardin d'acclimatation*—a lovely patch whose residents were acclimatized for eternity.[34]

The Treaty of Soledad was a direct consequence of these circumstances. In it, the Republic of Mexico agreed to allow allied forces to escape the deadly coast for cooler, higher elevations, beyond the reach of the *vómito.* Soledad was an extraordinarily generous concession by the government of an invaded country. After all, nature was doing the work of an army of thousands, sowing death and demoralization; because the disease process was not understood at the time, yellow fever, as an invisible killer, had a devastating effect on morale. Manuel Doblado, Mexican minister of foreign affairs, extracted significant concessions from the European allies in return. The most important, certainly, was the mere fact that representatives of Britain, France, and Spain signed the treaty; it was a de facto recognition of the legitimacy of the Mexican republic. Just as important, Doblado had probed and exploited differences among the allies, laying the groundwork for the rupture that would turn a joint European operation into "the French Intervention."

The process combined bluff, bluster, and warm family ties. Juan Prim, Spain's representative and commander of the Spanish forces, was related to Doblado through marriage. Prim's wife was Doblado's niece.[35] With both personal and diplomatic channels open, Prim and Doblado reached out to one another and, in a meeting on February 19, sketched out the core elements of the Treaty of Soledad. The allies would be allowed to advance to the safer climes of Córdoba and Orizaba while negotiations continued. If negotiations broke down, they would return to the deadly coast. Meanwhile, customs at Veracruz, the lifeline of the Juárez government, would be handled by Mexico. The treaty also affirmed that the allies did not intend to threaten the independence and sovereignty of the Mexican republic. President Juárez signed the agreement on February 23, the allies having signed in the days preceding.[36]

Soledad effectively fractured the alliance. The reasons were both political and practical. On the political side, since his arrival Prim had become convinced that there was no "monarchist party" in Mexico. To attempt to establish a monarchy there was a fool's errand. He openly shared these views with anyone who would listen. Finally, in a brief and brilliant letter to Napoléon III, he demolished arguments in favor of monarchy, incidentally explaining why the allied plan for Mexico would fail. Yes, Mexico had once been ruled by a monarch, but the real authority had been with the Spanish viceroys, who had garnered little affection; the experience had left no true monarchist sentiments. Nor did Mexico have a hereditary nobility, the traditional prop to monarchy. On the contrary, republicanism in Mexico was strong, and strongly supported by the American republic. Men with monarchist sentiments were rare in Mexico. If they had existed in any number, they would have manifested themselves upon the arrival of the European allies, but they had not, and they were now scattered in exile. More to the point, if Mexican Conservatives had wanted a monarchy, why hadn't they established one when they were in power? Then, in words that ought to echo down the ages, Prim recognized that a great power like France could do what it pleased in a place like Mexico, but would it last? Prim noted that France easily had power "sufficient to erect a throne in Mexico for the house of Austria" but that such a throne would crumble the day France ceased to defend it.[37] In a few well-argued paragraphs, Prim sketched the trajectory not only of the Mexican Empire but also of all future attempts at nation building by military might.

Prim's realism was also informed by practical considerations. It was by no means clear that European forces could fight their way from the coast. By the time Juárez signed the Treaty of Soledad, Spain had already sent a thousand men—sick from yellow fever—back to Havana for rehabilitation.[38] Sir Charles Wyke, Prim's British analog, tended to see things the same way. Prim's argument fed British disenchantment. The British were already deeply offended by the return of the trickster/robber Miramón and by French complicity in his return. The Miramón episode only deepened British suspicions.

In the end, realism won. The available options were that European forces could remain in Veracruz and lose soldiers to yellow fever, or they could lose soldiers fighting their way from the coast, or they could affirm Soledad, save lives, and buy themselves time. Only the third option made sense. Admiral Jurien found himself in the minority but lacked, for now, the resources to blaze an independent path.[39] He signed along with Wyke and Prim.

Differences emerged among allies back in Europe, too, fed by US diplomacy. In early March, William Seward, the US secretary of state, released a communication in European capitals defending Mexican sovereignty and pointing out the folly of destroying a country militarily in the name of order. European intervention would bring not order but disorder to Mexico.[40] Napoléon III was enraged by the Treaty of Soledad, starting with the fact that it implied recognition of the very regime he intended to bypass and subvert. On March 7 the newspaper *Moniteur universel* published an article written by Napoléon III in which he blamed Prim for all the mistakes committed by the allies in Mexico. Spain defended Prim. It could be fairly said that Spain, too weak to lead, preferred to subvert the alliance rather than permit France to take Mexico. In early April the government of Spain publicly approved Prim's conduct, effectively blessing the split among allies.[41]

In Britain, apart from a few disgruntled bondholders, public opinion was hostile to anything so ambitious as regime change. Benjamin Disraeli, speaking in the House of Commons, reminded his listeners that "England was the first nation to recognize the independence of Mexico" and that it would be odd for it now to strike a blow against it. "We see," he noted, "that the motive for the Intervention [has changed] in a very short time." The objective, he warned, had now become "to introduce new principles of government in North America and even to establish new dynasties."[42]

France had long since decided to go it alone if necessary. What it lost was the cover of European alliance. At about the time Napoléon III was publicly blaming Prim for everything that had gone wrong, General Charles Ferdinand Lorencez was arriving at Veracruz with an additional forty-five hundred men, effectively doubling what was now called an "expeditionary force." The move tipped the balance of forces in the Intervention clearly in favor of the French.

Meanwhile, the opportunism of Mexican Conservatives continued. Mere weeks after the banishment of Miramón to Cuba in late January, another Conservative Mexican general, Juan Almonte, appeared in Veracruz. Few Mexicans could lay a stronger claim to Mexican patriotism, at least in terms of lineage, than Juan Nepomuceno Almonte. Almonte was of Indigenous descent, the natural son of José María Morelos, hero of the struggle for Mexican independence from Spain. Almonte fought along-side General Santa Anna at both the Alamo and the battle of San Jacinto in the doomed effort to put down the Texas rebellion. After the loss of Texas, he served as Mexico's representative to the United States from 1842 to 1845. In that crucial period between Texan independence and annexation he warned in blunt terms that US annexation of the Republic of Texas would lead to war.[43] When the annexation resolution passed the US Congress, Almonte left Washington in protest, returned to Mexico, and prepared for war.[44] As Polk contrived to engineer war with Mexico, Almonte's vision seemed about to come to pass. After the war, Almonte remained vigilant, persuaded that US ambition would sooner or later have "the whole of Mexico . . . swallowed up by the United States."[45] Mexico needed allies. By 1856 Almonte, "the soul of the revolutionary clerical party," was in Europe, moving in the same circles as Gutiérrez and Hidalgo, representing a certain vision of Mexico in London, Paris, and Madrid.[46]

When Almonte returned to Mexico in March 1862, he expressed surprise when he learned that allied forces had not already reached Mexico City, but he was undeterred.[47] He issued a proclamation promising "firm government" and behaved as if he were head of state. He began working closely with the French, to the dismay of British and Spanish forces, and he expressed confidence, in late March, that European forces would arrive in the capital by the end of April.

Almonte's noisy arrival prompted the Juárez government to protest. The presence of a notorious Conservative like Almonte and his calls for regime change were a violation of the Soledad Treaty, in which the Europeans had affirmed that they did not intend to initiate political change. As if to drive the point home, forces loyal to the Juárez government captured another Conservative Mexican general, Manuel Robles Pezuela, as he was making his way to meet with the allies. He was shot on March 23 under the terms of a decree issued as the Intervention began, specifying death for any individual found to have aided the invasion.[48]

The execution sent a message and heightened the stakes, but it did not change attitudes. The French offered protection to Almonte, citing Robles's execution as justification, while Almonte decided to double down on his political ambitions, issuing a proclamation declaring himself "supreme chief of the nation." He also issued a paper currency and threatened merchants with confiscation if they refused to accept it as legal tender.[49] Two days later, on April 9, 1862, Sir Charles Wyke and General Prim met with the French. They insisted, without success, on the departure of the troublesome Conservative Mexican exiles. Six days later, Prim and Wyke concluded a separate agreement with the Juárez government, effectively separating their mission from that of the French. British and Spanish evacuations began immediately; when the final Spanish troop ship departed on April 24, the allied divorce was complete. France would go it alone.

3

Puebla

THE MEXICAN EMPIRE was founded on a lie—the lie that the people of Mexico would welcome a European monarch. Mexican exiles in Europe had cultivated this idea, then repeated it until it seemed true. It didn't hurt that it was a message certain powerful listeners wanted to hear.

This was not the first time that foreign adventure had been justified as a war of liberation—and it was far from being the last. The French Revolution had invented the concept of the war of liberation, using it to justify the invasion of the Rhineland, Italy, and the Low Countries with the promise of freeing their occupants from the tyranny of monarchy.[1] The invasion of Mexico was also justified as a liberation, though in this case the promise was to free the people from the tyranny of a republic.

General Manuel Doblado, the Mexican minister of foreign affairs, was having nothing of it. In a statement dripping with scorn, he insisted that "the Mexican republic has no need of the aid offered with such goodwill to the Mexican people."[2] He saw to it that the Treaty of Soledad made it explicit that the European intervention did not intend regime change.

Admiral Jurien, de facto commander of French forces, had seen that, unlike the Spanish, who were clearly hated by the Mexican population, the French were comparatively well regarded, so much so that he entertained the fantasy that Mexicans might rally to the French cause once the Spanish left. He was soon disabused of the idea, but it mattered little as the illusion would be nurtured by his successor. Napoléon III had lost confidence in Jurien after his role in the Treaty of Soledad and the disavowal of regime change as an objective. He used the pretext of troop reinforcement to replace Jurien with a more aggressive commander in chief.

The arrival of General Charles de Lorencez on March 6, 1862, marked the turn toward a much more confrontational style, which prompted France's final break with Britain and Spain. British and Spanish representatives Wyke and Prim concluded an agreement with the Juárez government that recognized the legitimacy of the Mexican republic as it affirmed its ability to work in good faith on the problem of debt. With Britain and Spain preparing their exit, France was free to pursue its vision of establishing itself as patron of Mexico.

As a first step, Admiral Jurien was promoted, but it was an "up and out" promotion—a mere preliminary to his replacement in favor of Lorencez. Jurien ultimately learned not only that France had disavowed the Treaty of Soledad, but also that he, Jurien, was being blamed for signing it.[3] Lorencez's aggressive moves were mirrored in the political moves of French diplomat Jean Pierre Dubois de Saligny, who had the full support of Napoléon III to pursue the campaign's political objectives. Saligny was an old hand in American affairs, dating back to the 1830s when he was secretary to the French Legation in Washington, D.C., before being appointed chargé d'affaires to the Republic of Texas.[4] In his role in Texas Saligny had articulated the racist outlook that Michel Chevalier would elevate to a philosophy of history. He was convinced that the Mexicans were a "degenerate" people who could never resist the vigorous expansionist impulses of the Anglo-Americans. Eager to head off Yankee imperialism, Saligny once proposed a Franco-Texan alliance against Mexico that would, not incidentally, secure French influence in the region. Before his recall from Texas, he was involved in a number of shady schemes, including a plan to buy the island of Cozumel, off the Yucatán coast; another would have awarded three million acres of west Texas land to a company promoting French immigration; yet another, more serious, would have sponsored the creation of a political party in Texas opposed to US annexation and willing to call on France to intervene to prevent it.[5]

In Mexico, Saligny's role was effectively that of political commissar, the man charged with watching over General Lorencez and serving as guarantor that the military means commanded by Lorencez matched the political aims of Napoléon III. Lorencez and Saligny got along well. Their partnership was founded upon certain shared values, notably utter disdain for the people of Mexico combined with complete confidence in themselves and, consequently, in French success.

On April 19, 1862, Lorencez announced a march on Orizaba from his camp in Córdoba. This signaled the end to the truce created by the Treaty of Soledad, as well as intent to march on Mexico City. Inevitably, clashes between Mexican and French troops would follow, but where and how? Lorencez entered Orizaba the next day having met little resistance. Nine days later, on April 28, Lorencez's forces encountered Mexican forces commanded by General Ignacio Zaragoza. This was the largest organized Mexican force on the road to the capital. Zaragoza and his forces were at the summit of Acultzingo, a position that gave the Mexicans a signifi-cant advantage.[6] Despite their opponents' benefit of terrain, the French easily dislodged the Mexican forces. The ease was deceptive. Zaragoza was leery of forcing a decisive encounter that would risk the destruction or capture of his army. After abandoning Acultzingo, he withdrew his forces to Puebla, arriving on May 3, leaving French forces to continue their march.

Even before the triumph at Acultzingo, on April 26, Lorencez exuded, at least publicly, only confidence in a swift and certain triumph. Privately he complained about shortages of equipment and about his soldiers—some lacked shoes, others lacked uniform pants, a few he dismissed as "children [who] could barely carry a rifle"—but he expressed only confi-dence up the chain of command.[7] In a boastful message to Paris he wrote, "We have . . . such a superiority of race, of organization, of discipline, of morality, of high-minded sentiments that I pray [you] to tell the Emperor that from this moment forward, at the head 6,000 soldiers, I am the master of Mexico."[8] He added that he expected to be in Mexico City by the end of May.

The swiftness and ease of the French advance only fed Lorencez's con-fidence and chauvinism, no doubt prompting flattering comparisons with the American invasion of Mexico fifteen years earlier. In 1847, during the US war with Mexico, General Winfield Scott landed his army of twelve thousand men at Veracruz in early March, took Puebla nine weeks later, and entered Mexico City in mid-September.[9] This feat earned praise from the era's greatest living commander—the Duke of Wellington, the man who had defeated Napoléon Bonaparte.[10] Lorencez was ahead of the pace of the Americans. He had needed only six weeks (to Scott's nine) to move his army of six thousand from Veracruz to the doorstep of Puebla. He was doing more, faster, with less.[11]

Comparisons with Winfield Scott and the Americans were misleading, however. In the 1846–1848 war, Mexican defensive efforts focused on American forces commanded by Zachary Taylor, invading from the north, until Scott opened a second front at Veracruz. Mexican resistance to Scott focused on Veracruz, Cerro Gordo, and Mexico City itself, allowing US forces to take Puebla with little difficulty. It would be different in 1862; General Zaragoza had prepared a rude reception for the French.

The city of Puebla rose to prominence under Spanish rule and manifests the classic features of Mexico's colonial cities. The city centers on a spacious plaza dominated by the cathedral and the main government building. Puebla's gridded layout, along with its many thick-walled convents, monasteries, and residences, facilitated the conversion of the city into a fortress. The construction of street barricades between sturdy buildings transformed Puebla into a defensive matrix with no evident weakness.[12] Puebla's twelve thousand defenders could readily find protected positions from which to fire; they could also rapidly and safely reposition themselves to counter any attack, thanks to protective walls and barricades.

On the evening of May 4, Lorencez halted his army at Amozoc, a few miles east of Puebla. Much of the population had fled toward Puebla, leaving Amozoc's dusty streets mostly deserted.[13] Lorencez conferred with his officers and arrived at a plan. Rather than attempt to take the fortress city of Puebla directly, they would force its defenders to submit by seizing the surrounding high ground. A hill a mile to the northeast of Puebla's city center, "Guadalupe" by name, rises three hundred feet above the city. If Guadalupe could be taken, the city below would be untenable, at the mercy of shot raining down from above. Rather than wait, Lorencez and his officers decided on a bold assault on Guadalupe the following morning, hoping that the defenders would be overwhelmed by the speed and ardor of the French attack. Two battalions of Zouaves, the legendary soldiers of French North Africa, would lead the charge. Their trademark red caps, billowy red pants with white gaiters, and short blue jackets with bright-red braiding, made them instantly recognizable—the elite, battle-hardened foot soldiers of French colonial military might. The Mexicans would tremble when they saw that the French were leading the attack with their best units.

The morning of May 5 began with an advance from the camp at Amozoc to the outskirts of Puebla, followed by a break for coffee. The Zouave assault on Guadalupe would be supported by ten cannons, a marine regiment, sharpshooters, and a mobile mountain battery. Other units protected the left flank, closest to the city, and communications to the rear.

General Zaragoza was indeed surprised by the French plan of attack, in part because Guadalupe was such a formidable position. Steep slopes

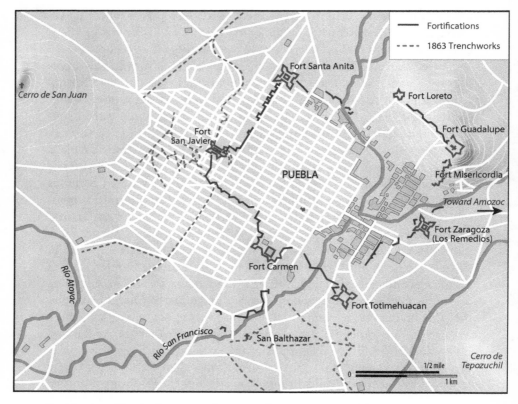

Puebla, site of battles in 1862 and 1863; to the east, Fort Guadalupe, the point of attack in 1862; to the west, Fort San Javier, the point of attack in 1863.

posed a daunting challenge to any attacker. At the summit of Guadalupe stood a convent, enclosed by thick defensive walls. Within the walls, artillery and infantry stood by to defend the convent fortress. Nor was Guadalupe a solitary position; Fort Loreto, atop a smaller hill northwest of Guadalupe, provided covering fire.

Once alerted to the French point of attack, General Zaragoza shifted infantry and cavalry to the flanks of Guadalupe.[14] The French assault began with an artillery barrage intended to weaken the walls of Guadalupe and the resolve of its defenders, but the distance of fire, as well as the angle of attack from the side and below, greatly reduced the effect of the barrage. For more than an hour French artillery fired upon the walls of Guadalupe without great effect other than to expend half of their ammunition.

Undaunted, Lorencez resolved to open the infantry assault. As the French clambered up the hillside of Guadalupe, Mexicans took up tiered positions in the convent courtyard. As French soldiers scaled the wall and hoisted themselves over the top, Mexican infantry across the courtyard opened fire, taking them down. Outside, at the base of the wall, a lone French bugler sounded the charge to thinning ranks as men fell around him.

After the initial assault, Lorencez prepared to commit two companies of Zouaves held in reserve, while Zaragoza sent reinforcements to support the defense of Guadalupe. Nature called off the slaughter—at four in the afternoon, a storm moved in, bringing giant hailstones with it. The flanks of Guadalupe became slick with mud and rain. Further effort was pointless. The assault ended.

Lorencez blamed the defeat of Cinco de Mayo on flawed intelligence, citing reports that French forces would be "welcomed as liberators" and showered with flowers. This might have been a plausible explanation upon his arrival in Mexico, but everything since then had shown—long before May 5—that this vision of the Mexican people thirsting for liberation and foreign monarchy was fantasy.[15] Even accounting for the power of fantasy, nothing could change the fact that Lorencez had given the command to attack an enemy of superior numbers in a fortified position. French losses reached 476, a sizable fraction of the force he commanded. Lorencez had nothing to show for it.

Lorencez carried into battle the reputation of the French army, widely regarded as the world's most powerful, and left it in shambles. Commentators compared it to Gulliver restrained by the Lilliputians.[16] Yet Lorencez's deadly blunders took nothing away from what Zaragoza and the defenders of Puebla had accomplished. The people of Puebla turned their military victory into a moral commentary on how far France had fallen from its founding ideals. Inside the city, a celebration with lights and music began. As the defeated French tended to their wounded in their encampment, they could hear the unmistakable melody of the Marseillaise, a song written during the French Revolution to celebrate the French nation rising to repel an invader bent on restoring monarchy.[17] In a note to his soldiers two days later, Mexican general Berriozabal drove the point home: "It's the justice of our cause that has given us victory. The love of country that saved France in 1792 saves again today. You have fought the finest soldiers of our time and you are the first to defeat them."[18]

In the aftermath of his defeat at Puebla, Lorencez had plenty to think about. The swift, uninterrupted march on Mexico City that he had imagined had vanished. Now he had to save his army from annihilation. Zaragoza planned to follow up Puebla with a pursuit of the French that would drive the invader out and bring the campaign to a close. As the news of victory at Puebla spread, Mexicans rallied to the cause. General Jésus González Ortega, governor of Zacatecas, committed an army of six thousand to Zaragoza. He also wrote to Saligny underlining the futility of the mission to establish a monarchy, noting that the "court of opinion" would judge him harshly, and France, too. Wouldn't it be better, he asked, "to abandon the idea to establish a monarchy in Mexico?"[19]

By the time Lorencez received a copy of Ortega's letter, he had retreated from Puebla to the relative safety of Orizaba to wait for reinforcements. A week after the battle of Puebla, General Zaragoza approached Orizaba at the head of an army of fourteen thousand—ready to offer a safe and honorable march to the coast in exchange for a promise to evacuate Mexico. By then Lorencez was already digging in. Barricades went up in Orizaba to protect a core of hospitals, arms depots, and barracks.[20] The French were turning Orizaba into the kind of fortress city that Zaragoza had made of Puebla.

In France, the news of French defeat had paradoxical effects. Wounded soldiers, some with horrific wounds, put a face on the defeat at Puebla. Some wrote to their families. Others wrote directly to Napoléon III. Fleury Bruchon, a veteran Zouave from North Africa, wrote that he had been "shot in the head, a penetrating wound" that left him weak on one side of his body. Auguste Vincent, also a Zouave, lost an arm to amputation. Jean François Ponsard had three serious wounds, "one in the face, another in the shoulder, yet another in the buttock." The wounds "ended" his "career" but he had received no compensation, nor had the others.[21] But instead of reinforcing the critics of an unpopular war, defeat rallied support for valiant troops. The legislative body of France's Second Empire voted to provide the means "to obtain a prompt and complete victory."[22] Lorencez, newly chastened by his experience at Puebla, tried speaking the truth. "I'm sorry to say that I still have not met a single supporter of monarchy in Mexico," he wrote, and he observed, belatedly, that his mission had been doomed by having the reactionary Almonte "in our baggage train" and the delusional Saligny as political commissar. "I am certain that nothing will be possible in Mexico with Almonte and [Saligny]," he wrote.[23] This was similar to the view that Juárez himself articulated. "The French intervention, with the alliance of Almonte . . . is lost in [public] opinion," Juárez wrote.[24] Among the people of Mexico, the French were known by their friends. Having chosen Almonte, they had tagged themselves as friends of savagery and reaction.[25]

However, instead of doubting the claims of Mexican exiles that a Mexican population seethed under republican rule, Napoléon III doubled down. "I know from twenty letters from Mexico . . . that the population awaited us impatiently as liberators," he wrote.[26] He backed Saligny with new vigor, asserting that if his advice had been followed, "our flag would be flying over Mexico City today." Lorencez became the goat, the weak link in an otherwise unbreakable chain of competence. If Lorencez "had succeeded in his attack at Puebla, everything that [the émigrés] had predicted would have happened."[27] It was a ridiculous assessment, using military failure to explain away both bad intelligence and stout Mexican resistance.

Avenging French defeat at Puebla was going to take time. For Mexico, this created an opportunity to snuff out the invasion by attacking the eighty-mile route connecting Lorencez's army at Orizaba with resources arriving at Veracruz.[28] Zaragoza's attempt to dislodge the French directly had failed, but attacks on their resupply could have the desired effect simply by making Orizaba untenable. Winning Mexico's independence from Spanish rule had required eleven years of insurgency; Mexico would put the same method to work against the French occupation.[29] Mexican insurgents would indeed disrupt the route to Orizaba in a move meant to demonstrate that even if the French succeeded in marching on Mexico City, they would never dominate the country.

French efforts to snuff out the Mexican insurgency led to atrocities and resentments that would plague the Intervention until its collapse. Mexican guerrillas had harassed French lines even before victory at Puebla. In April 1862 President Juárez issued a proclamation calling on all Mexican men, ages thirty to sixty years, to join guerrilla forces.[30] Also in April, Lorencez authorized a counterinsurgency force, calling upon a Swiss engineer named Stöcklin to organize it.[31] Stöcklin put together a mounted force of eighty, supported by forty-five foot soldiers drawn from Mexican dissidents as well as foreign adventurers like himself. He chose Medellín, just south of Veracruz, as a base of operations. Stöcklin's cavalry unit used their mobility to surprise and disrupt guerrilla operations while infantry followed up. As an irregular force, they operated unconstrained by the standards of war, becoming notorious for atrocities and acts of cruelty.[32]

The problems were not limited to European counterinsurgency forces. Their main Mexican ally, General Leonardo Márquez, was even worse.

Sent to Veracruz to escort a convoy, Márquez and his soldiers terrorized Soledad, some twenty miles to the southwest. According to the parish priest at Soledad, Father Savelli, Márquez and his men set fire to Soledad and robbed and raped its residents, sending them fleeing to the woods for their safety.[33]

Nor were French regular forces above atrocity. Even their Conservative Mexican allies reported abuses. Antonio Corona, a Conservative general, told Concepción de Miramón, "Barely had they arrived in our country when they started to commit an infinity of abuses, as if they were *conquistadores.*"[34] French forces committed atrocities at Huauchinango and Tulancingo. Huauchinango was sacked and burned "with the barbarity of another era" while at Tulancingo captive insurgents were shot.[35]

Defending supply lines in coastal areas brought the special challenge of yellow fever. Moving new arrivals to higher altitudes reduced the risk of sickness, but it also made control of the lowlands tenuous. Mindful of such challenges, the French drew upon forces already in the Caribbean, at Martinique and Guadalupe. Napoléon III also called upon North Africa, drawing down troops from Algeria.[36] Not only were Caribbean and North African troops thought to be resistant to yellow fever, they had the additional advantage of being redeployed without attracting the attention of the Napoléon's critics. These moves showed how empire could build upon empire.

Imperial connections also underpinned Napoléon III's appeal to the ruler of Egypt, Muhammad Sa'id Pasha, for an allocation of African troops for service in Mexico. Sa'id Pasha pondered Napoléon's request, then agreed. In early January 1863, 447 men boarded the frigate *Seine* at a port near Alexandria. The men came from an area described as "the extremity of Upper Egypt." One French officer referred to them as "black Abyssinians." One was from Somalia and another from Chad, but most came from Darfur and the Sudan/Ethiopia borderlands.[37] A few were "conscripted" off the streets of Alexandria by police acting as press gangs. Despite their diverse African origins, they were routinely referred to as "the Sudanese."[38]

Conditions on board the *Seine* were awful, especially because the ship was carrying nearly a hundred more passengers than it was designed to carry. Misery was compounded by a painfully slow crossing. In order to economize on coal, Napoléon III ordered transport captains to cross the Atlantic under sail. Upon arrival at Veracruz, the men were listless and depressed, having had no say in their assignment and knowing next to nothing about their fate.[39] Even their supposed resistance to yellow fever couldn't help them. Elementary observations ought to have raised doubts—creoles from Martinique did better than Blacks from Sudan—but the Black conscripts suffered the consequences of the triumph of racial ideas over medical science.[40] Within two weeks of their arrival at Veracruz, fifty-two of the soldiers and sailors were dead.[41] Even their commander, Major Jabaratallah Muhammad, succumbed.[42] No matter. The arrivals were immediately assigned to protect the first leg of the supply lifeline from Veracruz to Orizaba.[43]

Meanwhile, convoys of reinforcements from France had begun to sail in June 1862, within weeks of the news of the French defeat at Puebla.[44] Departures would continue through the spring of 1863: Brest, Cherbourg, and Toulon saw multiple departures. Here, too, poor planning and bad luck thwarted efforts. Ships were tossed during rough crossings. Large waves pushed one vessel, the *Aube,* to a 43-degree angle, creating chaos. Below-deck horses were pitched from their stalls, colliding with timbers and one another; some drowned as water streamed in. Injuries mounted. When the storm passed, the crew of the *Jura* heaved 120 injured horses overboard. Crews and passengers were relieved to reach safe harbor at Martinique, but because the vessels arrived in quick succession, the governor forbade them to disembark, fearing overcrowding. He sent them on to Veracruz, where they faced new perils, including a hurricane that beached one vessel and scattered others.[45]

There was no doubting French resolve, despite the setbacks. Napoléon III was keenly aware of the reputational cost of having been defeated at Puebla the year before. In fact, the setbacks increased French determination to succeed. "The defeat of Puebla and nine months of procrastination have cost us much of our prestige," Napoléon III wrote in a candid comment. "[We must] act with promptness and energy to strike the Mexican imagination." More than 30,950 men were transported in convoys from Europe and North Africa between June 1862 and February 1863. Added to the 7,542 men sent before Puebla and the 447 Sudanese conscripts, these numbers made the Mexican campaign—38,939 men in all—the largest transoceanic deployment of its time.[46] Numbers like these guaranteed that Puebla would fall. Defeat must be avenged. Napoléon III was taking no chances. He appears to have staked everything on the assumption that Puebla would be the final point of resistance, after which Mexico would fall peaceably under French authority. Recent imperial history would have counseled caution. Algiers fell in the first year of the

French conquest of Algeria that began in 1830, but resistance continued. Even the capture of resistance leader Abd el-Kadr seventeen years later did not end the insurgency. Worse, Napoléon III urged the practice of collective responsibility—making communities pay collectively for acts of resistance committed on their territory, "like in Africa." Such practices might create a surface calm but they built resentments, and when they involved atrocities committed against the civilian population, they expanded resistance.[47]

Despite such examples, Napoléon III insisted on the fiction that Mexicans were dominated against their will by a few evil men. The fact that Lorencez had been disabused of such ideas after his experience of Puebla hadn't changed Napoléon's views; it merely convinced him that he needed to change commanders.[48] General Elie Frédéric Forey was on board the first group of vessels bound for Mexico after the disaster of Puebla. Forey was a Bonaparte loyalist, having supported Napoléon III's coup against the French Republic in 1852. Napoléon III made sure that Forey understood that the strategic objective was to halt the expansion of the United States and to let no one, including the Mexican reactionaries like Almonte, get in the way of that objective. When he left Cherbourg aboard the *Turenne* on July 28, 1862, Forey took with him a wealth of experience in colonial warfare, dating back to the military campaigns to conquer and pacify Algeria in the 1830s. The Atlantic crossing took seven weeks, plenty of time to reflect on the gravity of the task he had taken on, but he gave no sign of hesitation when he arrived at Veracruz in September to take command of French forces. In February 1863 he announced the resumption of operations against Puebla.[49]

France had waited to assemble an overwhelming force before moving on Puebla. The catch was that Mexico had used this time well, too. Ignacio Zaragoza, the hero of Cinco de Mayo, had died of typhus a few months after his victory, but his successor, Jésus González Ortega, continued preparations for the inevitable return of the French. Ortega brought five thousand men from Zacatecas and nine thousand rifles by way of Guadalajara.[50] Mexico had even sought to win French soldiers over to their side, offering land in exchange for military service and a transfer of loyalties.[51] The city and its defenses now contained twenty-two thousand men ready to fight. Some of the most important preparations involved the city itself, building on Zaragoza's defensive strategy and, according to a French source, drawing on the expertise of an Italian engineer with Garibaldian sympathies.[52] The sturdy walls of Puebla's convents, churches, and monasteries were reconceived as nodes in a network of formidable redoubts. The rooftops of Puebla were fitted with crenelations. The beginnings and ends of streets were filled with rubble, forming barricades with parapets and gun embrasures. The defenders of Puebla were turning the rectangular blocks of the city into a nested set of fortresses, each block its own citadel.[53]

Outside the city, Forey concentrated his forces east of Puebla at Amozoc, the place from which Lorencez had launched his attack the year before on May 5. But unlike Lorencez, who had sought to capture the city by seizing the high ground of Fort Guadalupe, Forey intended to bypass Guadalupe and attack the city of Puebla directly—but only after he had surrounded, besieged, and starved it.[54] On March 17, 1863, Forey's forces moved westward out of Amozoc before splitting, "like two branches of a river," flowing north and south around Puebla, forming a "terrible circle" that would seek to strangle the city.[55]

With Puebla deprived of resupply of food and ammunition, Forey's focus shifted to point of attack. Assessing their own vulnerabilities, the Mexicans considered their southern defenses, anchored by Fort Carmen, as their weak point, partly because Fort Carmen was too far from Forts Guadalupe and Loreto to benefit from artillery support. Not only that, the southern fortifications were but a few blocks from the town square, bounded by Puebla's cathedral, government buildings, and market. If the French could breach defenses at Fort Carmen, they would be mere blocks from the heart of the city.[56]

Instead, Forey chose to attack Puebla from the west, where Fort San Javier anchored the city's defenses. Fort San Javier was a formidable redoubt, but it projected from the city, creating a salient vulnerable to attack from many directions. Forey's decision also grew from the conviction, carefully nourished, that the people of Puebla supported the Intervention. If that were true, it followed that once Puebla's defensive perimeter was breached, resistance would collapse and Forey's army would quickly take command of the city.[57] It was a plausible scenario, but it revealed a serious misunderstanding of the deep and flexible defensive strategy that Ortega and his army had devised.

Once Forey moved his command to the west and the French line of attack became clear, the defenders of Puebla repositioned their artillery to threaten the approaches to San Javier. By day, Mexican lancers threatened the French from the rear, by way of Cholula, but these attacks were easily fended off by French cavalry. By night, French sappers dug a network of trenches approaching San Javier in a zigzag pattern that would provide cover from Mexican fire.[58]

The French attack on the San Javier fort began on March 29. Forey offered the honor of leading the assault to the remnants of units that had fought in the failed assault a year earlier on May 5. The assault was a brilliant success. By the end of the day, San Javier had fallen, putting Forey on schedule to take Puebla by the anniversary of defeat the year before. But French joy soon turned to consternation. As the French occupied what remained of the fort, they came under intense fire from windows and rooftops of buildings barely a hundred feet away. In withdrawing from San Javier, the Mexican defenders had lured the French into a perilous position, making them the focus of withering crossfire. Almost immediately the French could envision the enormity of the undertaking before them. The people of Puebla would not rally to the invaders once the city's defenses were breached. Puebla's defenders were going to force them to take the city block by block. Some of the French soldiers had seen street fighting before, notably during the insurrection in Paris known as the June Days of 1848.[59] They knew what lay ahead. The conquest of Puebla would be slow, bloody, deadly work.

Block after block, Puebla's defenders executed a strategy of attrition that involved relinquishing territory only at great cost to the attacker.[60] French intelligence reports had insisted that San Javier was the only defensive position of any significance to the west of the city.[61] True enough, but this overlooked the fact that the massive walls of Puebla's buildings provided the built environment for a bloody defense in depth. Whenever French soldiers stepped into view on the street, they were targeted by Mexican fire from barricades at street level and from windows and rooftops above. Even building interiors brought no respite. When Colonel Longueville, under intense fire from a barricade, sought to lead his men to safety in a courtyard, they entered only to face a volley from the wall opposite. When Captain Melot and his men sought refuge in a residence, they found themselves trapped in a gunfight and outnumbered. They didn't dare return to the street. As losses mounted, they retreated and managed to fortify a bedroom. In desperation, they called on engineers to dig a supporting trench so they could exit and cross safely to the building across the street. Snipers on the rooftops forced an end to the digging. Out of options, Melot led his men back onto the street in a rush to overwhelm the barricade. When the attack failed, they had no choice but to fall back. They hoisted their wounded and carried them to safety, taking fire even in retreat.[62]

A week after the fall of Fort Javier, the Mexicans had yielded only two blocks, and each block taken exposed French forces to lateral fire from the blocks on either side. The casualties and the dismal pace were taking a toll on French morale, especially as the center of town—clearly identified by the cathedral spires nearly half a mile away—seemed impossibly distant. Even French soldiers taken prisoner by Mexican forces were becoming a morale problem. Captive soldiers found themselves well treated—an attractive alternative to combat wounds and death. The candor of their letters home broke through official accounts of valor against a perfidious enemy. "We are treated perfectly, thank God," wrote a captured officer. He offered praise for his Mexican captors. "They are very kind, several speak French, and they all sympathize with our misfortune," he wrote. In a letter to his parents, Lieutenant Duchesne of the 1st Zouaves offered a graphic description of wounds he suffered in combat on April 25, prior to his capture. The inventory of his wounds offers a vivid glimpse of the intensity of Mexican resistance. "I have been wounded in my right arm by grape shot, on the right leg by a ball, and in the face by rocks," he wrote. He hastened to reassure his parents not to worry. "We have fallen into the hands of a generous enemy," he wrote. "I evaded death by a true miracle and I am happy to have gotten out of it [with my life]." Of the five hundred soldiers involved in the fight that day, "barely seventy or eighty" escaped capture.[63]

Such stories had a way of getting into the local press in France, sapping already tenuous support for the war, and they had an immediate effect on troop morale. French commanders held a meeting on April 7 in which they recognized their soldiers' loss of confidence. They even discussed abandoning Puebla in favor of a march on Mexico City—a quite sensible idea, militarily speaking—but then rejected the idea for fear of the boost it would give Mexican forces to see them break off their attack.

They pressed on, but the defenders of Puebla made each yard count. "It's house by house, street by street," wrote once French officer. "[Our] artillery fires [and] makes a breach, the infantry rushes forward and all of a sudden an embrasure opens fire on us from behind . . . shells, grenades, mines—nothing is left out in this extraordinary defense." Mexican defenders were forced to abandon two more blocks toward the periphery. On April 19 they abandoned and destroyed four more blocks to create a killing field in front of San Augustín by exposing French attackers to crossfire from Santa Inèz. A week later the French halted their attack—reinforcements and resupply were about to open new options. Puebla's defenders, in fact, were desperate for resupply. General Ignacio Comonfort was leading an army to bring relief to the defenders of Puebla. By early May, Comonfort was on the outskirts of the city. On May 4, the eve of the anniversary of historic victory the year before, President Juárez visited Comonfort's army in a show of support, but May 5 came and went without victory. A few days later Comonfort was concentrating his forces at San Lorenzo, north of Puebla. His plan was to strike a blow at the rear of demoralized French forces, force them to break off their attack, then move to resupply Puebla. Before he could move, his army was surprised in a nighttime attack.[64]

Mexican losses on the night of May 7–8 were catastrophic. Comonfort's army was scattered and the supplies destined for the defenders of Puebla were seized by the French. The rout of Comonfort's army coincided with the arrival of reinforcements for the French, decisively shifting the momentum of the conflict. The attacking French were able to open a second line of attack, from the south of Puebla. On May 12 General Achille Bazaine's division began trench works in front of Fort Totimehuacan, southeast of the city. At dawn on May 16, Mexican defenders at Totimehuacan received convergent artillery fire across an arc from the west and the south. By 8 AM they were no longer able to return fire. With Totimehuacan silenced, the French turned their attention to Fort Carmen and Fort Zaragoza. By late afternoon the guns of Carmen and Zaragoza were silent, too.

Inside the city, General Ortega knew that Puebla was lost. With the southern forts down, he now faced an offensive across an arc of 180 degrees. With thinning forces and scarce ammunition, his priorities changed. After the disaster of Comonfort's army, Ortega commanded what was effectively Mexico's only large, conventional fighting force. His priority now was to preserve it. General Ortega appealed to Forey for a cessation of hostilities. Ortega would yield Puebla, in exchange for permission to vacate the city with soldiers, arms, and material under protection of armistice. Forey rejected this offer from "arrogant Puebla"—he insisted on unconditional surrender.[65] He would allow Ortega's army the honor of a final parade before French forces, after which Puebla would surrender arms and men.

At 1 AM on May 17, Ortega's forces began the destruction of weapons and ammunition. Controlled explosions took down ammunition stocks; cannon muzzles were spiked. Ortega sent a message that his officers would gather in front of Puebla's cathedral at 5:30 AM to offer themselves in

Napoléon III and Eugénie celebrate the fall of Puebla with fireworks at Fontainebleau; a pavilion on an island in the lake bears the names of French commanders Bazaine, Forey, and Douay. *Reproduced from* Le Monde illustré, *June 27, 1863.*

surrender. The defense of Puebla was over. On May 19, 1863, the French tricolor flag flew from the towers of Puebla's cathedral, Our Lady of the Immaculate Conception. Two weeks and one year after Mexico's glorious defeat of the French in 1862, Puebla had fallen.

The surrender of Ortega's army posed a problem for Forey. He was now in custody of an army almost half the size of his own. He decided to treat rank-and-file soldiers as a labor resource. Some he assigned to the demilitarization of Puebla, tearing down the formidable defenses constructed against the French; some he assigned to the construction of the railroad from Veracruz; nearly half were reassigned to fight in the army of Leonardo Márquez, a man without mercy, the most feared Mexican commander to rally to the Intervention. These assignments seemed to invite desertion, a tacit recognition of the impossibility of policing thousands of prisoners.

Forey took greater care with the Mexican officers. He saw them as particularly dangerous, the leaders of Mexican resistance. Although he resisted calls from Mexican Conservatives such as Almonte to execute them—and he rejected Saligny's call to send them to Cayenne, a remote place of secure confinement, the Guantanamo of its day—he recognized that their capture presented an opportunity to decapitate the Mexican insurgency and prevent the revival of organized resistance.[66] Accordingly, he decided to place an ocean between the captive officers and their bases of power. He would deport them to France. But even in this case, the numbers proved overwhelming. Over 1,500 officers had surrendered at Puebla, far more than Forey and his army could manage. When the day for the march from Puebla to Veracruz arrived, hundreds had already vanished; 950 remained. Four hundred more slipped away on the journey from Puebla to Veracruz; only 530 actually boarded at Veracruz, barely a third of those originally captured.[67] Forey's intuition that the officers represented the core of Mexican resistance would prove prescient.[68] Of those who escaped, several would go on to distinguish themselves as leaders of the Mexican resistance.[69] Among them were Mariano Escobedo and Porfirio Díaz.[70] Escobedo would roll up forces of the empire starting at the US border in 1866, and then, driving southward, capture Maximilian at Querétaro. As for Díaz, within days of his escape he would be back fighting the French at Tehuitzingo and Piaxtla. In 1866 he would retake Puebla and lay siege to Mexico City, forcing its surrender. Many years later he would serve as president of the Republic of Mexico.[71]

Mexican officers deported to France arrived at Brest in July 1863. General José Maria González de Mendoza, second in command at Puebla, was kept in Paris, where he could be put to use as the need arose. Most of the other captive Mexican officers, some five hundred of them, were farmed out to the French provinces. Brigadier generals were set up at Evreux. Colonels and lieutenant-colonels were dispatched to Tours; mere captains landed in places like Blois, Bourges, and Moulins—the lower the rank, the farther from Paris. A few were sent across the frontier to San Sebastián in the Basque country.[72] Some prisoners found romance. A lieutenant colonel sent to Tours met and married Marie Mathilde Seré. The married couple decided to live in Mexico, returning there in the summer of 1865.[73]

Meanwhile, in Puebla, Forey and his soldiers made their victory parade into the city. Forey's army did not receive the delirious welcome his informants had promised. On the contrary, as one of his officers described it, "We entered a dead city." The dreary reception he and his army received proved that they were seen as conquerors, not as liberators. Even an official reception was lacking—there were no town officials to greet them.[74]

All around them was rubble, not from their own bombardments—those had fallen in the western and southern parts of the city—but from the people of Puebla themselves, who had cobbled together barricades from whatever they could salvage around them. The "dismal silence" accompanied the conquering soldiers through vacant streets until they reached Puebla's magnificent *plaza mayor,* adjacent to the cathedral.[75] There, crowds moved among the arcaded buildings and through the square, for it was a Sunday, the siege was over, and life was returning to the markets. In the cathedral, the Catholic clergy of Puebla celebrated the arrival of the French with a Te Deum, a triumphant hymn of thanks.[76]

4

⌒⌐

Pacification and Resistance

A BLACK CARRIAGE ROLLED NORTHWARD out of Mexico City on the evening of May 31, 1863. Inside were Benito Juárez and Sebastián Lerdo de Tejada. The dismemberment of Ortega's army after the fall of Puebla two weeks earlier meant that there was no way to prevent the occupation of the capital. Congress met for a final time on that day to confer extraordinary power upon President Juárez.[1] That evening, Juárez and Lerdo departed.

What might the men have said to one another as they left the capital behind? It was a somber occasion and both men were famous for their reserve. After Rafael Martinez de la Torre met Juárez in 1855, he described him as "reserved and circumspect"—an assessment that varied little from person to person over years to come.[2] It was a reputation that traveled far, all the way to Paris. Andrés Oseguera, representing the Mexican republic in Paris, wrote admiringly in 1861 that "Juárez had the rare, quite rare, quality . . . of seeing things clearly and coldly."[3] Both Juárez and Lerdo had come up through seminary school—Juárez in his native Oaxaca, Lerdo at Puebla. Although seminary school implied a priestly vocation, it did not require it. It was an inevitable passage for young men of ambition growing up in a country where the Catholic Church had a monopoly on education.

Juárez left seminary for the secular Institute for Sciences and Arts in Oaxaca, a move that shifted his career prospects toward law and politics.[4] Lerdo also left seminary school (in 1841) to prepare for a career in law at the renowned Colegio de San Ildefonso, a residential college in Mexico City.[5] The Jesuit order had founded San Ildefonso and operated it until the order's expulsion from Mexico in 1767. After Jesuit expulsion,

Sebastián Lerdo de Tejada. *Museo Nacional de Historia,
Castillo de Chapultepec. Photo: R. Jonas.*

diocesan clergy—who, unlike the Jesuits, were accountable to the local
Catholic hierarchy—assumed responsibility for instruction. Yet even after
the Jesuits' departure, the institutional culture at San Ildefonso retained
the imprint of the Jesuit values of scholarly seriousness, discipline, and
rectitude. Lerdo, who rose to become rector of San Ildefonso in 1852, was
expected to embody those values during his tenure.[6] Both men had been
profoundly shaped by Catholic institutions in their youth; both would
commit much of their political careers to the substantial reform of the
place of the Catholic Church in national life.

As their carriage took them northward from the city, Juárez and Lerdo
were entering a political desert of unknown extent. They could not know

how long their exile from the capital would last or, indeed, whether they would ever return. More than four years later, on July 15, 1867, they would enter the capital again in triumph, riding in an open carriage. For now, they could only contemplate the bleak future facing them and the Mexican republic.

Until the fall of Puebla, the presence of those two men had provided a kind of symbolic unity in the capital, where it mattered the most. Now that presence was no longer tenable. Nine days after leaving the capital, Juárez and Lerdo halted in San Luis Potosí, where they would remain until the end of the year. The fact that they would pass six months unmolested there tells us much about the slow pace of the campaign of pacification of Mexico. It even gave rise to hopes of establishing at San Luis Potosí a functioning national capital to rival the occupation government that would be installed in Mexico City. They did as much as they could to project an image of normalcy. By June 16 the official newspaper of the Mexican republic, *El Diario del Gobierno de la República Mejicana,* had resumed publication from San Luis Potosí. It acknowledged the necessity of the departure from Mexico City but insisted that it would continue to fulfill its role and appealed directly to global public opinion by sharply criticizing the French Intervention as a "radical subversion of the rights of peoples."[7] By July 1863 their adversaries were writing the two men off. A French officer, Lieutenant La Tour du Pin, wrote that "Juárez . . . has been abandoned by his former partisans." He discounted the possibility that "anyone would organize a significant resistance."[8] In this he was soon to be proven wrong.

There were attempts to reconvene the Mexican national congress in San Luis, but by the end of 1863 it was clear that this would not be possible. This had consequences for Lerdo, whose original role was to embody the legislative branch in exile. Given the impossibility of reconvening, the legislature would have to cede its supremacy to the executive branch for the duration, a concession symbolized by Lerdo's decision to accept a position in Juárez's cabinet. The necessity of this move was borne out by what followed as the occupation settled in. For the next four years, Juárez and Lerdo would move no fewer than thirteen times, establishing residences in eight separate locations, sometimes for mere days, as they were pursued and displaced by occupation forces.[9] Such conditions made anything like normal government impossible. It took all the courage and ingenuity they could muster simply to remain on Mexican soil. Their primary aim was to prove, through mere survival, that Mexico endured.[10]

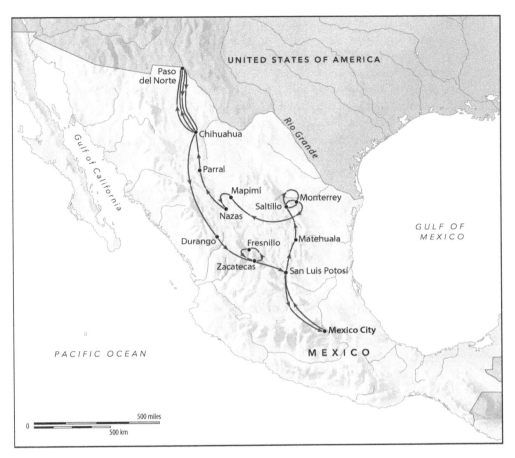

Internal exile of the Juárez government, May 31, 1863, to July 15, 1867. *Adapted from Andrew Knapp*, The Life of Sebastían Lerdo de Tejada, 1823–1889: A Study of Influence and Obscurity *(Austin: University of Texas Press, 1951).*

As Forey consolidated his power at Puebla, he ordered General Bazaine to advance on Mexico City. Bazaine's force moved out on May 25. Mexican leadership had no adequate force at its disposal to block his progress—the scattering of Comonfort's army in early May and the surrender of Puebla shortly thereafter had reduced Mexican resistance to insurgent forces.[11] Even Río Frío, where the road from Puebla narrows before opening out into the valley of Mexico, was undefended. Bazaine advanced on the capital unimpeded.

The departure of the Mexican government left Mexico City without a recognized authority. Sara Yorke Stevenson, an American who had taken up residence on the Calle San Francisco (today Calle Francisco Madero), witnessed isolated acts of violence during the interregnum. A Frenchman, bleeding from a head wound, stumbled into her home seeking refuge. He had been accosted on a nearby street and beaten. Another Frenchman was lassoed and dragged through the streets. Stevenson was not at all reassured by the rumor that the French were sending ahead their Mexican ally Leonardo Márquez, a man notorious for his cruelty. The prospect of more political violence prompted a series of delegations from the capital to Bazaine, urging him to hasten to the capital to prevent loss of life and property. Bazaine declined, citing strict orders not to enter the city.[12] Finally, on June 6, a week after the departure of Juárez and Lerdo, Forey authorized Bazaine to enter the capital. Bazaine's mission was to establish order and to prepare for Forey's ceremonial entry four days later.

Forey had a healthy respect for the power of pageantry. As part of the pacification of Puebla, he deployed his troops to form the honor guard for a gleaming Corpus Christi procession through the streets of the city, knowing the effect it would have on the population. The effect of priestly vestments, incense, and glistening ritual objects was magnified by the fact that public displays of religion had been proscribed since the Reform. The message was clear: the Church is returning to public life.[13] For the capital, he gave Bazaine detailed instructions for an entry that would make a similarly powerful impression on the people. As he was approaching the city from the east, he would enter by way of the *garita* San Lázaro, one of the gateways to the city. Once within the city, the soldiers of Bazaine's division were to stand at attention on either side of the ceremonial route, forming an honor guard and a human perimeter to restrain the crowds. Forey wanted triumphal arches along the parade route as well as poles trimmed with bunting, swag, and garlands—all guaranteed to draw the curious. Above street level, balconies and windows on his route were to be festooned with ribbons and banners.[14]

Bazaine executed Forey's orders to perfection. On June 10 at 8 AM, Bazaine positioned himself and his entourage outside the eastern entrance to the city, a few hundred meters from the *garita*. Moments later, Forey's column could be seen approaching by way of Peñón de los Baños (near where the airport stands today). Then an incident occurred that made it clear just how much weight General Forey placed on appearances. Bazaine had sent Colonel Blanchot forward to greet Forey and escort him to Bazaine's position. As Blanchot approached at a gentle gallop, he noticed the men around Forey gesturing frantically to slow down. Forey, it seems, had held a new uniform in reserve for just this occasion. The outfit included a uniform hat with spectacular white feather plumes; Forey was afraid that a coat of dust would ruin the effect. Properly cautioned, Blanchot returned to Bazaine at a walking pace. Forey's party followed at a distance.[15]

After Bazaine and Forey greeted one another, the procession proceeded to the *garita,* where artillery fired a salute, announcing their arrival. They were met by José Mariano Salas, a general whose military career stretched back to the independence era. Salas had served under the First Mexican Empire. He fought against the Americans during the Mexican-American War, was associated with the politics of Santa Anna, and briefly entered politics as interim president in 1846. When Juárez and Lerdo had left the capital the week before, forces favorable to the French Intervention had put Salas forward as their leader and spokesman.[16] In that capacity Salas greeted Forey and presented him with the keys to the city.

As the procession made its way through the streets of the city, Leonardo Márquez and his men were at its head. Anyone harboring doubts about

General Forey, on horseback center, reaches out to accept the keys to the city from a delegation of civilians while women and children scatter flowers. José María Calderón, *Entrada del general Forey a la ciudad de México el 6 de junio 1863. Museo de la Ciudad de México/Secretaría de Cultura/Gobierno de la Ciudad de México.*

what the Intervention would mean and reading the procession for clues could now set aside those doubts. In politics Márquez was a notorious Conservative; as a soldier he was known above all for his cruelty. A play on his name paid tribute to his ferocity—to friends and admirers Leonardo Márquez was "Don Leopardo" (Mister Leopard). In candid moments, his French allies acknowledged him to be a "vulture."[17] During the War of Reform, he had ordered the execution of Liberal officers taken prisoner after the battle of Tacubaya in 1859; more recently he and his men had rallied to the cause of the Intervention and in that capacity committed atrocities at Soledad.[18] Forey had been holding Márquez at arm's length for fear of the response he might provoke, but at the last minute he set aside those reservations. Márquez and his men led the procession into the city. They were followed by units of the French army and, finally, Forey himself. Forey was flanked on his right by General Almonte and on his left by Dubois de Saligny, the French political officer. A triumphal arch on the Calle de Plateros featured the names of Forey and Saligny, alongside the names of Almonte, Márquez, and other Mexican officers friendly to the Intervention. A triumphal arch on the Calle San Francisco featured portraits of Napoléon III and Empress Eugénie framed by flowers and trimmed with laurel.[19]

Forey would later write to Paris about the "delirious" reception he and his army received on June 10. France's soldiers, he claimed, were "literally crushed" under bouquets. The pro-Intervention newspaper *La Sociedad* noted that while most buildings were decorated, a few were not, suggesting perhaps the sincerity of the many. But even less self-interested witnesses noted a warm reception—"something very like spontaneous enthusiasm" is how the American Sara Yorke Stevenson put it, leaving room for a hint of doubt.[20] Writing years later, Ignacio Altamirano noted the ease with which loyalties transferred—not so much to the conquering French per se, but to the French and their Mexican allies who together represented the latest incarnation of an ongoing struggle. Conservative military leaders like Márquez had long ago made known their support for the Intervention. Now it was the turn of "all those who made up the civilian element of the Conservative Party," Altamirano noted. Government ministers and civil servants for the new administration would now be recruited from the established political families of Mexican politics— "the old political centralizers, the former supporters of Santa Anna, the rich, the clergy."[21] The Intervention was a foreign conquest, there could be no doubt, but it found strength when it grafted itself to established roots in Mexican society and politics.

The procession traversed the vast *plaza mayor* of the capital. Forey halted in front of the cathedral, dismounted, then ascended the steps toward the baroque façade that frames the central door. At the top of the steps, clergy in full regalia waited to greet Forey, Almonte, and Saligny. Cross- and candle-bearers led the procession into the church; they were followed by a group hoisting a white silk canopy, then the ranking clergy, then Forey and the other dignitaries. Inside, the cathedral was illuminated as for a holy day. The nave and transept were packed with congregants, ordered by rank and status. Forey, Almonte, and Saligny followed the procession into the sanctuary, a signal honor, and took their places to the right of the altar. A full orchestra was on hand for the celebration of the Te Deum, a prayer offered in gratitude for an extraordinary gesture of divine grace—a royal birth, victory in war, or in this case a national deliverance. Following the Te Deum, a trumpet sounded and the soldiers presented arms in salute. Then the recessional began following the established rules of precedence. Exiting the cathedral, Forey made his way to the Palacio Nacional, the official residence of the head of state, adjacent to the cathedral.[22]

Two days later Forey issued a manifesto to the Mexican people in which he set out the meaning of the French presence as being, above all, an opportunity to "show the flag of France, symbol of civilization." He dismissed Mexico's Cinco de Mayo victory the year before as a mere setback, puffed up into a great victory through the "boasting of a few military leaders." Puebla, far from being the "unassailable" city championed by Juárez and his government, had served as their "tomb."[23] The need to refer to Cinco de Mayo at all showed that the memory of Puebla could still sting, but he made an even bigger claim: "The military question is decided." Forey wanted to suggest that the occupation of the capital meant the end of the fighting, as might be the case in conventional warfare. Yet Forey knew better. He had served in Algeria, where the insurgency continued for years after the capture of Algiers.[24] In Mexico the insurgency was just getting started.

Nowhere was this clearer than at San Luis Potosí, where Juárez and Lerdo were setting up their government in internal exile, displaced from the capital but resolute in the justice of their cause. Forey's manifesto imagined power emanating from the capital, where he had taken command, but events were soon to reveal that Forey's power hardly extended beyond the ribbon of territory his forces controlled from Veracruz to Puebla to Mexico City. Everywhere else, power remained contested. Forey

Te Deum in the cathedral of Mexico City, celebrating the conquest of the capital, June 10, 1863. *Reproduced from* Le Monde illustré, *August 1, 1863.*

implicitly acknowledged this with a decree setting up courts-martial on June 20—ten days after his triumphal entry into Mexico City; the decree targeted "bands of armed evildoers" who would be sentenced without appeal and executed within twenty-four hours.[25]

Forey pressed on with the task of setting up a government, but here he bumped into the limits of bravado. His instructions called for a government with a clear national mandate; but without the ability to call upon representatives nationwide, he could only mobilize supporters in the capital. The best he could do was to create a council of thirty-five members, who in turn elected a triumvirate to exercise executive power. The council's choices for the triumvirate—two generals and a Catholic archbishop—represented a peculiar view of the nation, but it had the advantage of candor. It was like laying cards on the table.

Forey's triumvirate put an unmistakably reactionary stamp on the Intervention and tore away any remaining illusions that the French were honest brokers "above factions."[26] The archbishop named to the triumvirate, Pelagio Antonio de Labastida y Dávalos, wasn't even in the country. A vigorous opponent of the Reform Laws, Labastida had been forced into exile by the Mexican republic. He went to Rome, where he served as a tireless critic of the Mexican republic and an equally tireless promoter of monarchy. His stand-in until his return, Juan Ormaechea, bishop of Tulancingo, was somehow regarded as more reactionary than Labastida.[27] As for the generals, both Juan Nepomuceno Almonte and José Mariano Salas possessed solid patriotic credentials: they had fought against the Texas secession, they had shared in the campaign that led to victory at the Alamo, and they were veterans of the war with the United States.[28] But both men had supported General Santa Anna in his attempts to establish an authoritarian regime, which is to say that both men shared the conviction that the fundamental cause of Mexico's weakness was the republic itself, rather than entrenched opposition to it from the army and the Church. The Almonte-Labastida-Salas triumvirate stamped the Intervention as a continuation of the War of Reform.[29]

What came next was also tightly orchestrated. Napoléon III had insisted on a national referendum in which the people of Mexico would express a preference for monarchy or republic.[30] This apparently open-minded idea foundered on the impossibility of such a referendum. Instead Forey and his new provisional government organized an Assembly of Notables, 231 in all, who, it was claimed, represented the nation and could speak for it. Nearly half came from the Veracruz-Puebla-Mexico City corridor where the French and their allies had established military control, but just enough came from elsewhere (presumably they were already in the capital for other purposes) to give the Assembly of Notables the appearance of broad geographical representation.[31]

On July 11, after two sessions, they made their recommendation: Mexico should have a hereditary monarchy under a Catholic prince. The throne would be offered to the Habsburg Ferdinand Maximilian, a specificity that revealed a deeper choreography, but it contained a proviso. If Maximilian rejected the offer, the throne should be offered to a Catholic prince to be chosen in consultation with Napoléon III.[32] A delegation was named to carry the invitation to Maximilian. It left Mexico City on August 18, bound for Miramare, Maximilian's home near Trieste. The delegation scheduled a stopover in Paris for an audience with Napoléon III, with whom the real power lay.

In the meantime, the triumvirate of Almonte, Ormaechea, and Salas would rule as a Regency.[33] Their vision of the role of the Regency was activist. Until the newly created throne was occupied, power was theirs to use as they saw fit. They set about reforming Mexico by decree. On July 6 they declared themselves the "sole government to which obedience is owed" and forbade payment of taxes to agents of "the ex-government of Benito Juárez." They canceled, without indemnity, contracts concluded with the Juárez government. On July 13 they set up a censorship apparatus. Three days later they established an official news outlet: *El Periódico Oficial del Imperio Mexicano*. They restored a work ban for religious holidays, signaling the return of Catholic control to the rhythms of everyday life. They initiated a loyalty test, calling on "officials and leaders" outside the capital to appear before relevant military authorities to declare their support for "the Intervention and the Empire of Mexico."[34] Pressure to pledge loyalty was applied in Mexico City, too; Colonel Miguel Anza, taken prisoner after the fall of Puebla but subsequently released, was arrested in the capital for refusing to sign a loyalty statement. They harassed critics of the Intervention and deported some of them. On August 22 nine individuals thought to be hostile to the Intervention were arrested. For six of the nine, the arrest began with a knock on the door in the middle of the night, fostering a general sense of insecurity. Antonio Palacio y Majarol, Manuel Moralez Puente, Castillo Velasco, Manuel Payno, and Augustín del Río were taken to Veracruz and shipped to France. Also arrested was Réné Masson, former editor of *Le Trait d'Union*, a French-language newspaper published in Mexico City that was sympathetic to the Mexican republic. As a journalist, Masson had published signed pieces hostile to the Intervention. According to the report describing the arrests, Masson was "a dangerous man" who served as the hub for "all those opposed to the Intervention" whether in Mexico or abroad. He deserved "not the slightest leniency." The arrests of individuals critical of the empire made it clear that criticism would not be tolerated. No one was safe.[35]

The Regency took the opportunity to define the cultural program of the empire, too. Independence for Mexico was a core theme—ironic, given that Mexico was being conquered—but defenders of the empire contended that the Mexican republic was, if not a tool of the United States, then at least an inept defender of national autonomy. Associating the empire with independence meant connecting the empire with Anáhuac (Mexico before the Spanish conquest) and with independent Mexico (Mexico after throwing off Spanish rule). This idea was captured in a new coat of arms for Imperial Mexico, which included symbols evoking the Aztec past, the struggle for national independence, and "the Empire recently sanctioned" thanks to the "great idea" of Napoléon III to give "life and vigor" to the Latin race. They also announced the motto of the new empire: Religion, Independence, Union.[36] A new "Imperial Hymn" debuted at the capital's cultural showcase, the Gran Teatro. In three stanzas the hymn linked the empire to pre-Columbian Mexico and hinted at a brilliant past to be restored: "At the powerful voice . . . Anáhuac [arose], freed itself . . . and . . . began to shine."[37] The emphasis on independence and the pre-Conquista past concealed a contradiction—under the Imperial Regency at least, the empire meant a restoration of the rule of the Church and army.

The Regency benefited from support from the pro-interventionist press. Regular features in the Conservative newspaper *La Sociedad* explained what the monarchy would mean and why it was preferable to the republic, which had "enthroned immorality."[38] The monarchy would have a "new and Catholic power base" just like "the most illustrious [governments] of the civilized world."[39] The Intervention had brought about "a frank and fervent conversion of the Mexican people to Catholic, hereditary monarchy with an enlightened Austrian prince [at its head]."[40] Even before the creation of the Regency, *La Sociedad* had led the public critique of the Mexican republic by raising the specter of a socialist bogey led by "this ferocious party," which had concealed its "red flag" behind the "lying mask of reform." It assimilated the sale of Catholic properties to "the first dawn of communism" that prepared the way for an attack on the property of individuals. Worse, this "robbery" encouraged disrespect for religion, whose transcendent role was to bind Indigenous and *criollo* Mexico, to forge "the common chain binding our heterogeneous races."[41] Such press prepared the way for a decree on August 17, 1863, nullifying the confiscations of property by the Juárez government.[42]

The speed with which the regents were aligning the Intervention with a Catholic counterrevolution set off alarms among the French leadership. General Bazaine—the commander Forey had sent to capture Mexico City after the fall of Puebla—had been appointed to replace Forey as commander of French expeditionary forces in Mexico. Napoléon III wrote a letter of appointment to Bazaine, but in his reply Bazaine took the opportunity to warn that the Regency was vastly exceeding its charge and damaging France's image and interests. He also noted that Forey had failed to follow up on the occupation of Mexico City by extending military control to Mexico's provincial capitals, a charge that exposed a stubborn unwillingness to learn the lesson of Puebla. Occupying provincial capitals was the obvious next step from a military point of view, but Puebla had shown that the people of Mexico were anything but complacent about the Intervention. The immediate occupation of provincial capitals, however desirable from a political point of view, was simply unrealistic in the face of a burgeoning resistance.

Bazaine officially took military command from Forey on October 1, 1863. France's fourth military commander after Jurien, Lorencez, and Forey, Bazaine began preparations for a pacification campaign that would be both political and military. The aim of the military campaign was to suppress whatever forces remained loyal to the Mexican republic. The political pacification meant undoing the damage Forey had done when he accepted the embrace of Mexican reactionaries. Almost immediately Bazaine found his efforts thwarted by a formidable opponent. Archbishop Labastida, although abroad when he was appointed to the Regency, arrived in mid-October to assume his functions directly. In addition to being Mexico's highest-ranking prelate, Labastida brought with him an implicit papal authority—after all, he had spent his years of exile in Rome.[43] When he stepped off the boat in Veracruz, he used that authority to rally the bishops of Mexico to use the Intervention to restore the power and property of the Catholic Church in Mexico. Labastida's initiatives directly countered Bazaine's efforts to associate the new regime with reconciliation, an empire "above politics."[44]

Labastida tried to check Bazaine, too. He made it clear, in pointed terms, just how important clerical support had been to the Intervention

Archbishop Pelagio Antonio de Labastida y Dávalos.
Reproduced from Arturo Aguilar Ochoa, La Fotografía
durante el Imperio de Maximiliano. *México: Universidad
Nacional Autónoma de México, Instituto de
Investigaciones Estéticas, 1996.*

and what it would mean to lose it. "If your army was well received on its
arrival," he warned, "it [was] the work of the clergy." Labastida calculated the military value of the Church's support as equal to fifteen thousand soldiers—the number of men Bazaine would need in reinforcement
if he lost Catholic support.[45] Labastida also cultivated allies, notably
French diplomatic representative Dubois de Saligny, who shared Labastida's ideal of an ardently Catholic monarchy for Mexico.[46]

On November 17, 1863, Bazaine wrote a lengthy complaint to the French minister of war about Labastida's "systematic opposition" to efforts to calm political passions and take the country in "a more Liberal direction." Bazaine understood what his predecessors had not—that the new regime was to be above factions—whereas the many supporters of the Intervention saw it as a continuation of the War of Reform. For them, if the Intervention wasn't going to undo the Reform, what was the point?

Bazaine was surely aware that many Mexicans had bought former properties of the Catholic Church. Talk of restoring Catholic properties threatened their investments and risked driving them into the arms of the supporters of Juárez and the republic.[47] Bazaine was able to get Saligny recalled, depriving Labastida of a powerful ally. As for Labastida himself, Bazaine rallied the other regents, Salas and Almonte, to eject Labastida from the Regency or, rather, to allow Labastida to eject himself—Labastida threatened to boycott future meetings of the Regency now that the regents had (under pressure from Bazaine) renounced their edict restoring nationalized Church property.[48] Archbishop Labastida, who tended to regard himself as the incarnation of the Church in Mexico, could only complain that "the Church suffers today the same attacks . . . as during the time of the Juárez government."[49]

Bazaine had won, but the cost was high. He had alienated the most powerful cleric in Mexico. Six months earlier Archbishop Labastida had been at Miramare, reveling in his special relationship with Maximilian and Charlotte, celebrating Mass in their private chapel. Mere weeks after his triumphant return to Mexico, Bazaine had ousted him from his position as regent, a public rebuke and humiliation. He would soon show Bazaine what could happen to someone who crossed him.

Having halted the political hemorrhaging, Bazaine turned his attention to military matters. He commanded a force of forty-two thousand men under arms, with another fifteen thousand in supporting roles. He organized them into two columns, one commanded by General Armand de Castagny, the other commanded by General Félix Douay. He directed both columns to move north from the capital on independent paths. Both forces began their march from Mexico City on foot at the end of October; the generals and their staff followed on horseback a few days later.

Bazaine was eager to demonstrate the might of the French army, to win by intimidation rather than combat whenever possible. He also wanted to familiarize himself with the country, so he followed his troops into the field. When Bazaine left Mexico City on November 17, Douay, accompanied by the forces of the allied Mexican general Tomás Mejía, was already entering the city of Querétaro. General Castagny's column operated toward the west of Douay at a somewhat slower pace. On November 24 Castagny reached Acámbaro, where the allied Márquez division joined him; they then pushed on to Morelia together.

On the face of it, the French campaign was impressive. French forces moved smoothly, even gracefully, from point to point, settlement to settlement, establishing their authority wherever they went, without substantial resistance. The problem was persistence. The movement was like a vessel on the sea, pushing water aside cleanly at the bow, but the water rushes back at the stern as soon as the vessel passes. As French forces moved on campaign, forces loyal to the republic moved aside, avoiding confrontation, but moved back as soon as the French vacated. Pacification meant little more than temporary, localized occupation. Loyalty to the empire often lasted little longer than the presence of armed forces necessary to secure it. Lerdo de Tejada understood this perfectly and took comfort from what it portended. French operations showed that they had public opinion—especially European public opinion—in mind. Their aim was to avoid setbacks that would upset "their military self-esteem" and make it difficult to withdraw "without discredit." This meant that they would only occupy provincial capitals and key routes between them in order "to make Europe believe that they dominate these territories without challenge."[50] In time they would declare victory and go home. Given that the aim was the *illusion* of control, Mexico could take comfort from the occupier's lack of resources to control of the spaces in between. Time, resistance, and attrition would do the rest.

Bazaine's pacification campaign faced virtually no organized resistance until December, when republican general José López Uraga moved against two thousand Mexican troops serving the imperial cause under Leonardo Márquez. Uraga suspected that Márquez's army had a soft core. He knew that soldiers taken prisoner by the French after the fall of Puebla had been released on the condition that they join Márquez's division. Uraga was eager to demonstrate the fragility of Mexican forces that had rallied to the French. They might well desert, given the opportunity, especially if they could be attacked apart from their French allies.[51] He was to be disappointed. Uraga attacked with an army of eight thousand.[52] Márquez's forces were battered and Márquez himself was wounded in the cheek, but Uraga's army was turned back with significant losses. Morelia held in what was the first real test of what would become the army of the empire.

Uraga's defeat showed that the republic lacked the conventional military forces necessary to halt the pacification campaign. Indeed, Uraga would transfer his loyalties to the empire, but smaller acts of resistance were everywhere.[53] The Juárez government effectively declared open season on allied forces with its decree issued January 25, 1862. Although the decree aimed to discourage collaboration with the Intervention, notably by threatening death to anyone offering aid or assistance, allied commanders recognized that this same decree effectively authorized Mexicans to attack allied forces. The Soledad Treaty, which merely allowed Spanish, British, and French forces to move away from the coast, did nothing to change that. When Mexican insurgents attacked and killed three French soldiers who had strayed from camp, French commanders recognized that this was "a consequence of the decree of 25 January."[54]

The French were unbeatable in military formation, but if individual soldiers could be culled from the pack, local acts of resistance were possible. An artilleryman was poisoned shortly after his arrival at Veracruz in November 1862.[55] In the same year, Michel Larroude and Jean Antoine Volle were stabbed in separate incidents while on mission to Tampico. Paul Vico was out hunting turtledoves when he was killed with a blow to the head from a blunt instrument; his body was tossed in a river.[56] Antoine Villeneuve was in Santa Anna (Jalisco) when he was set upon, dragged into a cornfield, robbed, and killed. The body of François Chatel was found in a pit outside San Luis Potosí. Edouard Duer was out late alone when he was halted, surrounded, and stoned to death.

Attacking soldiers who strayed outside of protected zones was a common theme in these local acts of resistance, but not always. A soldier assigned to General Douay at Guadalajara was standing guard at night outside Douay's residence when he was picked off by a sniper. Soldiers sometimes went out in pairs; there was safety in company, but not always. Two soldiers wandered into a pulque bar on the Calle Tacuba just outside the capital; as they left, they were attacked by a group of men who beat and stabbed them and left them for dead. In a similar incident involving two soldiers leaving a *pulquería,* one was stabbed when he stepped aside to urinate.[57]

Resistance wasn't limited to Mexicans. Resistance also came from Europeans who began to arrive in 1864 as volunteers in service of the Mexican Empire. Sometimes resistance took the form of desertion; sometimes it took the form of an active denunciation of the empire while in uniform.[58] Some soldiers engaged in minor acts of resistance—insubordination, in fact—almost upon arrival. One soldier rendered himself unfit for combat through self-mutilation; another sold his military-issue saber; another sold his boots. Some Belgian soldiers were won over by Guillaume Wodon, a Belgian who had emigrated to Mexico fifteen years earlier and made his home in Morelia. Under questioning from his officers, a corporal revealed that Wodon had offered him one hundred dollars to go to the United States with a group of soldiers who were ready to desert.[59]

After a disastrous battle at Tacámbaro, where green Belgian volunteers were routed by a numerically superior republican force, the problem of desertion took on new forms. Belgians taken prisoner were separated from their officers, then turned loose in nearby settlements with a small daily allowance for support. Some supplemented their allowance by selling off parts of their uniforms. Others worked for pay, filling cartridges for the republican army or repairing the mobile printing press used to print an opposition newspaper.[60]

Prolonged contact with actual Mexicans had the inevitable effect of humanizing them. Relationships happened. Some became legend. Charles-Louis Blandinière, a humble clerk from Brussels, courted "a rich widow." They married and lived happily ever after.[61] The legend of "blue-eyed Mexicans"—still alive today in Mexico—is sometimes attributed to such interactions. Sometimes love ended in tragedy. A young woman became pregnant by her lover, a European soldier posted to Orizaba. Rejected by his lover's family, he took his own life on the steps of San Juan de Dios, the local church.[62] Suicide was its own form of desertion and not always a solitary act of despair. Pierre Eytabli and Henry Géraudan were in Mexico City on November 12, 1864, when they took their own lives, for reasons unexplained.[63]

Not all acts of resistance involved violence. Resistance could also take the form of intelligence gathering. Teófilo Martínez collected money for the resistance. Anacleto Leipa delivered corn and livestock to insurgents. Even symbolic resistance mattered—and could bring prison. Juan Trujillo was arrested in Jalapa and tossed into jail for the crime of carrying a portrait of President Juárez.[64] Sometimes vigilance offered a chance to settle old scores. Ingacio Velazquez was picked up after an anonymous denunciation.[65]

Some acts of resistance took place abroad. In fact, as Forey was setting up the Regency in the capital, Juárez attended to the foreign policy and diplomatic apparatus that would represent Mexican legitimacy abroad. He put Sebastián Lerdo in charge of foreign relations, a crucial position that positioned him as the contact for Matías Romero in Washington, and Jesús Terán, the man who would represent the Mexican republic in Europe. Both were talented men operating with limited means in difficult circumstances. Terán's charge was all the more difficult because of the complexity of the European political terrain. Terán represented an American republic in a Europe that was wedded to monarchy and hostile to democracy. Terán's reception in Spain provides an example. Lerdo drew up a letter of introduction to Queen Isabella, stating that Terán had full authority to represent Mexico, but in Madrid he got nowhere. The reforms carried out by the Mexican republic—especially those concerning the power and property of the Catholic Church—had created a bad impression in Spain and a offered a pretext to withhold diplomatic recognition. A similar letter addressed to Queen Victoria established his credentials in Britain without objection; the dispossession of the Catholic Church in Britain had happened centuries earlier and under a monarch—Henry VIII—so there could be no resistance on those grounds. In France, Napoléon III's aversion to republican politics meant that Terán could only work through back channels, which Terán did quite successfully while also fostering crucial support among French republicans. In Austria, Terán's first act was to lobby vigorously to persuade Maximilian not to accept the Mexican throne.[66] Taken together, Terán's unflagging efforts across Europe enhanced the reputation of an independent Mexican republic struggling under foreign occupation.

Juárez, Lerdo, Romero, Terán—these four men embodied the persistence of Mexico at home and abroad. They were seconded in these efforts by the work of individuals not nearly so well known—the men and women who refused to submit to European rule, whose everyday resistance made it impossible for the occupation and the empire to establish anything resembling normalcy.

Even so, the steady military progress of the enemies of the republic had immediate domestic political consequences. The speed with which French forces and their Mexican allies occupied key locations destroyed optimism that Juárez and his government could remain in San Luis Potosí.[67] For sixth months Juárez and Lerdo's presence there nurtured hope that San Luis might endure as a republican capital to rival the occupied capital of Mexico City. The dream ended on December 22 when Juárez and Lerdo were forced to exit San Luis to continue their movement northward by way of Matehuala. They would enter Saltillo on January 9. For the next three and a half years Mexican sovereignty would be itinerant. Wherever Juárez could be found, there, too, was the republic.

Bazaine was under instructions to establish a presence in provincial cities and towns and to use that presence to organize demonstrations in favor of the empire—the signs of popular support that Maximilian and Charlotte had insisted upon as a condition for accepting the throne. Early French military progress encouraged some local Mexican leaders, by conviction or opportunism, to rally to the imperial cause. In December Bazaine joined with General de Castagny to bring León, Lagos de Moreno, and Aguascalientes into the fold, while Douay moved on San Miguel Allende and Guanajuato.[68] Given the impracticality of organizing a national referendum, these events were organized as a substitute. They typically took the form of written statements in support of the empire, signed by local notables—figures of wealth and influence.[69] These *actas de adhesión* (testimonials of allegiance) were reproduced in the press to create a sense of momentum.[70] They were also communicated to the emperor-elect, Maximilian.

Anyone looking on from the outside could be forgiven for regarding these *actas de adhesión* with skepticism. No doubt there were monarchists in the provinces—they now had their moment to step out, thanks to the presence of foreign troops—but given that the testimonials in favor of the empire came during a military campaign, coercion could never be ruled out as a factor. Counter demonstrations were impossible. And what should we make of signatures like those on the *acta* from Ciudad Valles, near San Luis Potosí? Many names are written in the same hand, but next to each name is a cross in a different hand, indicating the assent of individuals who could not write their names but could scratch out an "X." The document is headed "Los Pueblos de indígenas de Ciudad de Valles"—the Indigenous peoples of the city of Valles.[71] Is the assent real or coerced?

Orchestrated or real, these testimonials of support for the empire worked where they mattered most—thousands of miles away. On December 26, 1863, Maximilian wrote to the regent Almonte, noting approvingly the recent testimonials in favor of the empire emanating from Morelia, San-Luis Potosí, Guanajuato, and Guadalajara—all way points in Bazaine's recent campaign. He also relayed his decision to accept the crown.

5

⌒◯

The Savior

CHRISTMAS EVE 1860 was magnificent for Maximilian and Charlotte, at least by appearances. It was their first in their new home, Miramare, a fairytale castle by the sea. Since their marriage in July 1857, they had been itinerant. In February of that year Maximilian's brother, Habsburg emperor Franz Joseph, had appointed Maximilian governor-general of Lombardy and Venetia, with its capital in Milan.[1] It was a plum assignment. Milan was a wealthy, highly cultured city, a jewel in the crown of the Habsburg Empire; Charlotte was eager to join Maximilian there as soon as they married.

Maximilian was twenty-five when he married; Charlotte had just turned seventeen. Maximilian had been an ardent suitor—daily bouquets during the courtship and a diamond bracelet at Christmas.[2] With their courtship complete, the newlyweds sought to win over the population of Milan with youthful charm and liberal administration. Maximilian and Charlotte made themselves visible around town, riding in an open carriage. They entertained brilliantly.[3] Charlotte found that she "adored" the Italians. Adopting the tone of a loving and indulgent mother, she told her grandmother that the Italians "are like children." "They have their faults," she conceded, "but that only makes me feel more strongly attached."[4]

But as a revived Italian nationalism threatened Austrian rule in Italy once again, Franz Joseph began to doubt that Maximilian's accessibility and progressive vision were what the situation required.[5] Ten years earlier, in 1848, struggles for republican rule and independence from Austria had been put down with brutal military force in Milan and Venice.[6] Now that Italian nationalism was resurfacing with new resolve, Franz Joseph was taking no chances. He opted for a firmer hand. Franz Joseph replaced his brother Maximilian with Count Ferenc Gyulai, a general.[7] Maximilian's rule had lasted barely two years.

Humiliated, Maximilian and Charlotte retreated to their property near Trieste, taking up residence in temporary lodgings while construction of their dream house went forward. They also occupied themselves with smaller projects. They bought Lokrum, an island in the Adriatic opposite Dubrovnik. Lokrum's main structure, an abbey, was in disrepair. They began to restore it.[8] Charlotte traded stocks. She rotated out of metals and into transportation stocks, advising her brother to do the same.[9] The new Habsburg family yacht, *SMS Phantasie,* launched in 1858; Maximilian, a naval officer, took it on a cruise to Corfu.[10] Maximilian and Charlotte undertook a cruise together to Brazil aboard *SMS Elizabeth,* but miserable weather even before they left the Mediterranean persuaded Charlotte to disembark at Madera; she promised to wait there while Maximilian continued the voyage without her. This was the first time they had been separated since their marriage, and Maximilian's mood was a regular theme of his letters. Maximilian wrote of his "Melancholie"—in the nineteenth century this was the mark of a rare and lofty spirit, a romantic genius capable of profound feelings, but in clinical settings it was also synonymous with depression.[11] By the spring they were reunited, preparing to settle into their magnificent new waterfront home on the Adriatic.

In the 1860s, Trieste was a cosmopolitan place, as port cities tend to be. It was also firmly under Habsburg rule. Italian and Slovenian were the dominant languages, but in the streets of Trieste it was not unusual also to hear Croatian, Greek, and, of course, German, the language of imperial power. Trieste provided access to the sea, and for that reason alone it was crucial to the Austrian/Habsburg claim to imperial status. After all, can a true empire be landlocked? Such considerations certainly informed Maximilian's decision to build his principal residence near Trieste. Maximilian had still been a bachelor in 1856 when he approved the architectural design for his home on a rocky promontory on the Adriatic Sea.[12] This means that Charlotte, whom he married in July 1857, had also married his sometimes romantic, sometimes gloomy, neo-Gothic vision of domestic life.

Miramare's most prominent seaward feature is a square, crenelated tower a full story taller than the three-story residence. Perhaps inspired by the cathedral bell tower of Seville ("my beloved Giralda"), perhaps inspired by Walter Scott, it establishes the profile of Miramare.[13] Below the tower, the crenelated roofline of the residence—punctuated by turrets at the corners—reinforces the defensive, castle-like design. Apart from a few decorative arrow slits, the sturdy fortress-residence look is set aside on the lower floors. The interior features much carved wood—wood-hewn balustrades with inserts of family coats-of-arms; coffered ceilings; a bedroom paneled in carved wood—even the private chapel featured an altar of carved wood and carved niches for the twelve apostles.[14] Charlotte personalized the castle by ordering artillery pieces embossed with the Miramare coat of arms.[15] The Italianate landscaping provided some relief from the somber interior and spoke to Maximilian's keen interest in botany.[16]

Maximilian and Charlotte were at Miramare when offered the Mexican crown. The timing was propitious, as a cascade of events enhanced the possibility of success. On December 20, 1860, representatives of South Carolina voted to secede from the American republic, announcing the fracturing of the United States, the possibility of civil war, and the long-awaited opportunity to confront Yankee aggression. In Mexico, the War of Reform reached a decisive moment on December 21 as republican forces triumphed in battle at Calpulalpan, removing the final obstacle to the occupation of Mexico City. Victory meant that the Reform, including laws supporting religious pluralism and civil marriage, as well as the breakup of the massive property holdings of the Catholic Church, would go forward. The triumphant return of President Benito Juárez to the capital, along with the hasty departure of Miguel Miramón, the darling of the Mexican forces of reaction, persuaded Mexican Conservatives that their cause was lost unless foreign powers intervened.

The idea of a European intervention in Mexico had been articulated before 1860. Santa Anna, as president of Mexico in the aftermath of the disastrous war with the United States, had attempted to secure the intervention of European powers as allies as early as 1853, but found little enthusiasm for it. In 1856 Tomás Murphy, a former Mexican representative to London, again put forward the idea of a European intervention. His timing was a bit better—France and Britain were fresh off their victory in Crimea, where they had halted the southward ambitions of the Russian goliath.[17] Might it not be the right time to blunt Yankee expansion with a European monarch in Mexico? Alexis de Gabriac, French minister to Mexico, put forward a similar idea in correspondence with Paris. The symmetry was obvious—Britain and France rallying to take down first one continental titan, then the other—but the timing was wrong. No one was ready to challenge the United States on its own turf; British, French, and Belgian textile mills relied almost exclusively on US cotton; no one wanted to antagonize an important buyer of European goods and supplier of raw materials.

The situation was different in 1860. France, Britain, and Spain would join in a military effort to force Mexico to pay its debts—in effect, three armies were to be engaged as debt collectors on behalf of European investors. This would be a good story already, were it not merely a cover story for an initiative that was grander still. For Napoléon III and Eugénie, egged on by Gutiérrez and Hidalgo, collecting delinquent debt was a pretext for a plan to conquer Mexico militarily and impose a European monarch as head of state. The only thing missing was a monarch.[18]

But was a European-style monarchy the solution, as Hidalgo and Gutiérrez imagined? Would the people of Mexico accept a foreign-born monarch? Even in an age of awakening nationalism, the idea that a people could be ruled by a foreign monarch remained alive. After all, Queen Victoria was of German lineage. The king of the Greeks was Bavarian. A not-quite-French Corsican named Napoléon Bonaparte had ruled France. Within monarchist ideology, alien lineage was an advantage. Only a foreigner—better yet, a foreigner raised to rule—could credibly claim a disinterested status above faction, above politics. But who would serve as monarch for Mexico?

Timing was everything. Personalities mattered, too. Late in 1857, José María Hidalgo had crossed paths with Empress Eugénie at the oceanside city of Bayonne in southwestern France. Hidalgo was an old friend of the family, a frequent household guest during Eugénie's childhood in Spain.[19] Eugénie's father was a Spanish noble, francophile, and Bonapartist; he fought alongside French forces after Spain was annexed to the Napoleonic Empire. Eugénie de Montijo was born in Granada in 1826 and educated in Paris at the Sacré Cœur convent school (today the Rodin Museum). She married well. Louis-Napoléon Bonaparte, nephew of Napoléon Bonaparte, had used his famous family name in 1848 to get himself elected president of France's Second Republic. Four years later he overthrew the republic and announced the restoration of the Napoleonic dynasty, taking the title Napoléon III out of deference for the son of Napoléon, who never ruled. Craving legitimacy as his uncle had, Napoléon III set out to marry the daughter of one of the established European ruling families. His overtures rejected, he proposed to Eugénie, a bright star of the Spanish nobility. She acquired the title "empress" when they married in 1853. It was a stroke of luck for Hidalgo that the woman he had known since child-hood was now married to the most powerful man in Europe.

They were reunited by the sea. Eugénie was fond of taking the air at the coastal resort of Biarritz; Hidalgo had stopped over on his way to take up a diplomatic post in Paris. Delighted to see an old friend from Spain, Eugénie invited Hidalgo to join her and her husband, the emperor of France, the next day on their yacht.[20] Thanks to this fortuitous encounter, Hidalgo became a regular in French imperial social circles; he used his position to stoke Eugénie's anxieties about the decline of Spain and the vulnerability of its empire to the predatory Yankee republic.[21] She hardly needed convincing. The annexation of Texas in 1845, followed by the disastrous Mexican-American War, was evidence enough. And the United States was known to be eyeing Cuba, still a Spanish holding.[22] Eugénie held mixed loyalties. For a time she supported putting the Spanish Bourbon Juan de Borbón y Braganza on the throne of Mexico.[23] Though that plan fizzled, she retained from Hidalgo the grand strategic vision whereby Spain and France shared a common racial heritage that obliged them to defend Latin peoples against the Anglo-Saxon race and the arrogant Yankee republic.[24]

For a time the Duke d'Aumale (of the rival Orléanist ruling family of France) was entertained as a prospect in a scheme whereby Britain, France, and Spain would guarantee the throne of Mexico, but the offer met with a firm refusal. It seems that Hidalgo himself was the one to imagine a monarch who, while not Latin himself, would fulfill the role of defender of Latinity. Spain at its apex had been ruled by a Habsburg, a fact that was evident throughout Latin America. As Hidalgo noted, the Habsburg "eagle with two heads" could be found on buildings across Spanish America thanks to two centuries of Habsburg rule.[25]

Mexican refugees had already approached and been turned down by no fewer than six potential monarchs before they encountered a receptive response from Ferdinand Maximilian, an archduke from one of the most distinguished ruling houses of Europe. He was younger brother to the Habsburg emperor Franz Joseph and, in a sense, that was the problem. As second in line to the throne, his talents seemed wasted. Franz Joseph's appointment of Maximilian as governor-general of Lombardy had offered an outlet to his ambitions, but his abrupt removal showed that he would always be at the mercy of his older brother. Meanwhile, the birth of a son to Franz Joseph and his wife, Empress Sisi, meant that Maximilian was no longer next in line to the throne.

Maximilian's wounded pride made him easy prey to Mexican imperial overtures, but so did dynastic preoccupations.[26] His voyage to Brazil might have been intended to clear his mind after Milan—his notes on botany and zoology reveal a mighty effort—but the dominant recurring theme was dynastic.[27] Crossing the equator on January 8, he noted in his diary that the *SMS Elizabeth* was "the first Austrian steamer [to cross] since steam has ruled the world," adding, "I can rejoice in being the first man of my house to enter the southern hemisphere." Maximilian was convinced that the future lay in America, but by what monumental dynastic neglect could it be that he was "the first lineal descendant of Ferdinand and Isabella" to visit the New World? As he approached the Brazilian island of Fernando di Noronha, he observed the intensifying traffic of seagoing vessels but also felt "grief not to [encounter a single] Austrian vessel among all those of various other nations."[28] He was convinced that America was "the cradle of the future," but this only heightened his alarm at Austria's apparent irrelevance there and highlighted the complacency of his Habsburg contemporaries, above all the complacency of his brother.

Ever since the revolutions of 1848 swept across Habsburg lands—to be brutally suppressed by calling out soldiers against civilians—Maximilian's brother Franz Joseph had associated the Habsburg name with reaction in Europe. In contrast, Maximilian was elaborating a modern, progressive alternative. Maximilian's modernity included a moral revulsion at American slavery, a "hideous" institution whose "germs of decay" corrupted everything it touched. Nor could he bring himself to overlook the hypocrisy with which some spoke of "the rights of man" when they meant only "the rights of white . . . men," denying rights to the enslaved.[29]

"One travels to learn," Maximilian noted in his diary. And so he had, but there was a redemptive aspect to his travels, too. The European vision of the Americas as a place to start over was already commonplace, but Maximilian's vision was spiritual, even sacramental. An Atlantic crossing, he noted, was like "a second baptism"—a eucharistic experience that could wash away "even the stains of blood."[30] In the old days, troubled souls joined a monastery. In modern times, they go to America.

For Maximilian, America wasn't only a place to start over. It held out the possibility of dynastic renewal. Unlike other crowns within reach— Poland or Greece—the crown of Mexico had a special allure because of the dynastic associations it conjured. Only in Mexico could he reconnect with the weighty legacy of Ferdinand and Isabella. It was a view shared by his spouse, Charlotte, and her father Leopold, king of Belgium. Charlotte and her father understood Maximilian's sense of frustrated ambition and even fed it. As Charlotte and her husband set out a decorative plan for their new home at Miramare, they found themselves returning to themes of lineage, destiny, sacrifice, and redemption abroad.

Miramare anchored the Habsburg Empire at the sea's edge, but it was more than a placeholder at a strategic imperial borderland. Maximilian and Charlotte planned the interior decorations of Miramare as the vision of their Mexican monarchy took shape. The decorations, some completed after their departure, reveal just how deeply and convincingly they inhabited their imperial fantasy, insinuating Mexico into a story of Habsburg redemption.[31] Two rooms at Miramare make the case. The Historical Room features paintings situating Maximilian and Charlotte within Habsburg family history. A ceiling fresco carries the title "The Triumph of Emperor Maximilian." The central subject is Maximilian, shown in three-quarters view, his left arm raised in an upward gesture, his index finger pointing toward an undefined future. His gaze follows his gesture.[32] The foreground teems with evocative detail. Maximilian is surrounded by allegorical figures representing the four continents—stock figures in Baroque allegory. Europa, on the right, wears a crown. In her left hand are drafting tools. She is the queen among continents and she is the builder. Her right hand touches her heart. She looks at Maximilian with eyes that can only be described as adoring.

From the lower left, Asia, Africa, and America emerge from frothy seas, bearing abundance. Africa offers feathers, Asia offers textiles, while America offers tropical fruit, a pineapple. Like Europa, they are transfixed by Maximilian. All of this is fairly standard allegory, but two additional details deserve our attention. The first is a female figure positioned between Europa and Maximilian. She holds the tools of a sculptor, like the others she is transfixed by Maximilian, and the bust she holds is recognizable as Maximilian's Habsburg ancestor Charles V. Why Charles? Because Charles served as Habsburg emperor at a time when the sun never set on the Habsburg Empire. Habsburg domains included not only much of eastern Europe, but also the Netherlands, Lorraine, Spain, and—most important of all—New Spain, better known post-independence as Mexico.[33] Finally, in the background, at top-center, the eagle of Mexico flies to Maximilian to deliver a scepter, the symbol of rule.

In vivid color, we notice one additional key detail—the artist's liberal use of cochineal red, most prominently in Maximilian's cloak. Cochineal red, also known as carmine, is a pigment produced from the body of an

Cesare Dell'Aqua, *The Triumph of Emperor Maximilian. Archives du Palais Royal Belge, BE-A0546/36, Impératrice Charlotte du Méxique, 203 De triomf van keizer Maximiliaan.*

insect indigenous to Mexico. Like turkey, tobacco, and tomatoes, it was a gift of New Spain to the world.[34] Here, it evokes the many accomplishments of the Habsburg dynasty.

The fresco represents what artists call an apotheosis—a culmination. It suggests that Maximilian's role as emperor of Mexico is no mere accident. It is historical destiny. It represents the apex of family history. It converts the self-regard of this vain and romantic prince into a solemn duty and a sacred trust.[35]

Maximilian and his artist are elaborating a grand vision of the Mexican Empire as a resurrected New Spain—a resurrection, by the way, that implies not just the reconstitution of the Habsburg Americas, but a reinvigoration of the Habsburg dynasty itself. In this respect, parallel to its fawning over Maximilian and his destiny, the painting also functions as a body blow to Maximilian's brother, Emperor Franz Joseph, who is rendered invisible, a nullity.

This is nowhere brought home more vividly than in the Throne Room, another neo-Gothic interior at Miramare. Here, too, Maximilian and Charlotte installed a work [not shown here] celebrating Charles V, depicted enshrined in the heavens where an angel offers one of many crowns representing his many domains; from below, Columbus and Cortés look on. In between, a map features the extensive Habsburg dominions of Charles V from the Old World to the New. In America, the *original* boundaries of New Spain are represented, including territories annexed by the United States as California, Texas, Arizona, and more—measuring what is lost but also offering a glimpse of the fuller ambition of Maximilian's Imperial Mexico, especially when we note that New Spain isn't labeled "New Spain" it's labeled "Mexico." The fresco captures the anti-Yankee resentments—and irredentist ambitions—of Maximilian and his sponsors.[36]

On the wall facing, a painting depicts portraits of Habsburg rulers and the Holy Roman emperors reaching back to Charlemagne.[37] At the summit are Maximilian and Charlotte, their portraits linked by a golden wedding band. They are claiming for themselves the energy and promise of the Habsburg family from the glory of Charlemagne to the present. Poor Franz Joseph! History passes him by. The reigning Habsburg is not even a sideshow—he doesn't figure at all.

The artistic program at Miramare captures the ambition and vanity of the imperial couple. It also conveys their plans for Mexico. Maximilian and Charlotte imagined themselves at the head of a political *Reconquista,* uniting a Mexico beset by internal divisions. Their ambition was to restore Mexico to its former glory, but also to reinvigorate the Habsburg line in doing so.[38] Charlotte championed this grand historical vision. Although she claimed that she'd "take it calmly" if the offer of the Mexican crown fell through, she was already imagining Maximilian "at the head of a great empire . . . restoring order . . . in the name of Charles V." She also promoted Maximilian's fraternal rivalry, speculating whether the "sun would set" on the Habsburgs of Europe.[39]

Given all of this, it's not difficult to understand the enthusiasm of Mexican Conservatives. If Maximilian's self-image harkened back to the Habsburg New Spain of Charles V, didn't that imply a restoration of everything that had been lost since independence? The confiscated property of the Catholic Church, the decline in status of creole elites in the name of republican equality—wouldn't these have to be reversed?[40] The grand vision of Maximilian and Charlotte implied as much.

Not everyone around the imperial couple shared their enthusiasm. Maximilian sought to enlist his younger brother, Ludwig Victor, in his mission to revive the Habsburgs and transform the Americas by way of Brazil. Maximilian encouraged Ludwig to pursue marriage with one of the daughters of Emperor Pedro II of Brazil. Pedro had no male heirs, which meant that Ludwig would be positioned as Pedro's successor. With Maximilian on the throne of Mexico and Ludwig Victor on the throne of Brazil, they would rule a newly resurgent Habsburg Empire from the Rio Grande to the Rio Plata. Ludwig declined.[41]

Disappointed by the Habsburg siblings but undaunted, Charlotte turned to her own siblings to capture the throne of Brazil. Charlotte had two brothers, Leopold and Philippe. Leopold's future was already mapped out. As the eldest, he was destined to succeed their father Leopold I, as Leopold II, king of Belgium. Philippe, however, was available. Charlotte sought to persuade Philippe to put himself forward for the Brazilian throne; she also conscripted Leopold to lobby Philippe on behalf of their grand vision. With Leopold on the throne of Belgium, Charlotte as empress of Mexico, and Philippe as emperor of Brazil, the Coburgs would be a new force in global politics and, through their alliance with the Habsburgs, dominant.

She pressed her case directly with Philippe, but also lobbied both Leopolds, father and son, coaching them in lengthy letters about how to approach Philippe. Her advice was coolly transactional. Brazil would make a fine placement for Philippe, she argued, and "a superb colonial outlet for Belgium."[42] It would also deepen the alliance of Habsburgs and Coburgs begun with the marriage of Maximilian and Charlotte. All Philippe had to do was to marry one of the daughters of Emperor Pedro of Brazil, it didn't matter which. "Try to marry him to one or the other," she urged her brother Leopold.[43]

Philippe had other ideas. He wasn't keen on Brazil, and he did not share Charlotte's grand dynastic vision. He resented Charlotte's Brazilian matchmaking but promised to forgive, noting, "We are such old and good friends." That said, given that Charlotte had so brazenly sought to interfere in Philippe's affairs, he felt entitled to comment on hers. He stripped away the embellishments that made her plans to rule Mexico seem like a noble undertaking. Peel back all the talk about Charles V and the revived Habsburg dynasty, Philippe noted, and Mexico was nothing but a "colonial affair."[44] Maximilian and Charlotte saw no distinction between rule over other Europeans and rule abroad, but Philippe did. Maximilian and

Charlotte would be better off with the crown of Poland. "Some crowns are heavy to wear; I hope the crown of Montezuma isn't one of them," he noted, before adding ominously, "I sincerely hope that one day you don't find that I was right."[45]

Philippe's grim warning was prescient, but late. As he was writing to his sister Charlotte, the Mexican delegation was arriving in Trieste, intent on offering the "crown of Montezuma"—heavy, as it turned out—to Maximilian and Charlotte. The seduction was about to enter its final phase.

6

The Seduction

By all appearances, Charlotte was troubled by none of the doubts that haunted Maximilian. Maximilian assured himself and those around him that his interest in the imperial throne of Mexico was conditional and that those conditions gave him a way out. The problem was that everything about his behavior said otherwise.[1] As forces from Spain, Britain, and France were descending on Veracruz late in 1861, Maximilian was meeting with his brother Franz Joseph in Venice to hash out the details of Maximilian's candidacy, including a cash advance to cover startup costs.[2] In January 1862, barely a month after allied forces arrived at Veracruz, Maximilian met with Juan Nepomuceno Almonte to draw up a preliminary agreement regarding the Mexican throne.[3] As Europe's most eligible monarchs, Maximilian and Charlotte were offered the throne of Greece, vacated in October 1862. Queen Victoria, it seems, had caught wind of their interest in Mexico and thought little of it. She urged her uncle, Charlotte's father, Leopold I, to make the ask regarding Greece, which he did in February 1863.[4] At about the same time, Charlotte's brother Philippe, working at cross-purposes with his father, encouraged Charlotte to reject the thrones of Greece and Mexico and to hold out for Poland. "It's better than Mexico," he told her.[5]

They declined. Their decision was made, in part, out of respect for engagements they had already made regarding Mexico. This attitude suggested just how firm a hold Mexico already had upon them. The little things were at least as telling. Maximilian would continue to insist that his acceptance was conditional, but he and Charlotte were already deeply involved in details about their new empire—details so trivial that they made sense only if the decision had effectively been made. By February 1863, not only had they settled upon a uniform for their court valets, they had placed an order for the outfits with a firm in Brussels.[6] They hired a tutor to teach them Spanish; by November they were writing to one another in Spanish.[7] Red curtains in the chapel at Miramare featured the Mexican eagle. Maximilian and Charlotte had made up their minds, at least in private.

Their Mexican seducers had kept up a subtle campaign throughout. Gutiérrez had visited Miramare to press his case in the summer of 1862, then followed up with a thank-you note wherein he repeatedly referred to Charlotte as "Your Imperial and Royal Highness" as if the matter was settled. He poured it on. "Never have I been more honored, never have I harbored more pleasant hopes for my country," he wrote.[8] He fed the momentum of inevitability by publishing an essay, "Mexico and the Archduke Ferdinand Maximilian of Austria," sending signed copies to European heads of state.[9]

Even God weighed in. As the French siege of Puebla was reaching its conclusion, Gutiérrez cast the imperial throne as a divine mandate that could not be refused. "Resolve to submit to Divine Will," he wrote. "[God] has placed this burden in [your] hands."[10] In early July, in the aftermath of the fall of Puebla, the exiled archbishop Antonio de Pelagio Labastida made the pilgrimage to Miramare.[11] In the private chapel at Miramare, Labastida celebrated Catholic Mass on Maximilian's birthday, July 6, while thousands of miles away the Assembly of Notables in Mexico City prepared to offer the throne of a new Mexican Empire to Maximilian. A few weeks after his visit to Miramare, Labastida departed for Mexico, ending his exile and reentering politics as imperial regent.

From Mexico City, Juan Almonte, now installed as regent, also dialed up the pressure. As Maximilian and Charlotte prepared to receive the delegation of Mexican notables in late September 1863, Almonte urged them to ignore signs of a burgeoning insurgency in Mexico. "[Don't] believe in a resistance that exists only in newspapers," he advised. The "phantom of resistance" would disappear. The people await "with impatience" the "liberating force" of the army. By the time this letter reaches "Your Majesty's hands," Almonte asserted, "imperial authority will be recognized over the great majority of the territory."[12]

Almonte followed up a few weeks later. Word had not yet reached Mexico of the visit of the Mexican delegation, but Almonte couldn't resist using the grand language due to an emperor. Again brushing aside inconvenient reports of resistance, Almonte assured Maximilian that "the entire country counts on [Your Majesty] and considers itself saved by your acceptance." Whatever resistance still existed, he asserted, was merely "theft and banditry [concealed] by a veil of false liberalism and lying patriotism." Turning the burgeoning Mexican resistance into an asset, Almonte argued that what the situation required was the emperor's presence in Mexico. It would have a calming effect and a real military value—worth more than a hundred thousand men "to the pacification of the country."[13]

The problem was uncertainty, and only Maximilian could fix that. "The presence of Your Majesty . . . is worth more than an army," Almonte wrote in late October. The people would express themselves freely only when there was clarity about the future. The arrival of Maximilian would put an end to a situation where "doubts are exploited by our adversaries." Early in 1864 Almonte turned up the heat, adopting a scolding tone as he shifted responsibility for disorder onto Maximilian. "I hope that this letter will not find Your Majesty still in Europe." The "widespread doubt" that Maximilian would accept the throne was "the last [remaining] weapon of our enemies."[14] Doubt was the enemy of the empire.

On October 1, 1863, the Mexican delegation appointed in occupied Mexico City arrived at Trieste. The mission was to offer the crown to Maximilian, but the members of the delegation represented several constituencies. The delegation included several persons eager to draw foreign investors to Mexico or to placate existing investors, including those who had bought Catholic properties.[15] Unlike Labastida, whose support for the empire was tightly linked to the aim of recovering Catholic Church properties, many of the delegates represented business interests. Tomás Murphy, Ignacio Aguilar y Marocho, and Joaquín Velázquez de León, in addition to Hidalgo, had backgrounds in banking and investments.[16] Antonio Escandón owned textile mills, sugar plantations, real estate (including Church properties), and railroad concessions.[17] Tomás Murphy was the son of a British financier who specialized in investments in Spain and New Spain; as Mexico's representative to Britain, he had been fielding complaints from British investors in Mexico eager to know when dividend payments would resume.[18] For men like these, the empire would provide the kind of political environment they saw as necessary for reassuring foreigners about the safety of their investments. In a sense, they were advocates for the vicar of Cranborne and other European investors who had pushed the Intervention—investors wanted safety of capital and reliable returns. The delegation consisted of men convinced that only European monarchy could provide the necessary security.[19] In that regard, it was relevant that of the eleven members of the delegation, four—Gutiérrez, Hidalgo, Antonio Escandón, and Tomás Murphy—were already in Europe when the decision was made to offer the throne to Maximilian; these men joined the Mexican delegation when it arrived in Europe. They were confirmed Europhiles, Mexicans in permanent exile or with foreign citizenship, *criollo* to boot, convinced that the more European Mexico became, the better off it would be.[20]

When Maximilian and Charlotte received the delegation at Miramare on October 3, they made certain that the welcome befitted an occasion of great magnitude, the founding of a New World monarchy. The delegation had spent the night in Trieste and made the five-mile carriage ride along the coast to Miramare. As the carriages rounded the circle in front of the castle, the delegates glimpsed the grand reception prepared for them. They were greeted by servants standing in two rows, dressed in rich liveries according to their role: some wore jackets of white suede with blue stitching and insignia; others wore black with silver embroidery and were outfitted with ceremonial swords. All wore knee breeches and silk stockings set off by shoes of patent leather. Most impressive were the halberdiers, standing immobile in red jackets with braided belts, white pants, and thigh-high boots. The spear and axe head of their halberds gleamed of silver; the shafts were wrapped in crimson velvet. In full beard and impossibly tall—"a species of giant," as one Mexican put it—they embodied a warrior masculinity that was both menacing and theatrical.[21]

The members of the Mexican delegation were led inside to a salon where Maximilian greeted them standing. An artist stood opposite, ready to capture the scene. Gutiérrez de Estrada, already convinced that Maximilian was indeed a savior—a "political Messiah"—took the lead, directly addressing Maximilian as future emperor of Mexico.[22] Prior to independence, he noted, Mexico had been a "prosperous . . . monarchical colony of Europe." Since independence Mexico had led a "sad existence" because it lost the "splendid legacy" of three centuries of rule. Mexico "did not know . . . how to preserve [this legacy] . . . under the Republic." His speech lavished praise upon Maximilian and Charlotte and acknowledged the sacrifice they were about to make, taking them "so far from this Europe which is the center and emporium of the civilization of the world." In addition to monarchy and Europhilia, the statement referenced Charles V and lauded Maximilian as "the worthy scion

Cesare Dell'Acqua, *The Mexican Delegation Appoints Ferdinand Maximilian of Austria as Emperor of Mexico*, 1867. *Museo Storico e il Parco del Castello di Miramare.*

of the illustrious dynasty" that had "carried Christian civilization to our own soil."[23]

Maximilian's reply invoked his romantic dynasticism ("It is flattering to our house that the eyes of your compatriots were turned toward the family of Charles V") and his desire to offer progressive monarchical leadership modeled on that of Napoléon III. Nonetheless, he stipulated that his acceptance depended upon "the whole nation expressing its will freely."

Ignacio Aguilar y Marocho remembered that he and the other members of the delegation were transfixed by Maximilian's "great blue eyes" as he spoke. After the formalities, they were led to an adjacent room where Charlotte and her ladies in waiting greeted them. Charlotte spoke to each of them in Spanish, asking questions that showed she knew something of each one. To Escandon she spoke of his railway interests; to Aguilar she repeated the flattering remarks of Mexican bishops Labastida and Munguía. Although they had made their acceptance conditional, everything about the imperial couple suggested they were fully committed. They had prepared minutely. Charlotte spoke knowledgeably of the history and geography of Mexico; Maximilian lapsed into the first-person plural as he spoke of the politics of Mexico—"We ought to do this" and "We harm ourselves by doing that"—speaking to the Mexican delegates as if he already saw himself as one of them, sharing their perspective as Mexicans.[24]

After the reception, the delegates returned to Trieste and then were back at Miramare that evening for dinner. They later recalled the banquet as exquisite, the conversation animated, the musical accompaniment from the adjacent room superb. They felt as though *they* were the ones being courted. Indeed, they were. Most of the delegates left the following day, but a few remained at the insistence of Maximilian, telling them that he wanted some Mexicans by his side "until he went to Mexico." They were invited to Miramare again, and as dinner ended on one such occasion, Maximilian noted that, as the water was calm, he and Charlotte would like their Mexican guests to join them at sea. They descended to the castle dock, where a vessel waited; everyone boarded and the crew pushed off. About two hundred feet from shore, the vessel stopped. With his guests gathered round, Maximilian blew a whistle. Immediately, two rockets launched from the castle, streaming sparks across the sky. As everyone turned shoreward to follow their flight, firework fountains in green, white, and red ignited at the foot of the castle—the fireworks' reflection turned the calm waters between the boat and the shore into a great, undulating flag of Mexico.[25]

Maximilian and Charlotte were tailoring their message according to time, place, and audience. Publicly and in diplomatic channels their acceptance was still conditional, they could step back at any time. In the company of the Mexican delegation, however, they behaved as if they were already emperor and empress. Over time the line between these audiences blurred. As events like the visit of the delegation to Miramare became public, it became harder to equivocate. It also became easier for third parties to muddy the message. So while Maximilian was keen on getting the public support of Britain for his Mexican Empire and insisted on it as one of their conditions for acceptance, in the press the matter was treated as settled. A write-up of the visit of the Mexican delegation published in *Le Mémorial diplomatique,* a major diplomatic weekly, treated British support as fait accompli. It even claimed that the Mexican Intervention was a fully European initiative. "The support of England and Spain has been assured for some time, that of Prussia and Italy can't be far behind; Sweden, Bavaria, Belgium, Greece, Holland, Portugal, Denmark, in a word, all of the states of the [European] continent associate themselves with this European act."[26] It was a vision of the Intervention that mirrored that of Mexican monarchists and Napoléon III—that this was the moment for all of Europe to rally to the cause of blocking American aggression by putting a European monarch on the throne of Mexico. It's certainly fair to ask whether the story was planted by forces eager to put an end to ambiguity and to lock down the future of the Mexican throne.[27]

Napoléon III himself had the central role to play in fulfilling the vision of Maximilian and Charlotte. Correspondence between Paris and Miramare revealed a willingness to maintain a shared discourse regarding Mexico. When massively reinforced French forces finally took Puebla in May 1863, then continued their march, entering Mexico City in June, the humiliation of Cinco de Mayo was erased and the matter of Mexican conquest was settled, at least for some. With the Mexican capital in French hands, Maximilian wrote to express his congratulations to Napoléon III; he cast Mexican defeat and occupation as a victory for Mexico "menaced by the American spirit of conquest." Mexican monarchists wrote to Charlotte, addressing her with the seductive title "Your Imperial Highness"—as if the matter were settled. But Napoléon III was taking no chances. Maximilian's acceptance of the imperial crown of Mexico was conditional—he could still back out. Napoléon decided to put the full persuasive power of Paris and Bonapartism to work. He invited Maximilian and Charlotte to visit Paris, with full honors, in March 1864.

The visit spanned more than a week and included a series of carefully staged events, beginning with a reception at the Tuileries Palace on March 5. Maximilian and Charlotte were welcomed as if they already were sovereign heads of state. As Maximilian and Charlotte approached the grand staircase, Napoléon III descended to meet them halfway, prompting courtiers to murmur and buzz regarding the unusually cordial reception. Napoléon III embraced Maximilian, then offered his arm to Charlotte, escorting her to meet Empress Eugénie, waiting in the adjacent salon.

That night Maximilian and Charlotte attended the theatrical debut of *L'Ami des femmes*, a new comedy by Alexander Dumas. They were seated in the imperial box. The days and nights to follow were packed with meetings, receptions, and performances. There was a trip to Versailles, where Napoléon III and Maximilian went hunting. There was a trip to the imperial residence at Fontainebleau. There were performances at the Opéra

Napoléon III and Empress Eugenie receive Maximilian and Charlotte at the Tuileries Palace. *Reproduced from* L'Illustration, *March 12, 1864.*

and the Comédie-Française, where Maximilian and Charlotte were guests of honor; when they appeared in their box, the audience turned and greeted them with an ovation.

The grandest event of all was a soirée at the Tuileries Palace, an event that showed how an empire can be consummated to music.[28] On March 7, Emperor Napoléon III and Empress Eugénie hosted a musical concert at the Tuileries featuring a selection of arias from Verdi, Donizetti, and Rossetti. Charlotte was so touched by the occasion that she saved the program, so it is thanks to her that we can read how Napoléon seduced Maximilian and Charlotte with twelve musical pieces. It started with an innocent toast ("Brindisi" from *La Traviata*), but it was the twelfth aria, from Verdi's *Ernani,* that drove the point home. *Ernani* is set in the Spain of Charles V. It was an inspired choice, and not only because Napoléon knew that Maximilian revered Charles as an ancestor and had taken him as his model. The *Ernani* story turns on a rebellion against Charles, who in the end brings peace and reconciliation through amnesty. The aria

"O Sommo Carlo" featured as the finale of the concert at the Tuileries. It pays homage to the new emperor Charles V, worthy successor to Charlemagne. Maximilian could not have missed the flattering allusion to his own status as emperor-in-the-making. Nor could he have failed to identify with a monarch who pacifies a rebellious people. This is how empires are made.[29]

Charlotte was ecstatic. She checked off the sites she had seen: "Fontainebleau, St Cloud, Versailles, Sèvres, les Gobelins." She gushed about seeing "*all* of the Louvre . . . the main churches." She was introduced to Baron Haussmann, Napoléon III's prefect of the Seine, the man responsible for the rebuilding of Paris as an imperial showcase.[30] He showed her "the new boulevards [and] the old ones." Haussmann even gave Charlotte a private tour of city hall.[31]

Not everything was seduction. There were important details to be worked out, too. Maximilian and Napoléon III huddled with Achille Fould, Napoléon's minister of finance; they drafted an agreement, partly private, setting out the terms of the relationship between France and the new Mexican Empire. They also hammered out key financial issues, including unpaid Mexican debt dating back to independence. A new Mexican loan with proceeds earmarked for repayment of investors was a brilliant way of creating enthusiasm for the success of the empire among investors and of satisfying the political establishments of Britain and Spain, partners in the Intervention. For France, this was also the moment to recoup the cost of the invasion and occupation—some 210 million francs taken from the proceeds of the loan. France had liberated Mexico; Mexico should pay for it.[32] Mexico would also have to pay ongoing occupation costs.[33] Maximilian, a man of vision, not finance, and too willing to trust Napoléon III in these matters, agreed in principle.[34] Only later would Maximilian learn that this arrangement was a ball and chain; repayment of debt plus repayment of occupation costs mortgaged nearly half of Mexican customs revenue.[35] Maximilian was putting himself at the head of a bankrupt empire, with meager prospects for improving cash flow.

Also part of their Parisian sojourn was a meeting with Mexican general José Maria González de Mendoza. González was one of hundreds of Mexican officers who had been taken prisoner after the fall of Puebla and deported to France in an effort to decapitate the Mexican insurgency. Most of the captive Mexican officers, some five hundred of them, had been sent to the French provinces.[36] Most of the generals were stowed at Evreux, but González was a catch; in the defense of Puebla, he had ranked second only to Ortega. Therefore, González and his staff were housed in Paris.

During a visit to the Tuileries, González performed a walk-on role wherein he announced that he had transferred his loyalties from the Mexican republic to the empire of Maximilian. His gesture was choreographed, designed to second the professions of loyalty to the empire arriving by mail from towns and cities across Mexico. Statements like the one from General González, combined with statements of loyalty from Mexico, helped to create an irresistible momentum in support of Maximilian, Charlotte, and their empire.

Everything about the Parisian visit had been arranged to suggest that Maximilian and Charlotte were entering an exclusive circle—the highest ranks of the European heads of state, now opening a branch office in the Americas. This political theater certainly redounded to the benefit of Napoléon III, who had cast himself in the role of kingmaker. Just like his famous uncle, this Napoléon was doling out coveted positions to worthy and admiring associates.

Still, there were cracks in the edifice, especially as Confederate and Union sympathizers in Paris jockeyed for advantage. The United States was at war with itself and unable to act militarily against the Intervention, but diplomatic protest and symbolic resistance remained possible. The US representative, William Dayton, had lobbied aggressively to prevent European recognition of the Confederacy and warned against French designs on Mexico.[37] Dayton was invited to attend the gala events for Maximilian and Charlotte, but declined to do so. His absence was a silent protest.

Lobbying also occurred at unofficial levels. Both London and Paris were favored places of exile for wealthy US Southerners seeking safety and comfort for their families far from the war. In Paris, official neutrality barely masked unofficial hospitality to Confederate families, who were "flattered and fêted" in the French capital. Confederate social events doubled as fundraisers for the Southern cause.[38] John Slidell, the Confederate diplomatic representative, could rely on the support of the Confederate families that had infiltrated imperial social circles, unofficially lobbying for French recognition of the Confederacy. Maximilian considered meeting with Slidell during his visit to Paris but thought better of it.[39] In London, meanwhile, oceanographer and Confederate officer Mathew Maury was cultivating relationships with British shipbuilders, with pacifist Anglican clergy, and with the British prime minister, Lord Palmerston. Maury also struck up an epistolary relationship with Maximilian, encouraging him to be bold as emperor and seize the opportunity of the Civil War to win back California for Mexico.

Amid the general excitement there were also worrying signs for the Mexican empire. Maximilian and Charlotte were putting together an army of European volunteers, but enrollments for volunteer regiments to Mexico were lagging expectations. Nor were investors lining up for the new Mexican loan. Leaders of minor German states, who traditionally looked to the Habsburgs for leadership, were not impressed. Some were scathing in their commentary. Why would an Austrian archduke, a Habsburg, lower himself to serve in Napoléon III's global empire?[40] The title "Emperor of Mexico" was exalted, but given his dependence on France and French soldiers, wouldn't Maximilian really be playing the role of a mere provincial prefect?[41] Wags couldn't help but comment that, in this particular drama, the Archduke Maximilian and his Archduchess Charlotte were cast in the role of archdupes.[42]

7

✍

Imperial Pageantry

PARIS WAS THE APOGEE OF THE MEXICAN EMPIRE. After Paris, anything would have felt like a letdown but, upon arrival in London, Maximilian and Charlotte encountered certain sobering realities that grandeur and flattery could not make vanish. Maximilian had set British support as a condition for acceptance of the crown of Mexico but in London Maximilian and Charlotte learned that public support would not be forthcoming.

British recognition of the Mexican empire posed serious diplomatic problems. Prime Minister Palmerston, though sympathetic to the idea of breaking up the American behemoth, was circumspect. As long as the outcome of the American Civil War remained uncertain, he dared not risk antagonizing the United States. Nor could he defy British public opinion, which was hostile to slavery.[1] As for Mexico itself, Palmerston held open the possibility of recognizing Maximilian's regime, but it depended upon Maximilian's reception there. Palmerston viewed racial dynamics in Mexico as favorable to Maximilian, who was positioning himself as champion of the Indigenous of Mexico, victims of *criollo* domination. "The Indian population," Palmerston would later tell Parliament, "are well disposed towards the Emperor. It is said that they have historical reminiscences which make them inclined to receive him, and I believe they have no particular regard or fancy for the Spanish race, by whom they were not over well treated."[2] For Palmerston, Maximilian's imperial indigeneity seemed like sound racial thinking, but it remained to be tested.

Even among dynastic friends and allies there were doubts. Queen Victoria was fond of "Max and Charlotte." She had not seen them since 1861, and she received them happily at Buckingham Palace, but she was skeptical regarding Mexico. "They are going to Mexico, which I cannot understand," she confessed to her journal. She also detected uneven enthusiasm for the undertaking. While Charlotte was enthusiastic, "[Maximilian] seems doubtful."[3]

In Brussels there was still shock that the crown had been accepted at all. The press characterized Maximilian as privileged and spoiled, a dilettante kept busy in exalted positions for which he was unqualified ("viceroy one day, admiral the next"), an airhead whose vanity made him tractable—a tool of Charlotte's ambition—prodded to accept a worthless "cardboard crown."[4] Although King Leopold supported his daughter Charlotte and her husband, his own government aligned with public opinion in opposing the adventure.

Things were no better at their final stop, Vienna, where an unpleasant confrontation awaited. While Maximilian and Charlotte were completing their circuit of European courts, Franz Joseph convened key relatives. Maximilian's grand—not to say grandiose—vision of a Habsburg renaissance in the Americas had set off alarms. With Franz Joseph presiding, Habsburg family leaders resolved that in taking the Mexican throne, Maximilian must renounce his rights of succession in Vienna. Maximilian felt ambushed by this demand, this *Familienvertrag,* this family pact, which he learned of just as they were departing Paris. A renunciation of succession rights had not been put forward before as a condition for accepting the throne, but now that he had pledged his word "on the advice of his imperial brother"—and after all the fuss and bother in Paris—it was.

Maximilian's naked ambition surely had something to do with Habsburg insistence that Maximilian renounce his place in the line of succession. Maximilian and Charlotte were convinced that Maximilian would make a better emperor than his brother. Mexico was their chance to prove it, but the endgame involved a triumphant return. Renouncing his rights of succession meant that there would be no turning back.[5] If his dream of a Habsburg Mexico failed, he would have nowhere to turn.

The Habsburg family pact risked a rupture between Maximilian and his family. It also forced Maximilian to confront his ambivalence about Mexico. It explains why, as the prospects for the empire began to crumble even before the couple had left Miramare, Maximilian found it so hard to halt the momentum, the sense of inevitability, that he and Charlotte had created. They had built their lives around this exalted vision. They were decorating their home with it. Now they would have to live it.

Back in Vienna, Maximilian announced that he would decline the throne of Mexico, putting the onus—and diplomatic embarrassment—on his brother.[6] After a gloomy final family dinner—a "hangman's meal," his mother called it—Maximilian and Charlotte left Vienna for Miramare.

The pact created a diplomatic crisis. If Maximilian refused to agree to the family pact, Franz Joseph would withdraw the permission he had granted Maximilian to accept the throne of Mexico. Eager to head off any misunderstanding with France, Franz Joseph sent a request to Napoléon III to intercede with Maximilian to agree to the family pact. Napoléon III and Eugénie felt betrayed when they learned that Maximilian might renege just two weeks after their grand reception in Paris. Napoléon III sent a telegram to Miramare appealing to Maximilian's honor and asking him to abide by the agreement. Empress Eugénie followed up with a stern letter to Charlotte emphasizing the consequences of a failure to follow through.[7] There was trouble on the other side of the Atlantic, too. In the United States, on April 4, the Senate and the House passed a unanimous resolution opposing recognition of a monarchy in Mexico. In London and Paris, investors were far from enthusiastic about the Mexican loan—a clear sign of a lack of confidence in the empire.

The pact also created a psychic crisis for Maximilian. For years, flattering titles, public fanfare, high-level diplomacy, appeals for soldier volunteers—even decisions about art and furnishings at Miramare and uniforms for court valets—had produced a relentless momentum toward the Mexican Empire. Now the family pact upset his equilibrium and forced him to confront his doubts. To decline the throne now would mean a very public humiliation. A delegation of Mexican monarchists was on its way, due to arrive at Miramare on April 10, 1864, to witness Maximilian's formal acceptance of the crown of Mexico. Maximilian still hadn't signed the family pact. As a serious, last-minute complication, the pact offered Maximilian an acceptable—albeit utterly humiliating—exit from the commitments he had made. Desperate to avoid global diplomatic disgrace, Franz Joseph made a trip from Vienna to Miramare the day before the arrival of the Mexican delegation. The brothers met, Franz Joseph secured Maximilian's agreement to the family pact, and on the rail platform awaiting his return ride to Vienna, Franz Joseph turned to his brother and they exchanged a final tearful goodbye.[8] It was the last time they would see each other.

The delegation of Mexican monarchists arrived at Miramare the next day, April 10, to witness Maximilian's formal acceptance. They brought with them additional signed testimonials—*actas de adhesión*—from Mexican cities and towns, signaling support for the new empire.[9] In lieu of a national plebiscite, this was intended to fulfill Maximilian's condition that the empire be an expression of popular will. Gutiérrez de Estrada, president of the delegation, offered a speech full of solemn historical references. He praised Napoléon III and his global vision; invoked Charles V and "the series of glorious monarchs" who had ruled according to the Catholic and monarchical traditions of the Habsburgs; invoked Anáhuac and praised "the noble and generous people" who discovered Mexico and "rooted out . . . the darkness of idolatry."[10] It was a speech that associated the greatness of Mexico with Habsburg rule and, by implication, cast the rule of Maximilian as a restoration, full of the promise of regeneration.

After Maximilian gave his acceptance speech (in Spanish), the Mexican flag was hoisted over the castle. The Austrian frigate *Bellona* fired a twenty-one-gun salute; the salute was relayed by a French frigate nearby and answered by guns at Trieste. The Mexican delegation joined the imperial couple in the private chapel of the castle, where a Te Deum, a hymn of praise and thanks, was performed by Monsignor George Rachich, the chaplain of Miramare and Maximilian's spiritual advisor.[11] Maximilian was so distraught that he excused himself from the remaining events, accepting only the company of his physician, Doctor Jilek. That evening Charlotte presided over the celebratory banquet alone. The crisis continued the next day. Maximilian was at breakfast with Jilek when Charlotte brought him a telegram. Maximilian brushed her aside with a brusque remark: "I don't want to hear anything about Mexico!"[12] On April 12 Charlotte was still alone when she received delegations from Trieste and surrounding towns arriving to offer their congratulations.

At 2 PM on April 14, a crowd watched and cheered as Maximilian and Charlotte descended the steps from the castle to the dock at Miramare.[13] As they boarded a launch that would take them to the ship *Novara*, Maximilian was sobbing and speechless, incapable of addressing the crowd. The *Novara* raised anchor along with the French escort vessel *Themis*. The royal yacht *Phantasie* led the farewell escort, which included six steamers representing the Trieste offices of Lloyd's. The flotilla passed by Trieste, where they were swarmed by fishing vessels, then made their way down the eastern coast of the Adriatic in order to pass by Lokrum and bid farewell to their private island home.[14] From there they continued south of the Italian peninsula, arriving at Civitavecchia on April 18.[15] Gutiérrez celebrated their arrival in Rome by hosting a grand reception at his palazzo on the Via della Pigna, where Maximilian and Charlotte stayed as guests during their two-day sojourn. Notable attendees included the king of Naples and Cardinal Antonelli, secretary of state for the Vatican.[16] The next day Maximilian and Charlotte attended Mass offered by Pope Pius IX in his private chapel in the Vatican. In the Sistine Chapel they listened as Pius gave a sermon on the superiority of the laws of God to the laws of man. It seemed like a banal topic for a sermon to heads of state, but it prefigured bitter disagreements yet to come. On April 21 Maximilian and Charlotte were back in Civitavecchia boarding the *Novara*. On April 24 they passed Gibraltar and entered the Atlantic. The crossing of the Tropic of Cancer was observed with a carnivalesque stage show—sailors costumed as gods and goddesses gave boisterous speeches, divine blessings were dispensed with sprays of water. Music and dancing ensued.[17]

Apart from such ritual entertainment, the imperial couple occupied their time setting out protocols for their new court.[18] In the absence of an opportunity actually to do anything, they focused on how they would like things to be.[19] They set out strict rules about who should wear what while standing where according to circumstance. For events of particular significance, such as Holy Week services and ministerial audiences, ushers and valets should wear "red livery with white stockings." For lesser occasions, such as "small dances and concerts," red livery with *black* stockings would suffice. They were mindful of security—during religious services at the palace chapel "a palatine guard would stand sentinel in the passageway behind the chapel, to prevent anyone from crossing." They fretted over the matter of precedence for the imperial *pelotón* when the emperor and empress traveled by carriage to a "grand gala." Seven carriages were to precede the imperial carriage, bearing the secretary of ceremonies, chamberlains, and ladies of honor in that order, in carriages pulled by two horses, with two footmen each, whereas the empress's grand chamberlain would have a team of four and the grand marshal of the court would have a team of six. Eight horses would draw the imperial coach, flanked by the Palatine Guard. Everything about court life was planned in exquisite detail. By the time the *Novara*'s anchor dropped at Veracruz on May 28, they had drafted some four hundred pages.[20]

There's no record of the reception Maximilian and Charlotte anticipated for their arrival, but the spectacle of their departure from Miramare—the spontaneous crowds of well-wishers, salutes from guns on board and on shore, the flotilla escort from Trieste—certainly served as a recent handy frame of reference. But when Mexico's new emperor and empress arrived at Veracruz, there was no one there to greet them. Almonte was late. Or the *Novara* was early. Either way, it was as if the *Novara* was just another merchant vessel or passenger ship arriving at Veracruz. Almonte was acting head of state. He had been appointed lieutenant-general of the empire, replacing the Regency until Maximilian's arrival. He had meticulously planned a reception, but he was still on his way from Córdoba when he learned of the arrival of the *Novara*. No one expected their arrival before the end of May, it was said. In any event, Almonte would not be there.

Charlotte put a good face on it. As they waited at anchor off Veracruz, she took the opportunity to write to her grandmother. She avoided discussing their embarrassing predicament by writing rapturously of their passage through the Caribbean. "I am delighted by the tropics; I dream only of butterflies and hummingbirds," she wrote. She was certain that the "New World" was not nearly so primitive as it was sometimes made out to be. It needed only the telegraph (still a novelty in 1864) and "a little civilization." "The look of Veracruz pleases me infinitely," she wrote. "It's a little oriental."[21]

If Veracruz reminded Charlotte of Cadiz, several recent visitors to Veracruz were less determinedly upbeat. They mention the sky full of vultures, scavengers that removed waste from the streets of the city and were protected by law. Others mentioned a shipwreck at *La Isla de los Sacrificios*, the remains of a vessel driven aground by a strong wind and left to rot. Nothing inauspicious in any of that.[22]

Juan Lainé, port captain of Veracruz, approached the *Novara* aboard a felucca. Given permission to board, Lainé was the first Mexican to greet their August Highnesses upon their arrival. As port captain, he assured them that he could guide the imperial frigate safely to port.[23] He certainly could, but the offer could be seen as disingenuous. High season for yellow fever had already begun. What if *el vómito* settled the matter of empire once and for all? It's not clear whether Maximilian and Charlotte grasped the import of Lainé's kind offer. If they had, they might have understood the profound hostility they faced and just how atypical the disgruntled monarchist *criollos* they had met in Europe actually were. Maximilian and Charlotte, having been warned not to stay in Veracruz "for their personal security," politely declined.[24] They would remain on board the *Novara* until General Almonte arrived to greet them.

Almonte arrived late that afternoon. He immediately visited the *Novara*, followed by the prefect of Veracruz and other officials.[25] For Maximilian and Charlotte, arrival at Veracruz gave them their first chance to gauge public opinion for themselves. In the days before opinion polling, public appearances were one of the better ways for political leaders to assess public support. After receiving the many *actas de adhesión* to the empire and after hearing about how much the Mexican people desired monarchy, the imperial couple could now judge for themselves. The signs were not auspicious. It was said that the people of Veracruz had been busily preparing decorations and triumphal arches for the imperial reception, but the early arrival of the *Novara* meant that the city was unprepared. According to one source, at news of their arrival flags, pennants, streamers, and bows appeared spontaneously.[26] It's likely that this is a mere cover story. It needs to be said that Veracruz was a republican city—Juárez had made it his capital during the War of Reform—and therefore hostile to the empire.[27] It may even be that Almonte's tardy appearance was due to his sense of insecurity, although the risk of yellow fever was reason enough to stay away. In any event, the reception at Veracruz was ill-prepared, even chilly.[28] Paula Kollonitz, who traveled aboard the *Novara* from Europe with the imperial couple and whose perspective likely approximates their own, described the reception as "glacial."[29] This did not prevent the French press from reporting a rapturous reception.[30]

During the crossing, Maximilian had contemplated staying in Veracruz a few days to acquaint himself with the city and its people. Instead, he was persuaded to leave on May 29, the day after their arrival, for fear of contracting yellow fever. At 5:30 that morning, as they prepared to leave the *Novara* for a reception on shore, Maximilian reminded his secretary, Angel Iglesias Dominguez, of his special solicitude for the Indigenous of Mexico. "From this point forward," he told Dominguez, "I want there to be no distinction between Indians and those who are not: they are all Mexicans and have the same right to my attention."[31] As they approached the shore, a "mephitic odor" grew stronger.[32] At dockside, city officials presented them with the keys to the city on a silver platter.[33] A perceptive witness noted that there were as many French among the dignitaries as there were Mexicans, apparently padding out the crowd. Maximilian and Charlotte were guided to an open carriage. The climbed in, then crossed the city to the train station, passing banners and arches along the way. The train departed, and by 9 AM they were in Soledad; by 10:30 they were in Loma Alta, the end of the forty-two-mile rail line. For the remainder of the two-hundred-mile journey to Mexico City, the imperial party with its eighty-five passengers and five hundred pieces of baggage would travel by coach and wagon.[34]

According to an itinerary prepared by Almonte, the first stop on their journey would be Orizaba, where they would attend a dinner for forty at 6:30 PM, but Almonte seems to have had an unrealistic idea of the speed with which a convoy of this size could move.[35] By 5 PM the imperial convoy had only reached Paso del Macho, more than thirty miles short of Orizaba. They pressed on, braving wind and rain. They were determined not to rest until they reached Orizaba, where, they were told, they would find a cooler temperature and a warmer reception. Darkness set in. The axle on their carriage broke. They switched to another carriage and pressed on past midnight. Orizaba now seemed out of reach; they would settle for Córdoba, fifteen miles closer and safely outside the coastal zone of acute yellow fever risk. As the caravan struggled toward Córdoba in the darkness, "a multitude of Indigenous" came out to greet them, lining the route with torches to light the way to the city. It was 2:15 AM.[36]

The torchlight reception at Córdoba was already considerably warmer than their reception in Veracruz. Triumphal arches stood at the four corners of the main square.[37] Despite the hour, Maximilian and Charlotte endured the formalities of an official reception, including the presentation of the keys to the city. By 3 AM the festivities were over. They could rest. The next day there was a Mass, a Te Deum, and a banquet for forty, establishing a pattern of such events that would continue as they moved toward the capital, each, like the restrained reception at Veracruz, a plebiscite, a test of the appeal of the empire. The scale varied, of course, and each city gave signs of the complexity of popular attitudes. At Orizaba, among the expectant crowd were many Indigenous, shepherded by their priests, sitting along the sidewalks "in bare legs and bare feet." "¡Ahí están!" went up the cry as the caravan came into view. Everyone stood to get a better view, but the disappointment was soon unmistakable. There were no magnificent horses, no golden reins, no superb carriage—instead, the imperial couple arrived in a four-seater with a folding top, the kind of conveyance sometimes used for cargo. No braided livery either—the driver of the carriage wore a wide-brimmed hat and a white jacket.[38] The imperial entourage arrived in a mishmash of carts, carriages, stagecoaches, and wagons—sturdy enough to survive ruts and mud but hardly the stuff of fairy tales. It gave the impression of a monarchy cobbled together, a makeshift monarchy, an improvisation.

The municipal prefect welcomed Maximilian as the "savior of this unfortunate people," but the "unfortunate people" themselves were perplexed by this motley assemblage. How should an emperor behave? Maximilian and Charlotte attended church the next day. As they left to return to their residence, it started to rain. Maximilian put on his hat and popped his umbrella as Charlotte took his arm—a charming scene, but one easily enacted by any provincial hidalgo. Maximilian wanted to be the People's Emperor, but the people wanted splendor and spectacle.

Puebla and Cholula were next on the itinerary from the coast to the capital. The glories of one of Mexico's finest cities were fully on display at Puebla—the colonnades framing the *plaza mayor,* the baroque cathedral, the sturdy convents with their magnificent courtyards—but this was a city conquered just a year earlier in bloody street fighting, and the remnants of combat were still visible.[39] Twenty drummers led the way through the city, followed by Maximilian and Charlotte and the rest of the imperial party in carriages. A large cavalry escort brought up the rear.[40] Press accounts describe buildings decked with bunting and the flags of Mexico, Austria, France, and Belgium.[41] Three massive triumphal arches, sponsored by various corporate entities, punctuated the route. The triumphal arch at Alguacil Mayor was more than three stories high and towered over adjacent buildings. Gawkers were leaning over building cornices, while at street level crowds on either side stood five and six deep, straining to catch a glimpse of the imperial couple as they passed by. Popular curiosity was genuine and the reception in Puebla was exuberant; the keys to the city were gold, the references to Charles V abundant. Puebla had been one of the first cities to issue statements in favor of monarchy, but it is worth recalling that Puebla and neighboring Cholula were both subjected to intense military pressure under the Intervention.[42]

On June 8 the imperial party moved on toward Cholula. An official account tells of some five hundred triumphal arches between Puebla and Cholula, such that the empress and emperor traveled "on a carpet of flowers" under "incessant arches of foliage."[43] Even allowing for hyperbole, there can be no doubt that a massive reception had been organized. With all parties aware that the reception of the imperial couple was a politically useful proxy for public opinion, nothing could be taken at face value, including journalistic accounts.[44] That said, the effect was telling. Tomas Mejía, a general who rallied to the empire, explained that he was skeptical of the Intervention and empire at first, but that the display of flowers and arches upon the arrival of Maximilian and Charlotte convinced him that popular enthusiasm was real.

A day after leaving Cholula, Maximilian and Charlotte were at the pass at Río Frío, with the valley of Mexico before them. A crowd went

Triumphal arch on Calle Alguacil Mayor. *ÖNB/Wien Pk 1128, 2.*

out from the capital to see them when they stopped to pay their respects at the shrine to the Virgin of Guadalupe on June 11. They entered the capital on the twelfth, passing under a portrait of Maximilian, painted in oils. Flowers, wreaths, and banners abounded, along with Mexican flags and ribbons in the national colors.[45] Maximilian and Charlotte toured the capital in an open carriage, past balconies draped with bunting. Pro-imperial banners greeted them along their route: "Oh, great Maximilian! The ancient throne of the Aztecs, awaits you!" "The pure Indian race has nothing to offer you except the scepter of Moctezuma!" "Come, exalted Prince, and be our firm support in the holy religion of Jesus Christ!"[46]

The banners captured cherished themes, themes that masked this novel empire in the trappings of history and tradition.

For the first time since their arrival, they were able to travel in a conveyance befitting monarchs. Charlotte favored a Paris couturier for her arrival outfit—a blue suit with white stripes. Maximilian wore a uniform. They passed under triumphal arches representing imperial values (peace) and provincial capitals (Zacatecas, San Luis Potosí) that had rallied to the empire. Perhaps most telling of all was an arch dedicated to Maximilian. It was to have been more than forty feet tall, with four columns and low-relief sculptures representing the Assembly of Notables, the delegation to Miramare, and the arts and sciences. At the very top would have stood Emperor Maximilian himself, flanked by effigies representing imperial values of equality and justice. Assembled, it would have presented a founding narrative of the empire, but time ran out, so instead the pieces offered a metaphor for an empire organized in haste.

Once the imperial couple had settled in, they made a point of making themselves visible by visiting sites—churches, schools, charitable institutions—around the capital. On June 13 they were greeted by a massive crowd when they visited the church of La Santa Cruz y la Soledad. Newspapers sympathetic to the empire reported endearing tableaux. According to the Catholic newspaper *Pájaro Verde*, the people showed a simplicity of belief that, combined with a shocking familiarity and a desire to touch, surprised the imperial couple.[47] An Indigenous woman embraced Charlotte at the knees, then looked up to see her smile. When courtiers intervened to push her away "so she wouldn't stain her dress," Charlotte objected, saying it was better for the Indigenous woman to have an experience to bring home to share with her family.[48]

Departments and districts and dioceses sent representatives to the capital to offer greetings. Octaviano Muñoz Ledo represented Guanajuato, welcoming the monarchy "as a symbol of peace and hope of reconciliation." Juan Ormaechea, bishop of Tulancingo, expressed the hope that the empire would bring regeneration to a country that "presented the pallid look of a cadaver." The representative of San Luis Potosí lauded the work of "raising a throne on the tomb of political hatred" and welcomed the empress as "a tender mother."[49]

If the intent was to impress Maximilian and Charlotte with warmth and enthusiasm, it seems to have worked. The reception was enthusiastic and sincere; so wrote Charlotte within weeks of their arrival. "We arrived without great trouble," she wrote, "in spite of the poor state of the roads

Maximilian and Charlotte pass through the San Luis Potosí arch, featuring an effigy of Charles V. *Reproduced from* Advenimiento de SS. MM. II. Maximiliano y Carlota al trono de México *(Mexico: J. M. Andrade y F. Escalante, 1864).*

and we were received with joy and affection by our new country." Within a month they had moved into Chapultepec Castle. They were already striving for comparisons that would help their European relatives understand Mexico. "It's a very beautiful country," Charlotte wrote. "It reminds me of Europe, especially Italy," she added. "If you could see what I see outside my windows, it's Palermo."[50]

Maximilian and Charlotte were eager to get to work, to prove that the empire could be a force for progress and order. For a time, things went their way. Prominent figures in Mexican society, perhaps moved by the imperial reception, perhaps acting prudently in the face of overwhelming French force, rallied to the cause. Mexican generals Uraga, Cadena, and Sandoval announced that they would serve the empire.[51] Eager to encourage such momentum and the image of the empire as a regime of reconciliation, Maximilian pardoned and ordered released some of those who had resisted the Intervention. Reconciliation would be a theme of Maximilian's empire—though not necessarily of his supporters. Implacable resistance would be a theme of President Juárez and his government. Collaborators with the empire faced serious punishment; a law passed on the eve of the Intervention, January 25, 1862, called for death for anyone convicted of aiding the invasion. On August 15, 1864, Colonel Quiroga nearly captured President Juárez and his government in Monterrey; had he succeeded, Quiroga would have deprived the resistance of its symbolic core.[52]

Developments in the United States in late August were also favorable to the empire. War weariness was pushing part of the US population toward a negotiated settlement with the Confederate rebellion. At its convention in Chicago, the Democratic Party was getting ready to nominate General George McLellan as its presidential candidate on a peace platform. A secure and independent Confederate States of America, alongside a United States weakened by disunion, would greatly strengthen the Mexican empire's chances of success.

The imperial couple had arrived in Mexico City in June 1864, but they moved to make their presence felt. Within days they announced an architectural competition for a monument celebrating Mexican independence. The call for proposals was to go out on the twentieth, giving enough time for architects and designers to present their projects and for a selection to be made in time for laying the first stone on September 16, Independence Day.[53]

Maximilian and Charlotte were also eager to cultivate relationships that would provide the foundation of court culture. For months they had struggled against attempts by others—the regents, the French, the press, the defenders of the republic—to define them and their empire. Now that they were finally in Mexico, the levers of power finally within their grasp, they could define their empire as they wished. Sometimes this involved making implicit comparisons between the Mexican republic and their empire. The Mexican republic had teetered on the edge of bankruptcy. Thanks to the millions generated by investors in Europe, Maximilian was able to contrast the penury of the republic with the brilliance of the empire.[54] The contrast was illusory, of course, because it was fueled by debt, but debt bought Maximilian and Charlotte the time they needed as they scrambled to produce the more durable prosperity their empire promised. Among the projects undertaken was the expansion and renovation of Chapultepec Castle as a site suitable for imperial receptions; they hired a European architect and interior designer for the purpose.[55]

Maximilian and Charlotte made a point of surrounding themselves with courtiers, advisors, ministers, and assistants of Mexican heritage, some notorious. Dolores Quezada Almonte (wife of Regent Juan Nepmuceno Almonte) and Manuela Gutiérrez Estrada (daughter of the Europhile monarchist José Maria) were counted among forty *damas de palacio*—Charlotte's inner circle—as was Mercedes Esnaurrizar de Hidalgo, the mother of José Hidalgo.[56] Such personages were the core of the social and political network underpinning the empire. The accoutrements were European. Officers appeared in civilian dress and women of the court dressed in European style. Such practices showed how the empire could bring European culture and sophistication to Mexico—a European graft on Mexican root stock. They hired Emilio Palant as their court composer, giving him the title "Director de la Música de los Bailes de la Corte." Palant composed "Recuerdo de Spa"—a lively piece in three-four time that recalled the Belgian resort town—and dedicated it to Charlotte. He also composed a polka in honor of one of Charlotte's European attendants, the Countess Bombelles.[57] Palant gave them what they wanted, the germ of a distinct imperial musical culture to feature at balls. The decorative arts were not neglected. Larger-than-life portraits of Maximilian and Charlotte were installed over the main hall, where they could preside over the scene. An eyewitness described the imperial balls at Chapultepec from memory—the swirl of elegantly dressed men and women with the imperial portraits hanging high above.[58]

Maximilian was eager to see the country and show himself to the people. He began a tour to acquaint himself with his new empire. For ten weeks, from August 10 to October 30, 1864, he made a circuit that included Querétaro, Dolores Hidalgo, Guanajuato, León, la Piedad, Morelia, Toluca—a counterclockwise loop in territory either recently pacified or overtly sympathetic to the empire. Maximilian took encouragement from the warmth of the crowds, which helped him convince himself that he had made the right decision and that public support was broad and deep. "The reception has been magnificent," he wrote from San Juan del Río on August 15. "The enthusiasm is indescribable," he noted in Celaya a week later. Charlotte relayed the story in her correspondence: Maximilian's tour was "a perpetual ovation."[59]

A fever with headaches and sore throat delayed him for a week, but he reached Dolores Hidalgo in time for the celebration of September 16, Independence Day. September 16 honors the day in 1810 that Miguel Hidalgo y Costilla, a Catholic priest, called upon the people to rise against Spanish rule. Hidalgo's call launched a struggle that would culminate in Mexico's independence in 1821. In honor of the occasion, Maximilian presided over a banquet for seventy. He gave a speech from the window of Father Hidalgo's house in which he invoked the reawakening of Anáhuac after Spanish occupation, and represented himself as the incarnation of a new era of Mexican independence. Symbolically, it was a risky move. Many of his Conservative supporters regarded independence from Spain as an unfortunate rupture, but independence—especially in face of the Yankee threat—was a core value for Maximilian's empire. Mexican Conservatives would have to get used to him seeking a middle ground, associating his empire with a strong and independent Mexico—a turbulent brew in which Anáhuac, Habsburg Mexico, independence from Spain, and anti-Yankee anti-imperialism blended into a single mission. By his lights, it was working. "The enthusiasm was indescribable," he noted once again, this time in a letter to his brother Franz Joseph. As he continued his tour, Maximilian was determined to encounter his critics, perhaps to win them over. Morelia was "the most dangerous and politically troublesome city in the empire," he wrote, but "I was received with enthusiasm such as I have never before seen in my life."[60] As Charlotte told the story in her own correspondence, the men wanted to carry Maximilian on their shoulders and the women had wanted to hug him, an intimacy that Mexicans had adopted from "Spanish customs" but not, she hastened to add, one that should be allowed by sovereigns.[61]

Maximilian was using his journey to assess public opinion and to understand something of the true condition of the country he now sought to rule, but it was also an opportunity for members of Mexico's ruling class to ingratiate themselves with the new head of state. For a banquet on September 27, Maximilian's host spared no expense to show that Mexico could match the best that Europe could offer. The banquet opened with turtle soup accompanied by a dry sherry, followed by a Jerez Amontillado. Next the servers brought out jellied ham paired with a Madera. Cutlets Soubise followed; Chateau Margaux was poured alongside. The menu listed eight possible entrées—in French—including pigeon compote, salmon mayonnaise, *suprême de volaille,* and a rabbit pâté; the wine pairings turned to Rhine wines and sauternes. They were rounded out by a vegetable course of salsify and artichoke followed by turkey and roast beef accompanied by champagne. Dessert consisted of cheese and fruit. After coffee there was the *pousse-café*—a choice of Chartreuse or cognac. A hand-lettered menu captured every detail.[62, 63] It was the kind of display calculated to manifest the keen discernment of those who rule, no vulgar display of wealth required. Power recognizes power through discreet references—fine restaurants, exotic locations, exquisite taste—that only money can buy. They are the secret handshake by which the wealthy and the powerful recognize each other.

The sumptuousness of the banquet contrasted sharply with the famine conditions Maximilian witnessed a few days earlier in Guanajuato, a consequence of the failure of the maize crop.[64]

As Maximilian proceeded on his tour, Charlotte ruled in the capital as Mexico's first de facto female head of state. During this time her considerable political skill, already evident to her family, became manifest to a much wider circle. In addition to managing day-to-day affairs, she used the opportunity to pursue a sophisticated campaign of public art intended to reinforce the association of the empire with the history of Mexico and the struggle for independence. When Charlotte and her husband arrived in the capital on June 12, 1864, September 16 was only three months away. Planning began almost immediately, with Charlotte taking the lead. On June 18 she met with Félix Eloin, imperial chief of staff, to sketch out plans for the occasion.[65] Given everything that had transpired since the arrival of the European powers at Veracruz three years earlier, it was important for the empire to situate itself within the tradition of Mexican independence, if only to obfuscate the painfully obvious fact that the empire represented the restoration of European control after four decades of self-rule.

The answer to the riddle was to emphasize certain key episodes in the story of independence. For this, the planning for September 16 drew astutely on Mexican history. Mexico had briefly been an empire once before, at the conclusion of the struggle for independence. Unlike the United States, where the struggle for independence culminated in a republic, in Mexico things turned out differently. Independence was realized in 1821 when Agustín de Iturbide, a general, entered Mexico City in triumph. Advocates for independence fought bitterly over whether Mexico should be a republic or a monarchy. When efforts to recruit a European—including the Habsburg archduke Charles—to serve as monarch failed, Iturbide took the crown for himself and adopted the title of emperor. Emperor Iturbide ruled imperial Mexico for less than a year before he was forced into exile.[66] When he returned from exile to retake his throne, he was arrested and executed.

Although this may seem an inauspicious precedent, it was a serviceable past, for Iturbide was undeniably a hero of independence and his reign served as a precedent, albeit brief, for the new empire, Mexico's Second Empire. It also established a mythical past. Under Iturbide's abbreviated reign, Mexico was independent for the first time since the arrival of Cortés; it also stood as one of the great empires of its time, alongside Russia, China, and Brazil. Mexico became a republic in 1823. For Mexican imperialists, everything since had been decline and dismemberment.

The centrality of Iturbide's story to the empire was already evident the year before Maximilian and Charlotte arrived. When the French entered the city in June 1863 and the Assembly of Notables offered the crown to Maximilian and the Regency ruled in his absence, the official observance of September 16 was muted, but the key elements were present. The Regency announced a new coat of arms for Imperial Mexico with symbols evoking the Aztec past, the struggle for national independence, and "the Empire recently sanctioned" thanks to the "great idea" of Napoléon III to give "life and vigor" to the Latin race. They also announced that the new empire would resurrect Iturbide's motto: Religion, Independence, Union.[67] At the Gran Teatro, the lyrics of a new "Imperial Hymn" told of how Anáhuac [pre-Columbian Mexico] awakened at "the powerful voice of Iturbide."[68] Iturbide's empire served to link precolonial to postcolonial Mexico.

When Independence Day arrived, Charlotte and the supporters of empire were ready with a full day of activities conveying a vision of an empire consistent with the history of an independent Mexico. On the morning of September 16, an honor guard lined the short route between the palace and the cathedral. At 8 AM, Empress Charlotte made her way to the cathedral in a carriage pulled by a team of six horses.[69] She was greeted at the main door of the cathedral by Archbishop Labastida, who blessed her and her retinue with holy water. Members of Iturbide's family were present; they followed Charlotte closely and took their places nearby. Soldiers who had fought for Mexico's independence were honored, too. A group of veterans of the wars of independence entered the cathedral, led by General José Mariano Salas, a veteran, a regent, and an advocate of the empire.[70]

Newspapers friendly to the empire also linked the anniversary with the rule of Iturbide and his motto "Union, Religion, Independence."[71] *La Sociedad* reprinted a speech given by the political prefect of Veracruz that linked Maximilian to the glories of the Aztec empire. In occupying the throne of "Moctezuma and Iturbide," Maximilian would help Mexico realize at last the benefits of independence after years of discord, reconciling "father and son, brother and brother." Maximilian's empire would embrace the struggle for independence, but also transcend it by linking to a deep and venerable Aztec imperial past.[72]

After the religious ceremony, the main event featured Empress Charlotte laying the first stone for a monument to Independence. The site chosen was on what was already known as the Paseo, the broad avenue linking the imperial residence at Chapultepec with the plaza mayor and the National Palace. Here, too, the project fulfilled more than one purpose.[73] The monument linked the empire with the history of Mexican independence while the Paseo brought a European-style boulevard modeled on the Champs-Elysées and the Vienna Ringstraße or, to English eyes, Rotten Row of London's Hyde Park.[74] The Paseo—soon to be renamed Paseo de la Emperatriz—was the promenade of choice for Mexican society every Sunday evening.[75] The monument would be conspicuously located on the Paseo, the "spine of the city" as one historian has put it.[76] The laying of the first stone of was solemnified by Archbishop Labastida, who offered prayers and blessed the stone with holy water. The ceremony closed with military music and an artillery salute.

The rest of the day featured events across the capital, planned by Francisco Mora, the gifted pageant-master of the empire. Theaters put on productions, free of charge. There were bullfights and gravity-defying tightrope performances in plazas around town, while other plazas had greased poles with money and clothing as prizes for anyone who could clamber to the top. Everywhere there were balloons and music, a circus on the main plaza and, in the evening, fireworks and still more free theater performances.[77]

As Maximilian's tour came to an end in late October, Charlotte prepared to meet him. Together they would stage a reentry to the capital. They were reunited at Toluca, some forty-five miles west of the capital, and prepared their return. On October 30, they entered Mexico City. Once again there was a grand reception, this time to welcome the imperial couple back to their capital. The two had made their point—although his itinerary touched only a fraction of Mexico's territory, Maximilian had shown that he could go to the people and not be troubled. He could even be received enthusiastically. That said, they were returning to face issues much more difficult than organizing a warm public reception.

8

The Empire Looks for Friends

THE EMPIRE HAD MANY ENEMIES. Some of them used to be friends. Inside Mexico, forces loyal to the republic and President Juárez wreaked military havoc and undermined the empire's promise of reconciliation, peace, and stability. Outside of Mexico, the United States was an implacable foe and would make its power felt in time. But when Maximilian and Charlotte arrived in Mexico in the summer of 1864, they couldn't imagine that their deadliest opponent would be an unarmed man, a prelate, Pelagio Antonio de Labastida, the archbishop of the diocese of Mexico.

At one time Labastida had been an ally of the empire, even an informal lobbyist. In 1863 he had made a cordial visit to the couple's new home on the Adriatic coast. In the private chapel at Miramare, Labastida had celebrated Mass on Maximilian's birthday. How could such a man bedevil their plans to remake Mexico?

Labastida was already an old hand in Mexican politics when he returned to Mexico from exile. In fact, his career was punctuated by major political events. As a young priest, he had criticized Mexican liberalism from the pulpit, gaining early notoriety. His promotion to bishop of Puebla came under the Conservative presidency of Santa Anna.[1] When Liberals drove Santa Anna from power and initiated the reforms that would include the nationalization of property of the Catholic Church, Labastida went into exile. He returned under the Conservative presidency of Miramón, then left for Rome once again when Miramón fell.[2]

As the Intervention advanced, so did Labastida's fortunes. In March 1863, as the second battle for Puebla was getting under way, Pope Pius IX appointed Labastida archbishop of the diocese of Mexico City, making him the leading prelate in Mexico—an unmistakable endorsement of the man and his politics. In June, after the fall of Puebla and the entry of the French into the Mexican capital, Labastida was appointed one of three regents.[3] Thus, by the summer of 1863 Labastida was at the apex of power. When he visited Miramare in July, he was the holder of the highest-ranking positions of church and state in Mexico. After visiting Miramare, Labastida returned to Rome, gathered his things, received papal instructions, and then made his way to Civitavecchia, where he boarded the steamship *Veracruz*.[4] He traveled in the company of fellow exiled clergy—among them Clemente Munguía, the bitterly reactionary bishop of Michoacán. Now that the Mexican republic had been chased from the capital, they could anticipate better days.[5]

Signs of trouble emerged early, within weeks of Labastida's return. The most obvious sign was a very messy public clash between Labastida and French commander Bazaine. Labastida's vision of the Regency was activist; he was part of a triumvirate, not a place keeper. By force of personality, Labastida dominated the other regents, Generals Almonte and Salas. Without qualms he would use his position to accomplish what he could. The Intervention would never have succeeded without the support of the clergy. One of the first steps to be taken, he insisted, was to annul the sale of Church properties.[6]

For Bazaine, the problem with Labastida was that he was alienating moderate Mexicans—the very people Bazaine hoped to rally to the empire.[7] Bazaine went to work splitting the triumvirate. He rallied Almonte and Salas and persuaded them that it was time to eject the archbishop. On November 17 Almonte and Salas announced that Labastida was no longer a member of the Regency.[8] Labastida had returned from exile a mere eight weeks earlier and his tenure as regent was already over. Thinking that the matter of the troublesome cleric had been resolved, Bazaine left on campaign.

Labastida did not go quietly. He waited until Bazaine had left on his campaign of pacification, then he mobilized an insurgency of his own. On December 26, Labastida summoned Mexico's upper clergy, its bishops and archbishops, to Mexico City. Most of them were in the capital already, preferring to avoid the complications of returning to their bishoprics while the insurgency and the pacification campaigns were under way. Egged on by Labastida, they used their power as leaders of the faithful to stir up opposition. When the Regency (minus Labastida) sought to reassure buyers of former Catholic properties that their titles were secure, Labastida and his bishops countered with a lightning bolt. On December 31 they issued a statement in which they forbade their followers to abide by the decrees of the Regency, on pain of excommunication from the Catholic Church. As for those who possessed former Church properties, they would be denied absolution at the moment of death if they did not return said property its rightful owner—the Church. The Supreme Court supported the bishops, going so far as to assert that the entire point of the Intervention had been to overturn the Reform.[9]

At 7:30 AM on January 3, 1864, a team of horses pulled limber and cannon into place in front of the Cathedral of Mexico City. The artillery crew detached the gun and positioned it so that it pointed directly at the cathedral's main door. This rather blunt confrontation between the Catholic Church and the occupying army had been precipitated by a recent announcement by Archbishop Labastida. The prelate had let it be known that the Catholic Mass offered for the benefit of the French army every Sunday morning since their arrival would not be taking place. The bishops' excommunication of those who supported the Regency included the French army, most of whom were at least nominally Catholic; they would not be welcome at the 8 AM Mass. During the absence of Bazaine, General Charles-Louis Neigre was the ranking officer in the capital. When he caught wind of the closure of the cathedral to French soldiers, Neigre sent a messenger to Labastida with notice that if the doors to the cathedral weren't open for the customary military Mass at 8 AM, he would use cannon to open them. A short while after the artillery crew positioned itself facing the cathedral, the doors swung open. Moments later, General Neigre and his officers arrived, entered the church, and took their places.

It was another humiliation for Archbishop Labastida, who had been forced to concede, quite publicly, that the threat of excommunication meant nothing to a twelve-pound field gun. But General Neigre couldn't ignore what this episode signaled for the future; the door in question was the same door General Forey had entered after the high clergy greeted him upon his triumphal entry to the city the previous June. So much had changed. Neigre sent word to Bazaine, who hastened back to the capital to deal with a deteriorating relationship between the Mexican Catholic hierarchy and the occupying army.

This incident occurred months before Maximilian and Charlotte arrived, and it ought to have sounded alarms for them. The same Catholic hierarchy who, in the person of Archbishop Labastida, had been so solicitous of them and the Intervention had already soured on the affair. Worse, they were rallying public opinion in Mexico against the French at the very moment when the French army was in the provinces pursuing those the Catholic hierarchy saw as its most formidable opponents. In Morelia, when a buyer of Church property died, local clergy refused to permit burial of the body. The claim was that only good Catholics could be buried in consecrated ground; a buyer of confiscated Catholic property clearly did not meet the standard. When Bazaine learned of this, he issued orders for the burial to take place and forbade, via the Regency, such acts of resistance on the part of the clergy. It took no great powers of perception to see that even though the empire had yet to be realized, disenchantment had already set in and its most powerful advocates had turned against it.[10]

After the arrival of the imperial couple, matters didn't improve. Labastida's stubbornness did not diminish; he and Maximilian and Charlotte began to look toward the imminent arrival of the papal nuncio to resume constructive discussions. In the late fall of 1864 Maximilian wrote impatiently to Gutiérrez in Rome, suggesting obliquely that he intervene with the Vatican. Maximilian had only arrived that June but had already formed a low opinion of the Mexican clergy, whom he regarded as "not at present" actually Catholic.[11] Mexico needed "a good concordat and nuncio" to form a mutually advantageous relationship, in which a reformed and reinvigorated Mexican clergy would consolidate Catholic support for the empire.

William Henry Bullock was on board the *RMS Solent* when it arrived at Veracruz on November 29, 1864, carrying Monsignor Pedro Francisco Meglia, bishop of Damascus and papal nuncio. Bullock was astonished when Meglia appeared on deck "in the full glory of his violet and green ecclesiastical trappings" before stepping onto the launch that would take him ashore. Bullock and Meglia had become regular dinner companions during the crossing. Meglia's table talk was "far from brilliant" but Bullock shared with Meglia a fondness for claret that relieved the monotony of life on board. A shared passion for hunting cockroaches in their cabins had moved their relationship along, so that when Meglia appeared in full regalia, it felt as though a great chasm had opened between them.[12]

Meglia arrived in Mexico City on December 7, 1864. The day offered an example of the enduring power of the Catholic clergy in everyday life. A pickpocket was working the crowd milling about in the large plaza in front of the cathedral. Pursued and nearly caught, the pickpocket sought refuge in the cathedral, where he cried out for the protection of "God and all the Saints"—thus invoking sanctuary. He tried to conceal himself by crouching under a pew, but French soldiers found him and forced him out at bayonet point. As the soldiers herded the suspect to the steps of the cathedral, a priest intervened and rallied the crowd in his defense. Sanctuary—entering a church to seek refuge from authorities—remained a common practice in Mexico, even in matters of petty crime. "In this country, no one may be arrested in a church, whatever the charge," an eyewitness claimed. Beyond the weight of tradition, the persistence of sanctuary was also driven by mutual self-interest. "Often a priest will share with the criminal the product of his theft." Expounding on dubious clerical practices in Mexico, the witness noted that "the clergy . . . sell prayers and crude images of the saints in plaster at monstrous prices."[13] There was no denying the profound integration of the Catholic clergy in Mexican popular culture; such practices seemed beyond the capacity of any concordat to change.

As for the nuncio, Bishop Meglia, the business of negotiations for the concordat didn't get started right away. It was as if, having made Maximilian and Charlotte wait months for his arrival, Meglia was determined to teach them patience by making them wait just a bit longer. There was ample pretext. Pope Pius had in recent years announced the dogma of the Immaculate Conception, with a feast day observed on December 8. Meglia thought it his duty to offer a High Mass as soon as convenient upon arrival. The anniversary of the appearance of the Virgin of Guadalupe to Juan Diego, a Chichimec man, is traditionally observed on December 12. The Guadalupe anniversary presented itself as the obvious occasion for high ceremony—the imperial coach traveling to the shrine; the Palatine Guard; a Holy Water blessing; a canopy entry; a chanted Mass.[14] All eyes were on Meglia as he officiated with the entire court in attendance. A celebratory banquet followed at which Meglia was seated in the place of honor, to Maximilian's right. Maximilian took the occasion to offer Meglia a gift of five thousand dollars, a princely sum, destined for the pope.[15]

All of this was designed to get negotiations going on the warmest possible basis, but when Maximilian invited Meglia to a private conversation to begin the negotiations that would lead to a formal agreement—a concordat—between the two states, Meglia presented Maximilian with a letter of introduction from Pope Pius. This would be normal diplomatic procedure—a newly arrived diplomat presents credentials to show proof of his authority to represent—but this letter directly addressed questions of policy that left no room for dialog. In the first sentence, which ran for an entire paragraph, Pius recalled the visit of Maximilian and Charlotte to the Vatican prior to their departure, then listed the sufferings of the Church in Mexico under the Reform, including the confiscation of Church property and the suppression of religious orders. The letter went on to express Pius's "ineffable joy" at learning that the "a prince of a Catholic family" was called to the throne, the expectation of "a prompt and just reparation" this news had raised, and the deep disappointment that followed. By the time the letter got around to its nominal purpose of introducing the nuncio, it had made it clear what would be required to secure a concordat—a Mexico in which the property and the primacy of the Church and its clergy had been fully restored.[16]

This was miles away from what Maximilian and Charlotte were willing to contemplate. They had grown up in a Europe where the status of the Catholic Church had been effectively modernized, even in historically Catholic countries such as Belgium and Austria. Modernization in Catholic Europe after 1789 included such mundane matters as the civil registration of births, marriages, and deaths, as well as weightier matters such as toleration for religious minorities (if not outright religious pluralism) and the presumption that the authority of the Church was subordinate to that of the state in civil matters.[17] But modernism was precisely the enemy according to Pius, whose encyclical *Quanta Cura*, with its "Syllabus of Errors," condemned liberal modernity. For someone like Maximilian, whose self-image was that of a devoted champion of modern progress and whose vision of empire was of a benevolent stewardship, this left no common ground.[18] It was probably pure coincidence that Pius issued *Quanta Cura* the day after his nuncio Meglia arrived in Mexico City, but anyone could be forgiven for thinking it was planned. Pius's "Syllabus" condemned modernity; Meglia, his envoy, was "the Syllabus made flesh."[19]

It seems that both Maximilian and Pope Pius IX shared the ambition to restore an idealized past and this superficially put them on the path to agreement, but they had different versions of the past. Maximilian idealized the reign of Charles V, for whom the sun never set on the Habsburg Empire, including Habsburg New Spain. This was clear even in the text of his proposal to the nuncio. Maximilian and Charlotte claimed for Maximilian and his successors "to exercise *in perpetuity* the same rights as the Kings of Spain exercised in the churches of America."[20] Maximilian did not see his empire as an ordinary colonial venture. In his exalted view, the empire represented the restoration of the rule of the Spanish Habsburgs.

Papal recognition of this vision was crucial to the imperial self-image. Pius seems to have embraced a corollary. If Maximilian's imperial vision harkened back to New Spain, wouldn't that imply the restoration of the status of the Catholic Church?

It was soon clear that the much-desired resolution of church/state differences would not occur. Meglia effectively seconded the positions articulated by Labastida—restitution of nationalized Church property, automatic legal authority for papal decrees, restoration of the privileged status of the Catholic Church. Maximilian and Charlotte could draw upon a number of recent models of church/state relations, all quite reasonable against the background of the previous half century or so, all of them rejected by Pope Pius.

By the end of the month Maximilian and Charlotte's patience had been exhausted. Maximilian wrote to his minister of justice and religions, Fernando Ramírez Escudero, complaining that Meglia lacked precise instructions from Rome, the kind that would allow him to negotiate a concordat. This wasn't precisely true; the problem was that Meglia's instructions weren't the ones Maximilian wanted. Maximilian insisted that a regularization of church/state relations could wait no longer; he asked Escudero to begin drafting policy apart from negotiations with the nuncio.[21] This was fine as an expression of his frustration and the need for a solution, but it overlooked the fact that what Maximilian desired most of all was the legitimacy that a concordat would bring.

The quarrel risked spilling into the open, causing further damage. The European press had already read the appointment of Meglia as an ominous sign. The Austrian press was generally sympathetic to Maximilian and Charlotte, but warned that Mexico's clerical party was waging a war against them and that the church property question threatened to derail the empire just months after their arrival. Some even accused Maximilian of wavering in the face of papal resistance.[22] In fact, Maximilian had given up on Meglia. On December 24, Charlotte met with Meglia for two hours in a last-ditch effort to get him to budge. Afterward, she concluded that he was "a mere puppet" of Labastida.[23] That same day Escudero delivered a letter laying out the empire's position on key points.[24] Within twenty-four hours Meglia responded with the same language he had been using since his arrival, expressing hostility to "the so-called laws of reform" and upholding "the sacred rights of the Church."[25] Two days later Maximilian lashed out in frustration. He sent a letter to Escudero in which he complained that "after more than seven months, further delay was impossible." The newspaper of record, the *Diario del Imperio,* published a statement in which the empire recognized as final the sale of ecclesiastical property carried out by the republic.[26] There would be no going back.

The fallout from Meglia's visit—notably Maximilian's public pronouncement regarding Church property—inspired a sense of betrayal among the Mexican clergy. At least with Juárez they knew who they were dealing with, but having labored to bring the empire about, the dreamed-of restoration of all that they had lost was not taking place. The Church had wanted a counter-revolution. The clergy acted as if the empire would deliver one. Instead, the empire now asked them to consolidate their losses and move on by ratifying the post-Reform status quo. Even before the arrival of the imperial couple, the Mexican clergy had followed Labastida in reasserting its authority, as if the Reform had never happened. Now, with the weight of the papal nuncio added to the forces of clerical reaction, the full weight of the papacy was aligned behind a burgeoning Catholic counter-revolution. Reports continued of clergy denying burial to buyers of nationalized Church lands. The empire countered with a decree declaring cemeteries open to all. When the president of Guatemala died, Meglia used it as an excuse to depart Mexico gracefully.[27]

As was so often the case, it was Charlotte rather than Maximilian who most keenly characterized the situation. The clergy were "gravely injured" by the position Maximilian had taken and had now formed a resistance to defend "all the old abuses." The Catholic clergy in Mexico needed reform; but to her eyes the existing clergy were beyond saving. "I think it's impossible that those presently making up the clergy are able to form the core of new one," she wrote. "What to do with them, that's the question."[28]

The obvious answer to clerical intransigence in Mexico was to bypass the clergy by going directly to the pope. With Charlotte's active encouragement, Maximilian created a commission for the purpose, consisting of three men: Joaquín Velázquez de León, imperial minister; bishop Francisco Ramírez y González, and Joaquín Degollado, lawyer and imperial adviser. In early February Maximilian let it be known that the commission would be sent to Rome with full authority to negotiate a concordat.[29] The commission's vision explicitly referenced a concordat concluded with Spain in 1851, which would seem to indicate its acceptability—after all, shouldn't what worked for one country work for another? The draft concordat included a few novelties: the Church was to grant Maximilian the rights enjoyed by "his predecessors"—that is, the kings of Spain, including his Spanish Habsburg ancestors—in the three hundred years following the *conquista*.[30] This meant that in matters involving power relations with the Catholic Church, Maximilian and his commission were elaborating a vision of the Second Mexican Empire as a restoration of New Spain. It was a boldly romantic—and candid—vision of what the empire could be, but that vision, along with a stipulation that the nationalizations carried out by the Mexican republic be accepted by the Church "for the good of the public peace and the tranquility of consciences" meant that the commission's initiative was dead upon arrival.[31] Maximilian and Charlotte wanted to believe that Labastida, Meglia, and the Mexican clergy were the source of their problems. They weren't. The Vatican of Pius IX was lining up squarely behind them.[32]

"The Finest the Mexican Clergy Has to Offer"

Just as Maximilian was beginning to despair of ever winning over the Vatican, salvation appeared in the form of Augustín Fischer. Fischer was a member of the Mexican clergy, but a man whose personal story reveals an extraordinary gift for self-invention. Fischer was born in Ludwigsburg, Württemberg, in 1825. His mother's occupation is unknown. His father was a butcher. Young Augustín was expelled from school at the age of twelve for unspecified acts of indiscipline. Admitted to a reform school, he was expelled for corrupting other children. He was apprenticed to a blacksmith, but failed. Having exhausted his options, he emigrated to Texas, where he found an environment more hospitable to someone with his talents.[33]

In Texas, Fischer worked for a time as an agricultural laborer, perhaps alongside the many German immigrants in New Braunfels. He was twenty-five when the discovery of gold at Sutter's Mill drew him to California. He seems to have washed out as a forty-niner. Somewhere along the way, Fischer, who was baptized Lutheran, converted to Catholicism and found his vocation—he next appears in the historical record in the diocese of Durango, Mexico, assigned to a parish as a Roman Catholic priest. Parish records in Parras show him administering holy sacraments to his flock as of January 1862.[34]

We have few sources that would enable us to flesh out the details of his existence in the twelve years that lapsed between his career as a prospector in the California foothills and his priestly vocation in Mexico, but one source places him back in Texas, working as a notary in San Antonio until accounting irregularities forced him to flee across the border.[35] This report at least explains his presence in Mexico, where stories of irregularities in his private life haunted him. He worked for a time as secretary to the bishop of Durango but was removed for indiscretions, which accounts for his reassignment to the parish in Parras.[36] What followed also yields insights. Intimacy with his housekeeper in Parras produced a small family—"the word made flesh," according to one of his detractors.[37]

Fischer's assignment as a modest parish priest in Parras proved decisive not only in his private life but also in his career, for it allowed him to insinuate himself within the powerful Sánchez Navarro family. The amount of land owned by the Sánchez Navarros was said to "approach the size of Portugal" and, indeed, the family comported itself at times as a sovereign power. Fischer had the good fortune to be introduced to Carlos Sánchez Navarro, the family patriarch, and from that encounter all good things would flow. Dolores Sánchez Navarro, the wife of Carlos, took Fischer into her confidence; it was said that he became her confessor. From such a position of influence and prestige, Fischer was within reach of the summit of power.[38]

When Maximilian and Charlotte arrived in the summer of 1864, they were eager to nurture relationships with Mexican notables by giving them titles and positions at court. Dolores Sánchez Navarro became one of Charlotte's ladies in waiting, and Carlos became a chamberlain. Augustín Fischer was just one introduction away from the apex of power in Mexico's Second Empire. In mid-1865, Dolores and Carlos Sánchez Navarro called Fischer to the capital.[39] The Sánchez Navarros wanted to put their abundant wealth in land to work in service of the empire. Somehow, Fischer set himself up as manager of the project, a position that put him in direct contact with Maximilian.[40] Sánchez Navarro, Fischer wrote, "offers the Government of Your Majesty two million acres of land." Fischer touted the lands as "most suitable" for immigrants, without specifying how. Given the paucity of water, the omission was significant, but immigration and farming were only part of the story, for as Fischer insisted, colonization there should be seen as a military measure, building "a military power on the North American border." German immigrants would arrive either from the United States or directly from Germany, where appeals for settlers went out from consular offices in Frankfurt.[41] Bachelors would be given one hundred acres; families would receive two hundred acres. Title to the land would be transferred after three years of occupancy and cultivation.[42]

Augustín Fischer. *Centro de Estudios de Historia de México Fundación Carlos Slim dependiente de Servicios Condumex S.A. de C.V.*

Though Fischer's German colonization plan seems to have borne little fruit, it was enough to get him the attention of Maximilian, who for his part seems never to have asked why a Catholic priest had been put in charge of a two-million-acre colonization scheme. In due course, Fischer was appointed court chaplain. By September Fischer was on his way to Rome carrying a letter of introduction in which Maximilian described Fischer as "one of the most distinguished members of the Mexican clergy."[43] Given Maximilian and Charlotte's low opinion of the Mexican clergy, the statement could be both true and meaningless.

Fischer's assignment was part of the story of how badly the imperial couple wanted an agreement with the Vatican that would confer legitimacy on their regime. Given the disastrous negotiations with the papal nuncio and the apparent failure of all other efforts to conclude a concordat, Fischer carried a weighty responsibility. For Fischer it was a triumphant return. When he left Europe in 1845, he was twenty years old and out of options, on his way to America in an effort to remake himself. In 1865 he was returning to Europe as a diplomat representing Mexico to the court of Rome.

Roman Intrigues

Fischer flourished in Rome. In November he had an audience with the pope.[44] He seems to have established a warm friendship with Cardinal Antonelli, secretary of state at the Vatican. Antonelli took Fischer in as a house guest at the Palazzo Braschi, Antonelli's residence on the Piazza di San Pantaleo. Fischer used his relationship with Antonelli to learn gossip, including gossip about Antonelli's mistress, which he duly passed on to Maximilian. For Antonelli, part of the attraction might have been that Fischer, like Antonelli, was a self-made man. Unlike his peers in papal service, Antonelli was not a priest, nor was he a member of the Italian nobility.[45] As for Fischer, rumors circulated about Fischer's mission—given the brevity of his association with the imperial court, some assumed his mission concerned his home diocese of Durango.[46] Eventually it came to be understood that Fischer was in town to pursue the concordat that had so far eluded Maximilian and Charlotte.

Advocates for the empire weren't the only ones active in Rome. The Mexican republic had a brilliant representative in Europe in the person of Jesús Terán. Terán had lobbied Maximilian before he left for Mexico, warning bluntly that the empire would fail. To no avail. When Terán learned of the failure of the mission of the papal nuncio to Mexico, he saw an opportunity. No one expected the Republic of Mexico to be on excellent terms with the Catholic Church, but the empire was the child of Mexican Conservatives and a Conservative government without the support of the Church would not survive.

As the nuncio was leaving Mexico City in April 1865, Terán was on his way to Rome. By May he had managed to arrange a conversation with Antonelli in which Antonelli, unaware that Terán was an agent of the Republic of Mexico, expressed the conviction that Maximilian would not be able to stay in power. It followed that it would not be prudent for the Church to be bound by an agreement.[47] In this manner, Terán acquired a fine piece of diplomatic intelligence sure to boost the morale of the embattled defenders of the Mexican republic. It was June 1865, Maximilian and Charlotte had been in Mexico barely a year, and Antonelli, one of the most powerful men in Europe, was already predicting the failure of their enterprise.

If Antonelli was as candid with Fischer as he was with Terán, neither man left a record of it. Fischer continued to cultivate his relationship with the pope's secretary of state and to enjoy his hospitality, which included fine dinners followed by excellent cigars. The relationship seems not to have moved along negotiations for the concordat, though Fischer did not hesitate to claim that it would, especially as his continued presence in Rome depended on such a prospect.[48] Maximilian's Imperial Mexican minister in Rome, Ignacio Aguilar y Marocho, remained a skeptic.[49] The same could be said for Archbishop Labastida, who had extensive contacts in the papal city thanks to his lengthy exile there. Both Labastida and Aguilar received regular updates from Monsignor Enrique Angelini, an old associate in Rome, who raised doubts about Fischer. Both men had reasons to hold a grudge; Fischer's mission had bypassed them. Neither man could shake Maximilian's confidence in Fischer. By January Maximilian was convinced that Fischer was succeeding brilliantly as his special envoy, despite "petty intrigues," and that his efforts would result in an agreement "very soon." This was very much the message Fischer had been feeding Maximilian. Fischer had made a good life for himself in Rome and was in no hurry to give it up. As long as Maximilian believed that Fischer's efforts would yield a concordat "very soon," Fischer could prolong a very agreeable sojourn in Rome at the empire's expense.

By January 1866 there was little progress. That didn't break Maximilian's confidence that things would go his way. He wrote to Gutiérrez to express confidence in the future, including a concordat. He was winning over the bishops of Mexico, who had "begun to understand the difficult position and good will of the Government," he wrote. Maximilian couldn't help but note that Gutiérrez, after Napoléon III the person most responsible for Maximilian's decision to go to Mexico, remained in Europe. "Why don't you come with your family to see our sweet and beautiful fatherland?" he asked. "It takes only twenty-five days to get from Paris to Mexico." Gutiérrez, it seems, shared Antonelli's pessimism about the future.[50]

By March, Enrique Angelini reported that negotiations for a concordat had been suspended, but he recounted a conversation he had had with Fischer the evening before in which Fischer, in a display of bluster, claimed to be meeting with the pope daily.[51] It was the kind of claim that strained credulity but also explained how Maximilian and Charlotte could cling to the hope that a breakthrough was imminent. Writing from Chapultepec Castle, Maximilian congratulated Joaquín Degollado for by-passing "obstacles and intrigues" and meeting directly with Pius and Antonelli. Maximilian was convinced that through Degollado's effort the eyes of the Roman Curia would be opened, "an immoral and greedy clergy" would be replaced along with its "feudal hierarchy," and true Catholicism would come to Mexico at last.[52]

In fact, the same Mexican clergy for which Maximilian had expressed such disdain was quite capably represented in Rome by Clemente Munguía, archbishop of Michoacán. Munguía had been banished by Juárez after the War of Reform for having compromised himself politically.[53] Like Labastida, Munguía had passed his exile in Rome.[54] Like Labastida, he had returned to Mexico with the empire, only to experience disappointment when the empire showed that the Reform would not be undone. Unlike Labastida, who remained in Mexico, Munguía returned to Rome as a self-appointed lobbyist and representative of the Mexican Church. Munguía's politics aligned perfectly with the politics of Pius IX as expressed in the "Syllabus." As the young bishop of Michoacán, he had refused to take a required oath under the Constitution of 1824. He eventually relented, but the episode clearly identified him with the most aggressive defenders of Church prerogatives. Under the government of Santa Anna, he was called to participate in discussions leading to a concordat, but actively subverted such efforts, shrewdly observing that although a concordat would stabilize Santa Anna's government—a Conservative government friendly to the Church—instability in Mexico served the Church's interests best, because weak government created the optimal environment for Church autonomy.

In Rome, Munguía continued his hostility to the empire. He opposed a concordat with the empire for the same reasons he had opposed a concordat with Santa Anna—a weak state meant a strong Church. He was coldly realistic, too, pointing out that the survival of the empire was far from certain; should the Mexican republic return, its leaders would rightly chastise the Mexican Church for collaborating with a foreign monarch. He was supported in this by Archbishop Labastida, who continued to circulate in imperialist circles in Mexico. "You know quite well the evil a con-cordat can do," he wrote to Munguía.

Fischer went on the offensive. He attacked Munguía's character and his conduct as bishop of Michoacán. Without giving specifics or proof, Fischer claimed that "very unfavorable rumors" circulated concerning "quantities of money" belonging to "pious funds" that had disappeared on Munguía's watch. Fischer repeated, with justification, the claim that Munguía saw political anarchy in Mexico as being more advantageous for the Church than a concordat, but he added a new claim—that political anarchy served as a "cover" for "messy" things that should not "see the light."[55] It wasn't just a matter of protecting the Church's freedom of movement in Mexico; it was about covering up misconduct and corruption.[56]

Fischer's attack combined elements of truth with slanderous specula-tion. Maximilian didn't need convincing. In an angry letter to Joaquín De-gollado in Rome, Maximilian complained that "according to persons who knew him well," Munguía was "completely atheistic" and a "sick soul" whose "only God is personal ambition."[57]

In the end it didn't matter. By the summer of 1866 the best argument against a concordat with the empire was the empire itself, which was per-ceived as weak and failing. The French were leaving. The Habsburgs halted the recruitment of additional Austrian volunteers, having caved in the face of pressure from the United States. The treasury of the empire was chronically empty; bankruptcy was averted only by occasional de-posits authorized by Bazaine, which were characterized as loans.[58] "The sick man has entered his final agony," wrote Munguía in June 1866. Then he offered a grim image to explain why the Church had no interest in a concordat. "It wouldn't be the best shroud for the deceased."[59] More than a vivid image of a moribund empire, Munguía's description worked as prophecy. A year later, not only would the empire be dead, the emperor would be, too.

Courting Indigeneity

At the time of the arrival of Maximilian and Charlotte, Bazaine's pacifi-cation campaign was not complete. The goal of the French military cam-paign had always been political as well as military. Control of territory mattered, but it was always immediately followed by a demonstration of support for the new imperial order. In practice, this meant that a prefect was selected from among prominent citizens; this was accompanied by a statement of support for the empire, an *acta de adhesión* signed by local notables and duly reported in the press.[60] These acts fit the narrative of salvation, the idea that the people of Mexico longed to be free—that they only needed an opportunity to express themselves openly and honestly. Their support for monarchy would reveal itself as a matter of course. In Puebla, for example, the testimonial included broad affirmations about Mexico and monarchy. "The great Mexican family cannot subsist on republican forms," the testimonial affirmed, "monarchy conforms to the spirit of the century, with national traditions, [and] with ancient custom."[61] Maximilian, desperate for signs of broad assent to the empire, had seized on the "acts of adhesion" produced in cities and towns in the wake of French occupation. But such assertions concealed the coercive aspect of these acts.

Not everyone was convinced. In the British Parliament, Liberal MP John Kinglake argued that these statements should not be confused with assent: "No doubt wherever a French army penetrated it would be easy to find persons called 'Notables' to offer a crown to an Archduke, but . . . beyond the reach of the French armies no one had expressed the slightest inclination for the introduction of the monarchical system into that part of the world."[62] Coerced assent was no assent at all.

Not all gestures were orchestrated, especially where the empire could insinuate itself into ongoing grievances. In Sonora, members of the Opata nation supported the empire politically and militarily, notably by helping the French hold the port city of Guaymas.[63] Their leader Tanori was awarded the rank of general for his efforts.[64] A group of fifteen hundred Cuatecoma operated around Puebla under the command of Captain Della Sala.[65] Most famous of all was General Tomás Mejía, of Indigenous Otomi descent, who, as a Catholic Conservative, rallied to the Intervention and brought his considerable following in the Sierra Gorda along with him.[66] He would die alongside Maximilian.

In Nayarit, Manuel Lozada rallied to the empire and brought three thousand soldiers of Cora tribal descent with him.[67] His and his supporters' allegiance owed much to an ongoing struggle for communal land rights, which had been undermined by Liberal reform, as well as a desire for regional autonomy.[68] According to the principle that the enemy of my enemy is my friend, he embraced the empire as a useful ally against the Liberal Mexican state. His allegiance was opportunistic—nimble, too; he would be one of the first to defect as the empire waned.[69] Imperial sympathies for Indigenous Mexicans prompted Indigenous appeals to the empire for redress

Tomás Mejía. *Wikimedia Commons.*

against landowners, though some of these appeals were based on spurious claims.[70]

The Indigenous of Yucatán were a special case. Yucatán was part of a broad base of support for the empire, important enough that Maximilian and Charlotte contemplated Yucatán as the core of a broader Latin American empire. A year after Maximilian's tour, Charlotte set out on a tour of her own, designed to cultivate support for the empire in Yucatán. She gave speeches, attended performances, and accepted handmade gifts from children.[71]

Indigenous interest in the empire was reciprocated. Even before they left Europe, Maximilian and Charlotte had expressed a keen interest in Indigenous Mexicans. Their interest drew upon their paternalist impulses—a sense of noblesse oblige—but also a romantic interest in the folkloric. Maximilian showed a pronounced preference for the Indigenous of Mexico, whom he professed to prefer to the *criollo* elite. Indians, in his view, were "the real Mexicans," and he made a point of reaching out to Indigenous populations. This was also a political calculation. Most of Mexico's population was Indigenous. By setting themselves up as champion of the Indigenous, the imperial couple might yet secure the foundation of the empire. Maximilian would later talk of "moralizing" the Indigenous population and cultivating their patriotism through land reform. Long before they left Europe for Mexico, Charlotte's father, Leopold, had speculated that "the Indian . . . with his penchant for religious practices" might be an important constituency. He even went so far as to suggest that reform of the Catholic Church would have to spare the lower clergy, given their influence on the Indigenous. Turned against the empire, "their influence on the Indians would be a terrifying calamity."[72]

For both Charlotte and Maximilian, respect for Indigenous Mexicans likely owed something to the necessary and pragmatic attitude toward ethnic pluralism they had acquired in Europe. The Habsburg Empire was an experiment in ethnic diversity—diverse peoples, customs, and languages were left untroubled provided they did not challenge an overarching Habsburg authority.[73] Pluralism and respect for difference, rather than obligatory conformity to a *criollo* civilizational ideal, might have served Mexico well.

Even the decision to renovate Chapultepec Castle supported efforts to woo Indigenous support, as the palace's association with Moctezuma made it the perfect setting for any effort to anchor modern monarchy in the Aztec past.[74] So did successful efforts to repatriate Aztec objects from Habsburg imperial collections. Shortly after Maximilian and Charlotte had installed themselves at Chapultepec Castle, they were visited by a delegation from the Texas-Coahuila borderlands representing the Kickapoo tribe.[75] The visit created an opportunity to incorporate indigeneity more firmly into the image of their empire. The Kickapoo were Algonquin who, under relentless pressure from US expansion, had descended the Mississippi and resettled in Texas—then a province of Mexico—only to find themselves caught up first in the Texas insurrection against Mexican rule, and then in the Mexican-American War.

The delegation's objective was to receive permission to resettle south of the US-Mexico border, in the new Imperial Mexico, but their ambition was easily instrumentalized, both in terms of Mexican Conservative political objectives and in terms of Maximilian's self-image. The Kickapoo were victims of US expansion and as such incarnated the devastation wrought by Yankee aggression—an aggression Maximilian and his sponsors had vowed to counter. Chased from their home in what is now the upper Midwest of Minnesota, Iowa, and Indiana, the Kickapoo now found themselves pursued beyond the US frontier into Mexico. In this, the Kickapoo embodied one of two ways that Native Americans figured in justifications for intervention in Mexico. In one, Mexico's instability was due, in part, to Indian raiding, notably in the northern states of Coahuila and Nueva Leon. In the other, Yankee aggression was to blame, driving refugees like the Kickapoo across the frontier into Mexico.[76]

By identifying a common external enemy, the Kickapoo could perform a valuable service to the empire. Internal differences made Mexico easy prey to foreign enemies. United behind the empire, Mexicans could rise against the foreign enemy, the Yankee. This outlook also highlighted the place of Indigenous peoples within the empire, implicitly criticizing the *criollo* elite who had ruled both before and after independence.[77] The Kickapoo visit embodied indigeneity as part of the ideology of the empire.

The Kickapoo delegation brought with them a large silver medal about two inches wide, bearing the image of Louis XV. On the reverse, an inscription: "To his faithful and beloved tribe of Kickapoos, King Louis XV." This medallion memorialized a Franco-Kickapoo relationship older than the United States itself, dating from the days when Kickapoo lands were part of what the French called Louisiana. Commentary at the time of the Kickapoo visit emphasized the victimhood of the Kickapoos, "forced to flee in the face of cosmopolitan foreign oppression," overlooking the fact that France had enabled that cosmopolitan foreign oppression when it sold the vast Louisiana territory to the United States in 1803.[78] Still, they had a point.

Jean-Adolphe Beaucé produced a painting to celebrate the meeting of the Kickapoo delegation with the imperial couple.[79] The painting is packed with meaning. On the wall in the background, three painted portraits preside over the scene. The two larger portraits in square frames on either side represent the French emperor Napoléon III and his spouse, the Empress Eugénie. In the center, in an oval frame, is a well-known portrait of Charles V, Maximilian's Habsburg forbear and his predecessor as ruler of Mexico. These are the sponsors of Maximilian, Charlotte, and their Mexican Empire. France provides military support, while Charles V provides the dynastic frame. On the left edge of the painting, a soldier stands guard with a halberd, a scene that might have occurred centuries earlier.

At the center of the painting, the Kickapoo delegation meets the imperial couple to present their case for resettlement under the protection of the Mexican Empire. The scene casts Maximilian's empire as a noble mission undertaken on behalf of the oppressed. The Kickapoo presence invoked the human cost of Yankee aggression, as well as the ambiguous status of the Indigenous within Mexico itself. After all, casting Mexico within a Latin racial frame willfully ignored Mexico's overwhelmingly Indigenous population.

In the center foreground, a minor tableau plays out between an Indigenous woman, her child, and Charlotte. The mother gazes with affection at her child as it crawls toward Charlotte, while Charlotte's eyes follow the mother, completing a sentimental triangle. The tableau also draws our attention to the carpet, of local production, which would have accentuated for European viewers both the exoticism of the moment and the extent to which Maximilian and Charlotte had adapted themselves to their new home. Their embrace of the Indigenous—their imperial indigeneity—also contributed to the image of their empire as an exercise in goodwill and

Jean-Adolphe Beaucé, *Visita de la embajada de indios kikapúes al emperador Maximiliano*, ca. 1865. *Reproduction ©Artstetten Castle, Lower Austria.*

self-sacrifice. One of Charlotte's European correspondents was impressed. "What enthusiasm the Indians have shown!" she remarked. "How Christian like . . . what immense good your example will produce!"[80]

Charlotte's philo-indigeneity was sentimental, often presented, as in the painting, in a maternal frame. Much of her work in public took the form of donations and visits to orphanages, part of a broader claim that the empire supported the needy classes, *las clases menesterosas*—effectively, the Indigenous community.[81] Maximilian's philo-indigeneity was intellectual—he sponsored major studies of Indigenous languages—but it was also populist, romantic, historical, even literary.[82] The Kickapoos were "true characters out of [James Fenimore] Cooper," he wrote to his brother. "[They are] authentic, savage, pagan, Indians," he added. They also helped link the empire to Anáhuac and the pre-Columbian past. "They ate here in the pine forest of Moctezuma," he told his brother, referring the woods surrounding Chapultepec, "in the same place where the Indian emperor gave his grand banquets."[83] These were also "noble savages"—more simple, honest, and direct than the *criollo* elites he had come to mistrust. The Kickapoo appeal played to Maximilian's keen sense of a moral obligation to serve. His elevation of them made them worthy of that moral sacrifice.

The empire's sponsors weren't quite sure where to fit this aspect of Maximilian's self-image, but his core constituents—the army, the Church, the large landowners—had little use for it.[84] Defenders of the republic saw it as insincere, as demagoguery designed to obscure what was at stake.[85] After all, the republic could look after its own. Benito Juárez, president of the republic, was Zapotec.

What these acts truly showed was the efficacy of military presence in securing the cooperation of the population. The emphasis on triumph after triumph and local testimonials of support following in rapid succession concealed the fact that large parts of Mexico remained outside imperial control and, by default, loyal to the republic. Signs of dissent were rare in the face of overwhelming military presence. This meant that the geography of support for the empire was limited by the practical limits of military occupation. In the north of Mexico, Tamaulipas, Nuevo León, Coahuila, Durango, and Chihuahua remained loyal to the republic, as did Sinaloa, and parts of Sonora in the west; in the south, Michoacán, Oaxaca, Tabasco, and Chiapas remained outside of imperial control. For the Intervention to succeed and the empire to prevail, these territories would have to be brought under control. But control could only be ensured by the presence of troops, and the size of the force at the disposal of the empire was entirely inadequate given the expanse of territory and the disposition of its population. Instead, in terms of authority, control was amoeba-like—dynamic and contingent on the movement and presence of troops.

Control of territory meant not only political power but also revenue for the new imperial state. State income depended upon taxation of goods. It followed that the movement of goods, notably through ports and from there to points beyond, had to be a state priority. Yet the telling fact was that the Intervention had secured only a limited commercial backbone. Goods arrived at Veracruz, where they were subjected to customs, after which they could be moved on. When Maximilian and Charlotte arrived, the commercial artery from Veracruz to Mexico City had been secured. From the capital, secure transit was ensured to the west as far as Guadalajara, by way of Morelia, and north to Zacatecas and San Luis Potosí, by way of Querétaro.[86] Viewed dispassionately, this was a clear picture of the weakness of the empire. Most other ports—Guaymas, Mazatlán, San Blas, Acapulco, Matamoros, to mention only the most important—remained outside imperial control or under tenuous authority.[87] True, Veracruz was by far the most important port and easily the greatest source of revenue, but the larger picture gave the lie to monarchist assurances that the mere presence of the imperial couple would remove all doubt and bring peace as the population rallied to the empire.

In contrast, the republic enjoyed revenue from ports still under republican control in the north as well as crossing-over locations such as Piedras Negras on the US-Mexico border, which mattered for arms shipments from Texas and beyond. Guaymas, on the Gulf of California, could be used for shipments from San Francisco, where a large Mexican-American community sent resources of all kinds, despite efforts by the French consul to stop them.[88] Juárez also made appeals to all good republicans willing to fight the good fight and defend republicanism in Mexico. From the beginning, Juárez wanted to internationalize Mexico's struggle. Now he was offering land and cash bonuses to those willing to fight.[89] The presence of foreign nationals fighting on behalf of the Mexican republic also greatly increased the chance of an unfortunate international incident. Floriano Bernardo, a Swiss-American, who led an insurgent group of twenty-eight men, was one of the first foreigners to die defending the Mexican republic.[90] His arrest and execution by French forces in January 1863 had greatly increased tensions, raising concerns of drawing the United States into the conflict.[91] All parties were keenly aware of the possibility that a death would serve as a tripwire, widening the struggle.

Bazaine had begun a new offensive in the summer of 1864 with the aim to capture Juárez, Lerdo, and the republican leadership or to force them to leave Mexican soil. The results of the offensive were impressive from a military point of view. Franco-Mexican forces entered a new tier of northern cities; Durango and Nuevo León came under imperial control. The last substantial fighting force available to the republic, commanded by General Jesús González Ortega, was decisively defeated at Majoma, in Zacatecas, in September.[92] Majoma capped Bazaine's summer campaign and opened the way for movements farther north, but Juárez remained elusive and on Mexican soil. He and Lerdo withdrew northward, forsaking Monterrey for Chihuahua, where new challenges awaited them.[93]

If there was a high point to the occupation—and a low point for the republic—this was it. Majoma seemed to signal the end of combat, at least in the conventional sense. With no real army left, the Mexican republic was vanquished militarily. There were rumors—eagerly seized upon—that Juárez was in the United States, having been chased from Mexican territory. From a distance, it was possible to convince oneself that the consolidation of power was complete. In Brussels, the semi-official *Echo du Parlement* asserted in November 1864 that "all of Nuevo León and the right bank of the Rio Bravo are occupied."[94] Given that the Rio Bravo (Rio Grande, in the United States) was the northern boundary of Mexico, the claim could imply the successful occupation of the country as a whole. This was far from true. The American Civil War was visibly reaching its end, the United States would soon turn its attention to the invasion of Mexico, and Bazaine worried that a skirmish involving US and French forces at the border might lead to war. He scrupulously kept French forces at a remove. It was telling that when it became possible to occupy Matamoros, opposite Brownsville (Texas), he refused to put French troops in harm's way. Bazaine sent General Tomás Mejía, a pro-imperialist. If US troops arrived and blood was shed, it would be Mexican blood, not French.

The Mexican defeat at Majoma was put to work on public opinion in France, too, where hostility to the Mexican adventure continued to grow. Bazaine seized the moment to make a grand gesture—it was time to begin to send troops home. Forces commanded by General L'Hériller advanced to Durango and San Juan del Rio, but Bazaine let it be known that they would be repatriated just as soon as Belgian and Austrian volunteers arrived. He was signaling to restive public opinion in Europe that operations were winding down.[95]

French Troops Enter Durango. *Reproduced from* l'Illustration, *December 21, 1864.*

Majoma, and the occupation of Durango that followed, also created an opportunity to fire up a new repertoire of images of enthusiastic crowds rushing to shower serene French soldiers with garlands and bouquets.[96] Taken together, the lessons of Majoma and Durango validated the message of Mexico as a good war—a short, decisive engagement with the French in the role of liberators.

It was not a message that held up well under scrutiny. In fact, the war was entering a much more brutal phase. Both the Intervention and the empire looked for ways to militarize the Mexican support that Mexican exiles like Gutiérrez and Hidalgo had insisted was there. In this nation-building narrative, if rank-and-file popular support could be mobilized and armed, the empire would have the kind of organic, patriotic, and popular support that would help it to thrive. French diplomats supported this view, too. "The people are in our favor," wrote Jules Doazan, French consul.[97] As political and military leadership imagined it, the forces of the Intervention would "clear dissidents" from an area and a locally recruited "rural guard" would maintain order.[98] But efforts to organize such village-based units in a "rural guard" routinely foundered in the face of indifference. Over time, European officers reported finding "little devotion to the empire" among the population. On the contrary, they frequently found caches of weapons, concealed by the populace but available to local insurgents. In the face of such evidence, they warned that creating and arming rural guard units was tantamount to "arming our enemies at government expense."[99]

Such observations underlined a related concern—the spread of forces of popular resistance determined to undermine the empire and occupation forces.[100] The destruction of conventional forces loyal to the republic meant that guerrilla forces—uncoordinated with one another, but united in their hostility to the occupier—would provide the backbone of resistance for Mexico. Within weeks of the fall of Puebla, Mexican officers who escaped French custody were back in their villages, calling to arms able-bodied men between the ages of fifteen and sixty.[101] These recruits functioned as a citizens' militia—in effect, as National Guard units—although arming them was often a bring-your-own-weapon affair. They also often lacked uniforms. With a basic outfit of white pants and white blouse, their allegiance might be marked by a flash of color—the red sash, vest, or hatband of the *chinaco* insurgent—the kind of marker, it should be noted, that could easily be attached, removed, or concealed. By comparison with European units they faced or even the soldiers of villages that rallied to the empire, they were informal partisan forces, often indistinguishable from bandits.[102] The ease with which defenders of the republic assembled, fought, then melted back into their communities potentiated reprisals. Imperial forces responded as conventional armies often do when confronted with an enemy who strikes and vanishes; they lashed out at civilians suspected of sustaining the enemy. With every such act, they associated atrocity and criminality with the regime they served.

The way had been prepared by men such as Colonel Charles Dupin, who took command of a counter-insurgency force at Tampico, on the Gulf Coast, in March 1864. Dupin was a grizzled veteran of several European and colonial wars of the mid-nineteenth century. After graduating from the École polytechnique in 1834, he joined the infantry and fought in

An auction catalogue depicting "Precious Objects from the Summer Palace of Yuen-Ming-Yuen," part of the Japanese and Chinese Museum of Monsieur Colonel du Pin, Paris, February 1862. *gallica.bnf.fr / BnF*

Algeria, Crimea, and Italy, before serving in China in the Second Opium War.[103] In China he participated in the looting of the Summer Palace and committed crimes against civilians, for which, it seems, he was punished.[104] This did not prevent him from profiting from his war spoils, which he sold at auction in Paris early in 1862. The auction catalog devoted to the "Japanese and Chinese Museum of Monsieur Colonel du Pin" filled 104 pages with items described as "found" in the Summer Palace.[105] Dupin understood better than most that war could be a lucrative undertaking.

It appears that Dupin's rehabilitation occurred in the aftermath of the French defeat at Puebla on May 5, 1862, when Napoléon III was scrambling to avenge the embarrassing defeat. Dupin was rehabilitated and, in March 1864, given command in Mexico, policing the states of Tamaulipas and Veracruz on the Gulf Coast. The results were predictable, given Dupin's entrepreneurial approach to war.[106] He took on soldiers of fortune—Greeks, Americans, French, Mexicans, Swiss—and gave them a direct interest in their success, notably by assessing cash payments from persons and communities in their path.[107] Dupin extorted eight hundred dollars from notables in the village of Medellín.[108] He accused the inhabitants of Valle de Purisma of making lances for Mexican cavalry and assessed a penalty of one thousand dollars.[109] When French troops were harassed as they passed through Ozuluama, Dupin assessed penalties in cash and in kind, under pain of destruction of the settlement.[110] In order to protect convoys from guerrilla attack, he ordered his men to create a defensive buffer by razing habitations on either side of the route.[111] Determined to deprive Mexican insurgents of resources, he torched the haciendas thought to have supported the insurgents sympathetic to the republic.[112]

Dupin became notorious, and not only for the brutality of his conduct. His outfit—an ill-fitting, braided uniform jacket and an exquisite sombrero—not only defied convention, it hinted at his dangerous unpredictability. In that, it was undoubtedly useful. He ruled Tampico and its hinterland through terror. It was an approach that gave him undisputed local control, but it was control that could be sustained only through his presence, and it utterly discredited the regime he served.[113]

On the west coast, General Armand de Castagny's campaign countered resistance with tactics that were at least as destructive as Dupin's. After occupying Durango in January 1865, Castagny moved west through Sinaloa toward the coast and the port city of Mazatlán. Castagny moved cautiously. He left a detachment at Veranos to protect his communications with Durango, but guerrilla forces led by Ramón Corona attacked Veranos as soon as Castagny and his main force left. The French suffered heavy losses; survivors were led away as prisoners. Castagny was unable to engage Corona directly, so he ordered reprisals against several communities suspected of supporting Corona, imposing brutal forms of collective responsibility. Ranchos were torched, and San Sebastián, a village

Colonel Charles Dupin, commander of counter-guerrilla forces. © *Musée de l'Armée, Dist. RMN-Grand Palais/Art Resource, NY.*

of four thousand, was razed in the name of "necessary rigor."[114] When the French soldiers taken prisoner at Veranos were found dead, a second column carried out reprisals against a string of villages including El Verde and Santa Catarina.[115] A deadly cycle of conquest, occupation, resistance, and reprisal devastated a host of small communities in the foothills of Sinaloa behind Mazatlán.

The case of Mazatlán itself is instructive, too. In the 1840s Mazatlán served as a hub for goods destined for Sonora, Chihuahua, Sinaloa, Durango, Nayarit, Jalisco, and Colima. And long before resort tourism made Mazatlán a cosmopolitan destination, it was home to Germans, French,

Americans, Spanish, and Mexicans who made a living as merchants, managing and profiting from inbound and outbound trade. Mazatlán was also home to shipbuilders and sailors, many of them French, engaged in coastal shipping north and south.[116] The military importance of such a location was obvious; the economic value was harder to realize. Forces loyal to the empire could take control of the port cities of Guaymas, Mazatlán, and San Blas, establishing a presence while cutting off customs revenue for the republic, but control of these ports on the west coast, like the control of Tampico on the east coast, yielded less than one might think. Ports can be choked from land as well as from sea, so while French troops, with help from the French navy, could control these ports, the hinterlands remained outside their authority, making trade insecure and dangerous. Stifled commerce testified to the power of popular resistance.

Mazatlán also gives us an insight into how the administration of the Mexican Empire was built. When Castagny arrived in Mazatlán, there were no local allies to be found. City police were "devoted to Corona," the leader of the insurgency. Judges were bought. Castagny claimed, not implausibly, that Mazatlán's elected officials collaborated with Corona against the French just as they had collaborated for years to move contraband goods through the port. To Castagny, this was evidence of the fundamental untrustworthiness of Mexican officials, whereas for the Mexicans it was merely the adaptation of established business relationships to military purposes in time of war. Castagny would later write of Mazatlán that there was not in all of Mexico "a city as crazy as this one."[117]

Castagny set out to remake municipal leadership in Mazatlán in the name of the empire. He dismissed the existing civil authorities but soon ran into a problem—the vacated positions drew no takers. "I couldn't collect enough honorable men," he complained. Castagny decided that if honorable men wouldn't step forward, he would compel them. He sweetened the pot for his appointees by threatening to imprison them for six months if they refused. Ladislas Gaona—whose name was testimony to Mazatlán's cosmopolitan heritage—was one of the appointees. When Gaona received notification in late January 1865 that he had been appointed to a judgeship, he begged off, claiming illness. On February 2, Gaona was threatened with imprisonment if he declined to serve. The next day he submitted his letter of acceptance. Thanks to such coercive measures, Mazatlán had its new imperial administrators. The appointments were subject to approval by Maximilian, who would never know the level of coercion applied to get the cooperation of the persons involved.

The story of Mazatlán shows that imperial administration rested on a fragile foundation of often unwilling participants.

Even more to the point, while Maximilian and Charlotte were crafting a superstructure of imperial elegance and pageantry in the capital, Dupin, Castagny, and others like them were operating in their name, reducing empire to the bare essentials of violence, intimidation, and coercive extraction.

9

Volunteers and Refugees

As Maximilian and Charlotte settled into their new imperial capital, thousands of young men across Europe were preparing to serve them. In fact, even before Maximilian and Charlotte found themselves succumbing to the charms of Parisian galas and grand imperial titles, they had put out the word that the new Mexican Empire was looking for volunteers to defend it. France had captured Mexico, but the French would not be staying. In the long run, the Mexican Empire would need its own soldiers to defend itself.

The groundwork for the recruitment of volunteers began at the end of 1861, weeks after Fort Sumter and *years* before Maximilian would formally accept the throne. On December 19, 1861, José María Gutiérrez visited Miramare, the first of many visits in his long courtship of Maximilian. Five days later, on Christmas Eve, Maximilian gave Gutiérrez his conditional acceptance; he would accept the crown of Mexico provided that it was the wish of the Mexicans themselves. The two men parted. Gutiérrez set out to publish a pamphlet that would rally public support for the empire.[1] Maximilian traveled to Venice, where he negotiated startup funds from his brother, Emperor Franz Joseph, as well as the assurance that he would have the authority to recruit volunteers from Habsburg domains for his imperial Mexican army.[2]

The meeting of brothers set in motion a process that would send thousands to Mexico. A parallel process was under way in Belgium. Together, the aim of the recruitment drive was to create an imperial force of eight thousand soldiers—two thousand from Belgium, the remainder from Habsburg lands.[3] Across Europe, from Barcelona to Belarus, young men answered the call. Why would thousands of Europeans volunteer to fight in a land they'd never seen, for a government that, at the time of their recruitment, did not yet exist? The answer helps us to understand the motives of the foot soldiers of European empires in the age of high imperialism, but also helps us to understand the allure of empire, how the needs of the multitude are yoked to the ambitions of the powerful.

Vienna's hot society ticket for early 1863 was an equestrian pageant to be held at the Spanish Riding School. The theme for the pageant was "Knights and Saracens." Archduke Wilhelm Franz chaired the blue-ribbon organizing committee, putting the weight of the ruling Habsburg family behind the event and proving that the Habsburg court still dominated Viennese high society. Emperor Franz Josef himself was lending sixty horses from the Riding School for the use of the performers at the gala.[4] Such a distinguished patronage would practically oblige the attendance of social elites and guarantee the success of the event. But this was to be no pointless display of splendor designed to feed the vanity of Viennese elites. "Knights and Saracens" was to be a charity event—proceeds would benefit the starving weavers of Silesia—tamping down criticism of what was otherwise a frivolous display of wealth and social power.[5]

Carl Khevenhüller-Metsch was in his early twenties when his cavalry regiment was posted to Vienna following months in remote locations. When Carl arrived in Vienna, he brought with him an ancient and storied name associated with high diplomacy and service to Holy Roman Emperors. As the eldest son of a noble family, Carl was guardian of the Khevenhüller-Metsch name and heir to family properties, but he yearned to make his mark. Carl was eager to break into highly choreographed Viennese society. Lineage would not be enough.[6]

Carl had other assets. He was good-looking. He was slender. His dark, wide-set eyes gave him the wounded look of a poet. He parted his thick, wavy hair in the middle to expose a tall forehead, which gave him a vaguely intellectual affect. But in fact he much preferred physical activity; he excelled at the athletic arts of fencing and gymnastics; he routinely won prizes at regimental equestrian events. The charity event played to his strengths. What better venue for a spectacular entry into Viennese society than a glittering pageant at the Spanish Riding School? Sisi, as the lovely young Empress Elisabeth of Austria was known, would be there, and she would draw the fashionable society she dominated. Carl had bought two fine and expensive horses since joining his cavalry unit—"Favorite," a thoroughbred mare, and "Mogudor," a chestnut gelding—but for this

Karl Khevenhüller-Metsch. *ÖNB / Wien PORT_00069735_01.*

occasion he wanted a horse beyond compare. He found a magnificent beast, priced at twelve hundred guilders, and went deeply into debt to buy it. With his looks, his riding skills, and an incomparable horse, Vienna would have to take notice.[7]

Carl's efforts were rewarded. The stunningly beautiful twenty-five-year-old Empress Sisi attended all the rehearsals. "All young people" were "in love" with her; her radiant presence inspired the performers, such that they "rode with a kind of exaltation." Among the performers were the Prince of Baden and the Duke of Württemberg of the German Con-federation alongside the great and notorious noble names of imperial Vienna—Metternich, Esterházy, Zichy, Erdódy. Even the emperor's brother, Archduke Ludwig Victor, would perform.[8] In such company, Carl Khevenhüller was positioning himself at the summit of court society.

The performance itself was a saga enacted on horseback. Historically, the Habsburgs had policed the Muslim/Christian borderlands of Europe, where the Ottoman and Austrian Empires met. The equestrian drama would recapitulate this history. Some performers were cast as Saracens, others as Knights. Costumes of colorful braids, sashes, tassels, brocades, and filigreed armor identified the opposing sides as they entered the arena. Intricate equine choreography showcased expert horsemanship per-formed as red, green, and black quadrilles. The pageant culminated in combats wherein Knights slaughtered Turks, Good destroyed Evil, Chris-tendom was defended, and order was restored.[9]

Carl's credit barely outlasted the fantasy. He missed payments on the debt he incurred to buy his horse. Soon he was being hounded by credi-tors. Then, in desperation, Carl did what any young person ruined by debt would do—he moved back in with his parents. In June 1864 Carl sought refuge at a remote, half-ruined family property at Riegersburg, close to what is now the Czech border. There he pondered his next move. Time was against him. The army would tolerate his absence for only so long, but if he returned to his unit his creditors would surely find him. His par-ents refused to cover his debts. Then, one day, in a moment of inspired maternal solicitude, Carl's mother suggested that he volunteer for Mexico. It was a brilliant idea. Mexico would put an ocean between Carl and his debt. It would give him a chance to start over.

The catch was that newspapers were publishing the names of volun-teers.[10] If Carl volunteered in Austria, his name would be released to the press, putting creditors back on the scent. Carl resolved to make his way west across Europe. He felt "a burden lift" when he crossed the border into Bavaria. He kept going, passing through the Rhineland, slipping into France. Somewhere along the way he learned of a troop transport for Belgian volunteers leaving from Saint-Nazaire, so he pressed on to Brittany. There, he boarded the *Floride*.[11] As the vessel pushed away on November 18, 1864, the burden of his youthful errors lifted. He was free.

The saga of Carl Khevenhüller was colorful, but far from unique.[12] From the beginning, both Maximilian and Charlotte knew that the French military presence would end; they would have to recruit their own soldiers to defend the empire. Recruiting, equipping, training, and transporting an army of volunteers would take money—lots of it. By March 1864, thanks to a loan organized in Paris, they had access to four million francs to finance their recruitment efforts.[13]

They also had a powerful family network to call upon. As early as December 1861—two and a half years before Maximilian formally accepted the throne—Maximilian was in conversations with his brother, Emperor Franz Joseph, about recruitment for Mexico.[14] Although the discussions were brother-to-brother, the arrangement was drawn up as a state-to-state agreement, published only after Maximilian's formal acceptance of the throne years later.[15] Franz Joseph agreed to support the recruitment of volunteers across the Habsburg Empire, a move that effectively opened much of central and eastern Europe to the effort. In western Europe, the recruitment drive was anchored by Charlotte's father, King Leopold of Belgium.[16] Between them, Leopold and Franz Joseph showed how, in the age of monarchy, the power of family could move peoples. With the active support of French emperor Napoléon III, recruitment effectively extended to all of Europe.

A royal nudge counted for something—it opened the door—but inducements would be necessary to make people walk through it. The promise of land as reward for military service was part of the recruitment pitch from the beginning. In offering compensation in land in exchange for military service, the recruitment drive borrowed from an old playbook and drew upon the image of New World abundance. In the 1820s, Brazil offered German recruits free land—tax-exempt for eight years—in exchange for military service in Brazil.[17] In the 1840s, a colonization project organized by members of the German nobility, the *Adelsverein,* lured thousands of Germans to Texas with the promise of land in "a new Fatherland beyond the seas"—no military service required. Hundreds died in harsh conditions in Texas, but a core survived; Fredericksburg and New Braunfels endured as German enclaves.[18] For the Mexican Empire, the objective was to raise two thousand volunteers in Belgium with the promise of retirement, pension, and land after six years of service.[19] The recruitment goal was three times as high in Austrian lands—six thousand men—with comparable incentives.

In April 1864, Baron Adolf Schiller von Herdern undertook recruitment efforts out of the Habsburg War Department. In the following weeks, advertisements calling for recruits to the österreichisch-mexikanische Freiwilligenkorps appeared in papers intended for wide readership (*Die Neue Freie Presse*) and for those targeting niche audiences (*Militär-Zeitung*).[20]

Recruitment appeals in Habsburg lands presented a rosy picture of the task ahead for soldiers in the new imperial Mexican army. A puff piece published in the *Wiener Abendpost* made the soldier's life in Mexico sound like a cakewalk. Yes, there was resistance, but French and volunteer forces had already made progress on every front; Juárez, it was claimed, had scarcely three thousand men at his command—true, but misleading; by the time the new wave of recruits arrived in Mexico, pacification might well be complete. Misspellings in the article—Durango became "Duanzo," Tamaulipas became "Tamauliovas"—might have raised doubts among attentive readers.[21] The essential point remained—volunteering for service in Mexico offered a path to land ownership and respectability.

The promise of land meant that the empire was recruiting subjects and settlers as much as soldiers. Not everyone was eligible. Recruitment was selective in matters of age and religion. Volunteers had to be under the age of forty and single (or childless widowers). As for religion, imperial recruitment imposed strict requirements. This was partly the legacy of the wars of religion—more than two hundred years after the Reformation, monarchist Europe continued to see danger in religious pluralism—but it was partly a concession to Catholic sensibilities and political realities in Mexico. Toleration of unbelief and religious minorities existed in Mexico, but these were values championed by the supporters of Juárez and the Mexican republic. For the empire's Conservative supporters, Catholicism was a prerequisite for good public order.[22] Volunteers had to be either Roman Catholic or Greek Orthodox, though an exception was made for recruits from the highly prized Hungarian light cavalry known as hussars. They could be Protestant.

Volunteers had to commit to six years of service, at the end of which they would receive acreage in Mexico proportionate to military rank. If by then they had soured on Mexico—or had come to disdain the yeoman existence—they would be offered repatriation, including transit from Mexico to Trieste and travel allowance from Trieste to home.[23]

Military leadership was reserved for those born to lead. In old-regime Europe, that meant that officers should be recruited among the sons of the nobility. Recruitment incentives for officers were particularly attractive, starting with immediate promotion and a raise. Austrian officers would step up a rank upon enlistment and receive wages 20 to 30 percent above current scale. Officers volunteered in abundance, so much so that the force was top-heavy with them. By the time the counting was done, officer volunteers exceeded need three times over.

Evidence doesn't exist to create an "average" profile of the motives of officer volunteers, but some better-documented cases provide some insight, mostly by showing how young men used enlistment as a bridge to something else, something that revealed itself only in time.

Franz Kaska was born in Horažd'ovice, southwest of Prague. He had made his way to Vienna as a young man to pursue an education. He had already earned a master's degree in pharmacy when he completed his doctorate in chemistry in 1863 at the age of twenty-nine. He saw opportunity in the Freiwilligenkorps, joining as an officer and pharmacist in 1864. In time he would become Maximilian's personal physician and confidant. After the collapse of the empire, he chose to stay in Mexico, where he made a fortune as a pharmaceutical wholesaler. Late in life he would become a guardian of the memory of Maximilian. His efforts drew the attention of Emperor Franz Joseph, who ennobled Kaska in gratitude.

Teobert Maler was born in Rome into a diplomatic family. (His parents were from Baden.) He studied architecture in the Rhineland, in Karlsruhe, then moved to Vienna, where he joined the architectural studio of Heinrich von Ferstel, noted for his work on the Votivkirche. Maler enjoyed a measure of financial independence, thanks to an inheritance, so it is likely that curiosity about the world, rather than dire financial circumstances, moved him to enlist in Maximilian's army at the age of twenty-two.

Once in Mexico, Maler was based in Puebla, where he served with distinction and rose to the rank of captain. He was transferred to Mexico City and served at Chapultepec. Maler developed a fascination for pre-Columbian culture; he studied Náhuatl with Faustino Galicia Chimalpopoca, a scholar of Aztec lineage. Maler, like Kaska, opted to stay after the collapse of the empire. He devoted himself to photography and to the study of the Yucatán, fields to which he made significant contributions. He lived out his days in Mérida.[24]

Kaska and Maler came from privilege. So did Count Theodor Széchényi, but it was heartache that took Széchényi to Mexico. He joined the Austrian volunteers to put thousands of miles between himself and the source of his pain, the Countess Johanna "Hanna" Erdódy. He made a nuisance of himself in Mexico, telling anyone who would listen how the lovely and talented Hanna had broken his heart. His romantic spite nearly killed him; he contracted diphtheria in Mexico and barely survived.[25]

Among laborers, poverty and despair were powerful motivators. Impoverished workers in Silesia and Bohemia signed up in such numbers that local employers began to worry about the loss of skilled labor. The anxiety was so great that newspapers tabulated and reported the occupations of departing workers. The loss of talent was unmistakable: 94 cobblers, 90 tailors, 65 masons, 61 bakers, 61 carpenters, 60 butchers, 60 weavers, 55 blacksmiths, 33 locksmiths, 26 millers, 23 saddlers, 17 gunsmiths, 17 carpenters, 17 miners, 10 bookbinders, 10 hatters, 9 plumbers, 9 rope makers, 9 turners, 9 tanners, 6 dyers, and 5 potters.[26] There was also a theologian.[27]

Although some volunteers were inspired by the possibility of adventure—the Austrian press called them *Europamüde,* "tired of Europe"—the sheer number of volunteers in skilled occupations suggests economic distress and despair.[28] Military service was always a fallback in tough times—and some volunteers had been declared unfit for service in the Austrian army.[29] The standards of the Freiwilligenkorps were more relaxed. Tired, poor, or yearning to be free, volunteers imagined something better in the New World. Volunteering meant free passage to a new life and a chance to roll the dice again. Once in Mexico, desertion was always an option, although not without risk. Toward the end of the empire, desertion became a serious problem, though it's difficult to say how many soldiers had contemplated desertion from the beginning.[30]

For Johan Galliol of Vienna, enlistment was a way to shake off creditors, just as it had been for Carl Khevenhüller. When his creditor caught up with him, he brushed him off with an antisemitic slur: "Jew, when you come for me, I'll be in Mexico, where you'll never find me!" Galliol never made it to Mexico. He was arrested on his way to the coast.[31]

Volunteers were remarkably diverse in ethnic origin, reflecting the diversity of the Austrian Empire. According to the *Militär-Zeitung,* the recruits included 151 Italians, 774 Upper and Lower Austrians, 628 Bohemians, 321 Moravians, 341 Hungarians, 87 Styrians, 34 Carinthians, 45 from the Kustenland [Trieste, Gorizia, Gradisca] and Istria, 35 Croatians, and 179 from Krain (Carniola—present-day Slovenia). The *Militär-Zeitung* also identified 67 "foreigners"—mostly from the German-speaking states of central Europe, including volunteers from Saxony, Hesse-Kassel, Thuringia, Bavaria, Baden, Hanover, Prussia, and Mecklenburg, but also from Russia, France, England, Naples, Modena, and Lombardy. The largest categories were listed, not by region of origin, but by ethnicity—Germans and Slavs. There were 898 recruits listed as "Germans"—presumably German speakers from non-Austrian parts of the empire. It's hard to know what to think about the 1,442 volunteers lumped together as Slavs—especially as some regions in the Austrian Empire with predominantly

Slavic populations—including Istria, Croatia, and Carniola—were counted separately. Taken together, the Slavs formed the largest single ethnic group among the volunteers, though the category was a catchall for Poles, Silesians, Bulgarians, Bosnians, Ukrainians, Belarussians, Russians, and more.[32] Some were political refugees; at least four hundred Poles enlisted because they had participated in the 1863 revolt against Russia and were desperate to get away from the Czarist police.[33] There were so many volunteers from Poland that Maximilian considered setting up a separate Polish volunteer corps, alongside the Austrian and Belgian corps. In the end he didn't, but one thing was clear about political refugees from Poland—given a choice between Siberia and Mexico, they would choose Mexico.[34]

Mobilizing and transporting volunteers became the new empire's first major logistical challenge. Thousands of men—scattered across Europe—had to be brought to an assembly point, provided uniforms and weapons, and transported to Mexico. Maximilian appointed Matthias Leisser to oversee these efforts. Leisser received an automatic promotion from the rank of major to colonel upon joining the imperial Mexican army. Colonel Leisser directed recruits in central and western Europe to make their way to the Breton ports of Saint-Nazaire and Brest, where they could book passage by commercial carrier to Mexico.[35] For volunteers within the Austrian Empire, Leisser negotiated discounted tickets on Austrian railways to bring volunteers to Ljubljana, the designated assembly point.

Today Ljubljana is a city of a quarter million residents, the charming, thriving capital of independent Slovenia. In 1864 the city of twenty-two thousand was known as Laibach, the German name for a provincial capital and railway hub within the Habsburg Empire.[36] By July 1864, just three months after the call for volunteers had gone out, more than a thousand recruits had enlisted. Leisser took responsibility for feeding and housing them in Ljubljana until sea transport had been arranged and they could continue to Trieste for embarkation. A brief ritual marked the transition into the Mexican imperial army. Volunteers swore loyalty "before God the Almighty" to "His Majesty, my Serene Prince and Lord, Maximilian the First Emperor of Mexico."[37]

As recruits for Imperial Mexico arrived, they swamped Ljubljana. Colonel Leisser organized clothing, meals, and local lodging with great skill, but managing a thousand young male recruits without military police was beyond anyone's ability. Worse, recruits were flush with cash, thanks to their enlistment bonuses. Drunkenness and disorder ensued. While some volunteers took the bonus and promptly deserted, many others burned through their bonus, then ran up tabs with merchants and taverns in Ljubljana. Even though Ljubljana merchants were grateful for Freiwilligenkorps spending, when the last troop convoy left Ljubljana for Trieste in March 1865, many debts remained unpaid.

Colonel Paul Zach of the imperial Mexican army promised to make good. He asked Ljubljana merchants to send him details of amounts owed, but money was lacking everywhere, not just in Ljubljana. At Trieste, the volunteers' embarkation point, Ernst Pitner was the officer responsible for managing troops as they arrived. Pitner stayed at local hotels, assuming that the Mexican Empire would pay for his lodgings. He was shocked to learn otherwise when he checked out; he had to borrow money from his sister at the last minute to settle his bill.[38]

Belgian Volunteers

The Belgian press, like the European press generally, sometimes drew a rosy picture of the invasion. These often consisted of stories of the defeat of forces of the Mexican republic and broad claims about new territory under imperial control. In November 1864 the *Echo du Parlement* asserted that "all of Nuevo León and the right bank of the Rio Bravo are occupied," giving the impression that the campaign of pacification was nearing completion.[39] But public confidence sometimes masked private caution. Despite obvious pride in his daughter and confidence in her political abilities, King Leopold of Belgium was developing private doubts about the Mexican enterprise and even greater doubts about Napoléon III. Cinco de Mayo at Puebla had shown that the French were anything but welcomed as liberators. The French invasion was making a hero of Juárez and the Mexican republic while resistance was turning Mexico into a military quagmire. "You are pulling his chestnuts out of the fire!" he wrote to Charlotte, using a folksy metaphor for saving someone's hide.[40] Leopold was skeptical of accounts of French forces dizzy with success. To his mind, Napoléon III, chastened by strong Mexican resistance and healthy political opposition in France, was looking for a way out.

These same doubts hampered recruitment efforts in Belgium. The inducements were similar to those offered in the Habsburg lands—an immediate promotion upon enlistment and the promise of Mexican land at the end of six years of service. Or, if preferred, repatriation to Belgium with a bonus. The vision of Mexico as a settlement colony was a bit more emphatic in Belgian recruitment appeals. The offer of lands to recruits emphasized the desire to promote colonization "as much as possible" with a promise that Belgian recruits who settled in Mexico would be encouraged to form a community of their own.[41]

Surely there were risks serving as soldiers, but these were downplayed, and some recruits were led to believe they would rarely, if ever, see combat. There were intimations that the Belgian volunteers would serve as Charlotte's own guard—that is, in a largely ceremonial role. Their regimental name—Régiment belge Impératrice Charlotte—allowed some ambiguity in the matter.

Meanwhile, some political and military leaders in Belgium saw Mexico as a marvelous opportunity to give young men some military experience. Others saw this as the beginning of a strong and lucrative trade relationship between Belgium and Mexico. A recruitment office opened at Audenarde, where a former abbey served as barracks.[42] The "Empress of Mexico" regiment, the first of four, met its quota of six hundred in just two weeks. According to Léon Timmerhans, a veteran officer, these early recruits consisted of former noncommissioned officers—that is, veterans—or young men eager to escape the boredom of office jobs, ready to "test themselves" in the face of danger.

Although recruitment was brisk at first, it soon flagged. Three subsequent regiments struggled to fill. The second regiment met its quota only on the day of its scheduled departure. The third and fourth regiments shipped out without meeting their quotas. Timmerhans claimed that recruits were put off by "ridiculous exaggerations" of health risks and fears of US intervention, perhaps the result of a Mexican disinformation campaign.[43] Political opposition was intense. The Belgian Chamber of Representatives emphatically rejected the idea of a *Belgian* expedition—the volunteers were joining as private individuals, mercenaries without government sanction. Hostility to the empire and its recruitment campaign ran hot. When the minister of war expressed sympathy for the recruitment effort, a deputy challenged him to a duel.[44]

As a parliamentary inquiry would later reveal, those running recruitment had roped in individuals "whose conduct wasn't entirely regular"—an ironic understatement intended to draw attention to the mix of characters, some with a shady past, who had signed up. When the recruits converged on Audenarde before shipping out, they overwhelmed the town, causing significant damage.[45]

Belgian volunteers in the imperial army. *War Heritage Institute, Brussels, DB-a-13783.*

And, in fact, to call the Belgian volunteers "Belgian" masks a significant reality—most recruits were Belgian, but many were not. Nearly eighty hailed from the German states of Baden, Bavaria, Saxony, and Württemberg; sixty came from the Grand Duchy of Luxembourg, a dozen from the Netherlands, fifty from France. Others were from well beyond, including Switzerland, Poland, Italy, Portugal, and Britain. Like the "Austrian" volunteers, the Belgian volunteers drew upon all of Europe.[46] Their occupations reflected an array of midcentury occupations: barrel makers, bootmakers, bakers, cabinetmakers, carpenters, cigar makers, coachmen, domestic servants, farmers, glove makers, gunsmiths, jewelers, matchmakers, miners, tinsmiths, weavers. Most listed no occupation. The typical age was between twenty and twenty-seven, but there were dozens of sixteen- and seventeen-year-olds and two boys of fifteen. Many of them, it was noted, lacked knowledge of military life or firearms.[47] What they had in common was a willingness—or the need—to try something new.

Women volunteered, too. Eight women joined as *cantinières*. It's not clear if they intended to start anew in Mexico, drawn by the promise of land, or if they were drawn by adventure. Five of them accompanied spouses; three were unmarried. All were married by the time they returned from Mexico.[48]

The Crossing

The logistical challenges were only beginning. Soldiers in the Mexican imperial army would need uniforms, but until they were designed and made, recruits for Mexico would wear the uniform of the Austrian imperial army. Meanwhile, lucrative military contracts for the new empire weren't going to Austrian firms, they were going to the French.[49] Count Franz Thun und Hohenstein, commander of the Austrian volunteer forces, routed his uniform inquiries through Eugene Taconet, a Parisian provisioner. Taconet responded with a price list and product samples. Tents that would accommodate sixteen enlisted men cost 212 francs each. An officer's tent was priced at 58 francs; an officer's bed would add 28 francs—shipping and handling not included. Manufacture would require three to four weeks, which meant that soldiers would arrive in Mexico before their tents did.[50]

Transport was also routed through French carriers. Thun contracted with the French shipping firm Compagnie Générale Transatlantique to get his army from Trieste to Veracruz. Compagnie Générale hired the *Bolivian,* a British vessel with home port in Liverpool, and sent it to Trieste to board the first group of recruits. The capacity of the *Bolivian* as a transport vessel was estimated at 1,150 men, at most 1,200.[51] Two military bands and many well-wishers were dockside when 1,400 soldiers and 46 officers boarded the *Bolivian* on November 19, 1864.

Shortly after leaving Trieste, Thun complained of crowding. "There are 120 men too many on board," he wrote, "with hygiene consequences for the vessel and the men." Conditions were so crowded below deck that the men traded places every four hours—half of them on deck, the other half below. Food was a problem, too. Portions, "especially the potatoes and dry vegetables," were too small. Thun threatened to put some of his men ashore at Gibraltar, rather than risk the crossing in such conditions.[52] Then he thought better of it and decided to press on, probably because it was easier than figuring out how to manage the soldiers he would maroon on Gibraltar. He consoled himself with the thought that he could offload soldiers once he reached the French Caribbean. Desertion was infinitely more difficult on Martinique.

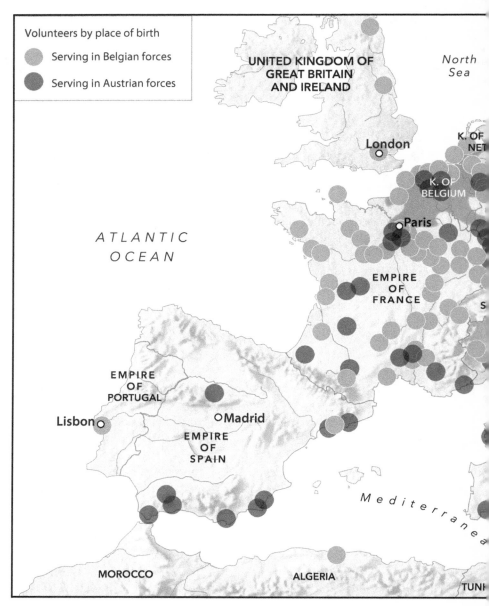

Volunteer soldiers by place of origin. Archival data for Belgian volunteers is complete; data regarding Austrian volunteers is partial, drawn from journalistic sources as well as reports of deaths, injuries, desertions, and repatriations. Belgian data team: Henry Grandy and Minh Phan.

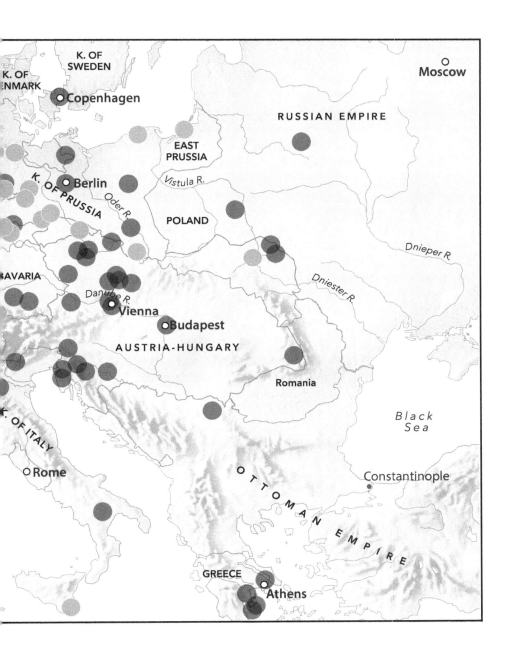

The *Bolivian* arrived at Fort-de-France, Martinique's port, on December 15, three and a half weeks after leaving Trieste.[53] Fort-de-France was a military colony with a population of about fifteen thousand. The *Bolivian* took on coal and offloaded a contingent of soldiers who would be shuttled to Veracruz separately. During the layover, Thun's volunteers could be accommodated in the barracks—a welcome change from life on board. The crossing had gone well for Thun, better than he had feared. After the *Bolivian* arrived in Veracruz, Thun could write that "except for a few drunks" the voyage was without incident.

About the time the *Bolivian* was leaving Martinique for Veracruz, another troop transport, the *Indiana,* was boarding troops at Trieste. Even before the *Indiana* reached the western end of the Mediterranean it was clear that discipline would be a serious problem. Soldiers had smuggled alcohol aboard in their bags, and officers struggled to get control of the "enormous drunkenness" on board. On December 24 a recruit died of what was diagnosed as an alcohol-induced stroke. He was buried at sea on Christmas Day just short of Gibraltar.[54]

Ernst Pitner, on a later crossing aboard the *Brasilian,* reported similar disciplinary problems, but at least the accommodations were better. In place of the "coffin-like" bunks of the *Bolivian* and *Indiana,* the *Brasilian* featured plank beds and hammocks for sleep. Pitner reported the luxury of a bath on December 26, though it should be noted that he had left Gibraltar nearly three weeks earlier.

Men unfamiliar with military discipline learned the rudiments en route. Men who had been loyal subjects of the Habsburg monarchy mere weeks before learned to salute Maximilian. Some who had volunteered to serve Maximilian and his empire died before they saw him or Mexico. When a volunteer succumbed to typhus during the crossing, his body was sewn into a hammock and draped with the flag of Imperial Mexico as other volunteers gathered round. The somber farewell included a few words from an officer followed by three cheers for Maximilian.[55] An officer read a prayer, and the body, laden with sand and iron, was let slip into the water.

While volunteers were departing Trieste, Belgian volunteers were beginning their journey. In October 1864, 950 volunteers traveled by rail from the barracks of Audenarde across France to St. Nazaire on the Brittany coast. At St. Nazaire they boarded the *Louisiane* and departed on October 16. What started with a pratfall—the commander of Belgian forces, Alfred Van der Smissen, stumbled while boarding and fell into the water—soon turned somber. Nine days into the journey François Crémin, a bugler, died of typhoid fever and was buried at sea—the first death among the Belgian volunteers. The *Louisiane* arrived at Veracruz after a voyage of twenty-nine days, including a stopover at Martinique.[56]

Recruitment faltered after the first voyage. Belgian public opinion was never enthusiastic about the Mexican Empire, and rumors of uncertain origin—that a vessel loyal to Juárez had tried to capture Empress Charlotte at sea, that the US Navy was stalking troop transports to sink them in the Gulf of Mexico—made the voyage seem even more dangerous.[57] Subsequent departures carried additional volunteers—400 on the *Floride*, 362 aboard the *Tampico*—but when the last of the volunteers disembarked at Veracruz in March 1865, the total fell shy of the volunteer target of two thousand.

Volunteers weren't all from Europe. In fact, whereas European volunteers professed a variety of motivations for serving the empire, many of them quite mundane, volunteers inspired by ideology could come from anywhere. Agnes Salm-Salm was a young American whose path to Imperial Mexico was singular. Agnes Joy was born in Swanton, Vermont, in 1840. By some accounts she joined the circus as part of an equestrian act, following a circuit that included performances in Cuba.[58] When the US Civil War began, she found herself in Washington, D.C.[59] There she met and married her prince, Felix Salm-Salm, a Prussian nobleman who left Europe by way of Antwerp and Liverpool, arriving in New York in 1854.[60] Prince Salm joined the 68th New York Volunteer Infantry Regiment as a colonel. Unsuited to conventional domestic life and unwilling to wait for her husband to return from war, Agnes joined Felix on campaign in the Union army. According to Felix, Agnes "shared my tent for months."[61]

Agnes and Felix were in Savannah when the war ended. Felix mustered out at Fort Pulaski on November 30, 1865. A week later the two were at the Savannah Freedmen's Bureau; Agnes took on Rachael Price, "a colored girl aged six years," as an indentured servant while Felix took on Alexander Fitzgerald, a "colored boy aged thirteen."[62] It seems that peace and domesticity made Felix restless. He soon decided "war was my element" and, rather than join the army of the Mexican republic, as some Union veterans did, he crossed over. He opted to offer his services "to the Emperor Maximilian of Mexico" for whose "person and civilizing task I had always felt great sympathy." He secured letters of recommendation, took leave of Agnes (what became of Rachael and Alexander is unknown), and made his way to New York where he boarded a vessel that would

Left: Agnes Elisabeth Winona Leclerq Joy Salm-Salm. *LC-USZ62-22178, Prints and Photographs Division, Library of Congress. Right:* Felix Salm-Salm. *LC-DIG-cwpb-046660 DLC, Prints and Photographs Division, Library of Congress.*

take him to Veracruz; by the beginning of July 1866 he had an appointment as colonel in the imperial army, tasked with coordinating Mexican forces with those of the Austrian and Belgian volunteers.[63] In fact, he arrived just in time to watch the imperial army come apart as soldiers, including officers, deserted to the enemy rather than risk capture and punishment.[64]

Six months after Felix's departure, Agnes learned that he was ill. She decided to join him in Mexico.[65] After some effort, she made a name for herself within the European expat community in Mexico City. Imperial Mexico was a more welcome environment than the United States for European Old World hierarchies; soon Agnes was known about town as "Princess Salm." Despite his German heritage, Prince Salm gravitated toward the forces of the Belgian volunteers, and both prince and princess adopted the silver and gray uniform of the Belgians.[66] Princess Salm also served the cause of the empire by putting her equestrian skills to work as a message courier. The combination of Old World title and New World femininity made her stand out in the capital. One of her admirers, Sara Yorke Stevenson, described her on horseback as "like a female centaur"— "picturesque" in her gray and silver uniform.[67]

Alarmism regarding Yankee aggression also brought some Canadian recruits to Maximilian's empire. The Canadian Left was skeptical of the empire and tended to see the conflict through the lens of democracy versus monarchy, but the Canadian Right was more receptive to anti-Yankee appeals, seeing Maximilian's empire as Canada's worthy ally "against the American menace."[68] The French Canadian population proved especially receptive to the image of the empire as a defender of Latinity. The image of the world divided along racial lines, reinforced by Protestant and Catholic difference, resonated among French Canadians as it mirrored a cleavage they experienced in their own lives. The French-language *Journal de Quebec* reproduced an article from the *Propagateur Catholique* to the effect that US policy toward Mexico was to promote civil war, the better to weaken and absorb the country.[69] Given that the US invasion of Mexico still lived in recent memory, the claim was plausible. The *Journal de Québec* sounded the alarm regarding US ambitions, arguing that a desire to expand had been the "dominant passion" of the United States for half a century. It would be foolish to expect that the Yankees could resist doing "everything in their power to extend their domination from Panama to the Arctic Sea." Only Mexico and Canada could restrain "the flight of the ambitious American eagle."[70] Although official Canada remained aloof, individual Canadians, notably from the École Militaire de Québec, made their way to Mexico to fight for Maximilian's Latin empire.[71]

The Quebecois volunteer Narcisse-Henri Faucher, a new arrival in Mexican City, best captured the polyglot nature and the varied motives of Maximilian's Mexico. "German noblemen, English merchants, Polish and Hungarian refugees—every kind of hero in search of his novel, his adventure, his social perch, an epaulette, a wealthy bride, a place at court . . . in the end . . . a bit of bread fallen from Maximilian's imperial table." It was as if "all of Europe had poured out its excess of adventurers."[72]

Canada, especially French Canada, showed that not all volunteers were European. California and the American Southwest showed that not all volunteers supported the empire. Juárez and the Mexican republic drew volunteers, too, notably from parts of the United States annexed from Mexico. Within weeks of the arrival of Spanish, French, and British forces in Mexico, Mexican Americans began to mobilize in support of the Mexican republic. Almost immediately a Spanish-language newspaper appeared. *La Voz de Méjico,* published in San Francisco, was the main communications link among Mexican American communities from Los Angeles to the Oregon border. The republican sympathies of *La Voz de Méjico* were clear from the moment the paper appeared in March 1862 with the watchwords "Liberty!" and "Reform!" emblazoned on its masthead. *La Voz de Méjico* enjoyed the patronage of the Consulate of the Republic of Mexico on Kearny Street in San Francisco.

La Voz de Méjico reported news from Mexico, such as forces loyal to the republic closing the road between the port of Acapulco and the Mexico City. It also reported news from California. Much of its content was reprinted from other newspapers, especially those of Latin America. A bitter condemnation of European pretensions in Mexico ("Today Europe seeks to impose its authority on Mexico") was borrowed from a Chilean newspaper.[73] When Maximilian's candidacy for the throne became public, *La Voz de Méjico* reprinted a profile from the Madrid newspaper *El País.* ("He is the direct descendant of Emperor Charles V . . . and Ferdinand and Isabel, who were the founders of Spanish rule in the Aztec lands.")[74] Not all the content was political. A serial novel, "Un Drama Misterioso," kept fickle readers coming back for more.

When the European alliance of Britain, France, and Spain came apart, *La Voz de Méjico* published the scathing open letter from General Juan Prim, commander of Spanish forces in Mexico, to Napoléon III, in which Prim contrasted the older Mexican exiles in Europe, the advocates of empire, with the "present generation" of Mexicans who had no interest in establishing a monarchy.[75] Mexican victory in defense of Puebla on May 5 led to celebrations in California and an enthusiasm for any effort to support the republic. A poem celebrating "El Triunfo del 5 de Mayo" occupied two columns of the front page. It honored the hero of Puebla, General Ignacio Zaragoza, compared Puebla to Waterloo, and assimilated victory at Puebla with the recovery of Aztec independence ("Eres mi patria, Anáhuac, todavía"; "Anáhuac, you are my homeland still").[76]

Victory at Puebla generated enthusiasm—and donations. From the community of Spanish Dry Diggings, Paula Martinez and Pastora Castillo each gave a dollar, as did Juan Cienfuegos and José Murrieta of Greenwood.[77] The settlement of Chinese Camp put together $48.50 for the month of January 1863. Half Moon Bay elected a "Patriotic Committee" to organize collections for the defense of Mexico.[78] Commentary in the pages of *La Voz de Méjico* drove home the point that the American war against the Confederacy and the Mexican fight against European domination were two aspects of the same struggle.

By the beginning of 1863 these early efforts to rally support for Mexico had led to the creation of a network of Mexican clubs, led by a Junta Central Directiva, committed to supporting the Mexican republic. They included Sonora, where Ignacio Carbajal was president, Columbia (Melchor Sanchez), and San Juan Bautista (Ignacio Villegas). Chilean Americans in the California foothills settlement of Murphy's gathered at the house of Marcelo Montes, where Onofre Bunster spoke of Mexico as a "sister republic" to the United States and urged the formation of a "Chilean Patriotic Union" to organize against "European nations, full of greed, ambition, and pride," seeking to oppress the Mexican people.[79]

From Los Angeles in southern California to The Dalles in southern Oregon, by way of Downieville and Sutter Creek in the Gold Country, Mexicans, along with Ecuadorians, Peruvians, Grenadians, and Chileans, mobilized to support the Mexican republic against European domination.[80] Each club had a treasurer and a recorder who handled recordkeeping and the monthly submission of donations to the Junta Central Directiva, while *La Voz de Méjico* reported their progress to their readership.

The mobilization of Mexican Americans was not limited to cash donations. Imperial control of port cities on Mexico's Pacific coast remained tentative, notably at Acapulco, where General Juan Álvarez organized republican resistance. Henri Kastau, an American of German origin, worked closely with Álvarez to move arms from San Francisco to Acapulco, where they could reach insurgents.[81] It seems that the weapons were bought with funds donated by Californians. Other weapons made their way to forces loyal to the republic at Ensenada and Magdalena Bay.[82]

Mexico needed money and weapons, but some supporters wanted a direct role in the fight. General Plácido Vega drew upon the network of Mexican clubs to recruit soldier volunteers in Pinole, Vallejo, Martínez, Petaluma, and San José. Mexican Americans stepped up, but so did Chileans and other hispanophone Americans, leaving homes in Fiddletown, Volcano, and Sutter Creek for San Francisco and, from there, Mexico.

The promise of land was used as a lure, as it had been in European recruitment. In August 1864 President Juárez had authorized the offer of land as well as pay to anyone willing to fight for Mexico. Acting on this plan, General Vega opened a recruiting office on Montgomery Street in San Francisco. By May 1865 the volunteers were ready to go; four hundred armed volunteers prepared to board the *Brontes* in San Francisco for the journey down the coast. Then the French Consul in San Francisco, Charles de Cazotte, intervened. The consul bribed the San Francisco chief of police, Edmund Burke, to halt the departure of the *Brontes,* citing an arms embargo against exporting weapons to Mexico. The US government has rescinded the embargo at the end of the American Civil War, but the enforcers claimed ignorance of the fact.[83] The interdiction stood. If volunteers were going to fight for Mexico, they'd have to get there on their own.

Confederate Exiles

At about the time the San Francisco police were blocking the departure of the *Brontes,* Jefferson Davis was apprehended in Georgia by Union forces. The president of the Confederate States of America was fleeing westward when he was arrested. The war east of the Mississippi was over. Davis hoped to reach Texas to continue the struggle against "Northern tyranny." Davis's war was over after his capture on May 10, 1865, but his flight typified the choices facing thousands of Southerners compromised by rebellion. Southern defeat had profound consequences for the Mexican Empire, too. Volunteers were arriving regularly from Europe, but the Confederacy had served as a buffer between the empire and US military might. That buffer was now collapsing, changing the scale and immediacy of the potential conflict. For Maximilian and Charlotte, concerns about the United States would now rival concerns about loss of support from the Mexican clergy and the Catholic Church. The imperial couple very quickly came around to the idea that the defeat of the US South created an opportunity to strengthen their empire. They would seek to recruit Confederates and their families as settlers who would stabilize and defend their empire both against the forces of the Mexican republic and against the intensified pressures they knew were coming from the US government.

The man they chose for the job was Matthew Fontaine Maury, a Confederate naval officer who had spent much of the war in Britain. Maury left Britain in early May 1865 as the collapse of the Confederacy appeared imminent. He learned about the flight and capture of Jefferson Davis when he arrived in Havana on May 22. Havana had been used for the transshipment of contraband goods during the war, but it was also a Confederate haven. Confederate associates in Havana warned Maury against his plan to return to the United States. He briefly considered going to Texas, where forces under General Edmund Kirby Smith still operated, before opting for Mexico, leaving for Veracruz on May 24.

Maury was far from the first Southerner to choose Mexico over life in the American republic. At the beginning of the US Civil War, many wealthy Confederate families moved to Europe. For those who chose to stay behind—or couldn't afford life in Europe—migration to Mexico was an alternative. The first wave of Confederate migration to Mexico came after the fall of New Orleans in 1862, which prompted the establishment of a Confederate enclave in Veracruz.[84] From California, William McKendree Gwin, Confederate sympathizer and former senator for California, was at the center of efforts to settle Sonora and exploit its silver mines.[85] Hundreds of Confederate sympathizers settled in Guaymas, on the Gulf of California, in 1864.[86] In Mexico City and suburbs, Colonel Andrew Talcott of Virginia was the hub of a social network of Confederate expats who had found their way to the capital.[87] Henry Watkins Allen, governor of Confederate Louisiana, crossed over into Mexico to escape punishment as an outlaw. By April of 1865 he was in Monterrey, writing confidently that the French "are rapidly conquering the country and in a few months all will be quiet in Mexico." All of this had happened in an ad hoc manner.[88] Maury's job would be to bring some order to the process as Maximilian's imperial commissioner of colonization.

Maury arrived in Mexico City in June 1865 and set about cultivating his relationship with the empire, laying out a plan for a large-scale Confederate migration to Mexico. For Maximilian, Maury was a "catch"—a cultivated and accomplished man, a man whose international reputation made him an asset for the empire. The two men met and talked, formalizing Maury's ideas. In early September, Maury formally turned his back on the American republic, renounced his American citizenship, and accepted an appointment as head of colonization for the empire.[89]

Besides being a distinguished scientist, Maury had the gifts of a promoter. As commissioner of colonization, Maury promised the imperial couple that two hundred thousand families were eager to make the move from the former Confederacy to Mexico.[90] In order to facilitate this migration, Maury's office developed promotional literature (in English) printed in volume for distribution. He also authorized the creation of colonization agencies in several American states: California, Texas, Missouri, Louisiana, Mississippi, Alabama, North and South Carolina, and Virginia.[91] Word got out through the press, too, notably in states not targeted for agencies. Matías Romero, Juárez's representative in Washington, forwarded a clipping from the *New Era,* published in Atlanta. *New Era* published a letter from Isham Harris, former governor of Tennessee, which

Confederate Generals gather for a portrait in Mexico. *Left to right:*
C. M. Wilcox, J. B. Magruder, Sterling Price, A. W. Terrell,
T. C. Hindman. *Duke University Library.*

highlighted the stories of prominent Confederates who had migrated to
Mexico, promoting migration through emulation.[92] Hearsay played a role,
too. Colonel Mitchel, a Confederate relocated to San Luis Potosí, passed
on to imperial authorities a letter from Texas claiming that "ten thousand
young men" were ready to come and join the fight to defend the empire.[93]
Confederate defeat, which might otherwise be seen as a grave setback for
the empire, might yet be turned to salvation.

Maury's promise of two hundred thousand families suggested perhaps
a million Confederate settlers in all. Maury's agencies were to facilitate

the departure and settlement of these Confederate refugees.[94] His efforts were seconded by the work of Henry Watkins Allen, a fellow Virginian. Allen had gone to Texas as a young man to fight in the war of secession against Mexico. After Texas, he was elected to the Mississippi legislature, became a plantation owner in Louisiana, and served the Confederacy as an army officer. While recovering from wounds suffered at Shiloh and Baton Rouge, Allen was elected governor of Confederate Louisiana. Declared an outlaw early in 1865, he fled to Mexico.

Allen, like Maury, was convinced that a great Confederate migration was taking place. He launched the *Mexican Times,* an English-language newspaper, with the help of an imperial subsidy, in anticipation of a large Confederate readership. After its debut in September of 1865 the *Mexican Times* became the promoter of the Confederate settler cause in Mexico. As the refugees arrived, the *Mexican Times* duly printed their names and states of origin, expecting to chronicle the massive influx as it unfolded. Nothing like the numbers Maury and Allen anticipated ever materialized—Southern discontent did not translate into such broad action—but it's thanks to the *Mexican Times* that we have a Who's Who of select Confederate émigrés and a map of their states of origin.[95]

Note the prominence of Texas and much of the Deep South, suggesting the importance of proximity to Mexico as a factor, but note, too, that Missouri, a border state, also sent many refugees.[96] The prominence of Missourians owed much to the bitterness of the fighting there, where citizens' militias aligned with the Confederacy carried out guerrilla actions that generated resentments that would long outlast the war. The fear of reprisals motivated many Missourians to find safety abroad.[97] Settlers also came from states without agencies, including Pennsylvania, New York, and Illinois. Note, too, the significant number of settlers from overseas as well as those arriving by way of Havana.[98] Habituated to living abroad and deterred by talk of Reconstruction, they were taking their chances in Mexico.

Maury's settlement policy imagined settler colonies scattered across Mexico, and the empire's official newspaper, *El Diario del Imperio,* noted that Confederate settlers were scouting numerous locations. "Hardeman and Roberts [of Texas] are leaving for Tepic and the Pacific coast," *El Diario* noted.[99] "Divine Providence has arranged everything," the article continued, taking an expansive view. The author of the article invoked Abraham's exhortation to Lot: "You have before you all the earth from which to choose."[100]

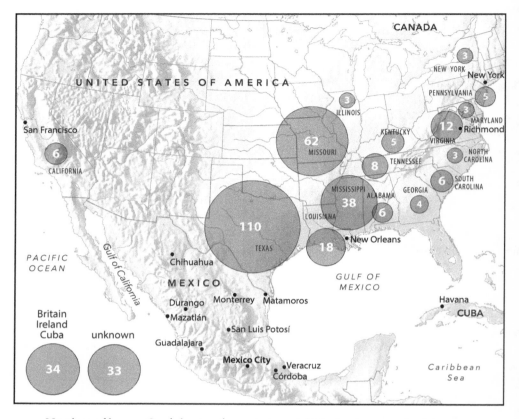

Numbers of known Confederate refugees in imperial Mexico, by state of origin.

But settlers often ignored policy. There were settlers elsewhere, but most settled at Córdoba, where there was a substantial Confederate community for a time. This was likely a reflection of the self-reinforcing effect of numbers as well as the result of promotion efforts—Córdoba was touted in pro-colonization literature.[101] Safety also was a concern. After all, settlers were arriving in the middle of a civil war.[102] Not only was there safety in numbers, Córdoba was on the corridor between Veracruz and Mexico City—the imperial lifeline and the most secure part of the empire. Córdoba was also where some of the finest land could be found. Former properties of the Catholic Church, nationalized by the Reform, were put to use by the empire, making them available for settler occupation.[103]

What shape would the colonies take? The earliest model dates from 1864, from the days of early optimism about the empire.[104] (Maximilian and Charlotte landed at Veracruz on May 29. The plan is dated December 12.) The plan shows a settler community planned in extraordinary detail, with Charlotte as patron and namesake. In the artist's scheme, grey represents land under cultivation. These lands radiate out, in classical style, from a planned town center with buildings and open space. The town center features a Catholic church facing off against a town hall. The imperial couple are invoked with namesake squares, incongruously drawn as semicircles. The town is served by a train station. The town center is outfitted with a park, a central plaza, and a fairground. Finally, the plan calls for farmhouses to be positioned on the periphery, like sentinels. Community defense is built into the design of the settlement, just as the community itself, joined by other communities similarly situated at intervals along the railroad, would be part of a system of protective settlements securing the railway.[105] Maximilian issued an imperial decree calling for "civil and military settlements" to be established on both sides of the railroad "not more than four or five leagues [12 to 15 miles] apart."[106] Maximilian's decree dates from the time when the Charlottenbourg plan was being drawn up. The railroad in question, the only one being built, was the line from Veracruz to Mexico City.

Work to establish this modern settler community began at a location just outside Córdoba. Such a meticulously planned community, let alone a *series* of such communities, was impossible during a time of war. Resources for grand projects were always lacking under the empire—in that sense, the community was just one among many grandiose plans drafted but never realized—but the kernel of the idea took shape near Córdoba. It featured a large town square "surrounded by a natural growth of trees."[107] It wasn't named Charlottenbourg, but it was a namesake community: Carlotta, the Mexicanized version of Charlotte.

Whether populated by Confederate refugees or European soldier-settlers, these settlements were to serve multiple purposes.[108] In addition to providing partial compensation to soldier volunteers and serving as defensive redoubts, they were also seen as invigorating the Mexican economy through the incorporation of a class of settler farmers of foreign origin. It mirrored what was happening in the corridors of power, where Maximilian created a shadow cabinet of outsiders—Europeans and Americans—who did the real governing in ministries nominally held by native Mexicans.[109] Charlotte wrote about settlers as part of her imperial

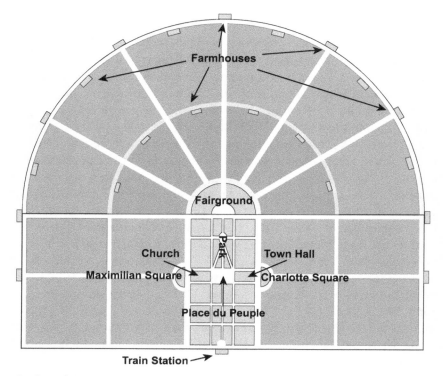

Charlottenbourg, model settler community. *Archives du Palais Royal Belge,*
BE-A0546/36, Impératrice Charlotte du Méxique, 315 Strijdmacht in Mexico.
Oostenrijks legioen en Belgisch Legioen. 1864–1866.

Zukunftspolitik—a grand vision of Mexico's future constructed through
emulation as "strong and honest" settlers set an example for "8 million
Mexicans."[110]

The problem, of course, was that settlement colonies were a betrayal
of the claim to defend Mexico from outsiders. Maximilian and Charlotte's
vision of themselves and their noble purpose depended upon trading Mexican land for the military service of foreigners, in the process betraying
the Mexican people. Immigration was not alien to Mexican planning.[111]
Mexican Liberals had imagined immigration as part of Mexico's future.[112]
In fact, within weeks of the arrival of Maximilian and Charlotte, the
Juárez government offered land as well as pay to foreigners willing to fight
the invasion.[113] But the form of immigration Maximilian and his allies

promoted, specifically the construction of settler colonies defined by ethnic and national origin—by race, in the language of the nineteenth century—raised the alarm.[114] The empire's vision of a rescued Mexico involved turning it into an archipelago of settlements—defensive enclaves on the model of Charlottenbourg—a reinvigorated *criollo* hegemony no longer exclusively Spanish, but pan-European.

The danger was clear. Even Mexican monarchists who had lured Maximilian and Charlotte to Mexico raised a warning flag. After all, Mexico's loss of Texas had started with American settlers who swore allegiance to Mexico only to revolt and form the breakaway Republic of Texas. The memory was raw and still painful. Writing about Confederate émigrés in 1864, José Hidalgo wasn't adamantly opposed to settlements, but he was wary and warned pointedly against a repeat of "what happened in Texas."[115]

Confederate settlers had an answer to such warnings. Promoters of the empire drew upon the pattern of Yankee expansion, their own hostility to republics, as well as the opportunity afforded by the distraction of the US Civil War, to posit an alternative vision of a "progressive" Mexico under the stewardship of a European ruling family. Resistance to Yankee aggression was where Confederate refugees and the Mexican Empire found common ground. This convergence of values was part of what made imperial Mexico a congenial environment for men like Maury. It's also what gave Maximilian hope that his empire might survive after all.[116]

Not only would the refugees modernize Mexican agriculture, they would also be ideologically aligned with the hierarchical politics of the empire. Even before Charlotte departed for Mexico, her father, King Leopold of Belgium, had assured her that Southerners cherished monarchical and aristocratic principles, a point that Maury would later echo.[117] The experience of the US Civil War, Maury asserted, meant that Southerners wanted nothing to do republics.[118] They would arrive as eager settlers and as confirmed political allies of the hierarchical politics of the empire.[119]

By all accounts, Confederates were on their way by the thousands, led by some of the biggest names in the Confederate pantheon: Sterling Price, John Magruder, James Slaughter, Alexander Watkins, and Kirby Smith.[120] Their example drew others in their wake. General Thomas Hindman of Arkansas crossed the Rio Grande with his wife, his freedmen, six mules, and a wagon full of tobacco for sale—enough, he hoped, to sustain him until he could get back on his feet in his newly adopted country.[121] Not all migrants arrived unimpeded. Confederate senator John B. Clark and

Colonel Luckett were part of a group that set out for Mexico but never made it. They were arrested by US forces at Matamoros and put in jail. There were also early signs that the promise of preserving slavery in Mexico would prove illusory. "All our Negroes decided to leave us upon arrival," Hindman wrote.[122] South could mean freedom, too.[123]

Brigadier General Joseph Shelby led a thousand men from his Missouri Cavalry out of Austin toward Coahuila.[124] He was joined at San Antonio by John Magruder and former Missouri governor T. C. Reynolds. Together they fed a vision of the South as bowed but not defeated. This fit with Maximilian's vision of settlers as part of Mexico's national defense. Carlos Sánchez Navarro had committed more than a million acres of land for the empire to use to lure settlers. An imperial decree established "military colonies" in Sonora, Chihuahua y Coahuila.[125] If disgruntled Confederate veterans settled along Mexico's northern frontier in sufficient numbers, they would prevent Union veterans from joining Juárez's forces. They would also serve as a human tripwire in the event of a war between the United States and Imperial Mexico. Many Confederates were convinced that a Yankee invasion of Mexico was imminent; it would touch off a war, but this time the Confederates would have France, Austria, Belgium, and Imperial Mexico as allies.[126] Allies of the empire even imagined Yankee invasion as a boon because it would ignite racial fears—"the terror of Saxon absorption" would cause Mexicans to set aside their differences and rally to the empire.[127] At best, Appomattox was a mere armistice; a greater struggle was yet to come.

Yet as this formidable exodus appeared to take shape, a strange crossing of paths occurred. A southbound crew of disgruntled but hopeful Confederates encountered northward-bound Austrian soldiers at Monterrey. The Austrians were deserters from forces commanded by Colonel Jeanningros. When Shelby asked the Austrians where they were headed, they answered, "To Texas!" "We do not hate Mexicans," they asserted. They hated what they had become. The empire had made "robbers of us." Shelby's party was headed south while the Austrians headed north. Yet for each, tyranny was at their backs, and freedom lay just ahead.[128]

Resettlement and the transfer of loyalty to Imperial Mexico implied a willingness to defend Maximilian's empire against the United States, a mutual enemy, but it came with a price. The prospect of wooing Southerners to Mexico to defend his empire persuaded Maximilian to betray his claim to rule as an enlightened, Liberal monarch. Maximilian's newest settlers would come with their families and households, but their allegiance would be all the greater if the empire would accommodate the migration of the Southern plantation economy.[129] They wanted assurances that the empire would protect their investment in enslaved labor. In August 1865, even before his appointment as imperial commissioner for colonies, Matthew Maury was writing to friends in Virginia, telling them to resettle in Mexico and to bring their slaves with them, with the promise of imminent legal support.[130] On September 5, 1865, Maximilian made good on the promise. He issued a meticulously crafted colonization law that restored slavery in all but name. The law allowed immigrants to bring laborers who, being indebted to the patron, could not legally terminate employment—nor could their children. The law designated the patron as the legal guardian for the indebted laborer's children and obliged them to remain in the patron's service through the age of twenty-five—by which time they themselves may well be indebted, thus establishing a perpetual cycle of servitude. Laborers who fled would be unemployable without a labor booklet signed by their employer; meanwhile, the empire undertook to return fugitives to their patrons. The law was prefaced by the lofty claim that "all men of color are free by the simple fact of treading the soil of Mexico."[131] True enough in a narrow legal sense—slavery would remain illegal—but in practice the claim was hollow.

Mexico had abolished slavery after winning its independence, by which time chattel slavery had virtually disappeared. Independent Mexico, however, had never quite come to terms with its history of peonage, a close cousin to slavery.[132] Indian labor anchored by debt had proven to be more lucrative than slavery and it didn't carry the stigma.[133] The Sánchez Navarro family had relied on thousands of peons to support their operations in Coahuila.[134] Their example, and the example of farming and ranching families like them, inspired the efforts of American settlers in Texas when it was still part of Mexico. José Antonio Navarro and Stephen Austin promoted such legislation in the Tejano legislature in the 1820s, with full knowledge that bringing laborers to Texas under multiyear contracts would enable slavery under the guise of contract law.[135] Indeed, the key stipulations of Maximilian's 1865 law—debt and hereditary service—may well have been lifted from Texas peonage laws of the 1830s. Matías Romero, Mexican ambassador to the United States, had flagged such legal sophistries in New Mexico and Arizona in 1861.[136] It was the ultimate betrayal of principle. Maximilian would allow servitude if it would save his empire. Indeed, Maximilian employed every means to assure plantation owners that they would have the labor they needed. In June 1865, when Peres de Almeida and Abdon Morales asked for the government's view regarding a plan to import Black and Asian labor (*negros y asiáticos*), a committee was asked to review the proposal. A variety of questions arose: How could this proposal be reconciled with the principle of equality before the law? From a humanitarian point of view it was unacceptable, but from an economic point of view it was the only way to develop agriculture in coastal areas, given the threat of yellow fever. Would the transport of Black and Asian labor draw the empire into a difficult situation with British cruisers policing the waters, committed to the suppression of the slave trade? Certainly, the laws of Mexico allowed the entry of all races, whether free or under private contract, but an exclusive agreement of the kind sought by Morales would hinder the imminent arrival of Southern plantation owners "with families and negros." In the end, the committee decided against the petition, largely, it seems, because it sought an exclusive contract to import such labor, which would implicate the empire in what would otherwise be a private matter.[137] A few months later Morales received a nonexclusive authorization to bring in "colonists, whatever their race" but at his own risk.[138] In a separate move, Maximilian authorized Manuel B. da Cunha Reis to create the Asian Colonization Company, which promised to import Asian labor on favorable terms, part of a turn to "coolie" labor that remained stillborn.[139]

These developments mirrored those north of the border. Union victory had meant the end of chattel slavery in the United States, but by then peonage was readily available as an alternative. Within months of Appomattox, such arrangements in the American South transformed enslaved labor into indebted service with little hope of escape.[140] The Mexican Empire was part of a broad effort to modernize bondage by looking to the past, to draw upon the ancient practice of peonage to envision a world where labor could be nominally free but bound in practice. Imperial Mexico charted a path to a bold new future where the conventional trappings of enslavement would vanish, to be replaced by the invisible bonds of debt.[141]

10

◁◯▷

Things Fall Apart

ERNST PITNER TRAVELED HALFWAY around the world as an Austrian volunteer, but when he reached his assignment in Mexico, he found himself momentarily transported back to the Alps. Pitner loved theater. At Trieste, the night before he boarded the *Brasilian* for Mexico, he had treated himself to a performance of *Un Ballo in Maschera* by "a very good Italian company." Now, assigned with his battalion to the northern Mexican border town of Matamoros in May 1866, he learned that a local company was putting on a production of "The Shepherdess of the Alps" ("La Pastora de las Alpas"). Lured by the promise of live theater, Pitner bought a ticket and went inside, only to find that "Shepherdess of the Alps" was truly bad—"a frightful play" whose visual climax was an alpine snow scene in which shredded cotton was dropped in great clumps from the rafters onto the stage below. Pitner walked out, returned to his lodgings, and wrote a letter about it to his mother.[1]

Pitner was born in Vienna into a minor aristocratic family whose male members pursued professional careers as doctors, lawyers, officers, and civil servants. His experience of Mexico, as related in letters to his mother, offers a candid, albeit idiosyncratic, take on the imperial folly. His first posting had been to Orizaba, where he quickly learned that the Austrian volunteers were no more welcome in Mexico than the French; that "the clerical party" was so disappointed by the empire that its hostility permeated local culture; that the local population was so reluctant to house imperial troops that they'd rather pay for them to stay at a hotel than face the consequences of lodging them themselves; that more than a thousand French deserters had joined the Mexican insurgency and were some of its most dangerous fighters.[2] After Orizaba he was posted to Campeche, in Yucatán, where he witnessed the execution of an Austrian volunteer for drunken insubordination. After Campeche, he was shuttled to Veracruz before his posting to Matamoros.[3]

Matamoros was a settlement chosen by nature and the special power that resides wherever water meets water. Positioned where the Rio Grande meets the Gulf of Mexico, Matamoros hosted contraband trade during the Mexican struggle for independence. Taxes followed trade. The Mexican government established a customs presence in Matamoros in 1823; the population more than doubled in five years, then doubled again by the time of the Texas secession.[4] The importance of Matamoros only grew after the American invasion and the Treaty of Guadalupe Hidalgo, which established the Rio Grande as the international boundary and Matamoros as a crossing-over place.

The American Civil War opened a new era. Given the Union blockade of Confederate ports—and especially after the fall of New Orleans to Union troops in April 1862—getting cotton to international buyers wasn't easy, but it was possible. Imperial Mexico was formally neutral in the war; its ports were open to commerce. Southern cotton could reach buyers if it could be moved to Mexico. Getting cotton to Texas, typically to Brownsville and from there across the Rio Grande to Matamoros, was one of the few ways Confederate cotton commerce could bypass the blockade.[5]

Getting the cotton to Matamoros wasn't easy. The cotton had to be hauled by mule teams over hundreds of miles of rough, rutted tracks. Arduous, slow land transport wasn't the only challenge. Goods had to be shuttled across the river from Brownsville on the US side, where Yankees, Confederates, Mexican republicans, and imperialists as well as "representatives of all the peoples of Europe" jabbered in a polyglot chorus, looking for a money angle.[6] Across the river in Matamoros, endless bales of cotton awaited shipment. Only light-draft steam vessels could navigate the serpentine final miles of the Rio Grande from Matamoros to the Gulf of Mexico. Once free of the Rio Grande, a fleet of oceangoing vessels waited, ready to carry the cotton to Havana for transshipment or directly to Europe to feed hungry textile mills. In addition to outbound cotton, a reverse trade in firearms and other manufactured goods from Europe (but also New York) made Matamoros prosper. By early 1863 as many as two hundred ships waited offshore to be loaded or unloaded, prompting one observer to comment that Matamoros had become the "great commercial and financial center" of the Confederacy, what New York City was to the

United States. Population doubled between 1863 and 1864.[7] Although there were far better ports on the Gulf for loading and unloading cargo, in those years and in those circumstances Matamoros would have to do.

Even after July 1863, when the fall of Vicksburg cut off the Trans-Mississippi District of Texas, Arkansas, and Louisiana from the rest of the Confederacy, a lively trade funneled through Matamoros. Matamoros was also a pop-up for privateers and merchants. One visitor said that Matamoros was built "as if everyone was leaving the next day."[8] It was a magnet for a loose collection of shady figures, a place where every deal was crooked.[9] Traders, spies, and deserters jockeyed for advantage as the makeshift settlement of Matamoros boomed with contraband trade.

When Pitner arrived in Matamoros early in 1866, he learned that Matamoros was awash in money. There were people "who made hundreds of thousands of dollars in the cotton trade" during the Civil War.[10] Scarcity and easy money promoted gouging: a chicken cost two dollars, a turkey cost four.[11] Wooden sheds slapped together functioned as grocery stores or saloons; tarps stretched above tables and chairs provided shade for restaurant patrons. Pitner saw Matamoros and Bagdad—a settlement nearer the coast—as classically American. "Everything of wood, everything provisional, everything practical, everything contrived for profit" and, although nominally part of Mexico, populated by "Americans, Spaniards, Italians, French, Germans, Greeks and, really least of all, Mexicans."[12]

Matamoros, its population swelling to thirty thousand by the spring of 1865, was the linchpin of the empire's northern border.[13] Financially, Matamoros was a great choke point for customs—though not as lucrative as Veracruz, it was crucial to capturing revenue from the Confederate trade. Militarily, it anchored the US-Mexico border, just as Brownsville, Matamoros's twin city across the river, was a node in the network of Juárist resistance.[14]

For all of these reasons, Matamoros risked becoming a flash point in a war between the United States and Imperial Mexico—or the United States and France. Although at times Napoléon III professed not to fear war with the United States, at least as long as the US Civil War raged on, it was an eventuality best avoided.[15] Even so, from the beginning of the Intervention, French commander Marshall Bazaine was so eager to avoid a clash with US troops that he kept his troops miles from the border, preferring to send units of European volunteers and Mexican imperial troops instead. With this in mind, he sent General Tomás Mejía, divisional general, to secure Matamoros for the empire in September 1864.[16] As the

US Civil War seemed to be approaching its end in the spring of 1865, Matamoros and other border towns grew in importance as crossing-over places. As early as March 1865—weeks before Confederate surrender at Appomattox—Confederate officers in Houston were in contact with General Mejía about shared interests.[17]

Even though trade through Matamoros tapered with the reopening of southern ports at the end of the war, the borderlands remained an area of concern. After the Emancipation Proclamation and fall of Vicksburg in 1863, the Trans-Mississippi West, especially Texas, had served as a haven for "refugeed slaves" and their owners—that is, for Southerners eager to protect their property in slaves from Union troops and emancipation.[18] Now, following Lee's surrender, there were rumors of Confederate soldiers making their way to Texas and from there to Mexico, preparing to use the empire as a base of operations from which to continue the fight. Partly for that reason, in May 1865 US general Philip Sheridan was given the mission to restore the Trans-Mississippi West to US control. Confederate general Kirby Smith surrendered before Sheridan arrived to take command, but rather than disband, Sheridan noted, Kirby Smith's men "marched off to the interior of the State [Texas] in several organized bodies." General Jubal Early had been observed crossing into Texas with similar intent.[19] By September 1865, Confederate veterans were warning of an imminent US attack "of sixty to one hundred thousand men" on Imperial Mexico and offering to fight on behalf of or alongside French forces in the borderlands.[20]

While some Confederate veterans contemplated emigration to Imperial Mexico, others were looking for ways to get back into the good graces of the US Army after having served the rebellion. General Lew Wallace reported to General Grant the content of conversations he had had with Confederate officers James Slaughter and John Ford at Point Isabel, Texas. As Wallace reported it, Slaughter argued that "the best way . . . to get honorably back into the Union was to cross the river, conquer two or three [Mexican] states . . . and . . . annex them, with all their inhabitants, to the United States."[21] Once again, Mexico was figuring in US plans to overcome internal conflict. The plan carried echoes of the deal Francis Preston Blair and Jefferson Davis had offered Lincoln and Seward in February 1865—bypass Reconstruction and reunite the States through war on Mexico.[22] Wallace put forward a plan with some of these elements, whereby Confederates could redeem themselves by joining a US expedition to march on Mexico City and depose Maximilian. Unlike the Confederate plan, Wallace's vision didn't involve annexing Mexican territory. Instead it envisioned reuniting North and South in support of Juárez and the Republic of Mexico, a crusade beneath the banner of the Monroe Doctrine.[23]

Indeed, Juárez was looking across the northern border. At the end of 1865, conventional forces at the disposal of the Mexican republic were quite modest, mostly the cluster of men commanded by General Mariano Escobedo. Escobedo's forces operated between Matamoros and Monterrey, using the US borderlands as an area of refuge, knowing that imperial forces would not pursue them as far as the US border.[24] But the border could also be used as a recruitment zone. Now that the US Civil War had ended, Juárez was eager to attract US veterans. He authorized General José María Carvajal to enlist up to ten thousand US veterans to serve in the Mexican army. The United States was interested in any plan that would block the departure of Confederates for Imperial Mexico, so US officers were ready to listen. Under the guise of a "Mexican Aid Society"— ostensibly to promote emigration—recruitment got under way, but then US secretary of state William Seward learned of the plan and scuttled it for fear it would disrupt negotiations with Napoléon III for a French withdrawal.[25]

Still, given the stakes and the proximity of forces, clashes seemed inevitable. In late November or early December, three members of the 23rd United States Colored Troops were captured by forces of the Mexican Empire south of the Rio Grande, a clear violation of Mexican territorial sovereignty. How they happened to be in Mexico is unclear, but General Douay described them to Bazaine as "irregulars"—an ominous term. In October Maximilian had issued a decree meant to intimidate and suppress guerrilla operations in support of Juárez and the Mexican republic. The "Black Decree," as it came to be known, specified trial by court-martial for members of armed bands; in event of conviction, death was to follow within twenty-four hours. If the captured members of the 23rd US Colored Troops were termed irregulars, they could be tried and executed under Maximilian's Black Decree. A stern message from General Sheridan to imperial general Mejía, rejecting such terms as "bandits, robbers, and outlaws" to characterize anti-imperial forces, seems to have settled things.[26] The captured men would not be tried as outlaws.[27]

As part of US efforts to support Juárez and the Mexican republic, Sheridan made every effort to convince Mexican imperial forces that a US attack was imminent. Given that Sheridan lacked the resources—and the

United States lacked the will after four years of civil war—skirmishes and small incursions kept the threat alive. According to the Austrian volunteer Ernst Pitner, in January 1866 "600 men of the negro troops of the United States" crossed the river and attacked Bagdad "in full uniform and led by their officers."[28] The number is exaggerated—it was probably closer to two hundred—but the provocation was real either way.[29] Mejía protested strenuously.[30] When asked for an explanation, US general Weitzel stated that he had sent the forces to Bagdad "at the request of [republican] General Escobedo." Their orders were "to preserve the peace and protect property and life in Bagdad"—a laughable assertion on its face, given that it involved crossing an international border and attacking troops stationed there.[31] But Weitzel was making a larger point. The United States recognized the republic, not the empire, and the republican general Escobedo had invited Weitzel and his men. Georges Clemenceau, who in those days was working as a journalist in New Orleans, reported on the notoriety Weitzel's troops had gained for their actions.[32] Mejía's outrage was irrelevant. Provocation was the point.

Eventually Weitzel evacuated his troops from Bagdad to Brownsville, but it was not the end of the story.[33] In fact, it became a model for US operations at the border. In June 1866 Sheridan massed troops near Brownsville and made a conspicuous show of a pontoon bridge, as if a military crossing was about to take place. Sheridan later claimed that such actions at Brownsville and Piedras Negras forced French and Austrian troops to withdraw from northern Mexico "as far down as Monterrey." He also claimed that these actions set up the dramatic triumph of Mexican republican forces at Camargo in June 1866.[34]

Camargo is a settlement not quite halfway between Matamoros and Monterrey, the capital of Nuevo León. In normal times there would be lively commerce between the capital and the coast, but by 1866 communications had dwindled. Republican forces did not control Monterrey, the empire did. Nor did they control Matamoros and its customs revenue, Mejía did, but they could raid commerce on the route between Monterrey and Matamoros, cutting its value. (Similarly, farther down the coast republican forces prevented goods from moving between San Luis Potosí and the port of Tampico.)[35] In April 1866 Colonel Van der Smissen, commander of Belgian volunteers, pointed out that "the state of Nuevo Léon is large, but the Empire only controls the capital (Monterrey); everything else is controlled by the enemy." The practical effect was devastating. Without commerce in Monterrey it was no longer possible to "pay civil

servants and court judges, to provide for the police and light the city."
Conditions continued to worsen. "The better commercial houses have already left, never to return," Van der Smissen noted, "and many others
are liquidating inventory." In a pattern repeated across Mexico, where
the empire controlled the ports and the provincial capitals, republican
forces controlled everything in between, cutting off the flow of goods and
choking off life in the cities.[36]

Ernst Pitner had been assigned to the defense of Matamoros as part of
Bazaine's plan to secure the frontier while avoiding war with the United
States. If there were to be a cross-border incident, better that it involve
Mexicans, Austrians, Belgians—anyone but the French. Bazaine also knew
that proximity to the border was an incentive to desertion for French
troops.[37] But the border was a lure for all European soldiers, not just the
French, and it became more attractive as pay fell farther behind. Six men
from Pitner's company crossed over to the United States with the promise
that they would "make a lot of money."[38] By the spring of 1866 Austrian forces had been so depleted by casualties and desertions that they
were to be evacuated to Mexico City, leaving Mexican imperial forces in
charge of Matamoros.[39] Back in Mexico City, the Austrian volunteers
would either to be reassigned within the imperial army or, though no one
was saying it at the time, repatriated to Europe.[40]

The fastest and safest route for the Austrian evacuation would have been
transport from Matamoros to Veracruz by sea, but Bazaine ruled out this
option, despite predictions that transport by land "will be the ruin of this
troop."[41] Sea transport would be costly and Bazaine had orders to restore
trade between Matamoros and Monterrey. A successful convoy of goods
would signal this restoration. Also part of the convoy was revenue from
the Matamoros customs office. The convoy would need a military escort
if it was to reach Monterrey intact. The Austrians would have to walk.

On June 7, 1866, the convoy of two hundred wagons and two thousand mules left Matamoros at a crawl, its progress limited by terrain and
rough roads. The military escort for the convoy, commanded by General
Feliciano Olvera, consisted of fourteen hundred Mexicans and three hundred Austrians, including Pitner. Their journey westward to Monterrey
would take them across nearly eight hundred miles on a route that shad-
owed the Rio Grande by way of Reynosa and Camargo before turning
south at Mier to Cerralvo and Monterrey.

Given the distance and the danger, Bazaine ordered a French force of
two thousand to leave Monterrey the same day, with a mission to meet

and reinforce the convoy from Matamoros en route.[42] General Mariano Escobedo, who served the Republic of Mexico as commander of the Army of the North, picked up intelligence about the converging forces. The pace of the Matamoros convoy gave him ample time to prepare Mexican troops. He sent a detachment under Gerónimo Treviño to harass and delay the French force out of Monterrey, so that he could confront the convoy from Matamoros before reinforcements from Monterrey reached them.[43]

Escobedo concentrated his forces outside Camargo, on the plain of Santa Gertrudis, where he waited with some fourteen hundred soldiers on June 16, 1866.[44] The next morning, at 6:30 AM, Escobedo's forces attacked the convoy. Fighting lasted barely an hour and concluded, in Escobedo's words, with "the complete destruction of the Austro-Traitor forces." It wasn't hyperbole. Olvera's soldiers were either dead or taken prisoner. Olvera evaded capture, but he and his cavalry escort were in full flight back to Matamoros.

The human cost was enormous: on the imperial side nearly 400 dead, 145 Austrian volunteers among them, some 200 wounded, against 155 dead and 78 wounded among Escobedo's troops.[45] The bigger story was the number of prisoners—more than a thousand captives. There were 143 Europeans among them, but most of them were *soldados traidoras*— native Mexicans regarded as traitors to the republic, many of whom would now be pressed into military service to the republic.[46] Weapons seized from the convoy included more than a thousand rifles, eight artillery pieces, including two mountain guns, and a large stock of ammunition. Escobedo's Army of the North had overwhelmed a larger Austrian / Mexican force.

Even if we discount Escobedo's triumphalist language about imperial soldiers "on their knees, begging for mercy," there is corroborating evidence to the effect that imperial forces had come apart.[47] Austrian volunteer Pitner, who was grievously wounded in the fighting, claimed to have watched as a battalion from Sierra Gorda "stuck the points of their bayonets into the ground" and surrendered with cries of "Viva la Libertad"— thus not only capitulating but vocally sympathizing with their captors, likely in a bid for mercy.[48] That's part of the reason the story of Camargo had such an impact. It meant that the army of the Mexican republic had recovered as a fighting force, capable of inspiring fear in conventional combat. In the three years since the fall of Puebla, the republic had rarely been able to field a significant conventional force and had had to rely on guerrilla tactics. That hardly mattered in the big picture. As Jésus Terán put it to an Austrian diplomat, in guerrilla warfare "one obtains victory [through a series] of defeats."[49] But Camargo showed that the army of the republic was once again able to go toe-to-toe with the enemy. Austro-Belgian-Mexican forces were beatable.[50]

Just three months earlier Bazaine had explained how he had set up what he called "great arteries" and "strategic lines" as a demonstration of the order brought by the Intervention. One artery ran east to west, from Veracruz to Guadalajara by way of Orizaba, Puebla, Mexico City, Lagos, and Querétaro. Two others ran northward: one from Querétaro to Saltillo and Monterrey, the other from Lagos to Durango. He confessed that control extended only "four or five leagues" to either side of these arteries, but it was a cherished proof of what had been accomplished.[51] What he didn't say was how much French forces were despised. According to a source friendly to the empire, French forces meant "despotism and depredation" to ordinary Mexicans. They were worse than the guerrilla bands; they were "universally hated."[52] So while Bazaine boasted of great arteries and strategic lines, what he was really defining were the narrow bands within which the French dominated. Outside those bands they faced a population frequently hostile, at best ambivalent. Camargo revealed the hollowness of Bazaine's boasts. In the weeks and months to follow, one by one these nodes on Bazaine's strategic lines fell.

Defeat at Camargo meant that Matamoros could not be held. Mejía withdrew from Matamoros just a week after Camargo—a significant win for the republic. Farther down the coast, Tampico fell a short time after.[53] News of the rout of imperial forces at Camargo had other cascading effects. The French force sent from Monterrey to meet the convoy was forced to retreat, but not everyone bothered. Seventy-nine members of the Foreign Legion, perhaps as much as 4 percent of the force, took advantage of the proximity of the US border—a day's march away—to desert.[54] They knew that there was strength in numbers. The usual punishment for desertion—court-martial and execution—simply couldn't be applied on such a scale.[55]

Meanwhile, some 140 miles west of Monterrey, imperial forces at Parras were forced to evacuate in the face of a popular insurrection.[56] The morale of imperial troops declined. Even before Camargo, Belgian soldiers at Monterrey had mutinied, shouting "Down with the Emperor! Long Live Liberty! Long Live the Republic!" as they circulated through the streets of Monterrey. Order was restored only by the arrival of two French battalions, dispatched from San Luis Potosí, many miles away.[57]

After Camargo, the dam broke. Monterrey was evacuated on July 26. Republican forces entered Guadalajara on August 1; they retook Saltillo a few days later. Public opinion, stifled during the occupation, now asserted itself more aggressively against the empire.

The image of the republican forces changed, too. To the general population, guerrilla forces were sometimes indistinguishable from bandits—living off the land, taking what they needed from the civilian population, fleeing when pursued by imperial forces.[58] The army of the Mexican republic could now begin to operate like a conventional army again. It would also enjoy more direct support from the United States. Now that imperial forces had evacuated Matamoros, the republic controlled the contested frontier from the Gulf of Mexico to El Paso del Norte (today Ciudad Juárez), greatly simplifying cross-border reinforcements and weapons shipments. It was rumored that Escobedo's army included 1,200 to 1,500 veterans of the Union army.[59] The truth was probably closer to 150 American veterans, but the point stood.[60] With US veterans in their ranks and a supportive American republic at their backs, the army of the Mexican republic could look southward with confidence.

At Chapultepec Castle, Charlotte and Maximilian followed events with a mix of despair and denial. Since autumn of the previous year, the news had been almost relentlessly bad. Charlotte's tour of Yucatán in November 1865, which was meant to show broad popular support for the empire, had to be shortened after mixed results. Also in November, US secretary of state Seward sent General John McAllister Schofield to Paris with a mission to persuade Napoléon III to withdraw French troops from Mexico; privately, Napoléon III acknowledged that "things in Mexico aren't going well." Negotiations for a concordat with the Mexican Empire had faltered, and the papal encyclical *Quanta Cura,* published in December 1865, seemed to slam the door shut—Charlotte read its condemnation of Liberalism as a direct commentary on Mexico and the progressive Catholic vision she and Maximilian championed. Personal tragedy also weighed. Charlotte's father, Leopold I, the person whose judgment she most trusted, had died.

The tragedy was soon compounded. A Belgian diplomatic delegation made a state visit to Mexico to announce the reign of Leopold's successor, Leopold II, Charlotte's brother. On March 5, 1866, as the delegation was returning to the coast, Mexican resistance forces seized the opportunity to attack at Rio Frío, a choke point on the route. The attack left one dead and four wounded. The political damage was immense. The incident heightened the sense of insecurity in Mexico, but caused a sensation in Europe, where it showed just how fragile the empire was.[61] The death of Baron Huart, an aid and friend to Leopold II, put "a pool of blood" between Leopold, his sister Charlotte, and her "imbecile" husband just as their empire staggered toward collapse.[62]

Even in mourning there was no comfort. Reports abroad of atrocities committed in the name of the empire laid bare the moral fragility of the regime and the culpability of its leaders. A few weeks after the Río Frío disaster, Charlotte received a brutally candid letter from an Orléanist relative, the Prince de Joinville, in which he cataloged charges of atrocity. "It's the blood spilled in the Mexican enterprise that wounds me deeply," he wrote. He recounted horrifying reports of Mexican dead, more than four hundred in Zacatecas in February alone and still others "hanged in error" in Tampico. He directly confronted the characterization of the victims as brigands, worthy of swift justice. "People say that [the victims] are brigands," he wrote, but "that's a flexible word." He closed with a stunning moral accusation. "I shudder to see you even indirectly responsible for these horrors. I shudder to see them committed by your army."[63] The criticism was unsparing and it was coming from a leading member of Charlotte's Orléanist family.

Long before Camargo, the end of the empire was in view. After Camargo, it seemed inevitable, as republican forces gathered momentum and Bazaine began to organize the evacuation of French troops. The only person who seems not to have understood the gravity of the situation was Maximilian, who in late May was writing imperious letters to Bazaine as "commander of my army," as if Bazaine answered to him, not to Napoléon III.[64] Disabused of that idea, Maximilian began to return, belatedly, to the task of creating a force directly under his control. A month later he was predicting that Imperial Mexico would have an army of forty thousand trained and equipped by October.[65] It was one of the first signs that Maximilian intended to remain to defend his empire, even if the French would not.

11

⁀੭

Charlotte Tries Diplomacy

THOUSANDS OF PEOPLE FILLED the streets of Mexico City. They were there to celebrate the emperor's birthday, July 6.[1] Many had journeyed for hours, coming from settlements in the valley surrounding the city, from Sultepec (90 miles), Temascaltepec (80 miles), and Zacualpan (100 miles); some had even traveled up from the Terra Caliente.[2] They converged on the National Palace, where hundreds packed the Salon Iturbide, the official reception area; hundreds more remained in the courtyard outside. Maximilian and Charlotte circulated among the throng. Still more, perhaps fifteen thousand in all, waited in the Plaza de Armas, the large plaza and parade ground known today as the Zócalo. Some played music, some brought greeting cards, others brought banners and bouquets of flowers. A few made short speeches.

There was no doubt that Maximilian's spirit needed propping up. The referendum from the streets had the desired effect. Writing about the experience later, Maximilian described himself as "quite moved" by the display of affection. He was especially moved by the presence of "10,000 indigenous"—an important constituency for a man who saw himself as their champion. He noted that some had come "from twenty leagues" (sixty miles) and the display of genuine affection showed that they appreciated "the hard sacrifice I have made for the good of my country."[3] In the days that followed, the empire's paper of record, *El Diario del Imperio,* ran stories of enthusiastic celebrations in the provinces, from Guanajuato to stubbornly republican Veracruz. In Jalapa, celebratory artillery fire, a military band, and an aerostatic balloon drew large crowds.[4] These stories were sure to catch the eye of the

190

emperor and add to the sense of a broad popular support for an empire under siege.

The enthusiasm, it turns out, was illusory. The birthday celebrations that Maximilian had found so genuine and so moving were, in fact, orchestrated. Archbishop Labastida, writing to a friend in Rome, offered a take on events that stripped away all sentimentality. Imperial prefects had "excited the Indians to appear in [the capital] with their flags and their music." The participation of hacienda workers had been coerced; they had been threatened with fines—coincidentally revealing the enduring power of the hacienda system. Despite such intense pressure, some workers refused to participate; Labastida dismissed them as "gutter workers"—the lowest of the low. As for the religious celebrations marking Maximilian's birthday, Labastida noted that they were well attended, but mostly out of fear that absences would be noted, entailing unpleasant consequences. Meanwhile Labastida noted bluntly, "The Empire cannot survive."[5]

That Labastida could be so candid about the fate of the empire—at least in private—provides the frame for what was to come, because no one did more to prolong the empire's death agony than Labastida. That the empire would survive another eleven months after Labastida's avowal of its certain death owed more to Labastida than to anyone else.

Not that Labastida was wrong in his assessment. Negotiations for the concordat continued to drag on, though purely for show. Now that the American Civil War had ended, the United States was addressing the Mexican situation directly and forcefully, albeit mostly in diplomatic terms, but making it amply clear that the empire would not stand. The opposition press in Mexico was openly discussing what might happen next, including the possibility that General Santa Anna might return—a clear sign that Conservatives were hedging their bets. Santa Anna's exile had taken him to New York, to Staten Island, where he followed Mexican politics closely and watched for an opening. The possibility that he might now be an agent of the United States or, at a minimum, a spoiler who would complicate Mexican politics alarmed Maximilian, who tried to dismiss Santa Anna's machinations as "burlesque" but acknowledged that he was haunted by the thought that Santa Anna might be conniving with Mexican clergy.[6] The specter of Santa Anna could be useful, too, in corralling the imperial couple and discouraging their abdication.[7] Dolores Almonte, the well-connected spouse of General Juan Almonte, frequently referred to Santa Anna in her letters to Charlotte, at one point directly assuring her that although her husband had recently visited Santa Anna: "Almonte is loyal."[8] The references could have been well-intended, but it's hard not to read them also as a subtle threat. Subtext: Santa Anna is in the wings, ready to take the stage. The possibility that the crown of Mexico might slip through their hands, to be given to someone else, had helped to convince Maximilian and Charlotte to accept the throne; it could just as easily be exploited to prevent them from abandoning it. Meanwhile, *La Sociedad* cast the return of Santa Anna as another instance of foreign meddling and reprinted speculation that Santa Anna was the "instrument" of France or of US secretary of state William Seward and the United States.[9] Since January, French intentions to withdraw had become difficult to ignore. Napoléon III was blaming French departure on Mexico's inability to fulfill its obligations— and shifting responsibility onto Maximilian. "Everything we hear from [Mexico] tells us that the Emperor lacks energy, that he spends his time on decrees . . . that cannot be carried out."[10]

The prospect of French withdrawal was daunting; even worse, imperial finances were teetering. Since May the imperial treasury had been unable to pay volunteer forces—they had to be shifted to Bazaine's payroll. On both military and financial matters, the support of Napoléon III was crucial. Unwilling to accept the increasingly dire—and blunt—warnings coming from Napoléon III and his proxies, Maximilian and Charlotte decided that Charlotte would go to Paris and make their case directly. The money situation was so grim, Charlotte's travel expenses had to be covered by drawing on funds set aside for flood relief.[11]

As Charlotte prepared to leave on her desperate mission, it was difficult to defend against the public perception that this was merely a ploy to extract the empress from an increasingly dangerous situation. It could even be seen as the first step in an eventual abdication. Charlotte's mission was anything but pro forma. She prepared for it minutely. In reading her correspondence, one easily forms the impression that her analyses and powers of observation are keener than her husband's. Principles were important to Maximilian and his self-image. He saw himself as motivated by principle and readily imputed the same to those around him—a generous sentiment that made him prey to the unscrupulous. Charlotte was more transactional, more political. She clearly saw how ambition and the human capacity for self-deception worked together. If she loved power more than Maximilian, she was probably more worthy of it, too.

Charlotte was the victim of a common attack against politically gifted women—namely, that it was childlessness, the empty womb syndrome, that made her restless and ambitious.[12] Her admirers grudgingly acknowledged her "virile" will, as if ascribing to her a masculine attribute was the only way to do her justice.[13] Charlotte's father, Leopold, mentor to both Queen Victoria and his own daughter, had put Charlotte's skills ahead of Maximilian's. She was "the better man of the two."[14] Indeed, while Charlotte could fulfill the "womanly" roles required of her at court, she didn't hesitate to step up when the moment called for a firm and sure political hand. Charlotte was a full partner in negotiations with the Church. When relations with the papal nuncio soured, it was Charlotte who sought to rescue them. In a private session with Meglia, she "made every possible representation to him in every possible tone: grave, gay, weighty, and almost prophetic," and when she saw the hopelessness of the situation, she wrote a candid letter to Gutiérrez seeking his intervention at the Vatican.[15] She was likely the architect of efforts to circumvent the nuncio by appointing a commission to go to Rome. When French efforts to disengage from Mexico became clearer and more insistent in 1866, Charlotte took the lead in drafting a statement outlining her position and that of her husband, detailing the commitments made and obligations owed by France to Mexico.[16] In the summer of that year she resolved to be the one to deliver it. She left Maximilian for the last time on July 8, expecting to return after six weeks. That night she wrote to Maximilian from Río Frío, remembering their tearful goodbye and imploring him "not to give up the dream."[17]

The pomp at Veracruz on July 12, 1866, was substantial, as if to underline that this was a matter of state and not a cowardly departure, a monarch slinking off. An honor guard of twenty-five Sudanese soldiers escorted the empress from the train station to the dock, where a 101-gun salute marked her departure.[18] As she stepped aboard the *Impératrice Eugénie,* she couldn't have overlooked the irony—the vessel was the namesake of the empress whose support, along with that of Eugénie's husband, Napoléon III, was the object of her voyage.[19] French officials had not been informed by Charlotte and Maximilian of her voyage; they would learn of it as her journey unfolded. And as news of her imminent departure spread, the empire found it necessary to issue a statement that she was leaving on "a special mission," in order to prevent rumor from filling the void. Too late. Defenders of the republic were jubilant; they insisted that Charlotte's departure was the beginning of the end, diplomacy being merely a cover story for her voyage home in disgrace.

This view rapidly entered republican political culture, thanks to a song, "Adiós, mamá Carlota," based upon a widely known melody.[20] Vicente

Riva Palacio, a writer, poet, and republican general, composed five stanzas of mocking lyrics, the first of which imagined *chinacos* (Juárist footsoldiers) singing "victory" as Charlotte departs.[21] Double entendres abound in later stanzas, and vulgar variations could be composed on the fly, earning "Adiós, mamá Carlota" a place in the repertoire of republican marching songs. In short order, "Adiós, mamá Carlota" became a song to be sung at the end of a night of drinking, as rowdy clients stumbled home.[22]

Charlotte's voyage to Europe had one goal: to save the empire. That she took the voyage rather than entrusting it to a diplomat was a measure of her seriousness. Everyone, including Maximilian, knew that no one would deliver the message more effectively or emphatically than Charlotte. But the act of leaving had a contrary effect on Mexican public opinion because it looked like the beginning of the end. A simple ditty, "Adiós, mamá Carlota," became the anthem announcing the end of the empire. Once let loose, nothing could be done to stop it.

Matters got no better in Europe. Charlotte arrived in France, at Saint Nazaire, on August 7, but her voyage had happened so quickly that none of the usual efforts to prepare public opinion and the press had taken place. What did her abrupt arrival mean? Was something wrong? Had she abdicated? Speculation filled the void. Lascivious rumor had it that Charlotte was pregnant and that the father was either the jaunty, mustachioed Colonel Van der Smissen, head of the Belgian volunteers, or the dashing Mexican colonel Miguel López.[23] Some newspapers denied her arrival altogether, dismissing it as a lie meant to harm the imperial cause. Others advanced credible alternatives. Given the death of her father in December, it was plausible that she intended to go to Brussels to handle family matters associated with the estate.[24]

When Charlotte stepped down the gangplank of the *Impératrice Eugénie* at Saint Nazaire, there was no official reception, other than a handful of Mexican imperialists residing in France. She made her way from Saint Nazaire to Nantes, where she spent the night, planning to leave for Paris in the morning. On the railway platform at Nantes, Charlotte was handed a telegram from Napoléon III. The French emperor claimed to be *souffrant*—bedridden, in fact—and promised that if she proceeded to Belgium, her presumed intended destination, he would have time to recover.[25] It was a brilliantly crafted message that feigned ignorance of her purpose (though he could guess), deftly imputed a less threatening one (family matters), and offered, were she to persist, an excuse for not seeing her. Charlotte persisted.

It got no better upon her arrival in Paris. The receiving party, sent by Napoléon III and Eugénie, missed her arrival at Montparnasse station; they had gone to the Orléans station by mistake. The contrast with the grand reception she and Maximilian enjoyed two years earlier was telling. She wasn't offered lodging in the Tuileries, so she checked in at the Grand Hôtel, near the site of the Paris Opera.[26] The latest news in Europe only added to the sense of cascading calamities. Austria and Prussia were at war. Austrian defeat at Königgrätz was shaking the foundations of Habsburg rule.[27]

Neither Napoléon III nor Empress Eugénie knew the precise object of Charlotte's visit, but they had a hunch. Empress Eugénie sought to head off an ugly confrontation by taking the initiative. On August 10 Eugénie went to meet Charlotte at her hotel, accompanied by a large retinue. Eugénie's husband, Napoléon III, having sensed that no good could come from this surprise visit and hoping to avoid meeting Charlotte, asked Eugénie to repeat his claims of indisposition. Charlotte would hear nothing of it. She would have her visit with Napoléon III. The next day a carriage from the imperial stables arrived at the Grand Hôtel to take Charlotte to Saint-Cloud, the imperial summer residence outside Paris.

The day went poorly. Charlotte presented her report to Napoléon III.[28] When he appeared unmoved, the conversation escalated. Charlotte insulted the French army, claiming it had succeeded only in exhausting Mexico's resources in a failed, three-year campaign of pacification. Not a single French soldier had ever even set foot in Tabasco, Guerrero, or Chiapas. The northern states were falling to Juárez and the forces of the republic, but Bazaine seemed not to care. The abrupt departures of French troops had shattered the confidence of the population in the future of the empire. Yes, under the Treaty of Miramare, Mexico had agreed to pay for the support of French forces, but not if the occupation secured only a third to a half of the territory.[29] The money borrowed to set up the empire had instead been consumed fighting an unending civil war. According to some sources, the conversation grew testy, and finally, in exasperation—and believing that the power to shame was her ultimate weapon—Charlotte blurted out a threat: "Fine, then we'll abdicate!" To which Napoléon responded coldly, "Then abdicate."[30]

The truth is probably more mundane. Apocryphal or not, the exchange captured a crucial truth. Abdication—which would have carried real weight if offered earlier because it would have left Napoléon III holding the bag—no longer mattered to him. The Intervention was an early example of "You break it, you own it."[31] Having broken the Mexican republic politically and militarily, the Intervention "owned" Mexico. But once Charlotte and Maximilian accepted the throne, Mexico was theirs and Napoléon III was off the hook. Abdication would have put Mexico back in France's lap, but by 1866 the end of the story was clear. Abdication was no longer a threat. In fact, it was desired.

Napoléon III decided to use time to wear down Charlotte. He hid behind his ministers—Charlotte would have to see them for an explanation, which meant that she would have to make an appointment and return. Charlotte returned to Saint-Cloud the next day (August 12) to see his minister of finance, Achille Fould, and minister of war, Jacques Randon, in a meeting presided over by Empress Eugénie. On August 14 the Ministerial Council met to discuss the situation and decided not to change its policy: both public opinion in France and US policy were against any further support for the Mexican Empire.[32]

Charlotte had failed, but she refused to say anything that would suggest as much in the letter she wrote to Maximilian the next day (August 15). Instead, she offered excuses for why her meetings hadn't produced immediate results. Charlotte, who had just turned twenty-six in June, offered an explanation of her own—age. Eugénie and Napoléon III were old, worn down, sick, even childishly senile.[33] Yet this could not change the fundamental fact that France was withdrawing support for the Mexican Empire and that without it the empire would collapse. A week later (August 22) Charlotte's patronizing tone turned defiant. On the eve of her departure from Paris, Charlotte wrote a long, disordered letter to Maximilian, suggesting that they were the victims of a vast conspiracy in which the decline of Austria and the abandonment of Maximilian and Mexico were premeditated, part of an effort by which Evil, embodied by Napoléon III, sought to destroy Good, represented by Maximilian. Apocalyptic references to Babylon, Mephistopheles, and Hell sat alongside quite concrete advice that Maximilian turn away from the French military and rely on "indigenous elements" for political support.[34]

Charlotte's letter mirrored themes she knew to be dear to Maximilian, notably his solicitude for "the indigenous race" of Mexico, the flip side of his sense of betrayal by *criollo* elites, both Liberal and Conservative. Maximilian now proposed land reform as part of a "restitution of rights of this loyal population." Land would "moralize" the indigenous, develop their patriotism, and bind them to the country.[35] Maximilian's indigenous populism was part of a confident conviction of an imminent "crisis" that would "destroy most of the states of the old and new world."[36] These views showed a rare and lively political imagination. Was Maximilian predicting a postcolonial reckoning? Or merely a penchant for an apocalyptic worldview? Either way, Maximilian's view stopped short of the paranoid vision Charlotte was beginning to set forth.[37]

Sleepover at the Vatican

Her journey from Paris to Miramare provided Charlotte with occasions to reflect on the past. In Italy she stopped at Villa d'Este—once the property of her father, King Leopold—on Lake Como. During her stay she wrote a nostalgic letter to Maximilian recalling their time as rulers of Lombardy, when they were newlyweds.[38] Then it was on to Venice, Trieste, and Miramare.

She seemed to recover her equilibrium at Miramare. Eloin, who ought to have known better, wrote to Maximilian that thanks to the flowers in the "enchanted garden" at Miramare, Charlotte was in "perfect health."[39] She and her entourage celebrated September 16, Mexican Independence Day. Her politics shifted, too. She had come to view the French departure from Mexico as a blessing. With the French gone, the empire could become fully Mexican, no longer a European imposition.[40] Mexican resistance would fade. The United States would drop its objections. Church, Liberals, Conservatives—everyone would rally to the empire.

This refashioned empire would still need the blessing of the Catholic Church. In desperation, Charlotte turned to Rome and Pius IX. A cholera outbreak made a voyage to Rome by sea impossible, so she voyaged by land to Bolzano, at that time an Austrian city, and from there to Mantua, Reggio Emilia, and Bologna. The Mexican delegation, alerted to her arrival, met her as she approached the city. Rome was dark by the time she arrived. It was close to midnight, with a hard rain falling. A coach took her from the train station to the Albergo di Roma (today the Grand Hotel Plaza) on the Corso. Soldiers from the papal army and the French army took turns standing watch.[41]

Cardinal Antonelli met her at her hotel the next day, September 26. His job was to deliver unhappy news, for although Charlotte and Maximilian had reimagined their empire as a thoroughly Mexican enterprise, this changed nothing in the eyes of the Catholic Church, whose property had not been restored. Charlotte broached the idea that the pope might prevail upon Napoléon III to continue his support. After an hour of conversation,

Antonelli had exhausted every possible variation of refusal.[42] His effort to spare Charlotte the trouble of a papal audience had failed. She insisted on seeing Pius.[43] That night she wrote to Maximilian expressing her confidence in a concordat but above all in Maximilian. She described a scenario inspired by Giuseppe Garibaldi and his role in rallying the people of Italy around King Victor Emmanuel. Charlotte wrote of her confidence that events in Mexico would play out similarly. She predicted that "the greatest victory will come to you as the dissidents [supporters of Juárez] . . . play the role of Garibaldi in Italy" and rally to Maximilian. In imagining such a historical reconciliation, Charlotte displayed both a lively political imagination and a faltering grasp on reality.[44]

The papal audience occurred the next day at 11 AM. Charlotte and her entourage moved through parallel ranks of Swiss Guards, then Charlotte's attendants left her with Pius for a private conversation that lasted more than an hour.[45] She presented the pope with a draft concordat. (She would later ask for it to be returned.)[46] She also revealed her conviction that members of her entourage meant her harm; they were in the pay of Napoléon III and intended to poison her. Back at her hotel, Charlotte asked to be left alone. Pius visited her the following day at her hotel—a rare and generous gesture of concern. Rome was still a papal city (it would remain so for another four years, until September 1870); the pope was head of state as well as spiritual leader, so the appearance of the papal coach on the Corso caused a stir, just as a royal coach might. Reactions varied: Monarch? Vicar of Christ? Celebrity? All of the above? Some turned to gawk; some bowed; some genuflected; some dropped to their knees; soldiers saluted. A few resisted quietly, stuffing hands in pockets, as if to forbid an inadvertent gesture that might convey recognition, let alone allegiance. Pius raised his hand in blessing as his coach turned into the carriage entrance of the hotel.[47]

Nothing is known of the outcome of that visit, but on September 30 Charlotte appeared abruptly at the Vatican. It was 8 AM and she insisted that she be taken to the pope. Pius was at breakfast. Charlotte declared herself famished; she had eaten nothing apart from fruit she peeled and nuts she shelled herself.[48] According to Egon Corti, Charlotte was offered food but refused to eat. Nor would she leave, for fear of encountering enemies plotting against her. Pius took her to see the treasures of the Vatican Library; he waited for her to become distracted, then slipped away. Charlotte refused to leave the Vatican grounds, though Antonelli insisted. Eventually a room was prepared for her and her personal assistant, Señora del

Pius IX visits Charlotte at the Albergo di Roma. *Reproduced from* L'Illustration, *October 27, 1866.*

Barrio.[49] In Corti's account, they spent the night surrounded by candle-sticks and the splendor of the Vatican Library. If true, it was a unique concession, given the persistent claim that no woman had ever spent the night in the Vatican.[50]

What is certain is that Charlotte's mental health was failing. A telegram from the Belgian Legation in Rome dated October 2 warned that the empress had experienced "a great excitement." The next day another dispatch to the Belgian Ministry of Foreign Affairs conveyed a hopeful tone. Charlotte had calmed somewhat after visiting Roman monuments, although there was concern that she had donated sixty thousand francs to Peter's Pence, the papal treasury.[51] It was an extravagant donation, equivalent to a quarter million dollars in 2020.

In the days that followed, Charlotte went to great lengths to thwart those who, she believed, intended to take her life. She had in her posses-sion a cup from the Vatican that she had taken with her. She wrote to Pius to ask permission to keep it, as she would drink from nothing else; she used it to drink water she took from Rome's fountains.[52] By October 4 she had been seen by several physicians. Their diagnosis as conveyed to Brus-sels was bleak: "Illusion impassible. Monomanie constatée. Excentricité continuelle."[53] The next day she was worse. A persistent fear of poisoning would not leave her. In her room at the Albergo, laying hens were lashed by the leg to a table; their eggs were her main source of food. Nearby was a coal stove used to prepare them.[54]

Her brother Philippe, the Count of Flanders, had been called to Rome. He arrived on the seventh. The next day sister and brother left the hotel arm in arm.[55] A carriage took them to the station, where they boarded a train to Ancona, on the Adriatic. From there they returned to Miramare by boat. On October 14, a telegram from Miramare to Eloin in Paris offered a medical summary: "State of the Empress grave; good physical health; doctors do not despair of curing monomania."[56] The best that could be said was that the doctors had not given up hope.[57]

1 2

Like Pinning Butterflies

IT WAS A MILD OCTOBER DAY in Orizaba—perfect for collecting. Maximilian dressed in bourgeois attire—a gentleman naturalist dressed in white and outfitted with broad hat and butterfly net. It was the perfect costume for a day of discoveries in the company of the naturalist Professor Bilimek and the learned physician Samuel Basch. Don José María Bringas, dominant proprietor at Orizaba and confirmed *imperialista,* had put his hacienda at Jalapilla at the disposal of Maximilian and his entourage. The grounds surrounding the white, arcaded compound were the ideal starting point for the trio to explore the countryside and its fauna on horseback.[1] At the sight of a unique specimen they would dismount and move in for the capture. Maximilian's jacket sleeve bristled with pins. His valet stood by, ready to hand over the specimen tray at the emperor's signal. The emperor then pinned each insect to the tray before handing it back to the valet. As the group rode off in pursuit of their next find, the specimens struggled in vain against their fate.[2]

Besides offering the prospect of a day without politics, the group constituted a mobile, German-speaking club—a welcome respite from the Spanish-speaking imperial coterie that had followed Maximilian from the capital. At a discreet distance, Carl Khevenhüller, an officer in the imperial cavalry, served as commander of an armed security detail.[3] His presence was the only intrusion on what was otherwise a resolutely apolitical exercise. Concepción Lombardo de Miramón, who watched the "unfortunate sovereign" from a distance, was not the only person to observe that the emperor was most at home in such pursuits. Maximilian fancied himself a naturalist. He was also an amateur taxidermist. A member of the Foreign Legion observed that Maximilian seemed happiest when he was stuffing tropical birds.[4]

Orizaba represented a hinge moment in the history of the empire. Maximilian and Charlotte had spent much of the previous year and a half trying to pin the French in place, seeking to counter ominous signs that the French were heading for the exit. In June 1865, when the fifty-five-year-old Marshall Bazaine married his Mexican sweetheart, the seventeen-year-old María Josefa "Pepita" de la Peña y Azcárate, the imperial couple allowed them to use the palace chapel for the occasion. They also saw an opportunity to anchor Bazaine and his army more solidly in Mexico. As a wedding gift, they gave the couple one of the finest pieces of real estate in the capital—the grand, eighteenth-century Palacio de Buenavista, today the Museo Nacional de San Carlos. The gift came with a condition, however. In the event that Bazaine returned to Europe, the property would revert to the state.[5] In effect, the gift to Bazaine and Pepita was a gilded cage.[6]

Maximilian and Charlotte's suspicions were well founded. Six months after his wedding, Bazaine received orders from Napoléon III to prepare for evacuation. "The very latest [date] for the repatriation of the Corps . . . is the beginning of next year," he wrote in January 1866.[7] Napoléon III promised to inform Maximilian and Charlotte also; when they received the news, both emperor and empress resisted. In the Treaty of Miramare they had been promised a longer period of support. But Bazaine's orders provided no wiggle room and the relationship between commander and emperor continued to deteriorate. At a dinner with Bazaine in February, Maximilian was put in the humiliating position of having to ask for an advance from the French treasury—imperial coffers were empty. The empire was running a monthly deficit of half a million dollars.[8] Merchants were losing confidence in the empire because it couldn't afford to pay its bills.[9]

Maximilian looked for ways to complicate the French departure. Just before Charlotte's departure for Europe, Maximilian brought two French officers into his administration. His ostensible aim was to make his administration operate efficiently. General Auguste-Adolphe Osmont was tasked with building a Mexican army of forty thousand soldiers in anticipation of the French departure. General Charles-Nicholas Friant was to head the Ministry of Finance.[10] Maximilian presented the change as a way to align the administration of the empire with Bazaine and the French military effort, though it certainly crossed his mind that having Osmont and Friant in his government would give him reciprocal leverage on Bazaine, forcing Bazaine to harmonize his efforts with those of Maximilian's ministers.[11] By the end of June, Maximilian was thrilled at the results. He claimed that the two had "done more in three weeks" than Bazaine had accomplished in three years.[12] Maximilian brought the two formally into his government.[13]

In addition to anchoring the French presence, the arrangement set up a possible abdication. If Maximilian were to leave Mexico, two of the most powerful ministries in the Mexican government would be held by French officers. Having arranged for Maximilian and Charlotte to assume political responsibility for Mexico, Napoléon III was unlikely to welcome the idea that it would all land back in his lap. Worse, to the extent that they were competent, Osmont and Friant only postponed the inevitable collapse. The point was to extract Maximilian gracefully from Mexico, not prop him up. Napoléon III had unexpected help from the United States. The United States saw the service of Osmont and Friant as a violation of French assurances made in April 1866—assurances not shared with the imperial couple—that France was operating a staged withdrawal.[14] Fresh from his encounters with Charlotte at Saint-Cloud, Napoléon III relayed to Bazaine the categorical refusal he had given to Charlotte—"neither a penny nor a man more" would be committed to Mexico. At the same time, he confirmed that it would be impossible for Osmont and Friant to remain in the service of the empire.[15] Although Maximilian would protest that their service was a visible sign of "the alliance between my government and the French government," the French generals were forced to resign.[16]

The move signaled a widening rupture. Napoléon III wanted out, but Maximilian and Charlotte wanted to hold his feet to the fire. He had promised things. They had acted on the basis of those promises. He should deliver. They shared a vision of the American republic as a threat. With the Civil War concluded, this threat was greater than ever. This was not the time to cower or run away. Maximilian wanted Napoléon III to convene a European "congress" whereby Europe would act in concert with Imperial Mexico against the United States.[17] France wanted to get out. Imperial Mexico wanted Europe to go big.

As Charlotte labored unsuccessfully in Europe to revive support for the empire, Maximilian was asserting his conviction that their empire would endure. The occasion was September 16, Mexico's Independence Day, and Maximilian gave an oration that once again inserted the empire within Mexican history and reassured his followers that he had no interest in abdication. He depicted the fight for independence as ongoing

("Mexico has already been fighting for a half century"), a subtle way of reminding his followers that his empire aligned with independence and the struggle against Yankee domination. The empire meant "true independence" as opposed to the ersatz independence of the republic. And he reaffirmed his commitment as a matter of Habsburg honor, because "a true Habsburg will not leave his post."[18]

As disagreements with the French deepened, Maximilian let himself be persuaded by Charlotte's Garibaldian scenario—their empire could be rescued by making it more thoroughly Mexican and populist. Maximilian stopped fighting the departure of the French. He began to see it as a necessity—the Mexican people would embrace his empire only if it were free of foreign entanglements.[19] But Maximilian's reconfiguration of his empire was also the product of spite. The desire to repatriate French forces safely had prompted Bazaine to work with forces representing the Mexican republic, notably by coordinating the evacuation of towns and cities, aiming to avoid clashes as French forces evacuated a city and republican forces moved in. There was also evidence that weapons and ammunition had been left in the care of republican forces.[20] When Maximilian learned of these actions, he was enraged: Why hadn't Bazaine coordinated with imperial forces so that they could occupy the evacuated cities?[21] In his spite, Maximilian turned toward the only remaining source of support—Mexican Conservatives.[22] Much later Maximilian would write to Vienna accusing Bazaine of a host of misfortunes and crimes, including selling government property to raise cash.[23] It was as ugly a breakup as one could imagine.

The rebound was no better. Maximilian had already begun to work with Téodosio Lares, a prominent monarchist whose impeccable credentials included having served as president of the Assembly of Notables that had given Maximilian the crown.[24] He was also a close associate of Archbishop Labastida. The association was telling.[25] Maximilian was once again abandoning his Liberal principles in order to save his empire. He was embracing the very reactionary forces that Maximilian and Charlotte had tried to keep at arm's length when they arrived in 1864. Maximilian brought Lares into his cabinet in August 1866, then promoted him to head of government the following month as part of his realignment with Mexican Conservatives.[26] Thousands of miles away, Almonte wrote approvingly that with a Conservative ministry, "the Emperor will be able to save the country and save himself."[27]

On October 18, news of Charlotte's crisis reached Maximilian. It arrived with shattering effect.[28] Two days later Maximilian announced his departure for Orizaba. The news of his departure immediately produced a political crisis. It was not unusual for Maximilian to leave Mexico City from time to time. He was fond of Cuernavaca and would go there, sometimes alone, sometimes accompanied by Charlotte, when he felt the needed a respite from the pressures of the capital.[29] Orizaba might plausibly provide the same, but the fact that Orizaba was on the road to the coast inspired fear that he intended to bolt, especially given the rumors of abdication. There was even skepticism about Charlotte's ill health, now seen as a pretext for Maximilian's safe exit. Maximilian's departure could bring the abrupt collapse of the empire, leaving his supporters exposed to reprisals. From the safety of his European exile, Gutiérrez Estrada had already foreseen a "bloody spectacle" wherein those who had called for the empire "become the sorry victims of cruel revenge" at its collapse.[30] Were those days about to come to pass? The prospect galvanized Mexican Conservatives. Before Maximilian could depart, his prime minister, Téodosio Lares, raced to Chapultepec. He delivered an ultimatum. If the emperor left, Lares would resign and take with him the rest of his cabinet.[31]

Bazaine was alarmed, too. He immediately realized that, in the face of such an abrupt and disorderly departure, he would be saddled with executive authority in Mexico, an unenviable position. The crisis was averted when Maximilian gave assurances that his journey to Orizaba did not signal abdication, but the episode revealed in stark terms that the end game had begun.[32]

Quite early the next morning, October 21, Maximilian departed in the imperial coach, escorted by three hundred Hussars. Over the next six days he and his entourage moved at a deliberate pace, staying at rectories and haciendas. While staying at a rectory in Acatzingo, the team of white mules used to pull the imperial coach was stolen under cover of darkness.[33] It was an embarrassment, but also a stark message about just how fragile the empire was becoming.

Maximilian's arrival at Orizaba opened a long, twilight period in the history of the empire, a period marked by confusion, doubt, and, finally, fateful resolution. From his arrival on October 27 until he announced his decision to stay, on December 1, rumor and speculation reigned. Partly this was fed by the emperor's own conduct. His instructions to sell furnishings and to see to the payment and evacuation of the European volunteers pointed clearly toward abdication. So did instructions he gave to arrange for his arrival in Europe.[34] An Austrian frigate, the *Dandolo*, was at Veracruz taking on his personal property and papers as cargo.[35]

Without mentioning the possibility of abdication, *La Sociedad* ran with stories about the possible return of General Santa Anna, in exile in New York, as a savior of Mexico.[36] The "jocular-serious ultra-liberal" periodical *La Sombra* offered a synopsis of the empire on its front page under the title "Darkness"; it doubled as an obituary of the regime.[37] Left and Right were united in their skepticism about the future of the empire. Such skepticism fed upon itself. It also spilled into the streets. From the capital, the Belgian consul wrote of a chaotic situation in which insurgents had begun to carry out reprisals, offering a glimpse of what could transpire should the empire fail. Across the land, functionaries and partisans of the empire were being singled out—their property, "even their houses in Mexico City," being requisitioned and sold as punishment. Confusion prevailed. "In the six weeks the Emperor has been in Orizaba," the consul wrote, "Mexico does not have a government."[38] The void created by Maximilian's departure from the capital was filled with speculation. There were rumors out of New York that Maximilian would abdicate in favor of General Ortega, preserving the empire.[39] Meanwhile, William Tecumseh Sherman and Lewis Davis Campbell prepared a US diplomatic mission that would take them to Veracruz in late November on the assumption that Maximilian was abdicating and would leave with the French.[40]

In fact, Mexico *did* have a government. It had two: the government of the republic, which had never left, and the empire. Maximilian seemed halfway out the door; certainly in his mind he was. After reaching Orizaba, his main concern was the well-being of those who had taken risks in support of the empire, especially the volunteers. Maximilian worked to ensure the safe return of the European volunteers and to guarantee that the financial obligations made to them were met. As for himself, he was haunted by the thought that if he left with the French, it would validate the claim that he had been a puppet of Napoléon III all along, and that his commitment to Mexico would last only so long as they propped him up. It was this concern that kept him in Orizaba, seeking to separate himself in space and time from the departure under way.

In his mind, his departure was justified not only by Napoléon III's betrayal, but also and primarily by Charlotte's condition. To return to Europe for her sake was beyond question.[41] No one would fault such a choice. But should he abdicate? Or should he leave Mexico while retaining his title and his power, such as it was, at least implying the intention to return? There was a possible scenario in which this was attractive. In June and July, Austria was defeated in a war with Prussia; defeat had made his brother Emperor Franz Joseph very unpopular. In Vienna, Franz Joseph was heckled by a hostile crowd. Cries of "Long live Maximilian!" rained upon him as he exited the Hofburg, his residence in Vienna.[42] At least part of the population was ready for a change at the top, ready to swap out the discredited Franz Joseph for the younger sibling. Maximilian was no longer next in the line of succession—his nephew Crown Prince Rudolf was—but if Franz Joseph could be brought to abdicate, Maximilian could rule as regent until Rudolf was of age.[43] Maximilian flirted with forces at home who conspired against his brother and wished to see Maximilian replace him.[44] This would be an astonishing betrayal of brother by brother, but it fit with what we know of Maximilian's vanity and ambition. Might Maximilian's dream of restored Habsburg glory, from the New World to the Old, yet be within reach? Would it give him another honorable motive for an exit from Mexico?

Exit on any terms was a prospect that terrified Mexican Conservatives. Apart from Santa Anna, whose return was rumored though unlikely, they had no one of Maximilian's stature, no one who could stand in the way of the return of the republic with all that that would entail for those who had compromised themselves by supporting the empire.

There seemed no chance of persuading Maximilian to stay, but until he departed there was still hope. Into this gap stepped Augustín Fischer. When Fischer was sent to Rome to negotiate a concordat early in 1866, he had failed. True to form, when he returned to Mexico in the summer he had claimed success.[45] Mexico would have its concordat in a few months, he boasted, when in fact he had accomplished nothing more than permission to convene Mexican bishops for further discussion.[46] Fischer certainly knew that in Rome, talk of a concordat with the empire was carried out in bad faith. Antonelli knew the empire wouldn't survive, while Munguía had already privately dismissed any possibility of a concordat with the remark that it could serve only as "a shroud" for a moribund empire.[47] Rather than endure the unpleasantness of saying no, Rome was spinning out negotiations until the inevitable—the collapse of the empire—occurred; but that didn't prevent Fischer from presenting papal consent to more talk as a great diplomatic triumph.

Fischer's return was perfectly timed to facilitate the marriage between Maximilian's empire and the ultra-Conservative, ultra-Catholic faction he had endeavored to keep at arm's length. Upon his return from Rome, Fischer was appointed secretary to the emperor, the equivalent of chief of staff. All communication to and from Maximilian would have to go through him. Now, in his role as gatekeeper, Fischer could influence the mix of visitors as he wished.[48] Since Charlotte's departure, Maximilian's dinners had become intimate, typically limited to his physician, Samuel Basch, and a friend, Stefan Herzfeld, along with Fischer.[49] As he transitioned into his political role as secretary to the emperor, he ceased to wear clerical garb; stories of his scandalous private life as a priest, which had by now reached the capital, did not imperil his status.[50] Fischer used his position to serve the clerical partisans of the empire.[51] His cause was helped inadvertently when a letter from Europe intended for Maximilian was intercepted and leaked to the press in late October. The author, Maximilian's assistant Félix Eloin, pointed out how Maximilian's departure before that of the French "would be interpreted as an act of weakness." The letter was sent from Brussels on September 17—that is, prior to the news of Charlotte's crisis, which had changed everything—but the message preyed upon Maximilian's sense of honor and landed with force, especially as it was splashed in newspapers in Mexico, the United States, and Europe.[52]

Embracing Mexican Conservatives was key to the political reconfiguration of the empire, but the departure of the French required a military reconfiguration, too, given that all units served under the ultimate authority of the French. Colonel Van der Smissen, commander of Belgian volunteer forces, wrote from Querétaro to lay out his vision for the army of the empire. He recommended that Belgian and Austrian volunteer forces be brought into a new, Mexican imperial army. This seems partly to have been a matter of self-defense, to prevent an inversion of hierarchies involving Europeans and Mexicans. Europeans had served under Mexican officers, notably in Matamoros, where Austrian volunteers served under General Tomás Mejía, but this seems to have been the exception—and done grudgingly.[53] French officers had flatly refused to take orders from Mexican generals.[54] As the ranking Belgian officer, Van der Smissen was sharply critical of efforts to amalgamate European and Mexican soldiers into a single imperial Mexican force when this involved putting Mexican officers in command of Europeans.[55] Whatever the reorganization of the imperial army might entail, Van der Smissen wanted to avoid the confounding of races.[56] Rank and military chain of command mattered, but they did not transcend race.

Van der Smissen also noted Maximilian's embrace of the Conservative cause, which he applauded. "I've learned here," he wrote from Querétaro, "that Your Majesty has just chosen ministers from the conservative party which alone represents . . . the principles of religion and property." Van der Smissen pointed out that, while Maximilian's step was laudable, it wasn't enough to bring Conservatives into his government. Conservatives in Mexico had withdrawn from public life in order to protect themselves from reprisal; putting a few Conservatives in the government wouldn't change that. What was needed was a dramatic event that would rally Conservatives and give them the courage to embrace the empire publicly.

Van der Smissen sketched the kind of event he had in mind. Maximilian must put himself at the head of a reorganized army. He must lead that army into battle with the enemy, while Van der Smissen himself would lead the victorious charge. In a fit of fantasy Van der Smissen sketched for Maximilian a glorious triumph. "I pray Your Majesty to let me lead the main attack," he wrote. "I give my word as a gentleman that it will be a brilliant victory: the enemy will lose all his artillery and at least 3000 prisoners. Throughout the Empire will arise an immense cry of enthusiasm."[57]

Van der Smissen was advising Maximilian to go for broke by putting himself at the head of the army. It was a stupid idea, but it undoubtedly appealed to Maximilian's romantic side. At its core, it was a remake of the old idea that Mexico harbored an imperial majority, who only needed a sign before rallying to the empire publicly. It's possible that Van der Smissen planted the seed for Maximilian's later decision to put himself at the head of an army and march to Querétaro. It also converged with a fantasy commonly cultivated by some members of Maximilian's inner circle—that the United States would have no objection to the empire as long as it was free from European influence.[58] The departure of the French, combined with the "Mexicanization" of the empire, would rally the people and set Maximilian free.

More seriously, the military problem posed by the French evacuation was addressed in part by the timely arrival of two military advocates of a Conservative/clerical empire. Leonardo Márquez and Miguel Miramón formerly had occupied such high-profile roles in the War of Reform that they were a liability to the empire; they had therefore been sent abroad "on mission" early in the empire. Now they were back, ready to prop it up. They arrived at Veracruz on November 10. Within days they were at Orizaba, arguing that a Conservative and truly Mexican empire could succeed where the Liberal empire had failed. They offered their swords in service.

Civilians weighed in, too. Three delegations arrived at Orizaba with the aim of persuading Maximilian to stay by showing popular support and offering money. The first carried a petition signed by the residents of Puebla, urging Maximilian to stay. Two delegations came from Mexico

City. The first consisted of representatives of the *ayuntamiento* (city council); the second included an ad hoc group of prominent citizens.[59] According to a source close to Maximilian at the time, the clergy and the *ayuntamiento* offered one million pesos each in support of the empire if Maximilian would return to the capital.[60]

Such lobbying dovetailed with the message Maximilian had received from his mother in which she had invoked his "honor" and duty as a Habsburg.[61] For someone of Maximilian's dynastic and aristocratic sensibility, the language of honor and duty had a powerful effect, even if it led to disastrous outcomes. Gutiérrez de Estrada chimed in from Europe in the same vein, going on about honor and courage and even discounting Charlotte's condition as justification for Maximilian's return. Gutiérrez, who couldn't bring himself to leave Europe to reside in the imperial Mexico that he had helped to create, was now preaching to Maximilian about his duty to remain there.[62]

Misinformation added to the confusion. An important element in this campaign was the assertion that if Maximilian did not abdicate, French forces would remain in Mexico until November 1867.[63] If that had been true, it would have given pro-imperial forces a year to organize their military. Colonel Alphons Kodolitsch insisted that Marshal Bazaine had assured him on November 18 that French forces would remain through November 1867 if Maximilian returned to the capital and continued to rule as emperor.[64] There were murmurs to the effect that Archbishop Labastida himself had assured Maximilian that the French would stay if he abandoned his plan to abdicate. Labastida denied such claims and felt obliged to do so in writing in a letter to Bazaine.[65] As for Bazaine himself, he later wrote by way of explanation to Napoléon III that he had only meant that the Foreign Legion would stay, as specified under the Treaty of Miramare. By whatever means this assertion was made, clarification came too late. By the time the matter was cleared up, the decision to return to Mexico City had been made.

Maximilian convened a council of state at 10 AM on November 25. Beyond convening the group and giving them their charge—to discuss the future of the empire—Maximilian did not participate.[66] Instead, he returned to the fields, hunting specimens while his fate and that of his empire were being debated. The decision to convene such a council but not to preside perfectly demonstrated how notions of honor and duty clouded Maximilian's thinking. He distrusted his own judgment and had difficulty making decisions but was willing to live—and die—from the consequences of decisions made by others. It also revealed his belief that a body packed with parti-sans of the empire would somehow have a disinterested discussion.

After Maximilian had left the room and the meeting got under way, the discussion broke clearly in favor of the Conservative/clerical faction, who agreed on the necessity of preserving the empire. These were the usual suspects—Conservative generals Leonardo Márquez and Miguel Miramón, and imperial politicians Téodosio Lares and José María Lacunza—who had a great deal to lose because of their prominent public support for the empire. Arguing in favor of abdication were the realists who saw that the situation of the empire was hopeless. They were right, but they were outnumbered.[67]

After the meeting, Maximilian issued a statement to be sent to all the courts of Europe. The statement laid out his assessment of the current sit-uation facing the empire, including his disappointment with Napoléon III and his broken promises. Above all it spoke to his concern about US de-signs on Mexico that threatened "the integrity of the national territory." Now, in the face of these challenges, he felt obliged to remain, fortified by "even greater self-denial than he had when he originally assumed the throne."[68] As always, Maximilian felt compelled to justify his action in the most high-minded and selfless terms. The statement was a reissue of Maximilian's appeal to Napoléon III to organize a European congress to mobilize an alliance against the Yankee empire, an initiative for which Napoléon III had no stomach. Not to be discouraged, Maximilian was appealing over the head of the French emperor.

From Orizaba came the resolution to stay. It involved reimagining the empire apart from the French, as an empire that was thoroughly Mexican. According to this logic, the problem with the empire was that it was foreign and felt like an occupation and would remain so as long as the French were present. Far from being the central prop to the regime, the French presence was bringing it down. The departure of the French would solve two problems. At home, it would allow the empire to become fully Mexican. Abroad, it would remove the stigma of foreign occupation and, in doing so, remove the main obstacle to US recognition of the empire.

At bottom, this was a reformulation of the idea that Mexicans deep down wanted an empire but could only express this desire in the right circumstances. The idea had not yet been fully discredited, even after years of popular insurgency against the empire. On December 3, a week after the discussions at Orizaba, Téodosio Lares and Luis de Arroyo, both leading figures in Maximilian's government, wrote to Bazaine that Maximilian

had decided "to maintain his government based exclusively on the resources of the country."[69] When the news broke, it was accompanied by
grandiose claims made on behalf of a reinvigorated empire. The "new
organization of the Empire" would feature four administrative divisions
each led by a governor who answered to the emperor. Divisional gover-
nors included José Salazar Ilarregui, a civilian, along with three generals
closely associated with the Conservative/clerical establishment—Mejía,
Miramón, Márquez.[70] The reorganization plan also elaborated a bold vision for Imperial Mexico and—somewhat paradoxically, given the desire
to placate the Americans—an aggressive reiteration of territorial claims
against the United States. Three of the territories included in the administrative reorganization were Arizona, California, and New Mexico.[71]
Supporters of the empire had long held that the Juárez government was
in the pocket of the United States, selling off bits and pieces to pay off
debts and appease the Yankee aggressor.[72] Now the empire was sharp-
ening the contrast, reinforcing Maximilian's self-image as the leader of a
resurgent Mexico that would claw back territory wrongfully annexed.[73]

Lares made it clear that the French evacuation should proceed at all
due speed. But getting rid of the French was the easy part. The previous
summer Maximilian had predicted that Imperial Mexico would have an
army of forty thousand men by October.[74] Six months later, he was nowhere
near that goal, although he was now making practical steps toward it.[75]

On December 12 Maximilian decreed the dissolution of the Austro-
Belgian volunteer units, accompanied by an invitation to remain and serve
in a new army constructed along Mexican national lines. The old racism, by
which European soldiers refused to serve under Mexican officers, would
vanish. Mexicans by birth and Mexicans by choice would serve side by
side under Mexican command.[76] Those who would prefer to return to
Europe could do so at government expense—although, characteristically,
this was a promise that the empire could not afford and would not keep.[77]

Maximilian was hoping to find recruits among the Austro-Belgian
units, but here he faced difficulties. The empire had already given plenty
of evidence of its inability to pay its soldiers. In May 1866 the empire was
forced to disclose that it couldn't pay the European volunteers; they had
always been on the French payroll, and the French were leaving.[78] Moreover, Baron Lago, the Austrian representative, instructed Austrian officers
to give "impartial advice" regarding the new Mexican army, which meant
talking candidly about "the precarious situation of the Empire." Except
for the cavalry (where nobles, perhaps more sympathetic to Maximilian,

dominated), most decided to return home.[79] Whether the frank messaging was necessary is hard to say, but the number of Belgian volunteers to remain suggests that it wasn't.[80] Only 55 chose to stay as soldiers in the imperial Army. Another 121 joined the imperial gendarmerie, presumably a function that involved less risk, but almost as many (80) had deserted by that point, or (17) decided to fight for the Mexican republic instead.[81] It also underscored just how hopelessly optimistic Maximilian had been in making the bold prediction that the empire would have an army of forty thousand men.

Bazaine was invited to attend a meeting on December 14. This gathering drew the cream of the military, religious, and civilian Conservative Party in Mexico—some thirty-five individuals in all—including Labastida, the archbishop of Mexico City, and Pedro Barajas y Moreno, bishop of San Luis Potosí; Carlos Sánchez Navarro, Mexico's largest landowner; generals Márquez, Portilla, and Galindo; Santiago Vidaurri, the anti-Juárist governor of Monterrey, as well as politicians Téodosio Lares and José María Lacunza. Maximilian had abandoned any pretense of occupying a position "above politics." He was now a creature of Mexico's clerical and Conservative forces.

The question of the survival of the empire was the topic, but given the makeup of the group, discussion was little more than a formality. Lares presided. José Maria Lacunza, reporting on resources available, asserted that revenues had produced $11 million and would reach $23 million "once the departments of San Luis, Zacatecas, and Jalisco were recovered" and $36 million when "the reach of the Imperial government reached the limits of the country." These were pie-in-the-sky aspirations, as was the claim that made by the minister of war that twenty-six thousand men were "immediately available."[82] General Márquez offered the opinion that these were "more than enough for victory."[83] Fischer argued for continuing the war.

Once again Bazaine stated the arguments against propping up the empire. He had commanded forty thousand French troops supported by an additional twenty thousand Mexican soldiers. He had had all the resources he needed, yet victory and the peace it would bring were elusive. To sustain the empire meant war, not peace. But this gathering was designed to present an overwhelming force in favor of the empire. Bazaine was vastly outnumbered.[84] It's worth noting that, besides the elite status of this pro-imperial group, they were all Mexican. For much of its life, the Mexican empire had been dominated by Europeans, starting with military commanders such as Bazaine. This body was explicitly designed to demonstrate that the reconstituted empire was fully and truly Mexican. This point is a useful antidote to the idea that the empire could be dismissed as a parenthesis in Mexico's history—"the French Intervention," as it is still sometimes called.[85] Apart from Fischer, the gatekeeper, and Bazaine, who had been called in as witness, the body that met on December 14 was Mexican. So, too, was the empire.

The decision to continue the empire was bolstered by promises of money and men.[86] Both would fall short.[87] The taxable population was limited to Mexico City and the (admittedly prosperous) settlements of Puebla and Orizaba along the narrow route to the coast. A lottery, of all things, was also put forward as a source of cash. It, too, failed. Even as Maximilian's body of wealthy and powerful elites predicted soldiers by the thousands and money by the millions, they couldn't pay the tabs they were running up with local vendors. When a market woman who had been supplying butter and milk to the imperial table on credit presented a bill of one thousand pesos, she was handed ten pesos and the promise of future payment of the balance.[88] In practice, the imperial army lived on forced loans (*prestamos*), which alienated the population and, in practical terms, rendered it indistinguishable from forces loyal to the republic, which employed similar measures.[89] In San Luis Potosí, a wealthy city with a large population of foreigners, General Mejía's forced contributions raised such an outcry among foreigners that he was forced to refund the sums taken.[90]

A special envoy from Napoléon III, General Castelnau, vainly sought to explain to Maximilian the hopelessness of remaining after the French departure, but to remain was the one thing that Maximilian, in his pride, was now determined to do.[91] He told Castelnau he wanted an honorable outcome and that this included calling a national congress to decide Mexico's future and the fate of the empire. Castelnau commended Maximilian for his generous sentiment, but he also pointed out its impracticality. A congress might have been possible a year earlier, when the territory was mostly under the control of imperial forces, but it was utterly impractical in the present context.

With the decision made, it was time for Maximilian to leave Orizaba and return to the capital. A great banquet was organized for the eve of his departure, with wine and champagne in abundance. The next day, as the imperial party prepared to depart, Father Fischer begged off. The indulgences of the night before had left him indisposed.[92]

13

Querétaro, Capital of Empire

THE TRICOLOR FRENCH FLAG was lowered in Mexico City for the last time at 10 AM on February 5, 1867. The *tricolore* had been hoisted over the Mexican capital every day after Forey's grand entrance on June 10, 1863, but at the end of more than three and a half years of military occupation, Marshall Bazaine and the remaining French troops were leaving Mexico City to begin their journey to the coast.[1] Two days earlier, Bazaine had issued a message via handbill to the people of Mexico in which he claimed that "all of our efforts have been to establish internal peace" and "never has it entered into the intentions of France to impose a government of any kind contrary to your wishes."[2] The word "disingenuous" doesn't quite capture the vacuity of Bazaine's attempt to characterize the violence visited upon the people of Mexico since the beginning of the Intervention in 1861. The point, it seems, was to say "goodbye" in some form. Napoléon III had ordered the departure, the Americans had insisted on it, and, after debate and reflection, so had Maximilian and his Conservative supporters. Of course, from the point of view of the Mexican republic, the French shouldn't have been there in the first place.

Even the monarchists were glad to see them go. Concepción Lombardo de Miramón, wife of the Conservative general, couldn't help but note the heavy silence of the streets, "full of onlookers" who witnessed the departure. She didn't hold back in her commentary. She noted that the French had arrived wearing "the mask of peacemakers" but "had played the role of conquerors." Mexico was far the worse for it. The French were now "leaving our homeland poorer and more unhappy than when they landed on the beaches of Veracruz."[3] She was right. The occupation had taken control of the customs houses and used the revenue to support military operations and to pay off investors. Occupations rarely enrich the occupied; the Intervention left Mexico more deeply impoverished. In politics it settled nothing.

Bazaine noted in his report of the events of the day that as the French paraded past the Imperial Palace, the windows remained closed, as if Maximilian had turned his back, ignoring their departure. In fact, Maximilian couldn't resist looking. He lifted the corner of a curtain so that he could see without being seen. He watched as the French paraded across the vast square in front of the palace. When the last French soldier passed from view, he let the curtain drop and said, "At last I am free."[4] It might have felt like that, especially as Maximilian had become so accustomed to blaming the French for the failures of the empire, but their departure also meant that he no longer had the French to blame.

Maximilian's return to Mexico City had been unrushed. He took a detour to Cholula to visit the pyramid—in part, an homage to Alexander

The French depart Mexico City, February 5, 1867 (in the background, the Imperial Palace). *Reproduced from* L'Illustration, *April 29, 1867.*

von Humboldt—before arriving outside the capital on January 5. Given that Maximilian's furnishings had been crated and shipped to Veracruz in anticipation of his departure, he occupied the Hacienda de la Teja as his residence until the Imperial Palace could be prepared.[5] It was here that former Liberal supporters Ramírez Escudero and Luis Robles y Pezuela took their leave, offering pointed advice to Maximilian that he should do the same. Archbishop Labastida also availed himself of imperial hospitality before taking his leave.[6] It's unclear whether he let on about his intention to abandon Mexico—one suspects not, given his role days before in persuading Maximilian to stay. Now that Maximilian had been coaxed back onto his throne, Labastida could prepare his own exit. Barely six weeks later Labastida would be in Havana, at a safe remove from the calamity he had prepared.

Maximilian, meanwhile, remained focused on the idea of a Mexican congress to determine the future of the country. Maybe it would result in a reaffirmation of the empire; maybe it would repudiate the empire and provide Maximilian with a graceful exit. It was pure fantasy, but he remained attached to the idea that overtures to Juárez and Porfirio Díaz to join a congress, combined with military initiatives against them, would coerce the desired result.[7]

Not only was a congress a fantasy, it was contradicted by Maximilian's own conduct, which clearly indicated a preference for destroying Juárez, given the opportunity. In late January, Miguel Miramón was leading his forces toward Zacatecas by way of Querétaro. He was at León when he wrote to his wife that he had certain information that Juárez (the "unconstitutional president") had entered Zacatecas on January 22 under the protection of General González Ortega. Miramón thrilled at the prospect of capturing both men. Juárez was the elusive incarnation of the resistance. As for Ortega, Miramón nursed a grudge against him ever since 1860 when Ortega defeated him militarily and took the capital in the name of the Reform and the republic. Miramón predicted that "things may not go well" for Ortega and that "he would be judged as a rebel"—that is, executed.[8]

Miramón's predictions proved correct, at least in part. At Zacatecas, Miramón enjoyed a stunning victory that seemed to augur well for the revived empire. Not only did he defeat republican forces there and enter the city on January 31; at one point he was close enough to Juárez, Lerdo, and José María Iglesias (minister of justice) to see them as they took flight, though he was unable to capture them. The republic avoided disaster, but it was an impressive victory for the empire just the same. When the news reached the capital, a buoyant emperor asked to visit Miramón's spouse. He entered her home, congratulated her on her husband's success, and offered spontaneously that he would like to be godfather of her child. (She was expecting.)[9]

The celebration didn't last long. Privately, General Miramón was despondent. He complained about the lack of resources available to his army. His army hadn't been resupplied for three days and his officers hadn't been paid in a month. He suspected that his letters to the emperor were being diverted, so he asked his wife to deliver a blunt message in person: "If you see an opportunity, tell him [Maximilian] that without resources his cause is lost."[10]

On February 3, Escobedo's army of seven thousand attacked Miramón' army of two thousand at the Hacienda San Jacinto. Miramón's forces fled in disarray, leaving money, supplies, artillery, many prisoners, and more than a hundred dead. Prisoners included French volunteers who had elected to stay and serve in the army of the empire rather than return to Europe. Escobedo had them shot as "filibusters" (mercenaries)—109 in all. As there were so many to be shot, the prisoners were executed in groups of ten, which meant that as some soldiers were executed, those who remained looked on, witnessing their own imminent fate.[11] Escobedo's actions showed that while the forces of the republic would treat European troops according to the laws of war, no such grace would be accorded those who volunteered to remain to fight for the empire. It also delivered a message. Volunteers for the imperial army now knew that if they were captured, they could expect no mercy.[12]

The war was entering a deadlier stage—and not just because of the summary executions carried out by Escobedo's forces. The empire had long before decided to regard its armed adversaries as traitors and punish them accordingly. Summary executions had been standard practice among imperial forces ever since the imperial decree of October 3, 1865—the notorious Black Decree—which specified that those caught with weapons in hand were to be considered outlaws. This was no idle threat. As recently as October 1866, General Ramón Méndez, operating in Michoacán, had defeated a republican force of eight hundred, taking one hundred prisoners in the process. The day after the battle, the prisoners were shot.[13] Maximilian intended a similar punishment for high-ranking political opponents. During Escobedo's rout of Miramón's army, Miramón lost several objects in his chaotic retreat. Among them was a letter from

Maximilian with specific orders that if Miramón were to capture Juárez or Lerdo or José María Iglesias, he was to try them and sentence them as rebels, but not to carry out the sentence without his permission.[14] The implication was clear. Without explicitly saying so, these men were to be threatened with execution, but their lives would be at the disposal of Maximilian alone. The letter and its stipulations would be used against Maximilian after his own capture.

Escobedo's steady advance was an ominous sign that Maximilian could not ignore. Only seven months earlier Escobedo's operations had been limited to little more than a thousand men, mostly confined to the territory close to the US border. But this was already a dramatic improvement over Escobedo's situation for most of 1864 and 1865, when he commanded a mere six hundred, a force that could do little more than harass European forces.[15] At Camargo/San Gertrudis, Escobedo commanded fifteen hundred in a bold, direct military confrontation that resulted in victory.[16] Now, following San Jacinto, Escobedo's army of seven thousand was moving steadily southward, gaining strength, recruiting soldiers, and occupying territory recently evacuated by the French.

Escobedo's advance, combined with the steady progress of other republican forces, gave the lie to the claim that the problem of the empire was the presence of French troops. The French were gone, but the crisis of the empire persisted. Worse, the summary executions carried out by imperial and republican forces revealed that the empire was not some neutral pole around which the people of Mexico could rally. It was merely one side in a deadly and deepening civil war.

Maximilian wrote a letter to Téodosio Lares, his head of government, setting out in clear terms how saddened he was by the recent turn of events. "I am profoundly moved," he wrote on February 9, "by the present situation of Mexico." It showed how bizarrely naive he had been about what the departure of the French would mean. "It was hoped that once the empire was freed of the French intervention, our action would make itself felt in a manner conducive to peace and the well-being of the people. Unfortunately the opposite has happened." He identified a host of woes—forced loans, taxes imposed in a way "more hateful than productive." And he concluded with a grave indictment of his own empire: "The Empire has neither moral nor material power in its favor . . . and [public] opinion forms in every way against it." As for the republican forces, he was forced to admit that although "[they have been described] unjustly as disorganized, demoralized, and driven solely by the desire to pillage," they instead had proven to be driven by valor and "sustained by the great idea of defending the independence of the nation." It was a truly insightful critique, but it would have been as true the day he arrived as it was then. It also suggested how willing he had been to shift responsibility for the evils of the empire onto the French, as if the horrors of the war until then were exclusively theirs. Now he acknowledged his own responsibility and in a dramatic conclusion noted that "the honor of my name and the immense responsibility that weighs on my conscience before God and history call upon me not to delay any further the great decision that will bring to an end so much misfortune."[17] But just as he had completed his eloquent argument in favor of abdication, he drew back. Instead, in his characteristic inability or unwillingness to decide matters of great importance, he concluded his letter by asking Lares what should come next.

In a response sent the next day (February 10) Lares began by stating that he had considered offering his resignation, only to draw back when he realized that he and the other ministers, like Maximilian himself, had resolved to stay. Lares was mirroring Maximilian's moves. Just as when Maximilian had contemplated abdication in October, Lares was using the threat of resignation to pin Maximilian in place.

Instead, Lares asserted, the solution was not abdication, but a renewed effort to engage with Juárez and the republic from a position of strength. But how was this to come about?[18] Lares evoked the horrors that would result from a siege of Mexico City and an assault by republican forces. Instead he suggested that Maximilian might consider going somewhere else, "to Querétaro, for example," where the empire could still count on many supporters. There, he should concentrate his forces under the command of his "most distinguished and loyal generals." Then, in an acknowledgment of bitter rivalry among imperial officers, Lares suggested that Maximilian overcome these rivalries by taking supreme command.[19] The point of it all, according to Lares, was to force the issue, to convince Juárez to begin direct talks to end the war.

Lares was imagining an endgame in which the empire might well dissolve itself. A negotiated settlement between Maximilian and representatives of a triumphant republic would bring peace with amnesty, by which supporters of the empire would be spared judgment and reprisal. Whatever the path forward, Lares wanted the unraveling of the empire to take place far away from himself—in Querétaro, for example.

The ploy worked. On the day that Maximilian received the Lares letter, he told his physician Samuel Basch in confidence that he should prepare for a two-week excursion to Querétaro.[20] On February 12 a rumor circulated in the capital that Maximilian would put himself at the head of his troops and leave the capital the next day. His objective was Querétaro, where Miramón had gone following his rout by Escobedo's army and where generals Méndez and Castillo were expected. Maximilian's aim was to concentrate his forces there, at a remove from the capital, and then confront the armies of the republic.[21] Querétaro offered other advantages; it was a wealthy city and by reputation Conservative and sympathetic to the empire.

A little after 7 AM on February 13, Maximilian left Mexico City for the last time. Before he left, he chose General Leonardo Márquez as his military chief of staff.[22] Márquez had been cultivating his relationship with Maximilian for some time, while defeat by Escobedo had greatly diminished the standing of his rival Miramón. Márquez had been a strong advocate of the idea that if Maximilian were to put himself at the head of a truly Mexican army—not an army of foreigners—it would attract the enthusiasm of the nation. Maximilian decided to take Márquez's advice. He left most of his European troops in the capital.

On the road to Querétaro, Maximilian was accompanied by a force of just sixteen hundred men. According to one source, half of them were raw recruits.[23] Like the money promised if Maximilian remained, the promised army of thousands of eager volunteers failed to materialize. Maximilian had been sold a vision of a people ready to rally to the imperial army if he would only put himself at the head of it. Among the men now beside him, however, there was little evidence of enthusiasm. In fact, there were persistent signs that rank-and-file soldiers had joined the army against their will.[24] By day, imperial officers were preoccupied by the threat of desertion. By night, rank-and-file soldiers were "always locked up in haciendas . . . to prevent them from running away."[25]

The threat of desertion haunted Maximilian's new army. It undermined the idea that a "people's empire" was in the making. So did attacks on his army, a sign of the popular insurgency against him. Just hours from the capital, the new imperial army encountered hostile fire. Three days later it was attacked more forcefully at San Miguel de Calpulalpan. It is unclear what conclusions, if any, Maximilian derived from such evidence. He willingly put himself in harm's way during these skirmishes, as if to invite death, but in that effort, too, he failed. Not all the evidence was gloomy. The day after the combat at San Miguel de Calpulalpan, the imperial army entered Soledad, where market day was in progress. According to locals, the market in Soledad had not been held for years, for fear of predation by guerrilla forces. Aware of the approach of the imperial army, they staged the fair as a sign of confidence in the empire and a show of support.[26]

As Maximilian approached Querétaro, he issued a proclamation to the army formalizing the reorganization that had put Márquez in command. He also reaffirmed the aim of the empire. "Our duty as loyal citizens" he wrote "demands us to fight for the two most sacred principles of the country." These principles were independence, "which is threatened by men who, in their blind egotism, dare to touch our national territory," and "peace and order, which we see disturbed every day in the most outrageous manner." These were veiled references to Yankee expansionism as well as to Juárez and supporters of the republic, who, it was said, weakened Mexico and served the purposes of the United States.[27] As for the call to defend "peace and order," it's worth noting that nowhere in the proclamation was there any talk of a congress. In Orizaba, Maximilian had made a great deal of a national congress as a condition of his decision to stay.[28] Like the conditions Maximilian had set forth at Miramare prior to his acceptance of the crown, this condition was set aside, too. The future of Mexico would be decided by brute military force.

Querétaro sits in a horseshoe-shaped basin—mostly open to the west, but bounded by hills to the north, east, and south. The road from Mexico City approaches the city from the southeast, before descending a steep grade to the city proper. On February 18 the imperial army camped at Colorado, just two miles from the city. The next morning the imperial party assembled at Cuesta China, attired in whatever parade garb they had packed. A welcoming committee consisting of a bevy of generals, among them General Escobár, imperial prefect of Querétaro, rode up from the city to great them.[29]

The procession descended to the city with Maximilian at the front, entering the city at 10:30 in the morning. Crowds had gathered to witness the event and balconies were festooned with bunting. Official accounts emphasized enthusiasm and splendor. The city was "profusely adorned with flags" and there was "not a door, window, balcony, or roof" not "covered with spectators."[30] The procession moved through the city, then made its way to the cathedral, where the emperor's arrival was celebrated with a Te Deum. After the service Maximilian held a reception. General Escobar (the prefect) took the occasion to give a speech in which he addressed Maximilian: "May God bless you, Sir, and may posterity proclaim you deservedly: Maximilian the Great."[31]

The generals organized a banquet in honor of the emperor later in the day, but Maximilian begged off, pleading fatigue. The banquet proceeded, but it became the setting for an ugly display. General Márquez, now commander of imperial forces, couldn't help but use the occasion to gloat and to get even for humiliation he had received from Miramón years before. Márquez had been subordinate to General Miramón when Miramón was president and Márquez was governor of Guadalajara. Miramón was enraged to learn that Márquez was using the power of his office to extort tribute from merchants shipping goods to the port of San Blas. He had Márquez arrested, stripped of his office and of the extorted money, then hauled to Mexico City for trial. Márquez nursed the memory of his humiliation and, now that he was Miramón's commanding officer, he couldn't help but use the occasion of the banquet to mock him, indirectly referring to Miramón's humiliating rout at San Jacinto. One witness described the speech as "malicious joy at Miramón's recent defeat.[32] Imperial forces had just been brought together. Grievances and personal differences were driving them apart.

The differences had telling consequences almost immediately. On February 20, General Ramón Méndez arrived from Michoacán with an army of four thousand men to add to the imperial army. Miramón wrote to his wife that Méndez had arrived accompanied by "half the population of Morelia," who followed the army "for fear of the republicans." Individuals and communities compromised by having collaborated with the occupation were seeking refuge.[33] The withering of the empire was setting off a humanitarian crisis.

Now that imperial forces had been brought together in Querétaro, a war council was called to decide upon a plan of action. Miramón noted that republican forces were in Guanajuato, Irapuato, and San Miguel Allende (all settlements within the state of Guanajuato, adjacent to Querétaro). Imperial forces should set forth immediately to confront them, he argued. Locally superior numbers of imperial troops would allow them to defeat republican forces one by one, before they could combine.

Miramón's idea was sound, but Márquez counseled caution. Let the republican forces concentrate, he argued, the better to destroy them with a decisive blow. This was terrible advice, but Márquez prevailed, with disastrous consequences. Even the terrain was wrong. Querétaro was fine as a base of operations, but it was surrounded on three sides by high ground, making it a dangerous place to await republican troops. Márquez had marched the imperial army into a basin. Now he was recommending that it stay there until sufficient republic forces arrived to make escape impossible.

These debates weren't just about strategy. Seniority, jealousy, and ancient grievances mattered. So did race. Concepción Miramón, Miguel Miramón's wife, claimed that her husband had tried to resign his position when he learned he would be subordinate to Márquez. He drafted a letter of resignation, but Maximilian talked him out of it. In a lengthy commentary, Concepción Miramón granted that Márquez was daring and courageous as a soldier, but as a commander he lacked imagination and foresight. Worse, Miramón remarked, Márquez "belonged to a family of mulattos." Even though "his skin didn't bear traces of the race to which he belonged," he carried within him racial characteristics that could not be effaced. The man known as "Mister Leopard" evinced deep racial traits. Márquez's "entrails bore witness;" they were "faithful heirs to the bloody instinct and cruelty of his ancestors."[34]

Concepción Miramón alleged that in addition to persistent racial traits, Márquez held a grudge against Maximilian. Shortly after his arrival in Mexico, Maximilian sent both Miramón and Márquez abroad on missions. At the time, Maximilian was trying to establish his empire at the center of Mexican politics. The reputations of both men as Conservatives sympathetic to clerical interests could not be aligned with Maximilian's vision of a Liberal empire. Miramón was sent to Berlin for military training. Márquez was sent as imperial representative to Constantinople, but his main task was to establish a Franciscan monastery in Jerusalem. The assignment was laughable on its face, given the peace-loving reputation of the Franciscans versus Márquez's own reputation as a brute. A man known in war as "the butcher of Tacubaya" and as a predator in his sexual conduct would never pass for an altar boy, no matter how pious the mission. The Liberal press had a field day mocking him. A comic sketched him dressed as a pilgrim, staff in hand. Márquez endured the ridicule, but in conversation with Concepción Miramón before his departure he vowed revenge: "Conchita, those who have done this to me will pay for it."

Maximilian seemed not to know about the bitter resentments and prejudices animating his commanding officers. He preferred to think the best of people and was reassured by the energy and pomp of his entry into the city. He wrote to the municipal leadership of Querétaro to express his gratitude for the "friendly and enthusiastic reception" he received. Maximilian preferred to employ the royal "We" but he dropped it on this occasion, though he continued to capitalize any pronoun referring to himself. "Please give thanks to the population in My name and [tell them] that all of My efforts, all of My labors will have no other object than to realize the happiness and peace of My country."[35] He wrote a letter brimming with confidence to his representative in Europe, Félix Eloin: "I received a friendly and enthusiastic reception from the [people of Querétaro] and likewise from the troops [who are] full of courage and devotion and ready to fight for our sacred principles."[36] In Mexico City, the English-language *Mexican Times* celebrated the arrival of Maximilian in Querétaro and marveled at the forces gathered there to begin a campaign against "the dissidents." It also offered the now-obligatory critique of the "French intervention," thus seeking to create a clean slate for the empire by foisting onto France the evils visited upon Mexico. The Intervention, the *Times* noted, had been a "great humiliation" for France; it joined the call for an investigation of the conduct of Marshall Bazaine.[37]

Shifting blame, no more than racism and old grudges, offered little in the face of the deepening gravity of the military situation. Mariano Escobedo's army of seventeen thousand was on the way south from San Luis Potosí. General Ramón Corona was leading eighteen thousand men east from Guadalajara. By March 6, Querétaro was surrounded by a thin line of republican troops. Two days later, Corona's troops arrived in force on the plains of Celaya, to the west of the city. On March 11, republican forces occupied the high ground all around the city. Querétaro's aqueduct, the city's main source of fresh water, was closed. The siege had begun.

Imperial hopes now rested upon republican forces depleting themselves by attacking soldiers of the empire in fortified positions. The convent of La Cruz anchored the eastern end of the city, and the Cerro de las Campanas (the Hill of the Bells) and the Hacienda de la Casa Blanca anchored the western end, the three points defining a defensive triangle. With Corona's forces encamped in the plains of Celaya to the west of the city, imperial forces fortified the Hill of the Bells, the high ground that dominates the plain. From this position they awaited—and hoped for—an attack. This would give the soldiers of the empire a great advantage, but that is precisely why republican forces were reluctant to attempt to take the city by force, imposing a siege instead.

With Querétaro cut off, time was on the side of the republic. There were insults and shots traded and occasional skirmishes with little result. With the western approach to the city mostly secure, republican forces could shift to the southeast, where they could control the road to Mexico

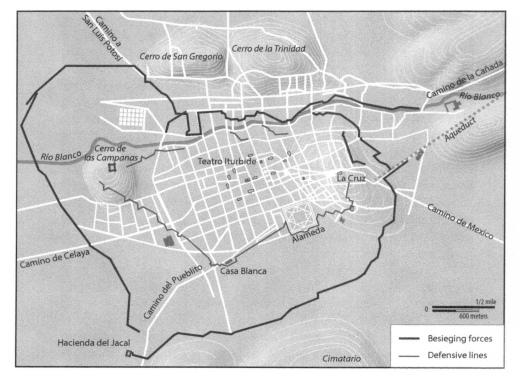

Querétaro.

City.[38] Maximilian and his generals established their headquarters at the convent of La Cruz, but here, too, republican forces refused to take the offensive on a large scale. On March 14 there was an artillery bombardment followed by infantry attacks from the northwest, from the south (Cimatario), and from the east toward the convent of La Cruz. The attacks were turned back and prisoners were taken, including an American officer who deliberately or by neglect did not remove his sombrero when presented to the emperor. Asked why he was fighting, the American replied, "Because I am a republican." He was part of a force of perhaps 150 Americans fighting in a unit called the "Legion of Honor." Their participation anticipated the engagement of the Lincoln Brigade on behalf of the Spanish Republic seventy years later.[39]

Four weeks after the arrival of the emperor and the concentration of imperial forces in Querétaro, little had been accomplished. Republican forces numbered twenty-five thousand and continued to grow. Imperial forces peaked at perhaps fifteen thousand and began to decline from casualties, sickness, and desertions. Military imbalance was only one problem. Querétaro is a wealthy city, but its resources were not unlimited. Rationing had begun. It was hard to imagine any outcome other than the gradual weakening of the city and its population until they fell to an assault. As options fell away, Maximilian continued to cling to fantasies and contradictory impulses. On April 10 there was a celebration of the anniversary of Maximilian's acceptance of the crown of Mexico in 1864. In a speech of thanks, he railed against "despotism and terrorism" and referred to the army of the republic disparagingly as "cohorts of social revolution" while repeating his conciliatory call for a national congress.[40]

There had been very little support forthcoming from Mexico City. The siege created a silence that was difficult to interpret except in ominous ways. In the capital, the press continued to praise Maximilian and talk up a negotiated end to the conflict. The clerical-Conservative newspaper *El Pájaro Verde* contrasted the approaches of Juárez and Maximilian, emphasizing that Maximilian was willing to sacrifice everything to the judgment of a national congress, and that Juárez would not.[41] Juárez, of course, was unwilling to grant the legitimacy of a false equivalence of republic and empire.[42]

Another council of war was called for March 20. Maximilian, characteristically, chose not to attend. This time his stated reason was that his presence might sway the outcome, but the pattern suggests a strange indifference to his own fate. This sense that he was a mere instrument in a larger plan could be read in scriptural terms, and although he seems not to have invoked such language, he certainly understood how it might be interpreted that way. Others would do so on his behalf after his execution. For Maximilian, the aim seems to have been to demonstrate that he acted not out of personal ambition but out of his desire and duty to serve.

The council discussed a plan for a massive breakout in the direction of the capital, but the idea was rejected as impractical. Even if the breakout succeeded, imperial forces, now outnumbered three to one, would be pursued all the way to the capital in a flight that could easily decay into catastrophic collapse.[43] Instead it was decided that Márquez would lead an elite cavalry group in a breakout that would reestablish communications with the capital.

Maximilian embraced this idea and within twenty-four hours drew up elaborate instructions.[44] First, Márquez was given the title "lieutenant-general of the empire," which gave him the power to speak for the emperor in all matters. Maximilian also drafted instructions for Márquez to carry and to give to others upon his arrival. As these instructions are quite detailed, they give us insight into Maximilian's state of mind and his expectations for the future.

First, politics. By this time Maximilian had lost confidence in Prime Minister Téodosio Lares, who had first suggested Maximilian's departure to Querétaro but who had done little to support imperial forces once they arrived there. Maximilian ordered him dismissed and replaced by Santiago Vidaúrri. Then, the war. In a sign that he anticipated a decline in security in the capital and did not expect to return any time soon, he ordered that certain valuable pieces of his personal property ("silver, carriages, horses, dishes, and the wine cellar") be inventoried and given to the English diplomatic mission for safekeeping. He also seems to have anticipated a prolongation of the siege. Complaining that quality reading material was not available in Querétaro, he requested that a "selection of good works" be brought back. He wanted "several copies of my speeches and letters" as well as a good map of Mexico. Also to be shipped—a "compendium of the laws of the Empire, the Military and Civil Code" as well as "the collection of official newspapers starting from the Regency up to this day." He also wanted "all decorations and medals" as well as the dies for them. Ditto for the dies for the imperial coinage. The trunk of his personal physician was also to be included.[45]

The impracticality of it all is astonishing. Did Maximilian expect Márquez—who was to escape besieged Querétaro in a mad dash at the head of an elite cavalry group—to return with a baggage train of maps, books, coins, dies, newspapers, and medals?[46] Did he expect republican forces to make way for his caravan as a personal courtesy? His instructions for the return to Querétaro had the nonchalance of an order for take-out.

Maximilian's capacity for faith in others also endured. Like Candide, for Maximilian, disappointment carried no lessons for the future. True, he expressed disdain for "the old wives" he had left behind in the capital and he dismissed Lares. But he merely transferred his confidence to others no more worthy—in this case, to Márquez. Márquez had created the disaster of Querétaro. Now he was being given a ticket out.

The date for the breakout was set for March 22. On the day before, the feast of San Benito, republican artillery fired celebratory shots in honor of Benito Juárez.[47] The next day Miramón led a diversionary attack toward the southwest, to the Hacienda del Jacal, from where he was able to haul back food and supplies.[48] That night, just after midnight on March 23, Márquez led twelve hundred of the best horsemen southward between El Jacal and Cimatario, the extinct volcano south of the city.

The Márquez sortie was successful. It even created confusion among republican forces who suspected that Maximilian might be among those who escaped. He wasn't, but the episode raised morale within the besieged city. True, their numbers were reduced by the departure of Márquez and the elite cavalry who accompanied him, but he would be back with cash and reinforcements in ten days, two weeks at the most.[49] There was now reason for hope.

The immediate effect of Márquez's departure was to hold imperial forces in place in the expectation of an imminent rescue; over the longer term, it meant the demoralization of imperial forces and a further reduction in their numbers. Republican forces continued to arrive, further shifting the balance of power against the besieged imperial forces and in favor of the republican forces encircling them. On April 1, a week after the departure of Márquez, Miramón ordered an attack to the north against San Gregorio hill. Forces led by Prince Salm, a Prussian volunteer, took the hill. As republican reinforcements arrived, the triumphant imperial forces withdrew. They hauled back some captured guns as trophies, but the victory was ephemeral and came at the cost of several dead and captured. The captured were shot. Their bodies were disposed of in a manner that was both brutal and profoundly demoralizing. Río Blanco flows through Querétaro from east to west. Republican forces dropped the bodies of the dead into the river east of the city, where they would drift downstream, terrorizing the population and spoiling the city's only remaining source of fresh water.[50]

Meanwhile, Márquez was nowhere to be seen. He had been ordered to send daily dispatches but none had been received. In fact, Márquez had arrived in Mexico City on March 27, just four days after his breakout from Querétaro.[51] Three days later, he left for Puebla, on the pretext that it was threatened by the forces of Porfirio Díaz.[52] Whatever his motives, he had abandoned his promise to return promptly to Querétaro.

None of this was known in Querétaro, and there was much speculation about what had happened and why his return might be delayed. There were also meetings to decide what to do, but these revealed new doubts and suspicions, regarding not only Márquez but also the remaining generals. Méndez and Mejía, both of Indigenous descent, expressed their suspicions about the ambitious creole Miramón, who seemed intent on repairing his reputation with heroic attacks, like the one on San Gregorio, which produced casualties but little of value. Méndez and Mejía advised Maximilian to escape to the Sierra Gorda, a mountainous, forested region northeast of Querétaro. There a loyal and sympathetic Indigenous population could sustain imperial forces indefinitely or, if need be, defend an escape to the coast.

But Maximilian could not bring himself to conclude that Márquez had betrayed him. He remained convinced that Márquez would appear at any moment. Rumors that Márquez was approaching circulated from time to time; these thoughts kept him pinned in place. On April 11 one such rumor prompted Maximilian to authorize an attack on the entrance gate to the city, the Garita de Mexico, convinced that Márquez would be approaching by that route.[53] The day ended with many casualties. Márquez was nowhere to be found.

In frustration, Maximilian authorized Prince Salm to break out in an attempt to get news from the capital. If he succeeded, he was to go to Mexico City and arrest Márquez if need be. The escape was scheduled for April 17, but it was poorly executed and encountered unexpected resistance. Again, on April 23 and 27, rumors of the arrival of Márquez prompted breakout attempts. On May 2 a rumor circulated that Generals Chacón, Olvera, and Márquez were approaching the city.[54] Such rumors were now greeted with skepticism. A few days earlier, an agent returned from the republican camp with news of Márquez, his march on Puebla, his subsequent defeat, and his retreat to Mexico City. There would be no rescue.[55]

By this time the hopelessness of the situation was becoming evident. Desertions were becoming routine. Out of an original force of more than ten thousand, Querétaro—and the empire—were now defended by fewer than five thousand men.[56] On May 5, republican forces surrounding Querétaro marked the fifth anniversary of the Mexican victory at Puebla with a loud celebration, followed by an attack on the city at 7 PM. The attack was turned back.

On May 13 it was decided that Maximilian would break out accompanied by high-ranking officers and a cavalry escort. The breakout was set for 3 AM on May 15. It was then postponed to the next day, but at 4 AM on May 15 Maximilian was awakened with the word that that republican forces had entered the convent of La Cruz. Roused from their beds, many members of the imperial party were able to escape and assemble on the plaza in front of the convent chapel.

Improbable as such an escape might sound, there are plausible explanations.[57] Samuel Basch, Maximilian's physician, was present during the attack and emphasized the confusion that accompanied it. He was not alarmed at the site of soldiers in republican uniform. He had grown accustomed to seeing soldiers in republican uniform in Querétaro, given that captured republican soldiers were conscripted into the imperial army and fought in their old uniforms. Besides, uniforms were rare given that "neither we nor the [republicans] had distinctive uniforms."[58] Even so, Basch was captured at La Cruz, while Maximilian escaped. It seems that the republican colonel Rincon Gallardo preferred not to have the responsibility for taking Maximilian prisoner and so allowed him and his immediate party to exit.[59] Not all had their horses, so the party proceeded on foot westward, in the direction of the Hill of the Bells. Masses of soldiers were closing in on their position when Generals Mejía and Castillo advised Maximilian to surrender. Lieutenant Colonel Augustín Pradillo improvised a white flag from a piece of tent material and began walking toward republican troops. General Corona, the highest-ranking officer present among the republican forces, accepted the surrender. Maximilian was told to mount his horse and return to the city under escort. On the way the group encountered General Escobedo with his staff. Maximilian presented his sword to Escobedo in a gesture of surrender.[60] After a brief exchange, Maximilian asked Escobedo for a private conversation, which Escobedo granted, and the two men distanced themselves from the group. "Would you allow me," Maximilian asked, "to make my way to the coast under escort and embark for Europe with the promise, on my word of honor, never to return to Mexico?" Escobedo replied that he could not do so. "Since that is how things are," Maximilian noted, "I hope that you will not allow me to be abused ("usted no permitirá que se me ultraje") and that you will treat me with the consideration due a prisoner of war." Escobedo replied enigmatically, "Eso es usted mío" (You are mine).[61]

14

◝◟◞

Empire on Trial

A LARGE CROWD GATHERED EARLY on the morning of June 13 in front of Querétaro's largest civic building. The words "GRAN TEATRO DE ITURBIDE" were painted in foot-high letters above three arched doorways. Given the immense interest in the trial of the captive emperor and his two generals Mejía and Miramón, the leadership of the republic had decided that Querétaro's theater, which accommodated hundreds of spectators, was the only practical venue.

It's hard to imagine a grander setting for such an event. The theater had been completed fifteen years earlier and was still relatively new. Tall wooden doors swung open to allow crowds to enter the lobby, where a chandelier lifted the eyes up toward a wrought iron balcony. Inside, the theater was all midcentury elegance. Box seats painted white with gold trim rimmed the U-shaped hall. A grand chandelier hung suspended four floors above the main seating area. Fluted columns supported the proscenium and framed the stage.

As the audience took their seats, they could see three stools on the left side of the stage facing a long table. Lighting came from four candelabras at the back of the stage and two on the judges' table, leaving the stools darker and partially backlit. On the right, Platón Sánchez, a lieutenant colonel, presided, supported by six uniformed captains. These were men of relatively modest rank, given the enormity of the occasion.[1] Perhaps that was the point—when it came to the tribunal, rank was incidental.

That the Teatro Iturbide was named for Mexico's first emperor was somehow fitting as a place of judgment for its last.[2] The crowd was eager to see the emperor, but when the coach arrived under armed escort at

Trial of Maximilian and Generals Mejía and Miramón. Museo Regional de Querétaro. Photo: R. Jonas

9 AM, only Generals Mejía and Miramón stepped out. Maximilian would plead indisposition, which may have been true as he suffered from ongoing health problems, but his main complaint was with the court-martial itself.[3] In his view, the key questions to be answered were political questions, which a military court was incompetent to answer. For a man accustomed to deference, everything about the trial seemed calculated to humiliate a man of his station.[4] The court decided to proceed without him.

At the time of his capture, it had not been obvious that Maximilian would be subjected to trial. A case could be made that, from Maximilian's point of view—and given the fading prospects of the empire—the point of the campaign all along had been political, not military. Once it became clear that the French intended to leave, Maximilian had looked for ways to mark himself off from the French. Impractical as it was, for a time he nurtured the idea of a national congress that would show real support for Maximilian and his empire.[5] Maximilian was keen to prove that he was not a tool of the French. The French—*they* were the occupiers. Maximilian was Mexican. That's why he stayed. A congress would prove that his power didn't rely on French bayonets. That was the political significance of the campaign.[6]

In his naïveté, Maximilian believed that, given the opportunity, he and Juárez could come to some kind of arrangement. The day after his capture, Maximilian told General Escobedo that he wanted to go to San Luis Potosí to speak with President Juárez; when Escobedo demurred, Maximilian followed up a few days later with a telegram to Juárez proposing a meeting.[7] This was not to be. Such a meeting implied the status of equals; Juárez would entertain no such idea. The gesture also reveals how badly Maximilian underestimated the gravity of the situation. Like Charlotte—who imagined that Juárez, like Garibaldi in Italy, would rally the people behind a national monarchy—Maximilian remained capable of magical thinking.[8] In his mind, the best outcome for Mexico would be for Maximilian and Juárez to hammer out an agreement to unite their movements, perhaps with Maximilian as head of state and Juárez as his prime minister.[9]

Although Maximilian was aware that execution was possible, he seems to have thought that the likeliest outcome was that he would be escorted to the coast. Concepción Miramón writes of a conversation between her husband and Maximilian early in their imprisonment. Maximilian came to her husband's cell with a fine bottle of cognac. He offered some to Miramón. The two men drank. In the conversation that ensued, Maximilian is said to have told Miramón, "No, General, don't think that an Austrian Archduke can be shot so easily; I'm sorry for you, but as for me, they'll put me in a . . . coach and send me to Veracruz."[10] Concepción Miramón doesn't give a date for the exchange, but calculations certainly changed on May 19. The night before, General Ramón Méndez, a prominent collaborator who had gone into hiding when Querétaro fell, was discovered in the basement of a private residence in the city. Méndez was responsible for atrocities, including the execution of one hundred republican prisoners in Michoacán the previous October.[11] He was executed at dawn.[12]

Méndez's execution put everything in a somber light. The day after the execution, General Escobedo summoned Maximilian. As Maximilian prepared for the meeting, the fate of Méndez and the possibility of execution were weighing on his mind; he left two documents with his physician, Samuel Basch, with instructions for how to handle them in the event he did not return. As it turned out, a lengthy conversation ensued between Escobedo and Maximilian. According to notes taken by his physician,

General Mariano Escobedo. Museo Nacional de Historia, Castillo de Chapultepec. Photo: R. Jonas

Maximilian used the occasion to enter into detailed negotiations for his departure. In return for safe transit to the coast, Maximilian would order the surrender of the final two bastions of the empire, Veracruz and Mexico City, and he would promise henceforth not to interfere in Mexican affairs. He also asked that imperial officers be spared.[13]

It's not clear how seriously Escobedo entertained such ideas, but a few days later he received explicit instructions; all three men were to be tried under the law of January 25, 1862.[14] This was an ominous turn. The law was drafted at the moment European troops arrived at Veracruz. It called for a court-martial and death sentence for anyone found to have aided the allies in any way. The law was designed to deter collaboration as "the Intervention" began, but it remained in effect for the duration, justifying the summary execution of prominent collaborators. Now, in the waning days of the empire, it was to be applied to Maximilian as well as to Miramón and Mejía.

The fact that there was to be a trial at all was something of a concession, because the law allowed for the execution of violators within twenty-four hours of arrest. In the days following their arrest, the prisoners took comfort from the mere fact that they were still alive, since, if they were going to be executed under the law, it ought to have happened promptly.[15] But this confidence was a misreading of the intent of republican leadership, which from the beginning understood the power of a trial in a global and historical context. A trial provided an occasion to educate the public—above all, international public opinion—regarding the crimes of the accused and the justice of the sentence to be passed. The charges were several: crimes against the independence and security of the nation; crimes against order and public peace; the violation of human rights (*el derecho de gentes*) and individual guarantees.[16]

Although immediate execution would have been within the law, Maximilian, in his naïveté, appears to have thought it would not be carried out. But officers of the Mexican republic had good reason to carry out a thorough trial. As President Juárez explained it, his government wanted to avoid the appearance of "precipitation and enmity" that the enemies of the republic could use against it. A trial would also mean that "the charges and defenses of the [accused] are recorded."[17] Even if Maximilian doubted that an execution would be carried out, people who were thousands of miles away could see the risks more clearly. In early April, weeks before Maximilian's arrest, Friedrich Hotze of Cincinnati wrote to Baron Wydenbruck, the Austrian representative in Washington. Hotze wanted Wydenbruck to petition Seward to intervene with Juárez so that, in the event of the capture of Maximilian, he would be treated as a prisoner of war, not as an insurgent.[18] It was one of the earliest such efforts; after Maximilian was captured on May 15 and the threat to Maximilian became concrete, a broad mobilization took place. Manuel Lozada, who had rallied to the empire as a protector of Indigenous rights, sought a pardon for Maximilian "in the name of all the Indigenous tribes of the Sierra Nayarit."[19] Giuseppe Garibaldi, the globally famous fighter for republicanism, and

Victor Hugo, the French literary giant, also drafted appeals to the Juárez government to grant clemency.[20] "Pardon him," urged Garibaldi, "as an example of the generosity of the people!" One of the editors of the *New York Herald,* George Church, urged Juárez to spare Maximilian, noting that "today Mexico has the opportunity to teach the world that it is more magnanimous than its enemies." Baron Magnus, the Prussian ambassador to Mexico, offered personal assurances that Maximilian would leave and never return. The Franco-Prussian War was looming and Maximilian's sense of betrayal by France was so great, Magnus argued, that if he were pardoned, he would return to Europe and enroll in the Prussian army to fight against France![21]

Matías Romero, Mexico's representative in Washington, argued against clemency, but he was plainly worried that the passage of time was working in Maximilian's favor. On June 8 Romero wrote to Juárez with a tone of impatience. "We have heard nothing about what has been done with Maximilian. It is necessary for him to be judged, condemned and not forgiven," he wrote. The US press favored clemency and was "treating us harshly." Fearing that the Mexican generals might be punished while Maximilian went free, he added, "There would be no justice in punishing [them] if Maximilian goes unpunished."[22] Romero seems to have underestimated Juárez, who never wavered despite multiple entreaties. Conchita Miramón, who had pleaded directly with Juárez, knew better. To her, the implacable Juárez was "like an Aztec idol"—that is, made of stone.[23] On June 13 Romero got his wish. The trial began.

The Trial

The defendants were tried together, but their legal defense was individual, and both Miramón and Mejía were questioned individually prior to the trial. (Maximilian refused.) When the proceedings got under way at the Teatro de Iturbide, the defense crafted by Mejía's attorney, Próspero Vega, advanced an argument in favor of clemency. "The sentence that you are going to pronounce will be a monument that honors yourselves," he argued. Referring to the deep political divisions in Mexico, he argued that Mejía was neither hero nor traitor, but something more complex calling for calm reflection. Vega tried to draw a distinction between the Intervention, which was foreign and treasonous, and the empire, which was fully Mexican. The empire was a de facto government. The true usurper was Napoléon III, not Maximilian.[24]

The fact that the men were tried side by side even though their cases were distinct encouraged the defendants to draw distinctions. Mejía, Vega pointed out, had never executed prisoners in his custody. (On this point, Miramón's record was notorious.) And he noted that Mejía had remained skeptical of the Intervention and aloof from the empire until "the flowers [and] the triumphal arches" convinced him that the empire was a matter of the national will.[25] Vega concluded his defense by calling for magnanimity from the court-martial, calling it an outcome that would honor the Liberal party's principles, notably its call for an end to the death penalty.[26]

Miramón's attorney, Ignacio Jáuregui, had a more challenging client. Miramón had made a career out of fighting the republic and the Reform, as well as their champion, Juárez. The trial would be used to hold him accountable not only for his service to the empire but also for his conduct as president of the republic.[27] Moreover, Miramón, as president, had concluded the disastrous transaction with the Jecker investment firm that had, arguably, saddled Mexico with the debt that had been used to justify the Intervention. Jáuregui began by establishing his republican bona fides, the better to bolster the argument he was about to make. He had lost a brother to the ferocity of Miramón and Márquez at Tacubaya during the War of Reform. If anyone was entitled to retaliation, it was Jáuregui. And he noted Miramón's affinity with the forces that had oppressed Mexico since the Conquest—the clergy, the army, the aristocracy—the very forces Juárez envisioned aligned against the revival of Anáhuac, Mexico before Cortés.[28]

Jáuregui's defense was historically rich. It spoke to the historicized view of the empire embraced by Juárez: the empire was not new; the empire was the return of the Spanish Habsburgs who had destroyed Anáhuac and imposed three hundred years of foreign rule.[29] It was, ironically, a view of the empire embraced by Maximilian himself, though in rosier terms. Where Juárez and most of his American contemporaries saw the return of a brutal, extractive colonialism, Maximilian insisted on a benevolent vision—the empire was the return of the Spanish Habsburgs who would restore Mexico to its former glory.[30]

Jáuregui's approach was unusual, especially as it involved dredging up the varied offenses against Mexico, its people, and the republic in which Miramón had been implicated. In the end, Jáuregui's defense rested upon three ideas. The first was the unacceptability of an ad hoc trial, which by definition involves a detour from the laws of the republic, which should weigh equally upon all. Jáuregui's defense also rested on the observation that the empire that Miramón served was an empire "of six months." It had taken shape with the departure of the French, was a fully Mexicanized empire, and was thus distinct from what had gone before, from the Intervention, during much of which Miramón had been absent. Finally, Jáuregui asserted that what happened in Querétaro was not sedition, but a war between two parties. Therefore, the rules of war should apply. Miramón is not a traitor, he is a prisoner of war, and if the aim was to pursue traitors, there was no shortage among "the spurious sons of Mexico," including Gutiérrez Estrada, Almonte, and Lares. As these men were beyond the reach of the law—or soon to be—the implication was that Miramón was being singled out solely because he was within reach. Finally, Jáuregui told the court that if it needed an example to follow, it should look northward to the United States where, in the aftermath of a bitter civil war, rancor had been set aside in favor of forbearance. Jefferson Davis was in prison, partly to protect him from popular vengeance, while General Robert E. Lee, the commander of rebel forces, was returning to civilian life.[31]

Miramón's second defender, Ambrosio Moreno, built on the idea that Miramón should be seen as distinct from those who hatched the idea of a foreign monarchy and conspired with the Europeans to bring it about. "When a handful of Mexicans voted for the establishment of a throne in Mexico, calling the Austrian archduke to occupy it, Miguel Miramón was not a member of this group; he wasn't even in the country," argued Moreno. And when he served the empire upon his return to Mexico, Miramón certainly made a political mistake, but it was not a crime. Miramón was exceptional in this regard, Moreno argued. He lacked the means to remain abroad while, upon his return to Mexico, his notoriety would prevent him from living modestly in obscurity; he had little option but to serve the empire. And when he served the empire, he never served alongside the French.[32]

As for Maximilian, his defense drew upon the service of several attorneys. Operating on the assumption that a conviction was inevitable, his legal team opted for a division of labor. Jesús M. Vázquez and Eulalio M. Ortega would present a defense at the court-martial; Mariano Riva Palacio and Rafael Martínez de la Torre would go to San Luis Potosí to lobby President Juárez for a delay of the trial and, failing that, a pardon.[33] When the session opened at the Teatro de Iturbide, Vázquez and Ortega attacked the constitutionality of the law under which the defendants were charged—the law of January 25, 1862—because the Constitution of 1857 had abolished the death penalty.[34] They also attacked the process. "Not a single witness has been examined, not a single document has been presented." They also warned that the charges against Maximilian were the result of the passions generated by war, not the sober reflection of men who upheld good republican ideals. Moreover, to impose capital punishment in his case would be ineffective, because the offender (Maximilian) is not an isolated man, but a figure within a party, an association, which would only reemerge in a new form.[35]

Ortega and Vázquez also referred to the example of the United States. "There is a great people on our continent, a profound teacher in the matter of free institutions," they wrote. In the treatment of Jefferson Davis, "a usurper of public power," the United States "presents a noble example to be imitated." Maximilian came to Mexico, they argued, believing "in good faith" that he was called to govern it.[36] The president of the Confederacy was, they argued, more culpable than Maximilian, yet he was treated with greater compassion.

The case against Maximilian was entrusted to Manuel Azpiroz, a lieutenant colonel, for whom we have a vivid description, thanks to Concepción Miramón, her powers of observation, and her deep animus toward the man who would order the execution of her husband. Señora Miramón arrived in Querétaro shortly after the arrest of her husband and sought permission to see him. She was directed to Azpiroz. She found him at his lodgings and later expressed her hostility through a detailed commentary on the man she met that day. "So I went to Azpíroz's house," she wrote. "He received me in shirt sleeves, wearing white pants [that were] quite dirty." On his feet were old slippers "revealing socks whose color I could not decipher." She guessed his age to be about thirty, adding, "I can't say anything about his manners, because he didn't have any. He received me lying on a sofa."[37]

Concepción Miramón had trouble concealing her enmity toward the man who controlled the fate of her husband. Whatever his personal habits, Azpiroz turned out to be a quite effective in his role as prosecutor. As he made his case before the tribunal in the Teatro de Iturbide, Azpiroz spoke directly to the conduct of the three men against the background of the law of January 25, 1862. Azpiroz hammered away at the contention that Maximilian responded to the will of the Mexican people. From the formation of the Assembly of Notables to the Regency, he pointed out how unrepresentative these bodies were and how they owed their authority to the military force supplied by the Intervention. In the face of the various overtures to accept the throne, he noted, Maximilian refused because it wasn't clear even to him that these invitations arose from the Mexican national will. It was only after receiving many testimonials—the Actas de Adhesión—from cities and towns did he accept the crown, although in doing so he failed to note that "all of the towns in which these votes were collected were invaded by French forces or by Mexican forces that were at the service of the French intervention." The Actas de Adhesión were orchestrated and coerced. Maximilian had chosen to overlook this when he accepted them as evidence that to "accept the imperial crown of Moctezuma and Iturbide" was to fulfill the wish of the people.[38]

Azpiroz went on to criticize the idea that somehow the empire could be separated from the invasion. "Even though [Maximilian] came without an army," Azpiroz noted, "the truth is that French forces seized part of our territory . . . protected his entrance, and lent him their support." Maximilian should be held accountable for the use of force, especially because he stood by as "settlements were looted and reduced to ashes." Azpiroz singled out for special mention the destruction visited upon the states of Michoacán, Sinaloa, Chihuahua, Coahuila, Nuevo León, and Tamaulipas. Worse, "this same foreign prince" denied republican forces the same consideration as belligerents that he was now requesting as defense against execution. Republican soldiers were treated as bandits, subject to immediate execution even when they surrendered. Azpiroz brought up the case of General José Arteaga, defeated at Santa Ana Amatlán and shot on October 21, 1865, just weeks after the Black Decree of October 3 calling for the execution of republican soldiers as insurgents.[39]

Azpiroz set the case of Maximilian apart from that of Jefferson Davis, echoing an argument made in Washington by Matías Romero. Romero defended the trial of Maximilian by pointing out how unlike his case was that of Davis. Davis was a mere rebel, Romero remarked. Maximilian was a rebel too, but he was not only that. If you want an analogous case in the United States, Romero argued, look to Andersonville prison camp where Captain Henry Wirz treated US prisoners of war with criminal contempt.[40] Wirz was tried, not for supporting the Confederacy, but for what we would call war crimes—specifically, the mistreatment of prisoners entrusted to him. Maximilian's "Black Decree" gave legal protection to those who killed republican prisoners of war; Wirz had boasted that he killed more Union soldiers than General Lee.[41] Wirz was executed on November 10, 1865.

The verdict of the court-martial was rendered on June 14. The three men were found guilty, a verdict that called for death. As the audience filed out of the Teatro de Iturbide, the accused were returned to their cells in the Capuchin monastery. Monasteries convert easily to prisons; they are constructed for the ages and the cells of nuns (or brothers) designed for penitential austerity easily serve as prisoners' cells. The cells at the Capuchin monastery carried pious names and so they remained at the time Maximilian, Miramón, and Mejía were committed to them. Maximilian was given the Santa Theresa cell, Miramón the Santa Rosa, and Mejía the somewhat obscurely named cell of Eleven Thousand Virgins (*Once mil Vírgenes*), in honor of the martyrdom of Saint Ursula.[42] The three whitewashed cells were similarly outfitted: a white pine table, a cot, chairs, and a water pitcher. Outside each room stood a sentry.

Mariano Escobedo set the date of execution for June 16. The three men prepared to die, but when the appointed hour came, no one arrived to conduct them to the place of execution.[43] A brief stay had been allowed.[44] The execution would take place on Wednesday, June 19.[45] There was relief at the announcement, but also anger. The three men had gone through the agony of preparing to die. Now they would have to endure it again. As Miramón saw it, the brief reprieve meant only that "they are going to kill us twice."[46] Maximilian used the time to thank his attorneys, to ask Juárez to pardon Miramón and Mejía, to ask his brother Franz Joseph to attend to the Belgian and Austrian volunteers, to write to the pope, and to arrange for the embalming and return of his corpse. He also wrote to Juárez to express the wish that his death would bring peace and tranquility to Mexico.[47]

There were final personal appeals to Juárez. Agnes Salm-Salm traveled for a third time to San Luis Potosí to appeal for clemency. Contrary to accounts of Juárez as unmoved and unmovable, Salm-Salm recounted a tearful Juárez. "It is not I who take his life, but the people and the law," he told her, as "tears ran down his face."[48] Concepción Miramón also made the journey to San Luis to make a personal appeal. Diplomatic appeals also failed.

On the day of the execution the prisoners awoke for Mass at 5 AM. Maximilian posted a final letter to President Juárez. He put a scapular—a religious object associated with protection from evil—in his breast pocket. The military escort arrived at 6:30 AM. The three men then entered the three carriages that would take them from the convent over rutted earth to the Hill of the Bells, the Cerro de las Campanas, to the west of Querétaro.

Maximilian's Firing Squad, 1867. Metropolitan Museum of Art, New York.

Mejía's wife had just given birth. She cradled the newborn in her arms as she watched her husband enter the carriage, then raised the infant to the window, running alongside as the carriage slowly pulled away.[49]

A troop of four thousand men had already established a protective cordon at the foot of the Cerro. The firing squad was in place when the carriages arrived shortly after 7 AM. The condemned alighted and walked to the place of execution. Maximilian gave the firing squad twenty pesos in gold with instructions to aim well. It was said that he was to have taken his place in the center, between Miramón and Mejía, but he offered the place of honor to Miramón instead.[50] Then Maximilian spoke. "I am going to die for a just cause, the independence and liberty of Mexico. May my blood end the misfortunes of my new country! Viva México!" Maximilian parted his blond beard, tossing each side over a shoulder to expose his chest.[51] Miramón also spoke. Mejía did not speak; he held a crucifix to his chest, then moved it aside as the order was given and the firing squad let loose its volley.

The day after the execution, General Escobedo ordered the firing squad to appear at Number 4, las calles de Cinco de Mayo in Querétaro for a photo portrait. The existence of the photo poses a riddle. Executioners often prefer anonymity as protection against reprisal. Yet these men allowed themselves to be posed carefully, with rifle crossing the body from right toe to left shoulder, left foot slightly forward, hands clasped in front. Their commanding officer stands to one side, his saber lowered, the tip touching the floor. We don't know who paid for the portrait or why it was thought that the moment should be preserved, but the singularity of the occasion was clear. More than five years after the allied landing at Veracruz, a *pelotón* of *mestizaje* had rendered justice to the blue-blooded scion who had come to rule them. With nothing to hide and nothing to fear, the men posed in full uniform with their weapons—bayonets fixed— looking directly at the camera.

15

Leaving Mexico

THE DRAMA OF QUERÉTARO—THE SIEGE, the surrender, the trial, the execution—was but one drama among many signaling the unraveling of empire. A parallel drama was unfolding in the capital, which largely lost communication with Maximilian after his departure for Querétaro and remained poorly informed of events there.

On March 27, just four days after his breakout from Querétaro, Márquez had arrived in Mexico City brandishing his new title—lieutenant-general of the empire.[1] He immediately imposed a forced loan on the population, an effort that was "largely successful."[2] Three days later, instead of returning to Querétaro as promised, Márquez left for Puebla, having given himself the mission to defend the city against the forces of Porfirio Díaz, who besieged the city.[3] Márquez failed miserably. Not only did Díaz take Puebla along with more than six hundred European defenders there, he also then turned to face Márquez. Díaz chased Márquez in his panicked retreat to the capital, arriving on April 14.[4]

Mexico City might well have fallen to a concerted effort, but Díaz chose not to take it by force.[5] His detractors claimed that he was afraid to try to take a city defended by European troops. It was a plausible argument. In his efforts to "Mexicanize" his army, Maximilian had taken only a handful of European soldiers with him to Querétaro, leaving behind many excellent soldiers to defend the capital. For Díaz, laying siege was also the prudent decision. Despite his recent success at Puebla, Díaz knew that it was easy to underestimate the challenges of urban warfare. Díaz also knew that the prize was not only the capital itself, but those within. Without sufficient cavalry, he wouldn't be able "control all the exits."

Austrian cavalry in the city, though seething under the command of Márquez, whom they regarded as untrustworthy and dangerously inept, posed a particular threat. Fast and feared, they could exploit the confusion of an attack, allowing prominent collaborators to escape. There was also the matter of Querétaro. The morale of those defending the capital would depend to no small extent on events in Querétaro, where the victory of Juarist forces grew more certain each day. Díaz, who had already made Chapultepec his headquarters, ordered the city encircled as he settled in for a long siege.[6]

Famine ensued within the capital. Grain vanished, as did stray dogs; horses were butchered. Hoarding was denounced. Ernst Tavera, an Austrian eyewitness, noted that "indifferent creoles" continued their evening promenades in the face of the suffering; wealthy backers of the empire were pressed to donate thousands.[7] Within a few weeks the situation became so desperate that the government ordered those possessing stocks of beans, lentils, rice, and corn to notify the government immediately or face denunciation before a War Council as "enemies of the people."[8] A makeshift butcher stand went up in the lobby of the Teatro Iturbide where rats and mice were sold, but as the economy ground to a halt under the siege, few could afford them. Death by starvation became a daily occurrence. One man's last willful act was to drag himself up the steps of the cathedral, where his lifeless body was later found.[9]

The state of siege blocked information as well as food. News got through, but it became difficult to disentangle truth from the rumor and falsehood that arrived with it. This perfectly suited General Márquez, who as Maximilian's lieutenant-general occupied a prominent and exposed position within the city as well as within national politics. He was determined to hold the European soldiers to their word to defend the capital as if his life depended on it—because it certainly did. Fearful of what the news of Maximilian's capture would do to morale in the capital, Márquez and the Conservative press withheld news of the fall of Querétaro for weeks.

In fact, the news of Maximilian's capture reached the US capital before it reached the people of Mexico City. In a letter to Matías Romero in Washington on May 26, Porfirio Díaz complained that the press in the capital "is still trying to deceive the people," denying reports of the fall of Querétaro and the capture of Maximilian.[10] In this Díaz was certainly correct. Just a few days before, the Conservative El Pájaro Verde ran a convincingly detailed account of the fall of Querétaro, followed by a disclaimer: "Estamos persuadidos de que todo es enteramente falso" (We are convinced that this is entirely false.)[11]

Márquez used confusion and the time it bought to extract money from rich supporters of the empire on the pretext that it would be needed upon the arrival of the emperor, who was expected at any moment.[12] Thus, in the absence of conclusive evidence that Maximilian had been captured—and in the presence of efforts to organize his escape—European troops remained loyal, albeit reluctantly, to General Márquez, even as he supported the most absurd fictions.[13] One rumor had it that Maximilian had escaped and was in the Sierra Gorda with General Mejía. In another, Maximilian had escaped and was on his way to liberate the capital.[14] The news prompted European troops to attempt a breakout from Mexico City on June 9, sustained by word that Maximilian was approaching. Finally, on June 17, one of the Austrian officers, Carl Khevenhüller, received a letter from Eduard Lago, the Austrian chargé d'affaires, attesting to the fact that Maximilian had been captured. Lago negotiated terms of surrender for the European troops—essentially, free and safe passage to the coast. The soldiers sought out Márquez, their commanding officer, for his permission. Márquez, informed of Maximilian's execution, signed a statement in which he acknowledged Maximilian's capture (though not his death), forthwith resigning as lieutenant of the empire.[15] (He would soon vanish.) The army of Porfirio Díaz entered Mexico City on June 21.[16]

But as the last bastion of the empire was falling, the empire of the imagination rose to take its place. In its final edition, the official newspaper of the empire, *El Diario del Imperio*, published a stirring call to its supporters. The piece carried the title "The Empire Lives On" and while it seemed to concede that the emperor had been captured, it insisted that the ideal endured. In a reassertion of the motto "The king is dead, long live the king" the article cited historical cases wherein monarchs had been captured, but whose monarchy survived them. What mattered, the author claimed, was that right prevailed: "The Empire with the strength of its principles and the power of its doctrines, and the goodness of its prince . . . triumphs and affirms itself."[17]

Evacuations

Alongside the events in Querétaro and Mexico City, a third drama unfolded as soldiers of the Intervention and the empire made their way out of Mexico. Some evacuating armies are victorious armies, but when the evacuating army has failed—as in the case of the European forces in Mexico—the risk is acute. The army acknowledges that it has failed its mission of conquest, and there is particular danger in that the population of the occupied country has a final opportunity for revenge. Sometimes there was no good solution for locals as power wobbled, shifted, and changed hands. In Matehuala, Gregorio Niño was assessed a penalty one thousand dollars for having given two hundred dollars to forces loyal to the republic who had threatened to confiscate some twenty thousand head of cattle.[18]

There were acts of reprisal—as there had been throughout the war and occupation—but those most vulnerable to reprisal were not the European occupiers but the Mexicans who had collaborated in the occupation. In general, these were individuals who had served in high-profile administrative or military roles and were left behind as occupying forces slipped away. Pedro Pruneda cites the cases of two officials who, after the evacuation of Durango, were charged with political crimes in Chihuahua and were executed.[19] In Oaxaca, Juan Pablo Franco, who had served as imperial prefect, was executed. An example was made of two villages accused of aiding the enemy—San Pedro Mixtepeque and la Galera were torched.[20]

Some European volunteers took advantage of the confusion of evacuation to take what they could. Back in the summer, Lieutenant Nestor Stassin took fifteen thousand francs from the regimental purse and deserted. In the view of Belgian consul Frederick Hooricks, self-dealing and corruption were common. "Very few" men could show "clean hands." He cited the example of soldiers buying animals in local markets, then reselling them to their unit at a profit.[21] A supply officer in Puebla took a thousand liters of wine intended for soldiers and sold it instead to merchants, pocketing the proceeds.[22]

Among the Austrian volunteers, Lieutenant Hofmeister was responsible for the funds allocated to the Austrian musical corps, $560 in all. In January 1867 he pocketed the funds and then, as his unit prepared to evacuate, he enlisted in the Imperial Mexican Army on the hunch—correct, it turns out—that he wouldn't be pursued.[23] The musical corps left their instruments at the prefecture of Orizaba.

The return of the troops was a complex enterprise. The European military presence had begun in December 1861. Since then, thousands of soldiers had arrived in dribs and drabs in the months and years to follow, with the final convoy of Habsburg volunteers arriving at Veracruz from

Trieste in May 1865.[24] Unlike the drawn-out arrival of these thousands, the departure of most of those soldiers would take place in just a few weeks. Thirty vessels departed France for Mexico between December 10, 1866, and January 11, 1867.[25] Their mission was to repatriate some twenty-five thousand men and their equipment. Of necessity, the evacuation included hundreds of European volunteers to the Belgian and Austrian corps. Maximilian's empire was insolvent and unable to pay for their return, let alone pay back pay, which in some cases amounted to hundreds of dollars.[26] Nor could they ensure their own safety as power passed from the empire to the republic on the route from Mexico City to Veracruz.[27] They threw themselves on the mercy of Bazaine and the French, who agreed to transport them to Brest and Cherbourg.

The convoys began with the departure of the *Rhône,* which left Veracruz on January 20, carrying many of the Belgian volunteers. The Austrian departures began the following day. The convoys continued until the middle of March, with ships leaving every day and sometimes two per day, until Marshal Bazaine left Veracruz with the last French forces on March 12.[28] Although the early departures headed for destinations like Brest and Cherbourg in northern Europe, later departures made for the Mediterranean, to the south of France (Toulon, Port-Vendres) or to North Africa (Algiers, Oran, Mers-el-Kébir), shuttling soldiers from one imperial deployment to another.

On average, the Atlantic crossing took thirty-nine days, though for vessels stopping over at Guadaloupe and Martinique the duration was closer to fifty-five days. Given the compressed time frame of the departures (fifty days from first to last) and the duration of the crossing, most of the French forces were still at sea when Bazaine, in the final vessel, departed. It was a massive undertaking. In just a few weeks, twenty-five thousand men were repatriated in the most ambitious transatlantic military crossing until the Great War.

Not all French soldiers returned with Bazaine's mass repatriation. Some chose to join Maximilian's army and were taken prisoner at Querétaro and held there. Others were held in Guanajuato, Zacatecas, or San Luis Potosí. All were released in the weeks and months to come.[29] A few stayed on and made their lives in Mexico. Thomas Vogel, a tailor by trade, took up residence in Aguascalientes and started a tailoring business. Pierre Barnoin married and stayed in Guanajuato.[30]

Apart from those repatriated with Bazaine in early 1867, there is no precise accounting of the whereabouts of all of the European volunteers.

There are, however, broad figures. Of the original six thousand "Austrian" volunteers, about thirty-six hundred repatriated. Of the remainder, some had been lost in catastrophic engagements like Camargo where, of three hundred Austrians engaged in protection of the convoy, only three were known to have reached Veracruz.[31] Many were casualties in lesser conflicts. Some one thousand were either prisoners or had deserted and joined the army of the Mexican Republic. About eight hundred chose to remain in the service of the empire. Of those who chose to remain as soldiers of the empire, most were captured either at Querétaro or Mexico City. They were released by the Juárez government in August 1867. They returned over the following year, "countless stragglers, individually and in small groups, half-starved and dressed in rags."[32] About a hundred chose to remain as civilians in Puebla.[33] The remainder were assumed dead.

A few survived only to die on the return voyage to Europe. Louis Schoenmaker joined the imperial Mexican army in January 1867, after serving in the Belgian volunteers. He served with distinction during the defense of Mexico City and received the Order of Guadalupe for military merit. When the city fell, he was taken prisoner by Porfirio Díaz. When he was released, he made his way to Veracruz and boarded the *Panama* along with other veterans of the empire's final combats. He died of yellow fever during a stopover in Havana.[34]

Many of those who completed the voyage to Europe arrived destitute, prompting awkward exchanges between officials in port cities and diplomatic representatives of their home countries. When the *Panama* arrived at Saint Nazaire in September 1867 carrying dozens of former prisoners, Alphons Kodolitsch, the ranking officer on board, told port officials in Saint Nazaire that he and his officers were penniless. He boldly asked for "at least 200 francs" per man, a sum that implied a request for back pay.[35] The request was denied. Everyone arriving aboard the *Panama* was shuttled to quarantine while the French Ministry of War was asked for guidance. Most on board were members of a nominally "Austrian" unit that included men of many nationalities. Were they the responsibility of the Habsburgs? What, for example, was to be done with forty-four Prussian volunteers? And twenty-seven Belgians? Six Italians? Vienna assumed responsibility for Habsburg subjects, but not for volunteers from other countries who served as "Austrian" volunteers. Confusion ensued. The Belgian consul in Paris refused aid to Belgian returnees; municipal authorities in Nantes, the nearest city, received notice that the Belgian returnees were to be released as indigents. As for those claiming status as Prussian subjects, the Prussian consul was on his way to verify their claims and rights to repatriation. Those rejected by the Prussian consul were likewise to be released as indigent. The Italian vice-consul authorized repatriation payments to six Italians. As for the Habsburg/Austrian volunteers, a special train was organized to take them as far as Strasbourg; from there they could make their way to Salzburg and on to Habsburg lands.[36] The Austrian press underscored the tragic aspect of their experience, "A horde of crippled and sick men, barely clothed . . . is marching through Germany . . . toward [home]. . . . More than half of those who went to Mexico . . . stayed there. Their bones bleached in the hot earth."[37]

Soldiers arriving at Bremerhaven were better off in the sense that they still had some cash, but once in town they were fleeced by poor exchange rates. At Le Havre, soldiers disembarked barefoot, wrapped in blankets. They received a bread ration, clothes, and 59 centimes a day for personal expenses.[38]

Arrivals at Trieste were tightly managed, in part because of memories of misbehavior when the volunteers departed for Mexico, but also because the soldiers were angry about missing weeks of back pay. Their mood was no better when they were given temporary lodging in barracks, where they were offered a chance to continue their military service, this time in the Austrian army. All but a few responded with derision. Those who declined enlistment were sent home with pocket money, characterized as an advance on what they were owed by Mexico. Volunteers from Venice were a special case. They were Habsburg subjects when they departed, but Venezia became Italian while they were away. They were stateless when they returned. Italy took them in.[39]

In Vienna, where Austrian national public opinion was shaped and articulated, the attitude toward anything associated with the failed Mexican adventure was ambivalent and sometimes cruel. When the news of Maximilian's execution broke, there was shock, but also a clinical nonchalance. In its obituary for Maximilian, *Neue Frei Presse* remarked that Maximilian "preferred to be first in Mexico, [rather] than second in his own country."[40] True enough, but cold. As for the returning volunteers, now commonly referred to simply as "the Mexicans," they could expect little better. Alphons Kodolitsch was warned of the hostile mood in a letter from his mother. "The Mexicans [the veterans] can expect nothing good," she warned. In the streets of Vienna, a clever but cruel play on words was making the rounds: "Mexikaner—mog sie kaner" (Mexicans—nobody likes them).[41]

Some returned disabled. Some never returned. Three hundred to four hundred families were without a husband or father. A "Support Committee for the Widows and Orphans of the Fallen in Mexico" formed to accept and disburse donations.[42] Archduke Karl Ludwig chaired the "Association to Support the Disabled soldiers Returning from Mexico." Donors were spurred on when the *Wiener Zeitung* began to publish the names of donors and the amounts donated. Not everything depended on private donations. The Ministry of War offered benefits to widows and orphans but the process was cumbersome, likely deliberately so; it required presentation of birth and death certificates as well as proof of financial need.[43]

Of the women who had volunteered to serve in the Belgian legion, two had married while in Mexico and one had given birth there. Juliette Kreitz had been wounded in the fighting at Morelia in 1865 and would be put forward for a medal of military merit.[44]

The Sudanese soldiers "loaned" by Egypt to Napoléon III returned at the same time, although, somewhat surprisingly—and unlike the European volunteers, who were ignored or worse—they were fêted in Paris before returning to Egypt. The Sudanese arrived in the French capital on May 4, in the middle of the festivities surrounding the Universal Exposition of 1867, which had opened the month before.[45] They were lodged at Les Invalides and, in contrast with destitute European volunteers, the French treasury came up with back pay. Their activities included a military parade through the city along a route that included the Austerlitz Bridge, recently reconstructed and enlarged. After six days in Paris, on May 10 they boarded the *Seine*—the same vessel that had taken them to Mexico four years earlier—for the voyage back to Alexandria.[46]

Not everyone leaving Mexico had played a combat role. Antonio Labastida, the archbishop of Mexico who had led the campaign to persuade Maximilian to stay, was among the first to depart, seizing the opportunity to leave as part of the French evacuation.[47] Labastida, of course, had deeply compromised himself by collaborating with the imperial project from the beginning. In exile in Rome, he had moved in Mexican royalist circles and was a major player, along with Gutiérrez and Hidalgo, in the campaign to put Maximilian and Charlotte on the throne. Once the Intervention was begun, he returned to Mexico only after Juárez and the chief officers of the republic had been chased from the capital. His efforts were crowned when he was named regent of the empire. By the end of 1866, with the empire collapsing and Maximilian nearly halfway to the

The Sudanese battalion crosses the Pont d'Austerlitz. *Reproduced from* Le Monde illustré, *May 18, 1867.*

coast, Labastida had connived with Lares, Fischer, and others to persuade him to stay, prolonging Mexico's agony. If the Juárez government drew up a list of prominent collaborators ripe for retribution, Labastida's name would have been on it, among those at the top. It wasn't necessary to be Mexican to feel resentment toward prominent collaborators like Labastida. Léon de Montluc, the French representative to Mexico prior to the Intervention, went so far as to write directly to Juárez, calling out unnamed Mexicans who fostered "fatal illusions" who ought rightly to be the "first victims" of their own conduct.[48]

Certainly Labastida felt his personal danger acutely. After convincing Maximilian in January to return to the capital for his final bid to save the empire, Labastida joined those heading for the exits. He left the diocese of Mexico City without an archbishop, just as he left Maximilian to his fate. His hasty departure didn't go unnoticed. When Labastida slipped away aboard one of the French evacuation vessels, the satirical newspaper *L'Orquesta* asked innocently whether Labastida had taken a new position as chaplain of French troops. By early March Labastida had reached Havana and safety. He wrote to Cardinal Antonelli, the papal secretary of state, to explain his departure and to announce his plans to travel to Rome to convey to the pope in person "other weightier reasons" for abandoning his flock. Whatever those weightier reasons might have been, they were not urgent; in the same letter, Labastida noted that he would be stopping over at Cádiz and Seville, unless His Holiness insisted other-wise.[49] The main thing for Labastida, it seems, was that he was no longer in Mexico.

General Leonardo Márquez was certainly the great prize to be obtained after the capitulation of the capital, but he managed to escape Porfirio Díaz and his soldiers. According to Sara Yorke Stevenson, when the cap-ital fell, Márquez evaded his pursuers by hiding in a cemetery, where he hunkered down in an unoccupied plot. He escaped his early grave and slipped away to Cuba, where he lived out his days.[50]

Confederate settlers interpreted the French departure much as everyone else did. Many had already been discouraged by what they found in imperial Mexico, which bore little resemblance to what they had been promised. Forces loyal to the Mexican republic were keen to discourage settlers, notably by enhancing their sense of insecurity. In May 1866 troops commanded by Brigadier General Luis Pérez Figueroa attacked and captured Confederate settlers near Orizaba. The captives—effectively squatters occupying dilapidated haciendas at Omealca and Toluquilla—protested that they were US citizens, though recently in rebellion, and demanded release. Then someone found colonization papers among the captives, along with other clear evidence of intent to become subjects of the empire. Figueroa and his men marched their twenty-nine prisoners to Oaxaca, using money taken from the captives to meet payroll.[51] The pris-oners were eventually released, but by then they had lost all stomach for the adventure of settlement. They returned to the United States, taking their harrowing story of captivity with them—likely as Figueroa intended—while the spirits of Confederate settlers who remained were considerably dampened.

Such incidents made it painfully evident that the empire could not pro-tect the settlers it had invited; the departure of the French truly signaled the end for all but a handful. Former Missouri governor T. C. Reynolds remained in Mexico City and General Joseph Shelby was still in Córdoba, but Governor Harris moved on to Cuba. General Jubal Early traveled down the road to Veracruz, where he caught a boat to Havana.[52] Major General Thomas Hindman, who had railed against "federal power" and vowed never to return to the United States, retracted his vow a year later and returned.[53] Return to the United States was out of the question for Judge Perkins, who, out of spite, had torched his plantation in Louisiana and "made a desert" of it before leaving.[54] He decided to try Paris. Con-federate Major John Edwards returned to New Orleans in March 1867, predicting the collapse of the empire in four months, a prediction that proved to be optimistic by a few weeks.[55]

Some Europeans made their way to Vienna in the hope of finding sympathy and compensation for their efforts. Agnes Salm had led efforts to gain clemency for Maximilian after his capture or, failing that, to plot his escape. After Maximilian's execution, she was deported to New Orleans; from there she made her way to Europe, where she joined her husband, Prince Salm, also deported. Keenly aware of the value of her story, she published a collection of journal entries and recollections in 1867, within months of her arrival. She made her way to Vienna, where in February 1868 she was able to secure an audience with Maximilian's mother, Archduchess Sophie. She told Sophie all that she knew and all that she had done and was awarded an annual pension of twelve hundred dollars.[56] She was widowed two years later when Prince Salm died in the Franco-Prussian War, his third war in ten years. She remained in Europe and married a British diplomat, Charles Heneage—they soon divorced.[57] After a storied life abroad, she was back in the States by the end of the century, bearing all the acquired prestige of European nobility. She gave interviews and made public appearances—billed as a "real American princess"—in Cleveland, Des Moines, and Chicago. She continued to scandalize, notably by riding a bicycle. She had some thoughts on empire to share, too. The United States, recently successful in the war against Spain, should withdraw from the Philippines.[58]

Augustín Fischer also made his way to Vienna, by a circuitous route. After Maximilian left for Querétaro, Fischer's power, which depended on proximity to the emperor, waned.[59] By one account Fischer sought appointment as bishop of Durango, which would have assured him of a comfortable existence after the fall of the empire, but Maximilian had soured on him. "Father Fischer lied to me," Maximilian said when he learned of Fischer's deceit involving the concordat.[60]

After the fall of Mexico City, Fischer was imprisoned in a former convent, La Enseñanza, along with other high-profile supporters of the empire. He retained possession of some portion of the imperial archives and was eventually released—having curried favor by promising to write a history of the empire from the republican point of view. When Habsburg officials asked him to relinquish the archives, he declined, offering to deliver them to Vienna himself. Once in Vienna, he seems to have sought a job at court; but he was widely regarded as having played a crucial role in persuading Maximilian to remain in Mexico, and therefore he was spurned. France was no more hospitable. In Spain, Alfonso XII offered him two high-status positions: chaplain at El Escorial and confessor to the queen. Fischer declined.[61] He lived for a time in Stuttgart, Tübingen, and Ulm. It is also said that Fischer bought Schloss Giessen—a castle in what is today part of Baden-Württemberg.[62] The story sounds improbable, but given that so much that is improbable about Fischer turns out to be true, one hesitates to discount it. By 1878 Fischer was back in Mexico, where he resumed his priestly vocation as pastor in Taxco, a lovely colonial mountain town known for its silverworks. By 1883 he was back in Mexico City, serving as pastor at San Antonio de las Huertas until his death two years later.[63]

Epilogue

The Hill of the Bells

Franz Kaska boarded the steamship *Prinz August Wilhelm* in Hamburg on a damp November day in 1903. The ship's manifest listed his profession as *Apotheker* (pharmacist), a modest descriptor that masked a complex life story. Kaska had booked a first-class cabin and insisted on registering as "*von* Kaska," for he was now a baron, ennobled in gratitude for service to the Habsburgs in both Mexico and Vienna.[1] The medals he wore gave proof.

When Kaska boarded the *Prinz August Wilhelm,* he might have intuited that this Atlantic crossing would be his last. He was portly, stooped, and bald except for a wispy half-crown of hair at the collar—nothing like the energetic young man who had left as a volunteer for Mexico nearly forty years earlier. Then again, the first-class accommodations carrying Baron von Kaska to Veracruz by way of Le Havre, Coruña, and Havana were a vast improvement over the narrow bunk he had endured when he shipped out from Trieste.

Kaska was fulfilling a duty of memory. No one embodied the dream of Habsburg Mexico better than Emperor Maximilian, but by 1903 Maximilian had been dead thirty-six years—cut down at the age of thirty-four. Kaska was fulfilling a promise as much to himself as to the memory of Maximilian when he returned to Mexico to participate in the solemn consecration of a memorial chapel. When he died in Mexico City three years later, the chapel ensured his memory.

Franz Kaska had joined the Freiwilligen Korps in 1864, but unlike so many volunteers who had returned maimed, penniless, and in rags, Kaska

257

was anything but down on his luck. His life story was one of adventure, wealth, and prestige. As a young man Kaska had wasted no time getting out of Horažďovice, his hometown west of Prague. He was in his early twenties when he reached Vienna, where he completed advanced degrees in pharmacy and chemistry. His education and profession assured him a comfortable life in Austria, but he chose adventure instead. He joined the volunteers as a pharmacist, ingratiated himself with Maximilian, and was on the verge of entering the inner circle of power when Maximilian undertook his final march to Querétaro. There's no evidence that he followed Maximilian on his final, desperate drive to save the empire. Like many other European volunteers, Kaska likely stayed in Mexico City as part of the force assigned to the defense of the capital. When the empire collapsed, Kaska declined repatriation. He accepted amnesty from the Juárez government and stayed in Mexico. He opened a pharmacy on calle Espíritu Santo (today Isabel la Católica) in Mexico City and built a wholesale pharmaceutical business. He prospered. In time he became one of the pillars of Mexico's Austrian expat community—a diverse group defined by shared culture of origin, an allegiance to Maximilian, and a determination to make a future in Mexico.[2]

To build a chapel to honor Maximilian was unthinkable in the aftermath of his trial and execution in 1867. Once taken into custody by the forces of the Mexican Republic, Maximilian was instrumentalized, to be jailed, tried, and condemned as the embodiment of the evils visited upon Mexico since 1861. There was little doubt about the outcome. As Maximilian awaited execution, international luminaries such as Victor Hugo and Giuseppe Garibaldi appealed directly to Juárez for mercy, to no avail.[3] Benito Juárez was determined that only the death of Maximilian—its finality captured by the new medium of photography—would send an emphatic message to Europe.

Even in death, the body of Maximilian remained contentious. When Austrian vice-admiral Wilhelm von Tegethoff, a personal friend from Maximilian's navy days, arrived in Mexico to retrieve the body in late August, a standoff ensued. The Juárez government wanted to know by what authority Tegethoff claimed Maximilian's body. Tegethoff responded that he acted on behalf of Maximilian's mother and brother—that is, in a strictly personal capacity. His request was refused for reasons that seem petty—he had no formal, written authority from the Austrian government to take custody. But given that the premise of the empire from the beginning had rested on simply ignoring the existence of the Republic of Mexico,

Juárez knew there was a point to be made. Mexico would not release the body until the republic was recognized formally, in writing, by the Austrian government or by Maximilian's family.[4] (Since they amounted to much the same thing, the distinction was moot.)

As this drama was playing out, Tegethoff was approached by Doctor Vicente Licéa, a physician from Querétaro. As Maximilian faced execution, he had asked that in death his body be embalmed so that his mother might gaze upon him a final time. Doctor Licéa was given the job, but the process turned to scandal when Licéa decided to sell pieces of clothing and locks of hair as a side gig. This commerce in souvenirs and relics seems to have gone unpunished, though not unremarked, until Licéa approached Tegethoff with a list of goods for sale.[5] The items included a ribbon of red silk, stained with blood; a bloodstained vest; a pair of white underpants with a bullet hole; a plaster death mask. Asking price? Fifteen thousand dollars. Tegethoff denounced Licéa to Mexican authorities. Licéa was arrested, charged with fraud, and imprisoned. At trial he presented himself as the faithful guardian of these personal effects, items that might otherwise have been sold by unscrupulous persons. He was convicted of fraud and sentenced to time served.[6]

By the time of the Licéa verdict, Tegethoff and Maximilian's remains were long gone. A formal letter had arrived in Mexico City as requested; it was presented to the government and Maximilian's remains were released. Tegethoff took custody on November 10, 1867; then he and Maximilian's body began the slow journey to the coast. At Veracruz, Maximilian's casket was placed in the sanctuary of a parish church, where it could be opened in Tegethoff's presence. The outer casket of wood was opened to reveal an inner casket of zinc, which opened to reveal a final casket of rosewood, which contained the body. Tegethoff verified the body as Maximilian's, the caskets were closed, and the journey resumed.

On the twenty-sixth of November, when Maximilian's remains were taken on board the *Novara* and the long voyage back to Vienna began, more than five months had passed since the execution, ample time to plan funeral arrangements. A grand reception awaited. A naval escort met the *Novara* in the Adriatic and accompanied it to the harbor at Trieste. Dockside, a funeral cortège, including musicians, led the procession of Maximilian's casket through the streets to the train station. A special funeral train to Vienna had been arranged. It would make a journey of five and a half hours, starting early in the afternoon and arriving in Vienna by evening. The timetable was shared by the press so that mourners could meet the train at one of eighty-six stops, three to thirty-eight minutes in duration, the longer stops for cities like Ljubljana, Graz, and Marburg. In the countryside, mourners waited by the tracks to pay their respects as the train rolled by.[7] In Vienna, ceremonies included interment in the Habsburg family crypt of the Capuchin church—admission by ticket only.[8]

The exaggerated punctiliousness with which the Juárez government had handled the transfer of Maximilian's remains to Tegethoff meant that animosity between Mexico and Austria only worsened. All major European powers followed Austria in breaking diplomatic relations with Mexico. Mexico's diplomatic isolation from Europe eased in 1869 when Prussia resumed normal contact, followed by Italy a few months later. France and England restored relations with Mexico only in the 1880s.[9] For Austria, it was later still. Emperor Franz Joseph, Maximilian's brother, would not countenance diplomatic relations with Mexico until Mexico atoned for its actions. Given the persistence of Habsburg resentment, the thaw in Austro-Mexican relations would have to take place at the level of persons, not states. When Franz Kaska left Hamburg for Mexico that wet day in 1903, he was nearing the end of efforts to mend relations.

In a strange way, it was Maximilian himself who restored relations between Austria and Mexico—posthumously, of course—because it was the necessity of working together on his memorial chapel that fostered reconciliation. Given that Maximilian's body had long ago been laid to rest alongside his Habsburg ancestors in the Capuchin crypt in Vienna, the memorial would be a cenotaph. Without the body, the structure and its location would carry the weight of meaning. They would have to speak on their own. The execution site in Querétaro was the obvious location for such a memorial. The Cerro de las Campanas (Hill of the Bells) had been chosen for execution because it was an easily secured location outside the city of Querétaro, with the hill as a backdrop for the execution itself. Today, Cerro de las Campanas is fully within the city of Querétaro, bounded on three sides by the Universidad Autónoma de Querétaro. But thirty years after the execution, the Cerro was still at a remove. More than a quarter mile of scrub and farmland separated the city from the execution site.

The idea of using the execution site to remember Maximilian, though discouraged officially, occurred almost immediately after the execution. A witness who visited the execution site three days later observed stones and crosses fashioned from sticks marking where Mejía, Miramón, and Maximilian had stood—a claim corroborated by photographic evidence.[10]

Another witness said that on the night of the execution "Indians from the area" had erected a memorial, including a "pillow of leaves" on the spot where the emperor's head first touched the ground when he fell.[11] Yet another witness recalled the pre-*conquista* practice of constructing memorials, *momuxtles* in Náhuatl, in memory of the dead. In time, memorial markers of carved stone took their place. Eventually these were enclosed by a half-height iron fence, an effort credited to Emilia Soto, a pious local.[12] A more substantial memorial would take years of effort.

As Kaska built his pharmacy business, he remained devoted to the memory of Maximilian and the empire, which he nurtured through newspaper articles and memorial masses celebrated on the anniversary of the execution.[13] The masses were celebrated at the church of Santa Brigida (demolished in the 1930s) in Mexico City; black-trimmed invitations bearing the imperial seal were printed. Kaska had sent them to known supporters of the empire as part of an effort to use the anniversary to keep a community of memory alive.[14] Such efforts dovetailed with those undertaken by the conservative Catholic establishment in Mexico, whose newspaper, *La Voz de México,* wove an elaborate redemption narrative around Maximilian with Maximilian himself in the role of redeemer.[15] This narrative dated back to the days following Maximilian's execution when it was claimed that Maximilian had been betrayed, like Jesus in Gethsemane, with Colonel Miguel López in the role of Judas. The story rested on a kernel of truth—Maximilian, in the interest of minimizing bloodshed, had tasked López with exploring options for surrender with Mariano Escobedo, commander of republican forces. López indeed met with Escobedo, at Maximilian's request. But the rumor alleged that instead López, in exchange for payment, had provided information that facilitated the nighttime assault of republican troops on La Cruz. Never mind that Escobedo went on record denying that López was culpable, never mind that Querétaro was teetering on the edge of collapse. The myth that the city had fallen because of treasonous betrayal—and had taken a pious vision of Mexico with it—was just too good to let go. Mexico, in the person of López, had proven itself unworthy of salvation. The dark forces of the republic had prevailed.[16]

This redemption narrative piggybacked on a lively ongoing interest in Maximilian, an informal and unsanctioned veneration of his memory— effectively, a popular canonization built upon celebrity, tragic betrayal, and remorse. A robust trade in relics included locks of Maximilian's hair as well as secondary relics—items said to have touched his cadaver.[17]

Meanwhile, Kaska cultivated his contacts, and in time he found a powerful ally at the highest reaches of political power in Mexico.

When Porfirio Díaz returned to power as president of Mexico in 1884, he and Kaska were already on friendly terms, though they had met as enemy combatants years before. As a young man, Díaz had made a name for himself for his role in the historic defense of Puebla on May 5, 1862. Díaz was taken prisoner after the fall of Puebla a year later, but like dozens of others he escaped, avoiding deportation to France. Within days of his escape, Díaz was back in the fight, serving as an officer in the Mexican insurgency. Díaz remained in opposition after the arrival of Maximilian and Charlotte. When Díaz was taken prisoner at Oaxaca in 1865, Franz Kaska was one of the hundreds of Austrian volunteers charged with se-curing the city and managing the prisoners, although it is unknown whether the men met face to face. Díaz eventually escaped to continue the fight. He commanded the Mexican forces that encircled Mexico City while Maximilian was entrapped and besieged at Querétaro.

Both men prospered after the fall of the empire—Díaz in politics, Kaska in business—and their social circles overlapped.[18] By the end of the 1890s they were hunting companions. Kaska was invited to social events hosted by Díaz and his new wife, Carmen Romero Rubio.[19] At some point one of the men broached the subject of the memorial chapel.

On the face of it, the construction of a chapel in honor of Maximilian was no more likely under Porfirio Díaz than under Benito Juárez. Díaz had served under President Juárez as a young officer. He fought to drive out the French and played a key role in toppling Maximilian. But unlike Juárez, whose Jacobin-style republicanism made him an implacable enemy of the Catholic Church, Díaz's relationship with Catholicism was more complicated. Anti-clericalism was obligatory in the republican politics of Mexico—and thus obligatory for Díaz—but that public posture contrasted with his pri-vate Catholic sympathies, a paradox not uncommon in republican circles. That Díaz would have been raised Catholic is not surprising—Juárez had been also—but Díaz came from a prominent and devoutly Catholic family in Oaxaca and remained in Catholic orbits. As a young man Díaz had contemplated a Catholic vocation, inspired by the example of his cousin and *padrino* José Agustín Domínguez, a parish priest.

The patriotic war against the United States in 1846 prompted a shift in young Porfirio's politics. As for many of his generation, the US inva-sion inspired an ardent patriotism. Díaz began to move in "Red" or "Ja-cobin" republican circles in Oaxaca. To the great disappointment of his family, Díaz abandoned his priestly vocation, joined the National Guard, and embarked on a military career. His cousin and religious sponsor, José Agustín Domínguez, effectively disowned him.[20]

Despite his lifelong association with Liberal politics and his service to the Juárist and republican cause during the empire, Díaz's association with Catholicism endured in private. By the 1880s this public/private paradox was obliterated when Díaz remarried in a way that signaled a reconciliation with the Catholic Church. Díaz's first wife had died from complications of childbirth in 1880. When Díaz remarried the following year, his marriage was blessed by Archbishop Pelagio Antonio de Labastida y Dávalos, patron of the empire and member of Maximilian's imperial regency.[21] With Archbishop Labastida and Franz Kaska, Díaz could now count as friends men who had once been among the most fervent enemies of the Mexican republic.

It is possible that this reunion of former foes was a predictable turn for canny survivors whose politics turned pragmatic in late middle age, but for Díaz there was likely something else drawing him toward the imperial legacy—namely, the imperial form itself. Díaz came to power in 1876 and, except for a four-year hiatus, would hold power until 1911. It was a period so dominated by the personality of Porfirio Díaz that it is remembered, simply, as the Porfiriato. As head of state, Díaz recognized the law when it suited him and ignored it when it didn't, subverting the Mexican republic in the name of order and progress. For Díaz himself, it is possible that he imagined his own brand of progressive presidentialism as a worthy descendant of Maximilian's liberal monarchy.

Whatever the mix of piety and self-interest, Díaz was sympathetic to the memory of Maximilian. He also wanted to restore diplomatic relations with Austria, the last of the major European powers to withhold recognition. He enlisted his friend Franz Kaska as go-between. Kaska broached the issue during a visit to Vienna in 1889, when he secured a private audience with Franz Joseph, brother of the late emperor of Mexico.[22] Franz Joseph was clear. The Habsburgs were not ready to forgive. They would insist on an act of contrition, a gesture to expiate the crime committed against Maximilian.

Powerful as he was, a public statement of apology was out of the question for President Díaz. In time, the idea for an alternative form of expression emerged. The construction of a memorial chapel became the means by which reconciliation could take place, but it would have to be handled with great delicacy. Díaz conferred upon Kaska the authority to

Porfirio Díaz, presidential portrait. *Museo Nacional de Historia, Castillo de Chapultepec. Photo: R. Jonas*

build a chapel. He also advanced the means. He put at Kaska's disposal funds drawn upon a New York bank, but with origins in discretionary funds controlled by Díaz. No Mexican official would take part in the effort to build the chapel. The mere fact of its existence—Mexican accommodation of a memorial chapel—would manifest a spirit of atonement.[23]

These efforts were crowned in October 1898 when Kaska voyaged to Querétaro to lay the first stone of the memorial chapel in honor of Maximilian.[24] In the intervening years, Kaska had used his connections in the expatriate business community in Mexico to generate support and to prepare public opinion. The month before the laying of the first stone, the French-language newspaper *Courrier du Mexique* carried an announcement of the proposed chapel, suggesting that the initiative came from Vienna by insisting that it was being built "at the direction" of Franz Joseph. Construction was moving forward "at the expense of some friends of the deceased emperor," which neatly obscured Díaz's role. The *Mexican Herald,* which served a resident American readership in Mexico City estimated at twenty-five thousand, carried the story of Kaska's voyage to Querétaro in its edition for October 25, 1898, claiming that the chapel would "have no political significance whatever." The *Herald* alluded to the potential for controversy ("there was a time when the authorities might have hesitated") but limited the official role simply to "granting permission" for "a pious mortuary memorial."[25] A German publication carried the *Herald* article in translation. Díaz's role was winked at everywhere but nowhere acknowledged.

The winking continued through other channels, including through private correspondence between Díaz and Carl Khevenhüller, like Kaska a veteran of the Freiwilligen forces, though of Carinthian noble descent. As with Kaska, Díaz's acquaintance with Khevenhüller went back to the final days of the empire. When Maximilian left Mexico City for Querétaro in 1867, he left Colonel Khevenhüller and his cavalry in the capital. Díaz's forces laid siege to the city, and it was Khevenhüller who negotiated the surrender of the capital to Díaz after Maximilian was captured.[26]

By the 1890s Díaz and Khevenhüller were exchanging letters. By 1900 Díaz was sending warm notes referring to himself as Khevenhüller's "devoted friend and servant" and offering "a wink in confidence" as they laid the groundwork for the memorial chapel.[27]

A Viennese architect, Maximilian von Mitzel, drew up the plans for an intimate chapel, with an interior space just thirty-four by twenty-one feet.[28] A foundation of stone and mortar construction, with a footprint approximately twice that of the chapel itself, compensated for the steepness of the hillside site. The foundation created a level platform for the chapel, but also served an aesthetic function: it set up an approach to the chapel by means of a graceful set of stairs, twenty-five in all. As visitors approached, the many steps would conjure a sense of purpose and invite an air of solemnity via the metaphor of ascent.

With chapel construction under way, work could begin on a program of sacred art that would complement the architecture. Two men, Tomás

Mejía and Miguel Miramón, had died alongside Maximilian on June 19, 1867, and the architectural plan for the chapel featured patterns of three throughout. The chapel was illuminated from the back and either side by three windows with Roman arches. The façade featured three crosses, one at each corner and one at the peak of the roof, etched with Maximilian's initials. Inside the chapel, the pattern of threes included the retable and altar. The repetition of threes, especially in the context of sacred architecture, inevitably invoked the crucifixion of Jesus, who, according to tradition, had been crucified flanked by two others. At the foot of the altar, three limestone blocks topped by marble slabs occupied the ground where the men had fallen.

A painting was commissioned and would be mounted behind the altar to complete the artistic program. The subject is immediately recognizable as a Pietà. Jesus is cradled in the arms of his grieving mother, as dictated by convention, but those very conventions draw our attention to significant departures. Jesus bears the features of Maximilian; Mary is a likeness of Archduchess Sophie, Maximilian's mother. We note, too, that the lap of Mary/Sophie is draped in an abundance of cloth such that Sophie's blue mantle is complemented by the white of Maximilian's shroud and, beneath it, a layer of red fabric. The combination of colors—blue, white, red—invoke the French flag. Ultimately, the painting argues, responsibility for Maximilian's death rests with France.[29]

Maximilian's brother, Emperor Franz Joseph, had commissioned the artist, Alois Delug, a member of the Academy of Fine Arts in Vienna. The dimensions of the space it would occupy, and thus the dimensions of the painting itself, were specified by Carl Khevenhüller. The critical importance of the chapel and the painting to the restoration of diplomatic relations between Austria and Mexico is underlined by the fact that Franz Joseph's final inspection of the Pietà occurred at the same time that he was apprised of the progress of negotiations with Mexico. Mexican atonement and the assertion of French culpability underpinned the restoration of good relations.[30]

President Díaz hoped to crown his efforts toward reconciliation with the attendance of an Austrian delegation, formally authorized by Franz Joseph, at the dedication of the chapel. Díaz loved pageantry and recognized the power of ritual, but in the end Franz Joseph demurred. Franz Joseph insisted, as a prerequisite, upon a formal, contrite letter from Díaz, but the existence of such a letter, should it ever become public, represented an unacceptable political risk. Díaz appealed to Khevenhüller to intervene on

Memorial Chapel interior, Cerro de las Campanas, Querétaro. © *Raymond Jonas*.

his behalf. Khevenhüller would attend and would do so with Franz Joseph's knowledge, but without his explicit authorization. The dedication would take place, but Austria would be represented only informally. Even so, Díaz stepped close to the line dividing public policy from private ceremony, notably by making his presidential railcar available to Khevenhüller and his wife for the trip from Veracruz to Querétaro.[31]

It was bright and sunny on morning of April 10, 1904, just as it had been on the morning of the execution in 1867. A journalist making his way to the Hill of the Bells for what he imagined would be an intimate ceremony was astonished to find the hillside filled with "thousands of people . . . [in] wide straw hats, white clothing and colorful sarapes." But what had appeared picturesque and folkloric at a distance turned mournful. A "deathly silence" took hold of the crowd as Monsignor Rafael Camacho, bishop of Querétaro, his back to the chapel doors, stepped forward to where he could be seen by those assembled below. Camacho, with embroidered vestments and gleaming crozier, was flanked by six assistants who were framed, in turn, by choirboys in red robes and, beside them, the episcopal choir of Querétaro. With a gesture, the Introitus began. As the voices of the choir cascaded to the valley below, the people dropped to their knees and clasped their hands in prayer.

As the officiant moved inside the chapel built to accommodate sixty, some seventy guests crowded in to witness, seated or standing. Among them were those who served the memory of Maximilian, such as Kaska and Khevenhüller, alongside descendants of the executed general Miguel Miramón, including a daughter and granddaughter. No officials from the Mexican government were present, though the wife of the governor of Querétaro was there with her three daughters.[32]

After an hour and a half, the ceremony ended. Attendees went to the porter's house next door to sign the guest book and jot down words of sympathy. Prince and Princess Khevenhüller presented Bishop Camacho with a gift—an oak cross trimmed with silver. The wood for the cross had been salvaged from the *Novara,* the ship that carried Maximilian to Mexico and carried his body from Mexico back to Trieste. The cross would eventually take its place above the chapel altar.[33]

The inauguration of the chapel fulfilled the obligation of memory, but questions surrounding its long-term status remained. In the enthusiasm to complete the chapel, its advocates had overlooked a key detail—the ownership of the land on which it stood. Permission to build the chapel had been obtained from Santiago Jimeno, who owned much of the Cerro, but the question of ownership had never been settled. Arrangements with Jimeno to construct the chapel had been worked out by Carl Giskra, a member of the Austrian diplomatic delegation in Washington. Giskra hadn't worried much about ownership and even conjured a fantasy in which Jimeno would donate the land. After all, given the modest footprint of the chapel and its location on a rocky, remote hillside, the actual value of the land and surroundings could hardly exceed three hundred dollars, even by generous estimate.[34] The problem now was that with the chapel completed and consecrated, the land on which it rested was unique, hallowed, and therefore . . . priceless. Jimeno was a reasonable man. He let it be known that he would settle for fifty thousand dollars (the equivalent of about 1.5 million in 2019 dollars).

Frustrated and angry, the Austrians approached President Díaz, who promised to do everything in his power to resolve the situation, but given the thorny politics of the chapel there wasn't much he could do. The governor of Querétaro couldn't be trusted to intervene discreetly. A plan to convert the entire hill into a public cemetery was thwarted by the bishop of Querétaro. To make matters worse, Doña Carmen, the pious wife of President Díaz, felt herself yielding to the imperial mystique. She planned a visit to the chapel. A scandal was avoided only when she was forbidden to do so.[35]

Giskra refused to be drawn into negotiations with Jimeno. Instead he tried to light a fire under Jimeno by feigning indifference. Jimeno countered by letting it be known that, as an American citizen with a primary residence in California, he was thinking of building a vacation home adjacent to the chapel—a travesty. Meanwhile, Jimeno, as guardian, was keeping the chapel locked, to be opened to visitors only on payment of an entrance fee.[36] The chapel was becoming a tourist attraction.

Giskra wrote to Vienna in frustration. Jimeno, who had no sentimental attachment to the property (he had acquired it through marriage), was no more than "a drinker, a player, and a blackmailer."[37] Despite Giskra's low opinion of Jimeno, he speculated about the persuasive power of a grand, courtly gesture. Maybe a medal from Vienna would win him over.[38]

Time was passing on. Prince Khevenhüller died in September 1905, barely a year after the consecration of the chapel. Franz Kaska would die in 1907. In frustration, President Díaz himself intervened. He had Ignacio Mariscal, his foreign minister, contact Jimeno directly with a message. In the interest of good relations with Austria, the government of Mexico, having built the chapel with its funds, intended to buy the land, too. The only question was whether Jimeno wanted to be a friend or an enemy of the government.

In November 1907, final, decisive negotiations took place between Giskra, Under-Secretary of State Algara, and the landowner, Jimeno. Three months later, a deal was struck. Santiago R. Jimeno, owner of Cerro de las Campanas, including the memorial chapel, sold this property to the federal government of Mexico for seventeen thousand pesos, about five hundred thousand in 2019 dollars. Mexican foreign minister Ignacio Mariscal notified the Austrian government that Mexico had acquired ownership of the land under and surrounding the chapel. A copy of the notarized transaction was included.[39]

In the end Franz Joseph got what he wanted—a memorial chapel, including grounds, paid for by the government of Mexico—thanks to the decisive intervention of Díaz. For someone of Franz Joseph's generation, raised in the aftermath of the French Revolution and the execution by guillotine of the Habsburg Marie Antoinette, the whole affair brought to mind the construction of the *chapelle expiatoire* in Paris, on the site of her interment and that of her husband, Louis XVI.[40] At the court of Vienna, internal documents referred to the project as the Sühnkapelle or Sühnkirche, the German equivalent of *chapelle expiatoire*—chapel of expiation or atonement. Even if Mexico rejected the notion of a "chapel of expiation"— expiation implied not just fault but a sin to be expunged—the fact that the chapel could be read that way was good enough for Vienna. The chapel on the Hill of the Bells erected and paid by the offending party fulfilled a solemn obligation.

It also transformed the meaning of Maximilian's death. The empire had been an ill-conceived farce, crafted by intellectuals using fine language to conceal their artifice, backed by men and women endowed with the power to act. The farce ought to have ended at Puebla, where the claim of monarchist Mexico was convincingly exposed as myth. But Maximilian and Charlotte, too heavily invested in their own fantasy to back away, served instead to revive it. From Puebla to Querétaro, they prolonged Mexico's agony for five years. For Charlotte the dream ended in paranoia and mental collapse. For Maximilian the end came in front of a firing squad.

Power is immortal. Although composed of transitory parts, it survives us and refashions us to suit its purposes. The arc of Maximilian's life was simply too vivid to let fade, too useful not to be grafted onto new desires. In death, Maximilian lent himself to the purposes of others just as he had in life. Time, architecture, and memorial masses celebrated each year on the anniversary of the execution reinvented the empire. Chapel and ritual elevated the empire of vanity to a sacred plane where it became a redemptive sacrifice and a triumph over death.

ABBREVIATIONS

ARCHIVAL SOURCES

NOTES

ACKNOWLEDGMENTS

INDEX

Abbreviations

AGN	Archivo General de la Nación, Mexico City
AMAE	Archives du ministère des Affaires étrangères, La Courneuve (Paris)
AMBAE	Archives du Ministère belge des Affaires étrangères, Brussels
AN	Archives Nationales, Paris and Pierrefitte
APRB	Archives du Palais royal belge, Brussels
BCAH	Briscoe Center for American History, University of Texas, Austin
BLAC	Nettie Lee Benson Latin American Collection, University of Texas, Austin
BMNAH	Biblioteca del Museo Nacional de Antropología e Historia, Mexico City
CEHM	Centro de Estudios de Historia de México, Fundación Carlos Slim
HRC	Harry Ransom Center, University of Texas, Austin
ÖSta	Österreichisches Staatsarchiv, Vienna
ÖSta KA	Kriegsarchiv, Vienna
SHD	Service historique de la Défense, Paris
WRC	Woodson Research Center, Fondren Library, Rice University, Houston

Archival Sources

AUSTRIA

Österreichisches Staatsarchiv (ÖSta)

Haus-, Hof-, und Staatsarchiv

OMeA NZA 32 Hoftrauer, Sterbefälle und Exequien, 1867–1868
32-1 Ableben von Kaiser Maximilian von Mexiko.

Ministerium des Äußerns

Politisches Archiv (PA)
PA IX Frankreich
10 Protokoll (1862–1863)
11 Protokoll (1864–1866)
12 Protokoll (1867–1870)
PA XXXIV Mexiko
12-2 Liasse I: Sühnkapelle in Querétaro, 1898–1901
12-3 Liasse II: Sühnkapelle in Querétaro, 1916
4 Mexico (1864–1867)
4-1 Berichte, Weisungen, Varia (1864–1866)
4-2 Protokoll (1864–1867)
SB Coburg
II-20 Familienkorrespondenz Sachsen-Coburg-Gotha, Korrespondenz,
1857–1881
UR Urkunenreihen FUK Habsburg-Lothringische Familienurkunden2526
Familienvertrag zwischen Kaiser Franz Joseph und Erzherzog
Ferdinand Maximilian anlässlich seiner Thronbesteigung in Mexiko,
Renuntiation des Letzteren auf seine Sukzessionsrechte in den
Erblanden und der Stephanskrone, 1864.04.09

Kriegsarchiv (ÖSTa KA)

Archiv der Truppenkörper (AdT)

Akten des Österreichisch-belgisches Freiwilligenkorps in Mexiko
Karton 1
Karton 2
Karton 7
Karton 8
Karton 9
Karton 14
Karton 15
Karton 19

BELGIUM

Archives du Ministère belge des Affaires étrangères (AMBAE)

Série Générale "Politique"

902 Personnel exterieur, Consulat de Belgique, Mexique, 1
902 Personnel exterieur, Consulat de Belgique, Mexique, 2
10296 Organisation de la tutelle de S.M. L'Impératrice Charlotte après le décès de S.M. le Roi Léopold II
11488 Conflit religieux Mexique, 1923–1932
13468 Charlotte
13916 Notes from sales catalog of the Parke Burnet Galleries (correspondence of Charlotte and Eloin)
Série B 68 I, II, III 1861–1866
Série B 68 III 1866–1944
Série B 68 IV Légion belge au Mexique, rapatriements; Maladie Impératrice Charlotte; séjour à Rome et Miramar
Série B 68 V Recrutement de troupes pour le Brésil, 1838
Série B 68 I, II, III 1861–1866 Enrôlements militaires à l'Etranger

Archives du Palais Royal Belge (APRB)

BE-A0546/36

Keizerin Charlotte van Mexico, Impératrice Charlotte du Mexique
15 Brieven aan de keizerin gericht door vorsten en prinsen, België: Leopold I koning der Belgen. 1849–1864. 1849–1864 346 stukken

16 Brieven aan de keizerin gericht door vorsten en prinsen, België: Prins
   Leopold hertog van Brabant en zijn echtgenote Marie-Henriette,
   aartshertogin van Oostenrijk. 1853–1867. 1853–1867
17 Brieven aan de keizerin gericht door vorsten en prinsen, België: Prinses
   Louise van België. Niet gedateerd.
30 Brieven aan de keizerin gericht door vorsten en prinsen, Groot-Brittannië:
   Victoria koningin van de het Verenigde Koninkrijk. 1850–1866.
   1850–1866
51 Brieven van particulieren aan de keizerin gericht: Juan Nepomuc de
   Almonte en zijn echtgenote Dolores. 1864–1866: met een brief van
   B. Fleury aan Dolores de Almonte, 12 juli 1866. 1864–1866
76 Brieven van particulieren aan de keizerin gericht: José-Maria Gutierrez
   de Estrada. 1862–1864 en niet gedateerd. 1862–1864 76
107 Brieven van particulieren aan de keizerin gericht: gravin del Valle de
    Orizava,1865 en niet gedateerd. 1865
114 Brieven en telegrammen gericht aan de keizer en de keizerin tijdens
    hun reizen in Mexico; Reis naar Orizaba en Jalapa. april 1866. 1866
115 Brieven en telegrammen gericht aan de keizer en de keizerin tijdens
    hun reizen in Mexico; reis in de provincie Yucatán. december 1865–
    februari1866. 1865
116 Brieven en telegrammen gericht aan de keizer en de keizerin tijdens hun
    reizen in Mexico; bezoek aan allerlei plaatsen. maart-april 1866. 1866
129 Aan Joaquin Degollado, 1865–1866 en niet gedateerd. 1865–1866
134 Aan Andrew Johnson, niet gedateerd (ca april 1865). 1865
139 Aan generaal Leonardo Marquez, 1866. 1866
159 Teksten van politieke aard: mémoire remis par moi à l'Empereur
    Napoléon à St-Cloud le 11 août 1866, met een kopie van dit
    memorandum en bijlagen. 1866
162 Reisaantekeningen: Relation der Reise fait (sic) vom 26ten Nov. Bis
    zur Rückkehr nach Vera Cruz novemebr 1865. 1865
175 Itineraria van reizen in Mexico, 1865–1866
176 Reis in Yucatán, 1865–1866
178 Reis van de keizerin naar Europa, 1867
183 Itineraria van reizen in Oostenrijk, Groot-Brittanië, Lombardië en
    langsheen de Dalmatische kust, 1862 en niet gedateer dreizen in
    Mexico, 1865–1866. 1862–1866
192 Kopies van brieven van Mexicaanse personaliteiten, 1862. 1862
196 Blad El Pájaro Verde van 31 maart 1866. 1866
203 De triomf van keizer maximilliaan, fotoreproductie van een doek,
    34×43, 5cm. 1 stuk

Archief Van Felix Eloin

207–299 Briefwisseling

207 Brieven aan keizer Maximilliaan gericht door maarschalk F.A.Bazaine (kopie), 19 januari 1866;kardinaal Alexis Billiet aartsbisschop van Chambéry, 15 december 1864; pater Augustin Fischer, niet gedateerd; J.M. Gutierrez de Estrada, 28 januari 1865, met in bijlage een brief van markies G.d'Audiffret, 27 januari 1865; Athinaïs Lory de Lafargue, 4 juli 1864; Robert Limelette Vander Linden, 19 september 1865 en 2 april 1866; P. Arnold de Thier, 30 november 1865; evenals een nota aan Eloin en een nota van Charlotte aan keizer Maximilliaan, juni 1866. 1864–1866

208 Brieven van keizer Maximilliaan aan Eloin, met bijlage; soms een Franse vertaling(van de hand van Eloin)van originelen in het Spaans; klad van verklaring afgelegd door aartshertog Maximilliaan van Oostenrijk aan de Mexicaanse afvaardiging die hem de troon van Mexico kwam aanbieden. 1864–1867. Minuten van brieven van Eloin aan de keizer. 1864–1867.

209 Notas en briefjes van keizerin Charlotte aan Eloin: meestal niet gedateerd, drie dateren van 1865. Met een brief van Eloin aan Charlotte, 5 februari 1868. 1865–1868

210 Brieven aan Eloin gericht door: Juan N. de Almonte, 1866. 1866

213 Brieven aan Eloin gericht door: Barandiarian, Mexicaanse diplomaat, 1865–1866. 1865–1866

217 Brieven aan Eloin gericht door: José Luis Blasio, 1868. 1868

218 Brieven aan Eloin gericht door: Edouard Blondeel van Cuelebroeck, Belgisch diplomaat, 1865–1866. Met twee verzoekschriften van de kerkfabriek van Onze-Lieve-Vrouw van de Zavel te Brussel, waarvan een ondertekend is door Blondeel en gedateerd is van Tacubaya 8 januari 1866, een andere gedateerd van 30 oktober 1865 en minuten van het antwoord van Eloin, 1866. 1865–1866

219 Brieven aan Eloin gericht door: graaf Charles-Albert de Bombelles, persoonlijke adviseur van keizer Maximilliaan, 1865–1868. En niet gedateerd. 1865–1868

229 Brieven aan Eloin gericht door: Luitenant-generaal baron P.E.F.Chazal, vleugeladjudant van de Koning, minister van oorlog, met een brief van Ernest Chazal, Belgisch officier; een brief gericht aan F. Hooricks, Belgisch diplomaat, en een persknipsel, 1864–1867. brief van A.Chaudoir, vice-consul van België te Mexico, 7 oktober 1865. 1864–1867

238 Brieven aan Eloin gericht door: M.Degollado, 1867 en niet gedateerd. 1867

247 Brieven aan Eloin gericht door: Augustin Fischer, adviseur van keizer Maximilliaan, 1866–1867. 1866–1867

255 Brieven aan Eloin gericht door: José Manuel Hidalgo y Esnaurrizar, Mexicaans diplomaat(en bijlage), 1864–1865 en niet gedateerd. En minuut van een antwoord van Eloin. 1864–1865

256 Brieven aan Eloin gericht door: Frederik Hooricks, Belgisch diplomaat. En minuten van Eloins antwoorden. En een nota betreffende het incident Hooricks-Eloin, 4 januari 1868, 1866–1868. 1866–1868

260 Brieven aan Eloin gericht door: Alfons Kodolich, Oostenrijks officier, 1865. 1865

261 Brieven aan Eloin gericht door: gravin paula Kollonitz, eredame van keizerin Charlotte. En minuten van Eloins brieven, 1864–1868.

266 Brieven aan Eloin gericht door: Charles-Joseph Loysel, Frans officier, attaché(nadien chef van) bij he tmilitair kabinet van keizer Maximilliaan (en bijlagen), 1864–1865. 1865

268 Brieven aan Eloin gericht door: Leonardo Marquez, Mexicaans generaal. Minuten van 2 brieven van Eloin aan-, 1864, 1869. 1864–1869

285 Brieven aan Eloin gericht door: Charles Rogier, Belgisch staatsman, onvolledige data.

292 Brieven aan Eloin gericht door: baron A.L.A. Van der Smissen, belgisch generaal, met een bijlage, 1865.

298 Minuten van brieven en nota's van de hand van Eloin: minuten van brieven en nota's van Eloin aan de keizer en aan allerlei personen of nota's die tot op memorandum gediend hebben, 1863–1867.

305 Minuut van de nota door Eloin aan Augustin Fischer overhandigd op 31 januari 1867, betreffende de schulden die het Mexicaanse ministerie van Financiën t.o.v. Eloin had.

315 Strijdmacht in Mexico. Oostenrijks legioen en Belgisch Legioen. 1864–1866. 1864–1866

318 Proclamaties. Pamfletten. Redevoeringen. 1865–1867. 1865–1867

FRANCE

Archives Nationales (AN)

AB XIX-171   Charles Dupin, "Memoires du Mexique," Dossiers du Mexique, Papiers des Tuileries

Archives du ministère des affaires étrangères (AMAE)

Quai d'Orsay (la Courneuve)

Affaires Diverses Politiques

Correspondance Politique, Mexico, vol. 45 (Tomás Murphy)

45 1856, janvier-juillet
53 1860, mars-decembre
...
69 1867,

Correspondance politique des consuls, 1826–1870

Mexique

1 1858–1860 La Vera Cruz, Tampico
2 1861–1862 La Vera Cruz, Tampico
3 1863–1864 La Vera Cruz, Tampico
4 1865–1866 La Vera Cruz, Tampico
5 1866–1867 La Vera Cruz (1867), Matamoros (1866), Mazatlán (1866), Tampico (1867)

Dubois de Saligny, Dossier Personnel

Service historique de la Défense (SHD)

GR 7 G Expédition du Mexique

86 Contre-guérilla du colonel Dupin, 1865
87 Contre-guérilla du colonel Dupin, Historique, Siège de Mexico, 1863–1867
88 Évènements de guerre au Mexique, de 1838 à 1861, Lois et décrets du gouvernement mexicain, Navires en partance, Prisonniers de guerre, Manifestes aux populations, Fonds secret, 1838–1861
89 Mémoires, Carte du Mexique, Documents divers, Pertes, 1862–1866
91 Embarquements (voie des transatlantiques—Saint-Nazaire), 1862–1864
92 Troupes à laisser au gouvernement mexicain, Légion étrangère, Prisonniers mexicains, militaires autorisés à rester au Mexique, Demandes de renforts, Cadres de détachement, 1866
95 Contingents belges et autrichiens, Rapatriement de l'armée, 1866
96 Officiers étrangers offres diverses, Demandes d'emplois, Corps sénégalais, Troupes de la marine, 1866
106 Affaires mexicaines, Organisations de l'armée mexicaine, 1863–1867
107 idem
108 idem

134 Armée mexicaine, 1864–1865
135 idem
224 Bataillon nègre, égyptien au Mexique, 1863–1867
225 idem
226 Contre-guérilla au Mexique (historique, engagements, contrôles, mutations, pièces individuelles), 1863–1867
227 idem
228 idem
229 idem
230 idem
231 idem
235 Armée mexicaine (volontaires austro-belges, escadrons légers de la frontière, régiment et ranger, bataillon de Cazadores), 1863–1867

Mexico

Archivo General de la Nación (AGN)

Segundo Imperio [55029]

Caja 01

Expediente 11, Asamblea de Notables
Expediente 16, Actas de Adhesión
Expediente 17, Actas de Adhesión
Expediente 20, Actas de Adhesión

Caja 02

Expediente 74, Colonización
Expediente 82, Regencia del Imperio

Caja 07

Expediente 1, Solicitud
Expediente 27, Itinerario de viaje del Emperador
Expediente 32, Itinerario del Viaje de SM; Cérémonial de la cour

Caja 018

Ministerio de Negocios Extranjeros
Expediente 12 Legación de México en Italia, Consulado en Florencia
Expediente 19, Legación de México en Italia, Consulado en Liorna
Expediente 38, Legación de México en Bélgica
Expediente 59, Legación de México en Prusia
Expediente 75a, Legación de México en Austria, Consulad en Viena

Caja 019

Ministerio de Negocios Extranjeros

Expediente 3, Legaciones extranjero en México

Caja 030

Expediente 1, Ministerio de Justicia

Caja 031

Expediente 2, Gabinete del Emperador

Caja 032

Expediente 1, "Al Emperador"

Caja 036

Expediente 1–71, Oficina Telegráfica del Gabinete

Caja 045

Expediente 1–78, Cuerpos Expedicionarios Franceses

Caja 047

Expediente 1–15, Legión Austro-Belga

Expediente 41–56, Legión Austro-Belga

Caja 048

Expediente 1, secretaria Privada del Emperador

Caja 051

Expediente 39, Gabinete Militar del Emperador

Proyecto de colonización franco-alemana en Guanajuato

Caja 054

Expediente 48

28 de septiembre 1866–16 octubre 1866

concesión de auxilios a familias de militares fusilados por disidentes

Caja 057

Expediente 49, Gabinete Militar del Emperador

Caja 061

Expediente 4 Miscelánea

Correspondencia y telegramas relativos a la deuda del ejercito expedicionario

Caja 064

Expediente 5 Miscelánea, las instrucciones para la construcción de un
monumento a los belgas

Biblioteca del Museo Nacional de Antropología e Historia (BMNAH)

Colección: Imperio de Maximiliano

Documento 375 Carta Maximiliano Señores Prefecto Municipal y Regidores de la Ciudad de Xalapa

Documento 382 Ceremonial. Disposiciones generales para la fiesta nacional del 16 de septiembre de 1865

Documento 387 Fiesta de Nuestra Señora de Guadalupe

Documento 412 Carta Alejandro Franchi

Documento 414 Carta Achille Bazaine

Documento 416 Carta Maximiliano a Ministro Mangino

Documento 428 Carta Maximiliano a Arzobispo

Documento 429 Carta Labastida a Sr. Doctor D. Pedro Espinosa

Documento 441 Carta a Mariano Escobedo, Brownsville Setiembre 20 de 1866 (cargamento)

Documento 442 Carta a Mariano Escobedo, Brownsville Setiembre 20 de 1866 (escándalo)

Documento 484 La toma de Querétaro

UNITED STATES

Woodson Research Center (WRC)

Charlotte and Maximilian Collection, eight boxes, including Charlotte and Maximilian Sheet Music

Briscoe Center for American History (BCAH)

Box 2A136   Juan Nepomuceno Almonte Papers, 1834–1865

Box 2Q230   Volume 713: Almonte's letters to Maximilian and others (2 copies), 1862–1866

Harry Ransom Center (HRC)

MS-2733   Maximilian and Charlotte Manuscript Collection, 3 boxes

Nettie Lee Benson Latin American Collection (BLAC)

Achille Bazaine Papers G500, Correspondencia de Achille François Bazaine, 1862–1867

Joaquín and Mariano Degollado Collection

Charles Ferdinand Latrille Lorencez Papers

Genaro García Broadsides and Circulars Collection, Series 1, 2, 3

Genaro García, Documentos Relativos a la Reforma y a la Intervención Francesa en México

78a Independencia, documentos relativos, 1744–1863
80b Intervención Francesa, Correspondencia miscelánea, 1846–1867
80b (2) Intervención Francesa, Correspondencia miscelánea, 1846–1867
80c (1) Intervención Francesa, Correspondencia miscelánea, 1846–1867
80c (2) Intervención Francesa, Correspondencia miscelánea, 1846–1867
80c (3) Intervención Francesa, Correspondencia miscelánea, 1846–1867
81 (1) Intervención Francesa, Documentos misceláneos, 1862–1867; documentos relativos a Maximiliano, 1865–1867
81 (2) Intervención Francesa, Documentos misceláneos, 1862–1867
81 (3) Intervención Francesa, Documentos misceláneos, 1862–1867
81 (4) Intervención Francesa, Documentos misceláneos, 1862–1867
81 (5) Intervención Francesa, Documentos misceláneos, 1862–1867
[Documentos incompletos o fragmentarios]
81b Intervención Francesa, Documentos misceláneos, 1862–1867
82a (1) Intervención Francesa, Estadística militar y económica, 1867–1869
82a (2) Intervención Francesa, Estadística militar y económica, 1862–1867
83a Intervención Francesa, Documentos misceláneos, 1862–1869
83a (1) Intervención Francesa, Documentos misceláneos, 1867–1869
83a (2) Intervención Francesa, Documentos misceláneos, 1867–1869
83a (3) Intervención Francesa, Documentos misceláneos, 1867–1869
83a (4) Intervención Francesa, Documentos misceláneos, 1867–1869

Jesús González Ortega Collection

1. Series, Correspondance
2. Series, Printed Materials

Reminiscencias históricas escritas por el general Mariano Ruiz

Notes

Prologue

1. Frances Leigh Williams, *Matthew Fontaine Maury, Scientist of the Sea* (New Brunswick, NJ: Rutgers University Press, 1963), 415–419.

2. David G. McCullough, *The Greater Journey: Americans in Paris* (New York: Simon and Schuster, 2011), 244.

3. William Henry Bullock, *Across Mexico in 1864–5* (London: Macmillan, 1866), 5–6.

4. For the letter to Maximilian, see Emmanuel Domenech, *Histoire du Mexique* (Paris: A. Lacroix, Verboeckhoven et Cie, 1868), 263–265; for Maury's letter to Octave Chabannes, see Gustave Léon Niox, *Expédition du Mexique, 1861–1867: Récit politique & militaire* (Paris: J. Dumaine, 1874), 752; Eugénie forwarded Chabanne's reply to Maury, expressing support for Maury's idea. See Egon Caesar Corti, *Maximilian and Charlotte of Mexico*, trans. Catherine Alison Phillips (New York: Knopf, 1928), 526.

5. Maury's interest in Mexico dated back to 1849. See his letter regarding proposed Tehuantepec railroad in J. D. B. De Bow's *The Commercial Review of the South and West* (1849), 1:16–17.

6. For details of Maury's arrival and promotion, see *La Sociedad*, September 5 and 27, 1865; for his office and budget, see October 8. For his salary, see Williams, *Matthew Fontaine Maury*, 427.

7. Matthew Fontaine Maury, "Decrees for the Encouragement of Immigration and Colonization" (Mexico City: Ignacio Cumplido, November 1865).

8. For details regarding formerly enslaved laborers, see Domenech, *Histoire du Mexique*, 265.

9. From a letter to Reverend Francis W. Tremlett, an acquaintance in England. See Williams, *Matthew Fontaine Maury*, 421–422.

10. Regarding some details, especially in the northern borderlands, see Todd W. Wahlstrom, *The Southern Exodus to Mexico: Migration across the Borderlands after the American Civil War* (Lincoln: University of Nebraska Press, 2015), 77–78.

11. Mexican Conservatives dubbed the American republic "la ladrona República"— the Robber Republic. See Concepción Lombardo de Miramón, *Memorias de Concepción Lombardo de Miramón* (Mexico: Porrúa, 1989), 515.

12. General Sheridan saw the Intervention as "so closely related to the Rebellion as to be essentially part of it." See Jay Sexton, *The Monroe Doctrine: Empire and Nation in Nineteenth-Century America* (New York: Hill and Wang, 2011), 143.

13. For the recovery of territory, see Williams, *Matthew Fontaine Maury*, 414.

14. On the place of the empire within the longue durée of the history of Mexico, see Erika Pani, *Para mexicanizar el Segundo Imperio: El imaginario político de los imperialistas* (Mexico: Colegio de México, Centro de Estudios Históricos, 2001).

15. Diary entry for September 20, 1845, Corpus Christi, in Ethan Allen Hitchcock, *Fifty Years in Camp and Field: Diary of Major-General Ethan Allen Hitchcock, U.S.A.*, ed. W. A. Croffut (New York: G. P. Putnam's Sons, 1909), 203.

16. David M. Pletcher, *The Diplomacy of Annexation: Texas, Oregon, and the Mexican War* (Columbia: University of Missouri Press, 1973), 39; Alfred Jackson Hanna and Kathryn Abbey Hanna, *Napoléon III and Mexico: American Triumph over Monarchy* (Chapel Hill: University of North Carolina Press, 1971), 11; see also Jay Sexton, *The Monroe Doctrine: Empire and Nation in Nineteenth-Century America* (New York: Hill and Wang, 2011); Eric Van Young, *A Life Together: Lucas Alaman and Mexico, 1792–1853* (New Haven, CT: Yale University Press, 2021), 106.

17. George M. Blackburn, "Paris Newspapers and the American Civil War," *Illinois Historical Journal* 84, no. 3 (1991): 182.

18. Percy F. Martin, *Maximilian in Mexico: The Story of the French Intervention, 1861–1867* (London: Constable, 1914), 416; cited in Frank G. Weber, "Bismarck's Man in Mexico: Anton von Magnus and the End of Maximilian's Empire," *Hispanic American Historical Review* 46, no. 1 (February 1, 1966): 53–65.

19. See, for example, the warning sounded by Domenech, *Histoire du Mexique*, 454.

20. See Henry Kissinger, *A World Restored: Metternich, Castlereagh and the Problems of Peace, 1812–22* (Boston: Houghton Mifflin, 1957); for a more recent take, see Glenda Sluga, *The Invention of International Order: Remaking Europe after Napoleon* (Princeton, NJ: Princeton University Press, 2021).

21. Carl Schurz, *The Reminiscences of Carl Schurz*, vol. 2 (New York: Doubleday, Page and Co., 1908), 201–202.

22. See "Conferencia con Mr. Seward, Washington, Octubre 9 de 1862," in Matías Romero, *Correspondencia de la legación mexicana en Washington durante la intervención extranjera, 1860–1868: Colección de documentos para formar la historia de la intervención*, 10 vols. (Mexico City: Imprenta del Gobierno, 1870), 2:395–396.

23. See, for example, Mauricio Tenorio-Trillo, *Latin America: The Allure and Power of an Idea* (Chicago: University of Chicago Press, 2017); Walter D. Mignolo, *The Idea of Latin America* (Oxford: Blackwell, 2005).

24. Mark Twain, *King Leopold's Soliloquy: A Defense of His Congo Rule* (Boston: P. R. Warren Co., 1905); Adam Hochschild, *King Leopold's Ghost: A Story of Greed, Terror, and Heroism in Colonial Africa* (Boston: Houghton Mifflin, 1998).

25. For Maximilian's reflections on the Americas, see Maximilian, *Recollections of My Life*, 3 vols. (London: Bentley, 1868), esp. 3:91–92, 111–112.

26. See the monumental work of Jan Bazant. Jan Bazant, *Alienation of Church Wealth in Mexico: Social and Economic Aspects of the Liberal Revolution, 1856–1875* (Cambridge: Cambridge University Press, 1971); see also Michael P. Costeloe,

Church Wealth in Mexico: A Study of the "Juzgado De Capellanias" in the Archbish-opric of Mexico 1800–1856, 2 (Cambridge: Cambridge University Press, 1967).

27. See, for example, "The Napoleonic Idea in Mexico," in *Blackwood's Edinburgh Magazine*, July 1864, 74–85.

28. For the Italian case, see Raymond Jonas, *The Battle of Adwa: African Victory in the Age of Empire* (Cambridge, MA: Belknap Press of Harvard University Press, 2011).

29. See, for example, the classic Fritz Fischer, *Germany's Aims in the First World War* (New York: W. W. Norton, 1967).

30. Not only Europeans were seduced by the idea that race was the key that unlocked the secret of power relations. The year 1910 saw the debut of *The Journal of Race Development*, an academic journal hosted by Clark University of Worcester, Massachusetts. As the title suggests, the journal took racial thinking as fundamental to serious scholarly understanding of international relations in the early twentieth century. A decision to rename it *The Journal of International Relations* in 1919 revealed as much as it concealed.

31. See Max Weber, "The National State and Economic Policy (Freiburg Address)," *Economy and Society* 9, no. 4 (1980): 428–449.

1. Rescuing the Latin Race

1. For the history of race and social hierarchy in Mexico, see Ben Vinson, *Before Mestizaje: The Frontiers of Race and Caste in Colonial Mexico* (New York: Cambridge University Press, 2018).

2. Manuel Covo and Megan Maruschke, "The French Revolution as an Imperial Revolution," *French Historical Studies* 44 (2021): 371–397.

3. On driving Islam out, see, for example, Mark Mazower, *The Greek Revolution: 1821 and the Making of Modern Europe* (New York: Penguin Press, 2021), xxxii. On Latin America, see Eric Van Young, *A Life Together: Lucas Alaman and Mexico, 1792–1853* (New Haven, CT: Yale University Press, 2021), 221, 434.

4. "fanatical": Egon Caesar Corti, *Maximilian and Charlotte of Mexico*, trans. Catherine Alison Phillips (New York: Knopf, 1928), 17. Victor Villavicencio Navarro, "Cuando la prensa incomoda al sistema político: La libertad de imprenta frente a la propuesta de José María Gutiérrez de Estrada de 1840," *Historia Mexicana* 69 (2019): 164–165; Frank J. Sanders, "Jose Maria Gutiérrez Estrada: Monarchist Pamphleteer," *The Americas* 27 (1970): 56.

5. In a letter to James Monroe, Thomas Jefferson spoke of "strengthening our title to Techas (Texas)" in the context of negotiations for Florida. See his letter dated May 14, 1820, in Thomas Jefferson, *The Papers of Thomas Jefferson: Retirement Series*, vol. 15: *1 September 1819 to 31 May 1820*, ed. J. Jefferson Looney (Princeton, NJ: Princeton University Press, 2019), 594–595. Jefferson had made the claim that the Louisiana Purchase included Texas. See Andrew Torget, *Seeds of Empire: Cotton, Slavery, and the Transformation of the Texas Borderlands, 1800–1850* (Chapel Hill: University of North Carolina Press, 2015), 28.

6. See "Mexico, National Colonization Law, August 18, 1824" and "Legislature of Coahuila-Texas, Coahuila-Texas State Colonization Law, March 24, 1825,"

both in Ernesto Chávez, *The U.S. War with Mexico: A Brief History with Documents* (New York City: Bedford/St. Martins, 2007), 47–52; David M. Pletcher, *The Diplomacy of Annexation; Texas, Oregon, and the Mexican War* (Columbia: University of Missouri Press, 1973), 66–67.

7. Van Young, *A Life Together*, 242–243.

8. For a survey of free-labor cotton in Texas of the 1850s, see Frederick Law Olmsted, *A Journey through Texas, or, a Saddle-Trip on the Southwestern Frontier: With a Statistical Appendix* (New York: Dix, Edwards Co, 1857), 87–89, 107–108, 138–140. On the inspection tour, see Manuel de Mier y Terán, *Texas by Terán: The Diary Kept by General Manuel de Mier y Terán on His 1828 Inspection of Texas*, ed. Jack Jackson, trans. John Wheat (Austin: University of Texas Press, 2000), 143–145; see also Torget, *Seeds of Empire*, 137–176.

9. On Alamán see Van Young, *A Life Together*, 243, 422. Stephen Austin to Edward Livingston, June 24, 1832, cited in Torget, *Seeds of Empire*, 155; H. W. Brands, *Lone Star Nation: The Epic Story of the Battle for Texas Independence* (New York: Anchor, 2005), 153.

10. Ten months earlier, Anthony Butler had assured Gutierrez of US respect for the independence of Mexico. See Butler to Gutierrez de Estrada, January 2, 1835, in William R. Manning, ed., *Diplomatic Correspondence of the United States: Inter-American Affairs, 1831–1860*, vol. 9 (Washington, DC: Carnegie Endowment for International Peace, 1932), 279–281.

11. See Ernest Wallace, George B. Ward, and David M. Vigness, eds., "The Constitution of the Republic of Texas, March 17, 1836," in *Documents of Texas History* (Austin: Texas State Historical Association, 2002), 98–106.

12. For early US diplomacy regarding Texas, see Timothy J. Henderson, *A Glorious Defeat: Mexico and Its War with the United States* (New York: Hill and Wang, 2007), 40.

13. On British and French relations with Texas: Elliot to Aberdeen, June 8, 1843, in Ephraim Douglass Adams, ed., *British Diplomatic Correspondence concerning the Republic of Texas,1838–1846* (Austin: Texas State Historical Association, 1918), esp. 205–207; François Guizot, *Histoire parlementaire de France: Recueil complet des discours prononcés dans les Chambres de 1819 à 1848* (Paris: Michel Lévy, 1863), 4:561–564, 5:19–25; Brands, *Lone Star Nation*, 499–500. For Belgium, see Francis Balace, *La Belgique et la guerre de sécession, 1861–1865* (Paris: Les Belles Lettres, 1979), 268.

14. See Lynn Marshall Case, *Edouard Thouvenel et la diplomatie du second empire* (Paris: A. Pedone, 1976), 365–366. For European cotton from the South, Shirley Black gives a figure of 93 percent. See Shirley J. Black, "Napoléon III et le Mexique: Un triomphe monétaire," *Revue Historique* 259, no. 1 (525) (1978): 72.

15. See Hook to Palmerston, April 30, 1841, in Adams, *British Diplomatic Correspondence*, 29–39.

16. Nancy Nichols Barker, "Devious Diplomat: Dubois de Saligny and the Republic of Texas," *Southwestern Historical Quarterly* 72, no. 3 (1969): 324–334; Torget, *Seeds of Empire*, 209–210; for Saligny and his plan for French settlement in Texas, see Pletcher, *Diplomacy of Annexation*, 81–82.

17. President Polk was kept informed of British and French positions. See Jacob Martin (in Paris) to Polk, December 1, 1845, in Wayne Cutler et al., eds., *Correspondence*

of James K. Polk, vol. 10: *July–December 1845* (Knoxville: University of Tennessee Press, 2004), 398–399.

18. See Kennedy to Aberdeen, December 5, 1844, in Adams, *British Diplomatic Correspondence*, 381.

19. See Josefina Zoraida Vázquez, "The Texas Question in Mexican Politics, 1836–1845," *Southwestern Historical Quarterly* 89, no. 3 (1986): 309–344.

20. Gutiérrez articulates a palpable embarrassment at the image of Mexico. José María Gutiérrez Estrada, "Excelentísimo Señor Presidente de la Republica, Don Anastasio Bustamente," in Justo Sierra, José María Gutiérrez Estrada, and Mariano Otero, *1840–1850, documentos de la época,* ed. José Colin (Mexico, DF: Editorial Rostra, 1948), 52; see also Villavicencio Navarro, "Cuando la prensa," 167; for more on Gutiérrez, see Clark H. Crook-Castan, *Los movimientos monárquicos mexicanos* (Monterrey, NL: UDEM, 2000), 38–39.

21. Gutiérrez Estrada, "Excelentísimo Señor Presidente," 85.

22. He was not alone. See, for example, Pedro Pruneda, *Historia de la guerra de Méjico, desde 1861 á 1867: Con todos los documentos diplomáticos justificativos* (Madrid: Elizalde y compañia, 1867), 8, 18.

23. Sierra, Gutiérrez Estrada, and Otero, *1840–1850, documentos,* 61, 112; Gastón García Cantú, *La Intervención Francesa en México* (Mexico: Clio, 1999), 47; Emmanuel Domenech, *Histoire du Mexique* (Paris: A. Lacroix, Verboeckhoven et Cie, 1868), 167–168.

24. See Van Young, *A Life Together,* 592–594.

25. Villavicencio Navarro, "Cuando la prensa," 183. For more on Tornel, see Will Fowler, *Santa Anna of Mexico* (Lincoln: University of Nebraska Press, 2007); on the difference between the monarchism of Gutierrez and of Lucas Alamán, see Van Young, *A Life Together,* 407.

26. Villavicencio Navarro, "Cuando la prensa," 182.

27. Lilia Díaz, "Los embajadores de Francia en el periodo de la Intervención," *Historia Mexicana* 38, no. 1 (1988): 6.

28. Sierra, Gutiérrez Estrada, and Otero, *Documentos de la época,* 76–77.

29. Quoted in Torget, *Seeds of Empire,* 186.

30. Santa Anna, in exchange for his life, agreed in a secret treaty to acknowledge the Rio Grande as the boundary. Van Young, *A Life Together,* 571–572.

31. Henderson, *Glorious Defeat,* 147–148; Amy S. Greenberg, *A Wicked War: Polk, Clay, Lincoln, and the 1846 US Invasion of Mexico* (New York: Knopf, 2012), 95–101; Matthew Karp, *This Vast Southern Empire: Slaveholders at the Helm of American Foreign Policy* (Cambridge, MA: Harvard University Press, 2016), 107–108.

32. On the possibility of total annexation of Mexico, see Henderson, *Glorious Defeat,* 175; letter from Nicolas Trist to President Buchanan, October 1847, in Rogelio Orozco Farías, *Fuentes históricas: México, 1821–1867: Documentos y escritos* (Mexico: Editorial Progreso, 1965), 111; Pletcher, *Diplomacy of Annexation,* 534.

33. On Sam Houston and the All-Mexico Movement, see Greenberg, *Wicked War,* 212–213.

34. John C. Pinheiro, *Missionaries of Republicanism: A Religious History of the Mexican-American War* (New York: Oxford University Press, 2014), 88–95.

35. Luis Weckmann, *Carlota de Bélgica: Correspondencia y escritos sobre México en los archivos europeos, 1861–1868* (Mexico: Porrúa, 1989), 96n. Advenimiento de SS. MM. II. Maximiliano y Carlota al trono de México (Mexico: J. M. Andrade y F. Escalante, 1864), 138; Frederic Hall, *Invasion of Mexico by the French and the Reign of Maximilian I, Late Emperor of Mexico, with a Sketch of the Empress Carlota* (New York: J. Miller, 1868), 99.

36. In this, his marriage to Countess von Lützow, daughter to one of Charlotte's ladies-in-waiting, was enormously helpful. See Esther Acevedo, ed., *Testimonios artísticos de un episodio fugaz, 1864–1867* (Mexico, DF: Instituto Nacional de Bellas Artes, 1995), 35; also Raphael Waldburg-Zeil, *Fernando Maximiliano de Habsburgo, 1832–1867: Perfil humano de un archiduque-emperador* (Madrid: Gunter Quercus, 2013), 59.

37. Ricardo Lancaster-Jones, "Imperialista Desengañado," *Historia Mexicana* 10 (1961): 663–664; José Fuentes Mares, *La Emperatriz Eugenia y su aventura mexicana* (Mexico: Colegio de México, 1976), 30–31; Carl H. Bock, *Prelude to Tragedy: The Negotiation and Breakdown of the Tripartite Convention of London, October 31, 1861* (Philadelphia: University of Pennsylvania Press, 1966), 27–28.

38. Corti, *Maximilian and Charlotte*, 33.

39. José Manuel Hidalgo y Esnaurrízar, *Recuerdos de juventud: Memorias íntimas de Don José Hidalgo, Antiguo Ministro de México en diversas cortes de Europa* (Mexico: El Nacional, 1887), 11; Luz América Viveros Anaya, "Recuerdos de juventud de un imperialista exiliado: José Manuel Hidalgo," *Decires, Revista del Centro de Enseñanza para Extranjeros* 17 (2017): 79; for the journey to Gaeta, see David I. Kertzer, *The Pope Who Would Be King: The Exile of Pius IX and the Emergence of Modern Europe* (New York: Random House, 2018), 115–118.

40. H. Hearder, "The Making of the Roman Republic, 1848–1849," *History* (London) 60, no. 199 (1975): 169–184; Kertzer, *Pope Who Would Be King*, 292.

41. For the ontological importance of Mexican indigeneity in defining the colonizer, see María Josefina Saldaña-Portillo, *Indian Given: Racial Geographies across Mexico and the United States* (Durham, NC: Duke University Press, 2016).

42. Michel Chevalier, *Society, Manners and Politics in the United States: Being a Series of Letters on North America* (Boston: Weeks, Jordan, 1839), 11; for context, see Reginald Horsman, *Race and Manifest Destiny: The Origins of American Racial Anglo-Saxonism* (Cambridge, MA: Harvard University Press, 1981). Sara Yorke Stevenson asserts that Chevalier visited Mexico; see Sara Yorke Stevenson, *Maximilian in Mexico: A Woman's Reminiscences of the French Intervention, 1862–1867* (New York: Century Co., 1899), 2; Alfred Jackson Hanna and Kathryn Abbey Hanna, *Napoléon III and Mexico: American Triumph over Monarchy* (Chapel Hill: University of North Carolina Press, 1971), 66–67.

43. This situates the European awakening to the challenge of US expansion in a much earlier period. See Sven Beckert, "American Danger: United States Empire, Eurafrica, and the Territorialization of Industrial Capitalism, 1870–1950," *American Historical Review* 122, no. 4 (2017): 1137–1170.

44. See Alexis de Tocqueville, *Democracy in America* (London: Saunders and Otley, 1835).

45. Torget, *Seeds of Empire*, 51.

46. See comments by Mexican Conservative Lucas Alamán in 1830 in Van Young, *A Life Together*, 417–418.

47. Greenberg, *Wicked War*, 128–129.

48. Michel Chevalier, *Le Mexique, ancien et moderne* (Paris: Maulde et Renou, 1851), 32.

49. Chevalier, *Le Mexique*, 38.

50. The key work is Alfred Thayer Mahan, *The Influence of Sea Power upon History, 1660–1783* (Boston: Little, Brown, 1898); for Mahan's views on race, see Robert Seager, *Alfred Thayer Mahan: The Man and His Letters* (Annapolis, MD: Naval Institute Press, 1977).

51. Torget, *Seeds of Empire*, 190–191.

52. See also James M. McPherson, *Battle Cry of Freedom: The Civil War Era* (New York: Oxford University Press, 1988), 105–106; Karp, *This Vast Southern Empire*; Horsman, *Race and Manifest Destiny*, 145–164.

53. For Houston, see "The Great War Meeting," *New York Herald*, January 30, 1848, cited in Greenberg, *Wicked War*, 212–213, 216–217.

54. Manuel Crescencio Rejón, "Observations on the Treaty of Guadalupe Hidalgo," in Chávez, *U.S. War with Mexico*, 126–128.

55. Forsyth to Cass, Mexico City, April 4, 1857, in Manning, *Diplomatic Correspondence of the United States*, 9:908.

56. Pasquier was in Chihuahua and Sonora in 1849 and 1850. Hippolyte du Pasquier de Dommartin, *Les États-Unis et le Mexique: L'intérêt européen dans l'Amérique du Nord* (Paris: Gillaumin, 1852), 7; see also Guy-Alain Dugast, *La tentation mexicaine en France au XIXᵉ siècle: L'image du Mexique et l'intervention française (1821–1862)* (Paris: Harmattan, 2008), 178–179. Tomás Murphy also sounded the alarm; see Díaz, "Los embajadores de Francia," 16.

57. Chevalier, *Society, Manners*, 16.

58. See Erika Pani, "Dreaming of a Mexican Empire: The Political Projects of the 'Imperialistas,'" *Hispanic American Historical Review* 82, no. 1 (2002): 1–31.

59. For a broad vision of the history of an idea, see Mauricio Tenorio-Trillo, *Latin America: The Allure and Power of an Idea* (Chicago: University of Chicago Press, 2017); see also Michel Gobat, "The Invention of Latin America: A Transnational History of Anti-Imperialism, Democracy, and Race," *American Historical Review* 118, no. 5 (2013): 1345–1375; Christina Carroll, "Imperial Ideologies in the Second Empire: The Mexican Expedition and the Royaume Arabe," *French Historical Studies* 42 (2019): 67–100.

60. See Maximilian to Eloin, August 28, 1866, APRB, BE-A0546/36/208.

61. Edgar Quinet insisted that the point of the Intervention was to destroy the American republic. See Edgar Quinet, *L'expédition au Mexique* (London: Jeffs, 1862), 17.

62. Alexis de Tocqueville, *Democracy in America*, trans. Arthur Goldhammer (New York: Library of America, 2004), 441, 475.

63. For an overview, see Mack Walker, *Germany and the Emigration, 1816–1885* (Cambridge MA: Harvard University Press, 1964), 87–88, 114–118; for calculations at the time of the Crimean War, see Andrew C. Rath, *The Crimean War in Imperial Context, 1854–1856* (New York: Palgrave Macmillan, 2015), 2; for elaboration of this fear two generations later, see Fritz Fischer, *Germany's Aims in the First World War*

(New York: W. W. Norton, 1967); see also Horsman, *Race and Manifest Destiny*, 35. Conversely, Russia saw the United States as a counterweight to Britain and France; see Joseph A. Fry, *Lincoln, Seward, and US Foreign Relations in the Civil War Era* (Lexington: University Press of Kentucky, 2019), 135.

64. See Rath, *Crimean War*; Hanna and Hanna, *Napoléon III and Mexico*, 15–19; Edward Shawcross, *France, Mexico and Informal Empire in Latin America, 1820–1867: Equilibrium in the New World* (Cham, Switzerland: Springer, 2018), 157.

65. By the 1860s, racial thinking would become a dominant organizational principle; see, for example, "Race Anglo-Americain: Histoire des États Americains," in *Annuaire des deux mondes: Histoire générale des divers états*, vol. 13 (Paris: Revue des deux mondes, 1864), 646.

66. For "la ladrona República," see Concepción Lombardo de Miramón, *Memorias de Concepción Lombardo de Miramón* (Mexico: Porrúa, 1989), 515; Chevalier, *Le Mexique*; Michel Chevalier, *Le Mexique, ancien et moderne* (Paris: L. Hachette, 1863); Pruneda, *Historia de la guerra de Méjico*, v; Erika Pani, *El Segundo Imperio: Pasados de usos múltiples* (Mexico, DF: Centro de Investigación y Docencia Económicas: Fondo de Cultura Económica, 2004), 41; Matías Romero, *Correspondencia de la legación mexicana en Washington durante la intervención extranjera, 1860–1868: Colección de documentos para formar la historia de la intervención*, 10 vols. (Mexico City: Imprenta del Gobierno, 1870), 2:290; Quinet, *L'expédition au Mexique*, 12–13.

67. Jules Doazan, French consul to Mexico, argued that the United States would bring despair to Mexico, making annexation by the United States "the lesser evil." See his letter dated January 7, 1860, AMAE, Correspondance politique des consuls, 1826–1870, Mexique, 1 1858–1860 La Vera Cruz, Tampico.

68. Robert Sencourt, *Napoleon III: The Modern Emperor* (New York: Appleton-Century, 1933), 270; Bock, *Prelude to Tragedy*, 44.

69. See the Conservative testimonial in Van Young, *A Life Together*, 614–615.

70. For Laws of the Reform, see Orozco Farías, *Fuentes históricas*, 173–179; for la Reforma, see Paco Ignacio Taibo, *La gloria y el ensueño que forjó una patria* (Mexico City: Planeta, 2017); Zachary Brittsan, *Popular Politics and Rebellion in Mexico: Manuel Lozada and La Reforma, 1855–1876* (Nashville, TN: Vanderbilt University Press, 2015), 37–38; Paul Vanderwood, "Betterment for Whom? The Reform Period: 1855–1875," in *The Oxford History of Mexico*, ed. Michael C. Meyer and William H. Beezley (New York: Oxford University Press, 2000), 349–372.

71. For Juárez, see Brian R. Hamnett, *Juárez* (London: Longman, 1994); for contrast, see José Fuentes Mares, *Juárez y la República* (Mexico: Editorial Jus, 1965); see also Richard N. Sinkin, *The Mexican Reform, 1855–1876: A Study in Liberal Nation-Building* (Austin: University of Texas Press, 1979).

72. Reports of the yield to Miramón vary from $700,000 to $1.4 million. See Bock, *Prelude to Tragedy*, 60; Gustave Léon Niox, *Expédition du Mexique, 1861–1867: Récit politique & militaire* (Paris: J. Dumaine, 1874), 720; for the lower figure, see "Conferencia con Mr. Seward, Washington, Octubre 9 de 1862," in Romero, *Correspondencia de la legación mexicana*, 2:446; Victor Daran, *Le général Miguel Miramon: Notes sur l'histoire du Mexique* (Rome: E. Perino, 1886), 84.

73. Michael Costeloe, *Bonds and Bondholders: British Investors and Mexico's Foreign Debt, 1824–1888* (Westport, CT: Praeger, 2003), 121–122; for reaction in

Europe, see Jesús Terán, *La Misión confidencial de Don Jesús Terán en Europa, 1863–66*, ed. Gabriel Saldívar (Mexico: Archivo Histórico Diplomático Mexicano, 1943), 94; Leonardo Márquez, *Manifiestos* (El Imperio y Los Imperiales) (Mexico City: Vazquez, 1904), 14.

74. See William H. Beezley, *Mexico in World History* (New York: Oxford University Press, 2011), 68; Erika Pani, "Republicans and Monarchists, 1848–1867," in *A Companion to Mexican History and Culture*, ed. William H. Beezley (Chichester, West Sussex: Wiley-Blackwell, 2011), 275; for treaty correspondence, see Manning, *Diplomatic Correspondence*, 1932.

75. This was the view of the bishop of San Luis Potosí as the Intervention began. See his letter to Antonelli dated November 7, 1863, from exile in Paris, in Luis Ramos et al., *Del Archivo secreto vaticano: La Iglesia y el estado mexicano en el siglo XIX* (Mexico, DF: Universidad Nacional Autónoma de México, 1997), 152.

76. Jesús de León Toral, *Historia militar: La Intervención francesa en México* (Mexico: Primer Congreso Nacional de Historia Para el Estudio de la Guerra de Intervención, 1962), 73; José M Vigil and Vicente Riva Palacio, *México a través de los siglos*, vol. 5: *La Reforma* (Mexico City: Herrerias, 1940), 443.

77. See report dated January 31, 1861, AMAE, Correspondence politique des consuls, 1826–1870, Mexique 2.

78. Domenech, *Histoire du Mexique*, 347; see also *La Correspondencia de España*, March 24, 1861.

2. The Vicar of Cranborne

1. Michael P. Costeloe, *Bonds and Bondholders: British Investors and Mexico's Foreign Debt, 1824–1888* (Westport, CT: Praeger, 2003), xiii.

2. Costeloe, *Bonds and Bondholders*, 280; Eric Van Young, *A Life Together: Lucas Alamán and Mexico, 1792–1853* (New Haven, CT: Yale University Press, 2021), 215–216.

3. Costeloe, *Bonds and Bondholders*, 115.

4. Carl H. Bock, *Prelude to Tragedy: The Negotiation and Breakdown of the Tripartite Convention of London, October 31, 1861* (Philadelphia: University of Pennsylvania Press, 1966), 469; Costeloe, *Bonds and Bondholders*, 165, 27, 173.

5. Costeloe, *Bonds and Bondholders*, 38; Napoléon III would later envision settler colonies fulfilling a similar function in Sonora. See Paul Gaulot, *Rêve d'empire; La vérité sur l'expédition du Mexique, d'après les documents inédits de Ernest Louët* (Paris: P. Ollendorff, 1890), 216.

6. Costeloe, *Bonds and Bondholders*, 193–197; see also Barbara A. Tenenbaum, "Merchants, Money, and Mischief: The British in Mexico, 1821–1862," *The Americas* 35, no. 3 (1979): 322–323.

7. Matthew Karp, *This Vast Southern Empire: Slaveholders at the Helm of American Foreign Policy* (Cambridge, MA: Harvard University Press, 2016), 12, 24.

8. For Asian sources, notably British India, see Michel Chevalier, *Le Mexique, ancien et moderne* (Paris: L. Hachette et cie, 1863), 442.

9. Charles Lempriere, *Notes in Mexico, in 1861 and 1862, Politically and Socially Considered* (London: Longman, Roberts, and Green, 1862), 109–111, 212.

10. Lempriere, *Notes in Mexico*, 230–231.

11. By 1861, 77 percent of customs receipts at Veracruz were committed to foreign investors by various agreements. See Silvestre Villegas Revueltas, "Charles Wyke y su misión en el México juarista," *Estudios de historia moderna y contemporánea de México* 32 (2006): 13.

12. Gustave Léon Niox, *Expédition du Mexique, 1861–1867: Récit politique & militaire* (Paris: J. Dumaine, 1874), 19–20, 151; for Wyke's mission, see Villegas Revueltas, "Charles Wyke y su misión."

13. Bock, *Prelude to Tragedy*, 79.

14. Villegas Revueltas, "Charles Wyke y su misión," 6–7.

15. José M. Vigil and Vicente Riva Palacio, *México a través de los siglos*, 5 vols. (Mexico City: Herrerias, 1940), 5:448, 452–453; Francisco Bulnes, *El verdadero Juárez y la verdad sobre la intervención y el imperio* (Mexico: Editora Nacional, 1956), 44; "Romero letter dated 6 February 1861," in Matias Romero, *Correspondencia de la legación mexicana en Washington durante la intervención extranjera, 1860–1868: Colección de documentos para formar la historia de la intervención*, 10 vols. (Mexico City: Imprenta del Gobierno, 1870), 2:284–286.

16. Emmanuel Domenech, *Histoire du Mexique* (Paris: A. Lacroix, Verboeckhoven et Cie, 1868), 393.

17. See "Cuestion de Mexico," an essay originally published in Madrid, republished in *La Sociedad*, June 26, 1863.

18. For the text of the Convention, see Niox, *Expédition du Mexique*, 731–732.

19. John Musser, *The Establishment of Maximilian's Empire in Mexico* (Menasha, WI: George Banta, 1918), 30–31; for Marx, see Karl Marx, "'The Intervention in Mexico,' *New York Daily Tribune*, November 23, 1861," in *Karl Marx on Colonialism and Modernization: His Despatches and Other Writings on China, India, Mexico, the Middle East and North Africa*, ed. Shlomo Avineri (Garden City, NY: Doubleday, 1968), 425–432.

20. Including key Pacific ports such as Acapulco as well. See Bock, *Prelude to Tragedy*, 218.

21. Spain had recognized Mexico's independence only fifteen years earlier, in 1836; France did not until 1830. See Van Young, *A Life Together*, 113, 204.

22. This followed earlier Spanish attempts to reconquer Mexico. See Van Young, *A Life Together*, 161.

23. Bock, *Prelude to Tragedy*, 219, 223.

24. Bulnes, *El verdadero Juárez*, 8.

25. See *Correspondencia de España* for March 24, October 14, and November 10 and 12. See also Jorge Mario Magallón Ibarra, *Proceso y ejecución vs. Fernando Maximiliano de Habsburgo* (Mexico: Universidad Nacional Autónoma de México, 2005), 368n.

26. Pedro Pruneda, *Historia de la guerra de Méjico, desde 1861 á 1867: Con todos los documentos diplomáticos justificativos* (Madrid: Elizalde y compañia, 1867), 91–95.

27. Niox, *Expédition du Mexique*, 59–60; Alfred Jackson Hanna and Kathryn Abbey Hanna, *Napoléon III and Mexico: American Triumph over Monarchy* (Chapel Hill: University of North Carolina Press, 1971), 40.

28. Amy S. Greenberg, *A Wicked War: Polk, Clay, Lincoln, and the 1846 US Invasion of Mexico* (New York: Knopf, 2012), 169–171.

29. Pruneda, *Historia de la guerra*, 93.

30. John C. Pinheiro, *Missionaries of Republicanism: A Religious History of the Mexican-American War* (New York: Oxford University Press, 2014), 96; on Winfield Scott campaign, see Will Fowler, *Independent Mexico: The Pronunciamiento in the Age of Santa Anna, 1821–1858* (Lincoln: University of Nebraska Press, 2016), 221–222.

31. At the same time, diplomatic initiatives in Washington were bearing fruit. Seward made it clear that the United States would not allow Spain to take territory or to change the government of Mexico against the will of the people. See Bulnes, *El verdadero Juárez*, 8–9.

32. See *Correspondencia de España*, March 24, 1861.

33. Niox, *Expédition du Mexique*, 74–75. Though Napoléon III had a low opinion of Miramón, writing that Miramón "only works for himself." See note dated November 30, 1862, BLAC, Genaro García, Documentos Relativos a la Reforma y a la Intervención Francesa en México, 83a (4).

34. General François-Charles du Barail, *Mes Souvenirs* (Paris: Plon, 1898), 337–338.

35. Sara Yorke Stevenson, *Maximilian in Mexico: A Woman's Reminiscences of the French Intervention, 1862–1867* (New York: Century Co., 1899).

36. Georges Bibesco, *Au Mexique, 1862: Combats et retraite des six mille* (Paris: E. Plon, Nourrit et Cie, 1887), 48–49; Bock, *Prelude to Tragedy*, 329–335; José Manuel Hidalgo y Esnaurrízar, *Apuntes para escribir la historia de los proyectos de monarquía en Mexico desde el reinado de Cárlos III hasta la instalación del emperador Maximiliano [y] Manifiesto justificativo de los castigos nacionales en Querétaro* (Mexico: Librería Española de Garnier Hermanos, 1868), 74.

37. For the text of Prim's letter of March 17, 1862, see Gaulot, *Rêve d'empire*, 46–49.

38. Bock, *Prelude to Tragedy*, 327.

39. Bibesco, *Au Mexique*, 48.

40. Hanna and Hanna, *Napoléon III and Mexico*, 73; Seward was already confident, however, that the Intervention would fail. See Joseph A. Fry, *Lincoln, Seward, and US Foreign Relations in the Civil War Era* (Lexington: University Press of Kentucky, 2019), 147.

41. See letter from Romero to Doblado, April 26, 1862, in Romero, *Correspondencia de la legación mexicana*, 2:150.

42. See report of Matías Romero, March 11, 1862, "Intervencion europea," in Romero, *Correspondencia de la legación mexicana*, 2:84–85.

43. David M. Pletcher, *The Diplomacy of Annexation: Texas, Oregon, and the Mexican War* (Columbia: University of Missouri Press, 1973), 128; Andrew Torget, *Seeds of Empire: Cotton, Slavery, and the Transformation of the Texas Borderlands, 1800–1850* (Chapel Hill: University of North Carolina Press, 2015), 254.

44. Timothy J. Henderson, *A Glorious Defeat: Mexico and Its War with the United States* (New York: Hill and Wang, 2007), 146.

45. Bock, *Prelude to Tragedy*, 41.

46. For "soul of the clerical party," see Manuel Ramírez de Arellano, *Ultimas horas del imperio* (Mexico: Tipografía Mexicana, 1869), xxii; Almonte's activities in Europe were tracked closely; see "Romero to Foreign Affairs," February 19, 1862, in Romero, *Correspondencia de la legación mexicana*, 2:56.

47. Helen Willits Harris, "The Public Life of Juan Nepomuceno Almonte" (thesis, University of Texas, Austin, 1935), 357.

48. Victor Daran, *Le général Miguel Miramon; notes sur l'histoire du Mexique* (Rome: E. Perino, 1886), 127–129; Harris, "The Public Life," 361.

49. See decree dated June 1, 1862, SHD, GR 7 G, 89; see also Vigil and Riva Palacio, *México a través de los siglos*, 5:543.

3. Puebla

1. See Jacques-Pierre Brissot de Warville, *Second discour de J.P. Brissot, député, sur la nécessité de faire la guerre aux princes allemands: prononcé à la Société, dans la séance du vendredi 30 décembre 1791* (Paris: De l'Imprimerie du Patriote françois, 1791).

2. See the first article of the Soledad Convention in Gustave Léon Niox, *Expédition du Mexique, 1861–1867: Récit politique & militaire* (Paris: J. Dumaine, 1874), 85.

3. Niox, *Expédition du Mexique*, 102.

4. See Saligny's letter of appointment to Texas in George Garrison, ed., *Diplomatic Correspondence of the Republic of Texas in the Annual Report of the American Historical Association for the Year 1908* (Washington, DC: Government Printing Office, 1911), 1271; he was recalled after several controversies, see 1388–1389.

5. For Cozumel, see Kennedy to Aberdeen, August 6, 1843, in Ephraim Douglass Adams, ed., *British Diplomatic Correspondence concerning the Republic of Texas,1838–1846* (Austin: Texas State Historical Association, 1918), 245ff; for French immigration, see David M. Pletcher, *The Diplomacy of Annexation: Texas, Oregon, and the Mexican War* (Columbia: University of Missouri Press, 1973), 81; Bernice Barnett Denton, "Count Alphonso De Saligny and the Franco-Texienne Bill," *Southwestern Historical Quarterly* 45, no. 1 (1941): 136–146.

6. Pedro Pruneda, *Historia de la guerra de Méjico, desde 1861 á 1867: Con todos los documentos diplomáticos justificativos* (Madrid: Elizalde y compañia, 1867), 146–147.

7. BLAC, Charles Ferdinand Latrille Lorencez, "Charles Ferdinand Latrille, Comte de Lorencez Papers," (n.d.), vol. 2, 12.

8. Niox, *Expédition du Mexique*, 155.

9. Pletcher, *Diplomacy of Annexation*, 494–498; Timothy J. Henderson, *A Glorious Defeat: Mexico and Its War with the United States* (New York: Hill and Wang, 2007), 166–167.

10. For more on Wellington and Scott, see Pletcher, *Diplomacy of Annexation*, 601n.

11. Expectations of a swift campaign were likely informed by the experience of General Miguel Miramón, who was welcomed enthusiastically at Puebla during the War of the Reform. See José M. Vigil and Vicente Riva Palacio, *México a través de los siglos*, 5 vols. (Mexico City: Herrerias, 1940), 5:356.

12. Niox, *Expédition du Mexique,* 161–162.

13. Georges Bibesco, *Au Mexique, 1862: Combats et retraite des six mille* (Paris: E. Plon, Nourrit et Cie, 1887), 133–134.

14. Niox, *Expédition du Mexique,* 164–165; Pruneda, *Historia de la guerra,* 147.

15. Such assurances had fueled a Spanish attempt to retake Mexico in 1829; it, too, failed. See Eric Van Young, *A Life Together: Lucas Alamán and Mexico, 1792–1853* (New Haven, CT: Yale University Press, 2021), 403.

16. See Coubertin to Lorencez, October 21, 1862, BLAC, Charles Lorencez Papers, vol. 1.

17. Paul Gaulot, *Rêve d'empire:La vérité sur l'expédition du Mexique, d'après les documents inédits de Ernest Louët* (Paris: P. Ollendorff, 1890), 65.

18. Berriozabal message dated May 7, reproduced in *La Cronista,* May 15. See Niox, *Expédition du Mexique,* 168–169.

19. Niox, *Expédition du Mexique,* 182; for more on Ortega and Liberal politics, see Brian R. Hamnett, *Juárez* (London: Longman, 1994), 102–103; for Ortega's larger role in organizing the resistance, see also letters of July 23, 1861, and January 19, 1862, in Jesús González Ortega Collection, BLAC; on Ortega's political ambitions, see Frank Averill Knapp, *The Life of Sebastían Lerdo De Tejada, 1823–1889: A Study of Influence and Obscurity* (Austin: University of Texas Press, 1951), 69.

20. Niox, *Expédition du Mexique,* 184–185.

21. For letters of wounded soldiers, see SHD, GR 7 G Expédition du Mexique, 89 Mémoires, Carte du Mexique, Documents divers, Pertes, 1862–1866.

22. See "Compte rendu de la séance du mardi 17 juin 1862," *Le Temps,* June 19, 1862.

23. Niox, *Expédition du Mexique,* 190.

24. Léon de Montluc, ed., *Correspondance de Juarez et de Montluc, ancien consul général du Mexique; accompagnée de nombreuses lettres de personnages politiques, relatives à l'expédition du Mexique* (Paris: Charpentier, 1885), 83.

25. From the safety of Brunoy, just outside of Paris, Gutiérrez insisted that the Intervention's only problem was a lack of clarity. These "struggles" would end once the French were in Mexico City and Maximilian was present. See Gutierrez to Baron du Port, Brunoy (Seine et Oise), July 16, 1862, APRB, BE-A0546/36 Impératrice Charlotte du Mexique, 192.

26. Meanwhile, in Washington, Matías Romero was pointing out that "[not]a single city had shown any sympathy for the invaders." Matías Romero, *Correspondencia de la legación mexicana en Washington durante la intervención extranjera, 1860–1868: Colección de documentos para formar la historia de la intervención,* 10 vols. (Mexico City: Imprenta del Gobierno, 1870), 2:344.

27. Niox, *Expédition du Mexique,* 213.

28. Matías Romero, Mexico's representative in Washington, reported on the success of Mexican attacks on convoys. See "Nota á Mr. Seward sobre los sucesos de México, 14 Agosto 1862," in Romero, *Correspondencia de la legación mexicana,* 2:343.

29. Insurgency had also brought success in the War of Reform. See Jesús Terán, *La Misión confidencial de Don Jesús Terán en Europa, 1863–66,* ed. Gabriel Saldívar (Mexico: Archivo Histórico Diplomático Mexicano, 1943).

30. See Proclamation aux Mexicains, AN, AB XIX-171, Papiers des Tuileries (1870), dossier Juárez.

31. Niox, *Expédition du Mexique,* 178, 245; Jean-Charles Chenu, *Aperçu sur les expéditions de Chine, Cochinchine, Syrie et Mexique: Suivi d'une étude sur la fièvre jaune par le Dr Fuzier* (Paris: Masson, 1877), 116; General François-Charles du Barail, *Mes Souvenirs,* 3 vols. (Paris: Plon, 1898), 345.

32. The Belgian press reported that these tactics were carried forward by Sudanese troops, "loaned" to the French by Sa'id Pasha, who punished and marked guerrillas by amputating hands and feet. See "Régiment Belge Impératrice Charlotte," *L'Écho du Parlement,* February 2, 1865.

33. See Savelli to Lorencez, June 7, 1862, in Lorencez, "Charles Ferdinand Latrille, Comte de Lorencez Papers," 2:29.

34. See Concepción Lombardo de Miramón, *Memorias de Concepción Lombardo de Miramón* (Mexico: Porrúa, 1989), 420.

35. See Eloin to Loysel, Mexico, July 31, 1864, APRB, BE-A0546/36, Archief Van Felix Eloin, 266 Brieven aan Eloin gericht door: Charles-Joseph Loysel.

36. Niox, *Expédition du Mexique,* 205; Taxile Delord, *Histoire du second empire (1848–69)* (Paris; G. Baillière, 1869), 81.

37. Richard Leslie Hill and Peter C. Hogg, *A Black Corps d'élite: An Egyptian Sudanese Conscript Battalion with the French Army in Mexico, 1863–1867, and Its Survivors in Subsequent African History* (East Lansing: Michigan State University Press, 1995), 21; for Abyssinians, see du Barail, *Mes Souvenirs,* 446, where he refers to "le bataillon des nègres abyssins."

38. There was a second attempt to bring soldiers "from Egypt or Abyssinia" organized by Felix Eloin at the behest of Count Bombelles, one of Maximilian's closest confidants. Eloin was authorized to offer Muhammad Sa'id Pasha up to one hundred francs per soldier. See Bombelles to Eloin, Mexico, May 28 [1866?], APRB, BE-A0546/36 Archief Van Felix Eloin, 219 Brieven aan Eloin gericht door: graaf Charles-Albert de Bombelles.

39. José Arturo Saavedra Casco, "Un episodio olvidado de la historia de México: El batallón sudanés en la guerra de intervención y el segundo imperio (1862–1867)," *Estudios de Asia y África* 55 (January–April 2020): 716–717.

40. They were also exoticized as "agile as panthers" in reports in the Belgian press. See "Régiment Belge Impératrice Charlotte."

41. The empire would later try to persuade Sa'id Pasha to send additional troops. Bombelles instructed Eloin to pursue an agreement, paying Sa'id Pasha up to 100 francs per soldier, all the while insisting the men were "free workers" and to exercise every precaution, so as not to give the United States a pretext to intervene. See letter from Bombelles dated May 28 [no year, likely 1865], APRB, BE-A0546/36 Impératrice Charlotte du Mexique, 176 Reis in Yucatán, 1865–1866.

42. Hill and Hogg, *A Black Corps d'élite,* 31.

43. For some Sudanese, Mexico proved to be a congenial environment. The *New York Herald* reported that "the negro was not treated altogether as a negro in Mexico." *New York Herald,* August 17, 1866, APRB, BE-A0546/36 Impératrice Charlotte du Mexique, 178 Reis van keizerin naar Europa.

44. The convoys brought a windfall to the Compagnie générale Transatlantique. See Service historique de la Défense, SHD, GR 7 G Expédition du Mexique, 91 Embarquements (voie des transatlantiques—Saint-Nazaire), 1862–1864.

45. Niox, *Expédition du Mexique*, 43.

46. For troop counts and convoy dates, see Niox, *Expédition du Mexique*, 736–740.

47. For Napoléon III commentary, see "Memorandum de Napoléon III, Suite du 14 Avril 1863," BLAC, Genaro García, Documentos Relativos a la Reforma y a la Intervención Francesa en México, 83a (2) Intervención Francesa, Documentos misceláneos, 1867–1869.

48. By the time Forey arrived, Lorencez was eager to get out of Mexico. Forey cautioned him not to move precipitously. "I know that your desire is to return to France, but I pray you not to leave Orizaba before my arrival." See Forey to Lorencez, Veracruz, October 4, 1862, BLAC, Charles Lorencez Papers, vol. 1.

49. Niox, *Expédition du Mexique*, 247–248.

50. See "Notes détachées et extraits de lettres sur le Mexique," Paris, July 17, 1862, SHD, GR 7 G Expédition du Mexique, 89 Mémoires, Carte du Mexique, Documents divers, Pertes, 1862–1866.

51. Niox, *Expédition du Mexique*, 249–250.

52. Paul Louis M. Laurent, *La Guerre du Mexique de 1862 à 1866: Journal de marche du 3ᵉ chasseurs d'Afrique, notes intimes écrites au jour le jour* (Paris: Amyot, 1867), 33.

53. Niox, *Expédition du Mexique*, 256.

54. In laying siege to Puebla, Forey was showing greater wisdom than Lorencez had and following the precedent of Comonfort in 1856. See Vigil and Riva Palacio, *México a través de los siglos*, 5:115–119; Hamnett, *Juárez*, 97–98; Victor Daran, *Le général Miguel Miramon: Notes sur l'histoire du Mexique* (Rome: E. Perino, 1886), 24–32.

55. Laurent, *La Guerre du Mexique*, 30–31.

56. This was the approach recommended by Napoléon III. See Gaulot, *Rêve d'empire*, 93; see also Juan de Dios Arias, *Reseña histórica de la formación y operaciones del cuerpo de Ejército del Norte durante la intervención francesa* (Mexico: N. Chávez, 1867), 655–656.

57. Niox, *Expédition du Mexique*, 257.

58. The lancers were from Nuevo León, their presence demonstrating the geographic breadth of Mexican resistance (Nuevo León is in the Mexican northeast). Laurent, *La Guerre du Mexique*, 40–41.

59. Laurent, *La Guerre du Mexique*, 57.

60. Rather than credit Mexican resistance, Domenech blamed Forey's timidity for the slow progress; see Emmanuel Domenech, *Histoire du Mexique* (Paris: A. Lacroix, Verboeckhoven et Cie, 1868), 106–107.

61. See note on Puebla defenses dated March 15, 1863, BLAC, Genaro García, Documentos Relativos a la Reforma y a la Intervención Francesa en México, 81 (2) Intervención Francesa, Documentos misceláneos, 1862–1867.

62. Niox, *Expédition du Mexique*, 263–264; on Longueville, see also Laurent, *La Guerre du Mexique*, 172.

63. For letters, see Eugène Lefèvre, *Documents officiels recueillis dans la secrétairerie privée de Maximilien: Histoire de l'intervention française au Mexique* (Paris: Armand le Chevalier, 1870), 278–280.

64. Domenech, *Histoire du Mexique*, 107–108; Jack Autrey Dabbs, *The French Army in Mexico, 1861–1867: A Study in Military Government* (The Hague: Mouton, 1963), 46–47.

65. Du Barail, *Mes Souvenirs,* 440.

66. For Saligny and Almonte, see du Barail, *Mes Souvenirs,* 442; see also Dabbs, *French Army in Mexico,* 49–50.

67. Niox, *Expédition du Mexique,* 282–283.

68. The fate of the prisoners remained an object of concern in the Mexican diaspora. In California, collections were taken up in support of the prisoners of war, not only from Puebla, but subsequently. See "Lista de donativos para los prisioneros de Guerra—Suscricion de las señoras de Los Ángeles," *La Voz de Méjico,* January 5, 1864.

69. See Guy P. C. Thomson, *Patriotism, Politics, and Popular Liberalism in Nineteenth-Century Mexico: Juan Francisco Lucas and the Puebla Sierra* (Wilmington, DE: Scholarly Resources, 1999), 89.

70. Díaz was early identified as a particularly talented general. See Blondeel à Rogier, Mexico, September 26, 1865, AMBAE, Série B 68 I, II, III, 1861–1866, Enrôlements militaires à l'Etranger; Légion Belge au Portugal, 1834.

71. For Díaz, see Paul H. Garner, *Porfirio Díaz* (New York: Longman, 2001), 243; for Escobedo, see Enrique M. de los Rios, *Maximiliano y la toma de Querétaro* (Mexico City: Las Escalerillas, 1889).

72. Epitacio Huerta, *Apuntes para servir a la historia de los defensores de Puebla que fueron conducidos prisioneros a Francia* (Mexico: Imprenta de Vicente G. Torres, 1868), 4–5, 30. For the return of the officers, see Service historique de la Défense, SHD, GR 7 G Expédition du Mexique, 91 Embarquements (voie des transatlantiques—Saint-Nazaire), 1862–1864.

73. See Oudriot à Bazaine Compagnie de Sureté de Mexico, Mexico, January 29, 1866, BLAC, Achille Bazaine Papers G500, vol. 17.

74. In July, Puebla notables would draft and submit a testimonial in support of the empire. See Actas de Adhesión, Puebla ("En la Ciudad de Puebla a 3 de Julio de 1863 . . ."), AGN, Segundo Imperio, Caja 01, Expediente 17, Actas de Adhesión.

75. Du Barail, *Mes Souvenirs,* 444.

76. James Frederick Elton, *With the French in Mexico* (London: Chapman and Hall, 1867), 19–20; Dabbs, *French Army in Mexico,* 50; Fernando del Paso, *News from the Empire,* trans. Alfonso González and Stella T. Clark (Champaign, IL: Dalkey Archive Press, 2009), 137.

4. Pacification and Resistance

1. Alfred J. Hanna and Kathryn Abbey Hanna, *Napoléon III and Mexico: American Triumph over Monarchy* (Chapel Hill: University of North Carolina Press, 1971), 86–87.

2. Letter to Manuel Doblado, October 24, 1855, cited in Frank Averill Knapp, *The Life of Sebastían Lerdo De Tejada, 1823–1889: A Study of Influence and Obscurity* (Austin: University of Texas Press, 1951), 35.

3. See Luis Weckmann, "Un gran archivo histórico mexicano en París," *Historia Mexicana* 8, no. 1 (1958): 94.

4. Brian R. Hamnett, *Juárez* (London: Longman, 1994), 21–22; Knapp, *Life of Sebastían Lerdo,* 5.

5. For San Ildefonso from an English perspective, see William Henry Bullock, *Across Mexico in 1864–5* (London: Macmillan, 1866), 94–95.

6. Knapp, *Life of Sebastián Lerdo*, 19–20.

7. See "Editorial," *Diario del Gobierno de la República Mejicana*, June 16, 1863; "La política francesa," *Diario del Gobierno de la República Mejicana*, June 16, 1863.

8. Letter, La Tour du Pin to Lorencez, Mexico, July 9, 1863, BLAC, Charles Lorencez Papers, vol. 1.

9. Knapp, *Life of Sebastián Lerdo*, 80–81.

10. The message of the itinerant government as a symbolic center for Mexican resistance spread far. See *La Voz de Méjico*, January 12, 1864. "[Whether established in San Luis Potosí] or elsewhere on national territory [we will be] the living representation that Mexico protests and will continue to protest against the unjustifiable violence of which it is the object."

11. For Juárez's take on the military situation, see his letters of May 27 and June 11, 1863, in Jorge L. Tamayo, *Epistolario De Benito Juarez*, 2nd ed. (Buenos Aires: Fondo de Cultura Económica, 2006), 358–361.

12. Sara Yorke Stevenson, *Maximilian in Mexico: A Woman's Reminiscences of the French Intervention, 1862–1867* (New York: Century Co., 1899), 91.

13. Gustave Léon Niox, *Expédition du Mexique, 1861–1867: Récit politique & militaire* (Paris: J. Dumaine, 1874), 286.

14. For the entry and Forey's instructions, see Auguste Charles Philippe Blanchot, *L'intervention française au Mexique: Mémoires* (Paris: E. Nourry, 1911), 412.

15. Blanchot, *L'intervention française*, 413.

16. Helen Willits Harris, "The Public Life of Juan Nepomuceno Almonte" (PhD diss., University of Texas, 1935), 392.

17. L'Hériller referred to Márquez as "this vulture always ready to pillage . . . thus . . . detested by everyone." See L'Hériller to Lorencez, Puebla, May 18, 1863, BLAC, Charles Lorencez Papers, vol. 1.

18. For Márquez's reputation, see Leonardo Márquez, *Manifiestos (El Imperio y Los Imperiales)* (Mexico City: Vazquez, 1904), 2–3, 111; Victor Daran, *Le général Miguel Miramon: Notes sur l'histoire du Mexique* (Rome: E. Perino, 1886), 79–80. Anton von Magnus reported joking references to Leonardo Márquez as "Don Leopardo"; see Magnus, *Das Ende des maximilianischen Kaiserreichs in Mexico: Berichte des königlich preussischen Ministerresidenten Anton von Magnus an Bismarck, 1866–1867*, ed. Joachim Kühn (Göttingen: Musterschmidt, 1965), 220; Ramírez de Arellano, *Ultimas horas del imperio* (Mexico: Tipografía Mexicana, 1869), 19; for Soledad, see BLAC, Charles Lorencez Papers, 2:29.

19. "El Ejercito aliado en Mexico," *La Sociedad*, June 11, 1863.

20. Stevenson, *Maximilian in Mexico*, 97.

21. Ignacio Manuel Altamirano, *Historia y política de México (1821–1882)* (Mexico: Empresas Editoriales, 1947), 118–119.

22. "El Ejercito aliado en Mexico."

23. "Proclama," *La Sociedad*, June 10, 1863.

24. As one newspaper would later put it, "They will make Mexico an Algeria— defeated, but never surrendered." See "Expedition dans le Michoacan du regiment belge Imperatrice Charlotte," *La Meuse*, May 16, 1865.

25. José Sebastian Segura, ed., *Boletin de las leyes del Imperio mexicano, ó sea Codigo de la restauracion* (Mexico: Imprenta literaria, 1863), 58; see 51–54, 60, for the text of Forey's decree.

46. For Saligny's career in Texas, see Nancy Nichols Barker, "Devious Diplomat: Dubois de Saligny and the Republic of Texas," *Southwestern Historical Quarterly* 72, no. 3 (1969): 324–334.

47. A significant number of Liberal leaders, including Lerdo and Juárez, had bought former Church lands, too. See Richard N. Sinkin, *The Mexican Reform, 1855–1876: A Study in Liberal Nation-Building* (Austin: University of Texas, 1979), 170–171.

48. They had done so on November 9, 1863. See Harris, "The Public Life," 410; see also José M. Vigil and Vicente Riva Palacio, *México a través de los siglos*, 5 vols. (Mexico City: Herrerias, 1940), 5:617; for the decrees, see WRC, Charlotte and Maximilian Collection, folder 11.

49. Gaulot, *Rêve d'empire*, 234–236.

50. See Lerdo to Sr. Gral. de División D. Jesús González Ortega, Sierra hermosa, Saltillo, March 16, 1864, BLAC, Jesús González Ortega Collection.

51. On the role of compulsion in the formation of Mexican forces, see Niox, *Expédition du Mexique*, 331.

52. Domenech, *Histoire du Mexique*, 162.

53. See letter from Godoy to Juárez, June 12, 1864, BLAC, Genaro García, Documentos Relativos a la Reforma y a la Intervención Francesa en México, 80c (3) Intervención Francesa, Correspondencia miscelánea, 1846–1867. Regarding Uraga's decision, Godoy writes "los motivos ostensibles de esta resolución son la falta de recursos." Godoy would eventually replace Manuel Rodríguez as Mexican consul in San Francisco. See Robert Ryal Miller, "A Mexican Secret Agent in the United States, 1864–1866," *The Americas* 19 (1962): 143; for more on Godoy, see Vigil and Riva Palacio, *México a través de los siglos*, 5:143, 272, 341; Juan de Dios Arias, *Reseña histórica de la formación y operaciones del cuerpo de Ejército del Norte durante la intervención francesa* (Mexico: N. Chávez, 1867), 262.

54. See Lorencez's letter from Córdoba dated April 19, 1862, in Dabbs, *French Army in Mexico*, 27.

55. Four were punished for their alleged involvement in the poisoning. Three men were executed; a woman was condemned to hard labor for life. See report from Veracruz dated January 1, 1863, AMAE, Correspondance politique des consuls, 1826–1870, Mexique, 3 1863–1864 La Vera Cruz, Tampico.

56. See Mort de Sergent VICO Paul, Guadalajara, July 19, 1864, SHD, GR 7 G Expédition du Mexique, 89 Mémoires, Carte du Mexique, Documents divers, Pertes, 1862–1866.

57. See "Etat nominatif des militaires qui ont été assassines au Mexique par des sujets mexicains," BLAC, Genaro García, Documentos Relativos a la Reforma y a la Intervención Francesa en México, 82a (2) Intervención Francesa, Estadística militar y económica, 1862–1867.

58. Timing was everything. An offer to serve in the republican army after the surrender of Querétaro was rebuffed. See letters from six officers to Escobedo sent the day after the fall of the city. In Benito Juárez, *Documentos, discursos y correspondencia*, ed. Jorge L. Tamayo (Mexico: Editorial Libros de México, 1972), 12:11.

59. Albert Duchesne, *L'expédition des volontaires belges au Mexique, 1864–1867* (Brussels: Centre d'Histoire Militaire, 1967), 433, 436.

60. Charlotte, moved to pity when she learned of Belgian privations, arranged for ten thousand francs (about two thousand dollars) to be sent to the prisoners. See letters dated April 28, May 9, and July 22, 1865, AMBAE, Série B 68 I, II, III 1861–1866, Enrôlements militaires à l'Etranger: Légion Belge au Portugal, 1834.

61. Duchesne, *L'expédition des volontaires*, 443, Blandinière at 685.

62. See the report on Pierre Vergne, Orizaba, May 19, 1864, SHD, GR 7 G Expédition du Mexique, 89 Mémoires, Carte du Mexique, Documents divers, Pertes, 1862–1866.

63. For Eytabli and Géraudan, see reports dated November 12, 1864, SHD, GR 7 G Expédition du Mexique, 89 Mémoires, Carte du Mexique, Documents divers, Pertes, 1862–1866.

64. See "Résumé des lettres prises dans les papiers du Colonel Jésus de la Garza," BLAC, Genaro García, Documentos Relativos a la Reforma y a la Intervención Francesa en México, 82a Estadística militar y económica, 1862–1867.

65. See "Liste nominative des prisonniers," BLAC, Genaro García, Documentos Relativos a la Reforma y a la Intervención Francesa en México, 82a Estadística militar y económica, 1862–1867.

66. Jesús Terán, *La Misión confidencial de Don Jesús Terán en Europa, 1863–66*, ed. Gabriel Saldívar (Mexico: Archivo Histórico Diplomático Mexicano, 1943), xvi–xviii, 14–15; see also Hanna and Hanna, *Napoléon III and Mexico*, 123.

67. General Negrete had evacuated San Luis, then sought to retake it when he learned it was defended by the troops of Tomas Mejía. He failed and lost much of his force. See Niox, *Expédition du Mexique*, 346.

68. Vigil and Riva Palacio, *México a través de los siglos*, 5:621; Niox, *Expédition du Mexique*, 341. Douay and Méjia were greeted "enthusiastically" in Querétaro; see Domenech, *Histoire du Mexique*, 154.

69. See, for example, the Actas de Adhesión of Puebla ("En la Ciudad de Puebla a 3 de Julio de 1863 . . ."), AGN, Segundo Imperio, Caja 01, Expediente 17, Actas de Adhesión.

70. Erika Pani, "Intervention and Empire: Politics as Usual?," in *Malcontents, Rebels, and Pronunciados the Politics of Insurrection in Nineteenth-Century Mexico*, ed. Will Fowler (Lincoln: University of Nebraska Press, 2012), 240–241.

71. See "Los Pueblos de indígenas de Ciudad de Valles," AGN, Segundo Imperio, Caja 01, Expediente 16, Actas de Adhesión.

5. The Savior

1. For Max and his brothers, see Károly Mária Kertbeny, *Spiegelbilder der Erinnerung: Erlebtes, Erschautes, Erdachtes aus den Papieren eines Fünfzigers. Vom Verfasser der "Modernen Imperatoren"* (Leipzig: Heinrich Matthes, 1868), 193–194.

2. For bouquets and bracelets, see letter from Charlotte to Aunt, Laeken, January 3, 1857, ÖSta, SB Coburg,4 II-20 Familienkorrespondenz Sachsen-Coburg-Gotha, Korrespondenz, 1857–1881.

3. Charlotte to Leopold, December 7, 1857, in Charlotte, *Lettres de Charlotte à Léopold, 1850 à 1868* (Brussels: Capron, 1988), 72.

4. Letter to her grandmother, January 31, 1864, in Luis Weckmann, *Carlota de Bélgica: Correspondencia y escritos sobre México en los archivos europeos, 1861–1868* (Mexico: Porrúa, 1989), 266.

5. The British ambassador to Vienna claimed that Maximilian was a "continual embarrassment." See Carl H. Bock, *Prelude to Tragedy: The Negotiation and Breakdown of the Tripartite Convention of London, October 31, 1861* (Philadelphia: University of Pennsylvania Press, 1966), 181.

6. The revolution for independence from Habsburg rule in 1848 had been repressed militarily, with great brutality. See Jacob Martin to James Buchanan, August 20, 1848, in Leo Francis Stock, *United States Ministers to the Papal States: Instructions and Despatches, 1848–1868* (Washington, DC: Catholic University Press, 1933), 10.

7. Lina Gasparini, "Massimiliano d'Austria, ultimo governatore del Lombardo-Veneto," *Nuova antologia* 377 (February 1935): 107.

8. Maximilian wrote frequently of Lacroma/Lokrum in his correspondence with Charlotte as he voyaged to Brazil. See HRC, MS-2733, letters from July 19, 21, 27, and 30, and August 11, 1860.

9. See Charlotte to Leopold, October 10, 1860, in Charlotte, *Lettres*, 83.

10. For the yacht, see *Illustrated Naval and Military Magazine: A Monthly Journal Devoted to All Subjects Connected . . .* , n.d., 387; for Corfu, see Anton von Magnus, *Das Ende des maximilianischen Kaiserreichs in Mexico: berichte des königlich preussischen Ministerresidenten Anton von Magnus an Bismarck, 1866–1867*, ed. Joachim Kühn (Göttingen: Musterschmidt, 1965), 36.

11. See HRC, MS-2733, letters, April 8, 1860.

12. Raphael Waldburg-Zeil, *Fernando Maximiliano de Habsburgo, 1832–1867: Perfil humano de un archiduque-emperador* (Madrid: Gunter Quercus, 2013), 132–133.

13. Maximilian, *Recollections of My Life*, 3 vols. (London: R, Bentley, 1868), 2:15.

14. For Maximilian, such features invoked "the spirit of Charles V." See Maximilian, *Recollections*, 178.

15. Charlotte to Leopold, December 20, 1860, in Charlotte, *Lettres*, 88.

16. Gasparini, "Massimiliano d'Austria, ultimo governatore del Lombardo-Veneto," 109.

17. On the Crimean alliance and the United States, see Nancy Nichols Barker, *Distaff Diplomacy: The Empress Eugénie and the Foreign Policy of the Second Empire* (Austin: University of Texas Press, 1967), 20.

18. On Cuba and monarchs for Mexico, see Christian Schefer, *La grande pensée de Napoléon III: Les origines de l'expédition du Mexique (1858–1862)* (Paris: M. Rivière et Cie, 1939), 7, 21.

19. Egon Caesar Corti, *Maximilian and Charlotte of Mexico*, trans. Catherine Alison Phillips (New York: Knopf, 1928), 36.

20. Bock, *Prelude to Tragedy*, 43.

21. Regarding Eugénie and Spain, see esp. Barker, *Distaff Diplomacy*, 9–11, 20; José Fuentes Mares, *La Emperatriz Eugenia y su aventura mexicana* (Mexico: Colegio de México, 1976), 10–16.

22. For US and transatlantic interest in Cuba in the 1820s, see William R. Manning, ed., *Diplomatic Correspondence of the United States: Inter-American Affairs, 1831–1860* (Washington, DC: Carnegie Endowment for International Peace, 1939), 60, 89ff; for Cuba and the revolutionary Caribbean, see Vanessa Mongey, *Rogue Revolutionaries: The Fight for Legitimacy in the Greater Caribbean* (Philadelphia: University of Pennsylvania

Press, 2020); for Cuba and hemispheric slavery, see Matthew Karp, *This Vast Southern Empire: Slaveholders at the Helm of American Foreign Policy* (Cambridge, MA: Harvard University Press, 2016); Sven Beckert, *Empire of Cotton: A Global History* (New York: Knopf, 2014).

23. Barker, *Distaff Diplomacy,* 88.

24. Corti, *Maximilian and Charlotte,* 77; Fuentes Mares, *La Emperatriz Eugenia,* 84.

25. H. José Manuel Hidalgo y Esnaurrízar, *Apuntes para escribir la historia de los proyectos de monarquía en Mexico desde el reinado de Cárlos III hasta la instalación del emperador Maximiliano [y] Manifiesto justificativo de los castigos nacionales en Querétaro* (Mexico: Librería Española de Garnier Hermanos, 1868), 18; Fuentes Mares, *La Emperatriz Eugenia,* 84–85.

26. There is evidence that Gutiérrez, sensing an opening, was in contact with Maximilian immediately following his dismissal as governor-general of Lombardy-Venezia in 1859. In a letter he wrote to Charlotte from Rio in April 1860 Maximilian refers to a "Signor Gutieres." See HRC, MS-2733, letter dated April 2, 1860.

27. They also reveal the enduring power of the example of Alexander von Humboldt. See Alexander von Humboldt, *Political Essay on the Kingdom of New Spain: A Critical Edition,* 2 vols. (Chicago: University of Chicago Press, 2019).

28. Maximilian, *Recollections,* 3:90, 92, 91.

29. Maximilian, *Recollections,* 3:103–104, 111–112.

30. Maximilian, *Recollections,* 3:119, 120.

31. Arturo Gómez Camacho and Ernesto de la Torre Villar, "La Intervención Francesa," in *La intervención francesa en la revista Historia Mexicana,* ed. Erika Pani (Mexico: Colegio de México, 2012), 24–25. Camacho and Torre Villar discuss the archival and historiographical complexity surrounding the imperial couple.

32. APRB, BE-A0546/36, Impératrice Charlotte du Mexique, 203 De triomf van keizer maximilliaan.

33. Maximilian worshipped Charles V, a devotion only intensified by a trip to Seville in 1851. See Maximilian, *Recollections,* 178.

34. See, for example, Marcy Norton, *Sacred Gifts, Profane Pleasures: A History of Tobacco and Chocolate in the Atlantic World* (Ithaca, NY: Cornell University Press, 2008).

35. For "dieser romantisch-eitle Prinz," see the remarks of Julius Frobel, a politician close to the court, quoted in Magnus, *Das Ende,* 306.

36. Maximilian discussed recovering the territories lost to the United States, notably with Matthew Maury in October 1863. See Frances Leigh Williams, *Matthew Fontaine Maury, Scientist of the Sea* (New Brunswick, NJ: Rutgers University Press, 1963), 414.

37. Gasparini, "Massimiliano d'Austria, ultimo governatore del Lombardo-Veneto," 109.

38. French marshal Bazaine would characterize Maximilian as "a German dreamer." See Gustave Léon Niox, *Expédition du Mexique, 1861–1867: Récit politique & militaire* (Paris: J. Dumaine, 1874), 596.

39. Charlotte to Leopold, January 27, 1862, in Charlotte, *Lettres,* 104.

40. On the move from principles to active politics among Conservative Mexicans, see Gastón García Cantú, *La Intervención Francesa en México* (Mexico: Clio, 1999), 28–29.

41. Corti, *Maximilian and Charlotte,* 280.

42. Charlotte to Leopold, February 9, 1863, in Charlotte, *Lettres,* 122.

43. See Charlotte to Leopold, December 17, 1863, in Charlotte, *Lettres,* 129.

44. See Philippe to Charlotte, February 22, 1863, APRB, BE-A0546/36, Impératrice Charlotte du Mexique, 16 Brieven aan de keizerin gericht door vorsten en prinsen, 1853–1867.

45. Philippe to Charlotte, October 11, 1863, APRB, BE-A0546/36, Impératrice Charlotte du Mexique, 17 Brieven aan de keizerin gericht door vorsten en prinsen, België: Prinses Louise van België.

6. The Seduction

1. The courtship of Maximilian had begun years before, in 1857. See Egon Caesar Corti, *Maximilian and Charlotte of Mexico,* trans. Catherine Alison Phillips (New York: Knopf, 1928), 72.

2. Helen Willits Harris, "The Public Life of Juan Nepomuceno Almonte" (PhD diss., University of Texas, 1935), 338; Corti, *Maximilian and Charlotte,* 139–140.

3. Alfred J. Hanna and Kathryn Abbey Hanna, *Napoléon III and Mexico: American Triumph over Monarchy* (Chapel Hill: University of North Carolina Press, 1971), 99.

4. See letters dated November 12, 1862, February 8, 1863, July 11, 1863, and August 9, 1863, APRB, BE-A0546/36, Impératrice Charlotte du Mexique, 15 Brieven aan de keizerin gericht door vorsten en prinsen, België: Leopold I koning der Belgen. 1849–1864.

5. Letter from Philippe to Charlotte, Brussels, February 26, 1863, APRB, BE-A0546/36, Impératrice Charlotte du Mexique, 16 Brieven aan de keizerin gericht door vorsten en prinsen, België: Prins Leopold hertog van Brabant en zijn echtgenote Marie-Henriette, aartshertogin van Oostenrijk. 1853–1867.

6. Albert Duchesne, *L'expédition des volontaires belges au Mexique, 1864–1867,* 2 vols. (Brussels: Centre d'Histoire Militaire, 1967), 110–111.

7. See HRC, MS-2733, letters from November 14, 17, and 19, 1863.

8. Letter from Gutiérrez to Charlotte, August 24, 1862, APRB, BE-A0546/76, Impératrice Charlotte du Mexique, 76 Brieven van particulieren aan de keizerin gericht: José-Maria Gutierrez de Estrada.

9. Napoléon III received his copy in July 1863. See Gutiérrez de Estrada to Napoléon III, July 15, 1863, AN, AB XIX-171 Papiers des Tuileries (1870).

10. Letter from Gutiérrez to Charlotte, May 2, 1863, APRB, BE-A0546/36, Impératrice Charlotte du Mexique, 76 Brieven van particulieren aan de keizerin gericht: José-Maria Gutierrez de Estrada. 1862–1864 en niet gedateerd.

11. Angel Pola, *Los traidores pintados por si mismos* (Mexico: Eduardo Dublan, 1900), 71.

12. See letter from Almonte to Maximilian, September 27, 1863, BCAH, box 2Q230, vol. 713.

13. See letters from Almonte to Maximilian, October 8 and 27, 1863, BCAH, box 2Q230, vol. 713.

14. Letters from Almonte to Maximilian, January 9 and February 9, 1864, BCAH, Juan Nepomuceno Almonte Papers, 1834–1865, box 2A136.

15. Jan Bazant, *Alienation of Church Wealth in Mexico: Social and Economic Aspects of the Liberal Revolution, 1856–1875* (Cambridge: Cambridge University Press, 1971), 150–151, 267–268.

16. Barbara A. Tenenbaum, "Development and Sovereignty: Intellectuals and the Second Empire," in *Los intelectuales y el poder en México*, ed. R. A. Camp et al. (Mexico: El Colegio de México, 1991), 84–85, 87.

17. Enterprises often owned with his brother Manuel. See Bazant, *Alienation of Church Wealth*, 187.

18. Tenenbaum, "Development and Sovereignty," 84; Michael P. Costeloe, *Bonds and Bondholders: British Investors and Mexico's Foreign Debt, 1824–1888* (Westport, CT: Praeger, 2003), 158. Murphy was himself a creditor of Mexico with payments in arrears. See Silvestre Villegas Revueltas, "Charles Wyke y su misión en el México juarista," *Estudios de historia moderna y contemporánea de México* 32 (2006): 19.

19. In fact, the Intervention made the investment environment worse. See William Henry Bullock, *Across Mexico in 1864–5* (London: Macmillan, 1866), 19.

20. For the Escandón family, see Bazant, *Alienation of Church Wealth*, 86–87, 183.

21. *Advenimiento de SS. MM. II. Maximiliano y Carlota al trono de México* (Mexico: J. M. Andrade y F. Escalante, 1864), 78–79.

22. José Manuel Hidalgo y Esnaurrízar, *Un hombre de mundo escribe sus impresiones: Cartas de José Manuel Hidalgo y Esnaurrízar, ministro en París del Emperador Maximiliano* (Mexico: Editorial Porrúa, 1978), 34.

23. *Advenimiento*, 72–76; see José M. Vigil and Vicente Riva Palacio, *México a través de los siglos*, 5 vols. (Mexico City: Herrerias, 1940), 5:614; Frederic Hall, *Invasion of Mexico by the French and the Reign of Maximilian I, Late Emperor of Mexico, with a Sketch of the Empress Carlota* (New York: J. Miller, 1868), 72–76.

24. *Advenimiento*, 81.

25. *Advenimiento*, 81.

26. *Le Mémorial diplomatique*, October 11, 1863.

27. It is worth noting, in this regard, that supporters of the empire considered "subsidizing" *Le Mémorial*. See Eloin to Hidalgo, Palacio de Mexico, August 24, 1865, APRB, BE-A0546/36, Archief Van Felix Eloin, 255 Brieven aan Eloin gericht door: José Manuel Hidalgo. *Le Mémorial* eventually received twenty thousand francs. See letter from November 7, 1865, same folder.

28. Paul Gaulot, *Rêve d'empire: La vérité sur l'expédition du Mexique, d'après les documents inédits de Ernest Louët* (Paris: P. Ollendorff, 1890), 274.

29. Maximilian and Charlotte continued to use *Ernani* as an imperial emblem once in Mexico. See BMNAH, Colección: Imperio de Maximiliano, Documento 382 Ceremonial. Disposiciones generales para la fiesta nacional del 16 de septiembre de 1865.

30. For Haussmann and the rebuilding of Paris, see David Pinkney, *Napoleon III and the Rebuilding of Paris* (Princeton, NJ: Princeton University Press, 1958).

31. Charlotte to Leopold, March 26, 1864, in Charlotte, *Lettres de Charlotte à Léopold 1850 à 1868* (Brussels: Capron, 1988), 131.

32. Hanna and Hanna, *Napoléon III and Mexico*, 172–173.

33. Corti, *Maximilian and Charlotte*, 325.

34. *L'Etoile belge* reported that the firm behind the loan was Glyn, Mills and Company of London. It's unclear if there were other loans. See *L'Etoile belge*, March 23, 1864.

35. See report dated March 14, 1866, from Inspecteur Générale des finances to Marshall Bazaine, AN, AB XIX-171 Papiers des Tuileries (1870).

36. For prisoners in Tours, see letters from A[ristide] Auber dated August 19, 1863, AN, AB XIX-171 Papiers des Tuileries (1870).

37. Lynn Marshall Case and Warren F. Spencer, *The United States and France: Civil War Diplomacy* (Philadelphia: University of Pennsylvania Press, 1970), 400–403; Hanna and Hanna, *Napoléon III and Mexico*, 116–119; Don H. Doyle, *The Cause of All Nations: An International History of the American Civil War* (New York: Basic Books, 2014), 160–164.

38. According to Elihu Washburne of Illinois. Quoted in David G. McCullough, *The Greater Journey: Americans in Paris* (New York: Simon and Schuster, 2011), 244.

39. For Maury, Maximilian, and Slidell, see Frances Leigh Williams, *Matthew Fontaine Maury, Scientist of the Sea* (New Brunswick, NJ: Rutgers University Press, 1963).

40. As Charlotte's father put it, "You have saved him from difficulties which would have been inextricable for him without you." See letter, July 11, 1864, APRB, BE-A0546/36, Impératrice Charlotte du Mexique, 15 Brieven aan de keizerin gericht door vorsten en prinsen, België: Leopold I koning der Belgen. 1849–1864.

41. Corti, *Maximilian and Charlotte*, 232.

42. Duchesne, *L'expédition*, 111.

7. Imperial Pageantry

1. Joseph A. Fry, *Lincoln, Seward, and US Foreign Relations in the Civil War Era* (Lexington: University Press of Kentucky, 2019), 150; Lynn Marshall Case and Warren F. Spencer, *The United States and France: Civil War Diplomacy* (Philadelphia: University of Pennsylvania Press, 1970), 549.

2. See "The Empire of Mexico," *London Times*, July 29, 1864.

3. See entry for March 14, 1864, in Victoria, *The Letters of Queen Victoria: A Selection from Her Majesty's Correspondence and Journal between the Years 1862 and 1878*, ed. George Earle Buckle (New York: Longmans, 1926).

4. Albert Duchesne, *L'expédition des volontaires belges au Mexique, 1864–1867*, 2 vols. (Brussels: Centre d'Histoire Militaire, 1967), 285–286.

5. Egon Caesar Corti, *Maximilian and Charlotte of Mexico*, trans. Catherine Alison Phillips (New York: Knopf, 1928), 335.

6. Egon Caesar Corti, *Mensch und Herrscher: Wege und Schicksale* (Graz: Verlag Styria, 1952), 312.

7. See letter from Eugénie to Charlotte reproduced in Corti, *Maximilian and Charlotte*, 833.

8. AT-ÖSta, HHStA Urkundenreihen Habsburg-Lothringische Familien-urkunden 2526, Familienvertrag zwischen Kaiser Franz Joseph und Erzherzog Ferdinand Maximilian anlässlich seiner Thronbesteigung in Mexiko, Renuntiation des

Letzteren auf seine Sukzessionsrechte in den Erblanden und der Stephanskrone, 1864.04.09.

9. For context, see Erika Pani, "Intervention and Empire: Politics as Usual?," in *Malcontents, Rebels, and Pronunciados: The Politics of Insurrection in Nineteenth-Century Mexico,* ed. Will Fowler (Lincoln: University of Nebraska Press, 2012), 240–241.

10. For the text, see Frederic Hall, *Invasion of Mexico by the French and the Reign of Maximilian I, Late Emperor of Mexico, with a Sketch of the Empress Carlota* (New York: J. Miller, 1868), 85–90.

11. *Advenimiento de SS. MM. II. Maximiliano y Carlota al trono de México* (Mexico: J. M. Andrade y F. Escalante, 1864), 110.

12. Paul Gaulot, *Rêve d'empire: La vérité sur l'expédition du Mexique, d'après les documents inédits de Ernest Louët* (Paris: P. Ollendorff, 1890), 299, 301–302.

13. *Advenimiento,* 150.

14. Hall, *Invasion of Mexico,* 99.

15. *Advenimiento,* 113–114.

16. For hosting in Rome, see the letter from Charlotte to her grandmother dated March 1864, in Luis Weckmann, *Carlota de Bélgica: Correspondencia y escritos sobre México en los archivos europeos, 1861–1868* (Mexico: Porrúa, 1989), 269.

17. Paula Kollonitz, *The Court of Mexico: Originally Published as Eine Reise Nach Mexiko Im Jahre 1864 (Vienna, 1867),* trans. Joseph Earle Ollivant (London: Saunders, Otley, and Co., 1868), 59.

18. See, for example, design number 19, in Maximilian Emperor of Mexico and Charlotte Empress of Mexico, *Reglamento para el Servicio y Ceremonial de la Corte* (Mexico: J. M. Lara, 1865), n.p.

19. They seem to have borrowed from various European courts. See "Cérémonial de la cour," AGN, Segundo Imperio, Caja 07, Expediente 32, Solicitud.

20. Robert H. Duncan, "Political Legitimation and Maximilian's Second Empire in Mexico, 1864–1867," *Mexican Studies/Estudios Mexicanos* 12, no. 1 (January 1996): 38.

21. Letter "En vue de Veracruz le 28 mai 1864," WRC, Charlotte and Maximilian Collection, box 1, folder 1, Charlotte to Grandparents, 1846–1865.

22. James Frederick Elton, *With the French in Mexico* (London: Chapman and Hall, 1867), 9; the vessel might have been the French corvette *Chaptal.* See General François-Charles du Barail, *Mes Souvenirs,* 3 vols. (Paris: Plon, 1898), 336–337.

23. *Advenimiento,* 151.

24. For personal security, see Almonte letter dated February 18, 1864, BCAH, box 2Q230, vol. 713: Almonte's letters to Maximilian and others, 1862–1866.

25. Anselmo de la Portilla, *De Miramar a Mexico: Viaje del Emperador Maximiliano y de la Emperatriz Carlota, desde su Palacio de Miramar cerca de Trieste, hasta la capital del imperio mexicano, con una relacion de los festejos publicos con que fueron obsequiados au Veracruz, Cordoba, Orizaba, Puebla, Mexico, y en las demas poblaciones del transito* (Orizaba: J. Bernardo Aburto, 1864), 82.

26. See Eco del Comercio de Veracruz, May 31, 1864, reprinted in Portilla, *De Miramar a Mexico,* 62.

27. For colonial Veracruz, see Danielle Terrazas Williams, *The Capital of Free Women: Race, Legitimacy, and Liberty in Colonial Mexico* (New Haven, CT: Yale University Press, 2022).

28. Concepción Lombardo de Miramón, *Memorias de Concepción Lombardo de Miramón* (Mexico: Porrúa, 1989), 473.

29. Paula Kollonitz, *Un viaje a México en 1864* (n.p.: Libros de Mexico, 2020), 43.

30. See *l'Illustration*, July 23, 1864; see also Esther Acevedo, ed., *Testimonios artísticos de un episodio fugaz, 1864–1867* (Mexico, DF: Instituto Nacional de Bellas Artes, 1995).

31. Portilla, *De Miramar a Mexico*, 81–82; Angel Iglesias Dominguez had accompanied him aboard the *Novara* from Miramare to Veracruz.

32. Kollonitz, *Un viaje a México*, 87.

33. Lombardo de Miramón, *Memorias*, 473; she also mentions the coldness of the reception.

34. Kollonitz, *Un viaje a México*, 44.

35. For detailed itinerary, see Almonte letter dated February 8, 1864, BCAH, box 2Q230, vol. 713: Almonte's letters to Maximilian and others, 1862–1866.

36. *Advenimiento*, 173.

37. *Pájaro Verde*, June 18, 1864, reprinted in *Advenimiento*, 178.

38. *Advenimiento*, 190–191.

39. Kollonitz, *The Court of Mexico*, 105–106. Some of the damage dated to the War of Reform.

40. *Advenimiento*, 215–216.

41. Portilla, *De Miramar a Mexico*, 147.

42. For acts of adhesion, see *Advenimiento*, 66.

43. *Advenimiento*, 241.

44. Though even jaundice-eyed, Kollonitz regards these demonstrations as sincere. See Kollonitz, *The Court of Mexico*, 97–98.

45. It's difficult to judge the spontaneity of these decorative efforts. At least some of the work was contracted out. See "Correspondencia sobre el mal entendido y el adeudo con Felipe Lefebvre por el adorno de las calles por las que entraron el Emperador y su esposa," July 27, 1864, AGN, Segundo Imperio, Caja 31, Expediente 2, Gabinete del Emperador.

46. See *La Voz de Méjico*, June 25, 1864.

47. *Pájaro Verde* was also known as "el periódico de monseñor Munguía." Munguía, bishop of Michoacán, was reactionary in his politics. See "El Pájaro verde," https://hndm .iib.unam.mx/consulta/publicacion/verDescripcionDescarga/558ff93a7d1e3252 308614e3.pdf.

48. *Pájaro Verde* account reproduced in Portilla, *De Miramar a Mexico*, 259–260; for the politics of Mexican newspapers from the viewpoint of a contemporary foreigner, see William Henry Bullock, *Across Mexico in 1864–5* (London: Macmillan, 1866), 101.

49. Portilla, *De Miramar a Mexico*, 266–272.

50. Charlotte to Marie-Amélie (grandmother), June 26, 1864, WRC, Charlotte and Maximilian Collection, box 1, folder 1.

51. For Uraga, see Charlotte to Marie-Amélie, July 24, 1864, WRC, Charlotte and Maximilian Collection, box 1, folder 1; for Cadena, Sandoval, and Uraga, see Jack Autrey Dabbs, *The French Army in Mexico, 1861–1867: A Study in Military Government* (The Hague: Mouton, 1963), 97–99.

52. Mario Treviño Villarreal, *El principio del fin: La Batalla de Santa Ger-trudis* (Monterrey, Mexico: Honorable Congreso del Estado de Nuevo León, 1999), 17; Juan de Dios Arias, *Reseña histórica de la formación y operaciones del cuerpo de Ejército del Norte durante la intervención francesa* (Mexico: N. Chávez, 1867), 88.

53. See memorandum, Palais de Mexico, June 18, 1864, and Cabinet de l'Empereur, Palais de Mexico, August 29, 1864, APRB, BE-A0546/36, Archief Van Felix Eloin, 298 Minuten van brieven van de hand van Eloin.

54. Maximilian received eight million francs out of the loan. See Gustave Léon Niox, *Expédition du Mexique, 1861–1867: Récit politique & militaire* (Paris: J. Dumaine, 1874), 360. The loan barely touched the 270 million francs specified as the amount France was to be reimbursed for military expenses under the Treaty of Miramare.

55. They hired Carl Gangolf Kayser, architect from Vienna, to plan the expansion, and Julius Hofmann (also Austrian) for the interior design. See David Pruonto, "Did the Second Mexican Empire under Maximilian of Habsburg (1864–1867) Have an 'Austrian Face'?," *Austrian Studies* 20 (2012): 102–103; Ferdinand Anders, *Maximilian von Mexiko, 1832–1867: Ausstellung auf Burg Hardegg, 13. Mai—17. November 1974* (Vienna: Enzenhofer, 1974), 155.

56. Érika Pani, "El proyecto de Estado de Maximiliano a través de la vida corte-sana y del ceremonial público," *Historia Mexicana* 45, no. 2 (1995): 427.

57. See Rice University Manuscript Collection, "Charlotte and Maximilian Sheet Music," MS 356, box 7.

58. Carl Khevenhüller, *Con Maximiliano en México: Del diario del príncipe Carl Khevenhüller, 1864–1867,* ed. Brigitte Hamann (Mexico: Fondo de Cultura Económica, 1994), 114.

59. For enthusiasm and illness, see Weckmann, *Carlota de Bélgica,* 310–311; for core themes of Maximilian's empire, see Pani, "El proyecto," 445.

60. For the speech, see *La Sociedad,* September 20, 1864, cited in Duncan, "Political Legitimation," 57; Corti, *Maximilian and Charlotte,* 434–435.

61. Letter, October 23, 1864, WRC, Charlotte and Maximilian Collection, box 1, folder 1.

62. HRC, MS-2733, box 2, folder 15. Though the menu does not specify a location, the banquet probably took place in León. See letter from Maximilian "near León" to Charlotte the following day, MS-2733, box 2 folder 7.

63. Was this the occasion where Maximilian requested the anti-Conservative song "Los Cangrejos" mentioned by Paula de Arrangoiz? See Francisco de Paula de Arrangoiz y Berzábal, *México de 1808 Hasta 1867* (Mexico: Porrua, 1968), 592.

64. Bullock, *Across Mexico,* 348.

65. *L'Etoile belge* reported that Eloin had been assigned to administer the mines of Mexico. It seems that his role was that of a trusted adviser to Charlotte's father, Leo-pold I, on loan to play a similar role in Mexico. See *L'Etoile belge,* March 23, 1864.

66. For the persistence of support for Iturbide, see Eric Van Young, *A Life To-gether: Lucas Alaman and Mexico, 1792–1853* (New Haven, CT: Yale University Press, 2021), 151.

67. See "Escudo de armas del Imperio" in Segura, *Boletin de las leyes del Im-perio mexicano,* 295–296.

68. For Latin race and "Himno Imperial," see *La Sociedad,* September 28, 1863, 3.

69. Amparo Gómez Tepexicuapan, "Carlota en México," in *Más nuevas del imperio: Estudios interdisciplinarios acerca de Carlota de México*, ed. Susanne Igler and Roland Spiller (Frankfurt: Vervuert, 2001), 33–34.

70. For a sketch of the program for the celebration, see "Aniversario de la proclamación de la Independencia," *La Sociedad*, September 13, 1864, 3.

71. Juan Gómez de la Fuente, "Fiesta de la independencia," *La Sociedad*, September 16, 1864, 2–3.

72. For monuments and memory at the centenary, see Mauricio Tenorio Trillo, "1910 Mexico City: Space and Nation in the City of the Centenario," *Journal of Latin American Studies* 28, no. 1 (1996): 75–104.

73. Pruonto, "Did the Second Mexican Empire," 103; it was one of many public works projects planned by Maximilian and Charlotte. See Raphael Waldburg-Zeil, *Fernando Maximiliano de Habsburgo, 1832–1867: Perfil humano de un archiduque-emperador* (Madrid: Gunter Quercus, 2013), 150–151.

74. For the preponderance of French influence, see Mauricio Gomez Mayorga, "La Influencia francesa en la arquitectura y el urbanismo en Mexico," in *La intervención francesa y el Imperio de Maximiliano cien años después, 1862–1962*, ed. Arturo Arnáiz y Freg and Claude Bataillon (Mexico: Asociación Mexicana de Historiadores, Instituto Francés de América Latina, 1965), 185–186.

75. For Rotten Row, see Bullock, *Across Mexico*, 99.

76. Trillo, "1910 Mexico City," 94.

77. "El 16 de Setiembre en Veracruz," *La Sociedad*, September 24, 1864, 2–3. For an example of Mora's meticulous planning, see BMNAH, Colección: Imperio de Maximiliano, Documento 382 "Ceremonial. Disposiciones generales para la fiesta nacional del 16 de septiembre de 1865" and Documento 387 "Fiesta de Nuestra Señora de Guadalupe."

8. The Empire Looks for Friends

1. For examples of his political engagements while bishop of Puebla, see Rogelio Orozco Farías, *Fuentes históricas: México, 1821–1867: Documentos y escritos* (Mexico: Editorial Progreso, 1965), 245–249.

2. For Mexican bishops in exile, see Riccardo Cannelli, "México visto desde el Vaticano en la época de la Reforma (segunda mitad del siglo XIX)," in *Las leyes de Reforma y el estado laico*, ed. Roberto Blancarte (Mexico City: Colegio de Mexico, 2013), 240.

3. John Musser, *The Establishment of Maximilian's Empire in Mexico* (Menasha, WI: George Banta, 1918), 59.

4. Luis Ramos, María Guadalupe Bosch de Souza, Ana María González Luna, and Archivio vaticano, *Del Archivo secreto vaticano: La Iglesia y el estado mexicano en el siglo XIX* (Mexico, DF: Universidad Nacional Autónoma de México, 1997), 12.

5. For Munguía, see José M. Vigil and Vicente Riva Palacio, *México a través de los siglos*, 5 vols. (Mexico City: Herrerias, 1940), 5:xlix–l, 228–232; for Munguía's later career and that of Labastida, see Brian Stauffer, "The Routes of Intransigence: Mexico's 'Spiritual Pilgrimage' of 1874 and the Globalization of Ultramontane Catholicism," *The Americas: A Quarterly Review of Latin American History* 75 (2018): 291–324.

6. See "Discurso de Labastida ante la Regencia, 20 Octubre 1863," in Orozco Farías, *Fuentes históricas*, 297.

7. Sara Yorke Stevenson, *Maximilian in Mexico: A Woman's Reminiscences of the French Intervention, 1862–1867* (New York: Century Co., 1899), 118.

8. Egon Caesar Corti, *Maximilian and Charlotte of Mexico*, trans. Catherine Alison Phillips (New York: Knopf, 1928), 273; Jack Autrey Dabbs, *The French Army in Mexico, 1861–1867: A Study in Military Government* (The Hague: Mouton, 1963), 82.

9. Gustave Léon Niox, *Expédition du Mexique, 1861–1867: Récit politique & militaire* (Paris: J. Dumaine, 1874), 350–351.

10. Niox, *Expédition du Mexique*, 349, 354.

11. Arnold Blumberg, "The Mexican Empire and the Vatican, 1863–1867," *The Americas* 28, no. 1 (1971): 3.

12. William Henry Bullock, *Across Mexico in 1864–5* (London: Macmillan, 1866), 4–5.

13. See the anonymous commentary, "Mexico," November 4, 1863, SHD, GR 7 G Expédition du Mexique, 87 Contre-guérrilla du colonel Dupin, Historique, Siège de Mexico, 1863–1867.

14. BMNAH, Colección: Imperio de Maximiliano, Documento 387 "Fiesta de Nuestra Señora de Guadalupe." For imperial ceremonial and Francisco Mora, imperial master of ceremonies, see Érika Pani, "El proyecto de Estado de Maximiliano a través de la vida cortesana y del ceremonial público," *Historia Mexicana* 45, no. 2 (1995): 434.

15. Eugène Lefèvre, *Documents officiels recueillis dans la secrétairerie privée de Maximilien: Histoire de l'intervention française au Mexique* (Paris: Armand le Chevalier, 1870), 13; see also Anton von Magnus, *Das Ende des maximilianischen Kaiserreichs in Mexico: Berichte des königlich preussischen Ministerresidenten Anton von Magnus an Bismarck, 1866–1867*, ed. Joachim Kühn (Göttingen: Musterschmidt, 1965), 51.

16. For the text, see Lefèvre, *Documents officiels*, 14–17; see also Alfred Louis Adolphe Graves Van der Smissen, *Souvenirs du Mexique, 1864–1867, par le général baron Van der Smissen, . . .* (Brussels: J. Lebègue, 1892), 42–50.

17. Cannelli, "México visto desde el Vaticano," 245–246.

18. During his visit to Brazil, Maximilian was critical of "the total lack of spiritual activity" in the monasteries, which he saw as "dirty shrines in which people lay up old booty." He imagined the pope as a partner in reform. See Maximilian, *Recollections of My Life*, 3 vols. (London: R. Bentley, 1868), 3:120.

19. For "syllabus made flesh," see Jose Antonio de Larrinaga, "L'Intervention française au Mexique vue par les principaux journaux canadiens-français du Québec, 1861–1867" (MA thesis, University of Ottawa, Canada, 1976), 130.

20. See "Puntos propuestos al Nuncio de S S," no date but apparently December 25, 1864, BLAC, Genaro García, Documentos Relativos a la Reforma y a la Intervención Francesa en México, 83a (1), Intervención Francesa, Correspondencia miscelánea, 1867–1869. Emphasis in original.

21. See letter from Maximilian to Fernando Ramírez Escudero, December 27, 1864, in Samuel Basch, *Recollections of Mexico: The Last Ten Months of Maximilian's Empire*, ed. Fred D. Ullman (Wilmington, DE: Scholarly Resources, 2001), 23.

22. Josef Wiedenhofer, "Die öffentliche Meinung in Österreich zum Abenteuer Kaiser Maximilians I. von Mexiko" (diss., University of Vienna, 1979), 97.

23. Corti, *Maximilian and Charlotte*, 456.

24. For the main points presented to Meglia, see "Puntos propuestos al Nuncio de S. S.," BLAC, Genaro García, Documentos Relativos a la Reforma y a la Intervención Francesa en México, 83a (1), Intervención Francesa, Documentos misceláneos, 1867–1869.

25. Francisco de Paula de Arrangoiz y Berzábal, *México de 1808 hasta 1867* (Mexico: Porrua, 1968), 600–601.

26. Blumberg, "Mexican Empire and the Vatican," 7.

27. Blumberg, "Mexican Empire and the Vatican," 9.

28. Niox, *Expédition du Mexique*, 405.

29. Blumberg, "Mexican Empire and the Vatican," 9–10.

30. The commission's vision substantially recapitulated what Maximilian and Charlotte had proposed to the Papal Nuncio Meglia. See de Paula de Arrangoiz y Berzábal, *México de 1808*, 599–602.

31. See articles 2 and 9 of "Proyecto de convenio . . . ," in Ramos et al., *Del Archivo secreto vaticano*, 234.

32. The papacy had recently lost nearly all of its land to Italian unification, so the issue was fresh. See Lynn Marshall Case, *Franco-Italian Relations, 1860–1865: The Roman Question and the Convention of September* (Philadelphia: University of Pennsylvania Press, 1932), 297–298.

33. Magnus, *Das Ende*, 57–58.

34. Lucas Martínez Sánchez, *Coahuila durante la intervención francesa, 1862–1867* (Saltillo: Gobierno del Estado de Coahuila, 2008), 14.

35. Magnus, *Das Ende*, 58.

36. Some sources identify Fischer as a Jesuit, a claim difficult to reconcile with his assignment to a parish. Jesuit archives have no record of him.

37. For his work as secretary to the bishop of Durango, see Charles Houston Harris, *A Mexican Family Empire, the Latifundio of the Sánchez Navarros, 1765–1867* (Austin: University of Texas Press, 1975), 299–300; for "word made flesh," see Basch, *Recollections of Mexico*, 125.

38. Harris, *Mexican Family Empire*, xvii, 300.

39. Martínez Sánchez, *Coahuila durante la intervención*, 14.

40. Fischer acknowledged that much of the land was suitable only for pasture ("die für keinen andern zweck verwendet werden können als für Weideland") but claimed that water was available from the Sabine River—which flows in Texas, but not in the lands in question. See Fischer to Maximilian, undated, APRB, BE-A0546/36, Archief Van Felix Eloin, 208 Brieven van keizer Maximilliaan aan Eloin, met bijlage.

41. See "16 agosto 1864–17 septiembre 1866 Legación de México en Prusia: Correspondencia informe comunicado por el cónsul de en Fráncfort, H. Stiebel, sobre colonización en el Imperio," AGN, Segundo Imperio, Caja 18, Expediente 59, Ministerio de Negocios Extranjeros.

42. See Fischer to Maximilian, APRB, BE-A0546/36, Archief Van Felix Eloin, 208 Briefwisseling, undated, but likely 1865 when, according to Anderson, the Sánchez

Navarro offer was made. See William Marshall Anderson, *An American in Maximilian's Mexico, 1865–1866*, ed. Ramón Eduardo Ruiz (San Marino, CA: Huntington Library, 1959).

43. Corti, *Maximilian and Charlotte*, 536.

44. Magnus, *Das Ende*, 57–58.

45. David I. Kertzer, *The Pope Who Would Be King: The Exile of Pius IX and the Emergence of Modern Europe* (New York: Random House, 2018), 49.

46. CEHM, IX-1. 4–8. 507.1, Enrico Angelini to Ignacio Aguilar, Rome, December 9, 1865.

47. See letter dated June 3, 1865, in Jesús Terán, *La Misión confidencial de Don Jesús Terán en Europa, 1863–66*, ed. Gabriel Saldívar (Mexico: Archivo Histórico Diplomático Mexicano, 1943), 28. See the reply from Lerdo de Tejada, dated August 15, 1865, in which he congratulates Terán.

48. Corti, *Maximilian and Charlotte*, 622.

49. Although Fischer would strive to remain on friendly terms with Aguilar. See his "estimado amigo" letter to Aguilar shortly after his arrival in Rome. See letter, Fischer to Aguilar, Rome, December 9, 1865, CEHM, Correspondencia Ignacio Aguilar y Marocho, IX-1. 4–8. 507.1.

50. CEHM, IX-1. 5–8. 619.1, Enrico Angelini to Ignacio Aguilar, Rome, January 8, 1866; CEHM, IX-1. 5–8. 631.1, Maximilian to Gutiérrez Estrada, Rome, January 16, 1866.

51. CEHM, IX-1. 6–8. 744.1, Enrico Angelini to Ignacio Aguilar, Rome, March 15, 1866.

52. See Alcazar de Chapultepec, Maximilian to Joaquín Degollado, March 9, 1866, BLAC, Degollado Collection, series 1, folder 1, Letters from Maximilian.

53. For Munguía and suspected ties to the Conservative newspaper *El Pájaro Verde*, see Kristine Ibsen, *Maximilian, Mexico, and the Invention of Empire* (Nashville, TN: Vanderbilt University Press, 2010), 46.

54. Riccardo Cannelli, "México visto desde el Vaticano en la época de la Reforma," in *Las leyes de Reforma y el estado laico*, ed. Roberto Blancarte (Mexico City: Colegio de Mexico, 2013), 244–245.

55. See letter from Labastida to unidentified recipient dated May 9, 1866, in which he discusses Fischer's conduct, ASV, Segretaria di Stato 1866 R. 251, fasc. 12, in Ramos et al., *Del Archivo secreto vaticano*, 326.

56. Corti represents Munguía in benign terms. See Egon Caesar Corti, *Maximilian and Charlotte of Mexico*, trans. Catherine Alison Phillips (New York: Knopf, 1928), 622.

57. See Alcazar de Chapultepec, Maximilian to Joaquín Degollado, May 29, 1866, BLAC, Degollado Collection, series 1, folder 1, Letters from Maximilian.

58. Niox, *Expédition du Mexique*, 565.

59. "Reservada," June 12, 1866, ASV Segretaria di Stato 1866 R. 251, fasc. 12, from Munguía, in Ramos et al., *Del Archivo secreto vaticano*, 340.

60. For reports of these *actas*, see *Diario del Imperio*, January 1 and 14, 1864 (Guanjuato), February 2, 1864 (San Francisco del Rincón), May 19, 1864 (Aguascalientes), etc.

61. See "Puebla," AGN, Segundo Imperio, Caja 01, Expediente 17, Actas de Adhesión.

62. For Kinglake's remarks and Palmerston's rebuttal, see "The Empire of Mexico," *London Times*, July 29, 1864.

63. Niox, *Expédition du Mexique*, 530, 662–663.

64. For Tanori, see Wilhelm von Montlong, *Authentische enthüllungen über die letzten ereignisse in Mexico . . . Auf befehl weiland Sr. Majestät des kaisers Maximilian nach dokumenten* (Stuttgart: Hoffmann, 1868), 161–162.

65. Carl Khevenhüller, *Con Maximiliano en México: Del diario del príncipe Carl Khevenhüller, 1864–1867*, ed. Brigitte Hamann (Mexico: Fondo de Cultura Económica, 1994), 134, 143, 155; see also *Militär Zeitung*, October 7, 1865; Adalbert Andreas Schönowsky von Schönwies, *Aus den gefechten des österreichischen freicorps in Mejico: Kampf gegen die Cuatacomacos im jahre 1865* (Vienna: Verlag der Österreichischen militärischen zeitschrift, 1873).

66. Brian Hamnett, "Mexican Conservatives, Clericals, and Soldiers: The 'Traitor' Tomás Mejía through Reform and Empire, 1855–1867," in *Bulletin of Latin American Research* 20, no. 2 (2001): 198–199.

67. Local militias could be a way to organize Indigenous power as well as a tool of criollo authority. See Paul H. Garner, *Porfirio Díaz* (New York: Longman, 2001), 40.

68. For a comprehensive view, see Zachary Brittsan, *Popular Politics and Rebellion in Mexico: Manuel Lozada and La Reforma, 1855–1876* (Nashville, TN: Vanderbilt University Press, 2015); see also Amy Robinson, "Manuel Lozada and the Politics of Barbarity," *Colorado Review of Hispanic Studies* 4 (2006): 79, 91; for Lozada and the "Religión y Tierras" movement, see Jean Meyer, "El Ocaso de Manuel Lozada," *Historia Mexicana* 18 (1969): 535–568; for a grudgingly favorable view of Lozada, see Bullock, *Across Mexico*, 326–331; for the Liberal take on Lozada, see Richard N. Sinkin, *The Mexican Reform, 1855–1876: A Study in Liberal Nation-Building* (Austin: University of Texas, 1979), esp. 109–111.

69. Brian R. Hamnett, *Juárez* (London: Longman, 1994), 216–217.

70. Brittsan, *Popular Politics*, 102.

71. Douglas Richmond, "The Failure of Mid-Nineteenth-Century Liberalism in Yucatán, 1855–1876 (1)," *Journal of Caribbean History* 45, no. 1 (2011): 14–15. On Charlotte's tour, see "Baile Popular a S.M. La Emperatriz de Mejico por El Pueblo de Mérida," APRB, BE-A0546/36, Impératrice Charlotte du Mexique, 176 Reis in Yucatán, 1865–1866. Though Yucatán was thought to be sympathetic to the empire, Maximilian's special envoy to the imperial governor there was intercepted by rebels and killed. See Luis González y González, "El Indigenismo de Maximiliano," in *La intervención francesa y el Imperio de Maximiliano cien años después, 1862–1962*, ed. Arturo Arnáiz y Freg and Claude Bataillon (Mexico: Asociación Mexicana de Historiadores, Instituto Francés de América Latina, 1965), 109.

72. González y González, "El Indigenismo de Maximiliano," esp. 108–109; see also Erika Pani, *El Segundo Imperio: Pasados de usos múltiples* (Mexico City: Centro de Investigación y Docencia Económicas, 2004), 119–120; Khevenhüller, *Con Maximiliano*, 131–132. Maximilian to Eloin, August 28, 1866, APRB, BE-A0546/36/208; letter from Leopold to Charlotte, July 11, 1863, APRB, BE-A0546/36, Impératrice Charlotte du Mexique, 15 Brieven aan de keizerin gericht door vorsten en prinsen, België: Leopold I koning der Belgen, 1849–1864; letter from Leopold to Charlotte, February 24, 1865, APRB, BE-A0546/36, Impératrice Charlotte du Mexique, 15 Brieven aan de keizerin gericht door vorsten en prinsen, België: Leopold I koning der Belgen. 1849–1864.

73. Raphael Waldburg-Zeil, *Fernando Maximiliano de Habsburgo, 1832–1867: Perfil humano de un archiduque-emperador* (Madrid: Gunter Quercus, 2013), 90.

74. Robert H. Duncan, "Political Legitimation and Maximilian's Second Empire in Mexico, 1864–1867," *Mexican Studies/Estudios Mexicanos* 12, no. 1 (January 1996): 53.

75. The visit occurred in January 1865. On the painting, see Jaime Soler and Esther Acevedo, eds., *La fabricación del Estado, 1864–1910* (México, DF: Museo Nacional de Arte, 2003), 49.

76. For Native Americans as refugees, see, for example, Charles Lempriere, *Notes in Mexico, in 1861 and 1862: Politically and Socially Considered* (London: Longman, Roberts, and Green, 1862), 232; on Native American raiding, see Corti, *Maximilian and Charlotte,* 363.

77. For an example of early overtures to Indigenous peoples, see "La Clase indigena," in *La Sociedad,* September 28, 1863, 4.

78. For commentary on the Kickapoo visit, see Auguste Charles Philippe Blanchot, *L'intervention française au Mexique: Mémoires,* 3 vols. (Paris: E. Nourry, 1911), 287.

79. Beaucé worked in Mexico in 1863–1865. See Ibsen, *Maximilian, Mexico,* 65.

80. See letters from Madame de Bovée to Charlotte, July 12 and August 10, 1864, in Luis Weckmann, *Carlota de Bélgica: Correspondencia y escritos sobre México en los archivos europeos, 1861–1868* (Mexico: Porrúa, 1989).

81. See *Advenimiento de SS. MM. II. Maximiliano y Carlota al trono de México* (Mexico: J. M. Andrade y F. Escalante, 1864), 237–238.

82. Of sponsored works, see Francisco Pimentel, *Memoria sobre las causas que han originado la situación actual de la raza indígena de México y medios de remediarla* (Mexico: Imprenta de Andrade y Escalante, 1864); see also Manuel Orozco y Berra, *Geografía de las lenguas y carta etnográfica de México: Precedidas de un ensayo de clasificación de las mismas lenguas y de apuntes para las immigraciones de las tribus, por el lic. Manuel Orozco y Berra* (Mexico: Imprenta de J. M. Andrade y F. Escalante, 1864); González y González, "El Indigenismo de Maximiliano."

83. José Iturriaga de la Fuente, *Escritos mexicanos de Carlota de Bélgica* (Cuernavaca: Instituto de Cultura de Morelos, 2012), 61; cited in Soler and Acevedo, *La fabricación del Estado,* 49.

84. On criollo mistrust of Indigenous Mexicans and their susceptibility to demagoguery, see Eric Van Young, *A Life Together: Lucas Alaman and Mexico, 1792–1853* (New Haven, CT: Yale University Press, 2021), 391.

85. González y González, "El Indigenismo de Maximiliano," 109.

86. Niox, *Expédition du Mexique,* 377.

87. If they came under imperial control, they produced no revenue, because Republican forces kept them bottled up. See "Mémoire remis par moi à l'Empereur Napoléon à Saint Cloud le 11 Aout 1866," APRB, BE-A0546/36, Impératrice Charlotte du Mexique, 159 Teksten van politieke aard: mémoire remis par moi à l'Empereur Napoléon à St-Cloud le 11 août 1866, met een kopie van dit memorandum en bijlagen.

88. Robert Ryal Miller, "A Mexican Secret Agent in the United States, 1864–1866," *The Americas* 19 (1962):137–138; on control of the ports, see Niox, *Expédition du Mexique,* 410.

89. See decree of August 11, 1864, in Orozco Farías, *Fuentes históricas*, 312.

90. Vigil and Riva Palacio, *México a través de los siglos*, 5:569.

91. For Floriano Bernardo, see "Correspondencia de Puebla," *Siglo Diez y Nueve*, January 27, 1863; "Gacetilla ¡Crimen Atroz de los Invasores!," *Monitor Republicano*, January 20, 1863; also undated memo, apparently January 1863, BLAC, Genaro Garcia, Achille Bazaine Papers G500, Correspondencia de Achille Francois Bazaine, 1862–1867.

92. Vigil and Riva Palacio, *México a través de los siglos*, 5:656; Pedro Pruneda, *Historia de la guerra de Méjico, desde 1861 á 1867: Con todos los documentos diplomáticos justificativos* (Madrid: Elizalde y compañia, 1867), 292; Niox, *Expédition du Mexique*, 421–422; Edmund Daniek, *Sie zogen nach Mexiko: Ein Denkmal für die österreichischen Freiwilligen unter Kaiser Maximilian, 1864–1867* (Vienna: Amalthea, 1964), 49.

93. Frank Averill Knapp, *The Life of Sebastián Lerdo de Tejada, 1823–1889: A Study of Influence and Obscurity* (Austin: University of Texas Press, 1951), 91.

94. See "Mexique," *Écho du Parlement*, November 18, 1864.

95. On L'Hériller's proposed return, see Niox, *Expédition du Mexique*, 428; for Charlotte's critical reaction, see H. de Reinach-Foussemagne, *Charlotte de Belgique, impératrice du Mexique* (Paris: Plon-Nourrit, 1925), 240–241.

96. The Juárist press saw things differently. See "Periodicos Juaristas," *La Sociedad*, September 19, 1864, 2.

97. As Jules Doazan wrote to the minister of foreign affairs, "les populations sont en notre faveur." See letter of August 31, 1863, AMAE, Correspondance politique des consuls, 1826–1870, Mexique, 3 1863–1864 La Vera Cruz, Tampico. But see also letter of March 17, 1864.

98. See Bazaine circular dated November 28, 1864, SHD, GR 7 G, Expédition du Mexique, 227 Contre-guérilla au Mexique.

99. See Thün to Bazaine, Puebla, June 23, 1866, ÖStA KA, AdT Mexiko Österreichisch-belgisches Freiwilligenkorps in Mexiko, 1864–1867, box 7.

100. By the beginning of 1866, these rural guard units were the nucleus of insurgent bands in such locations as Aguascalientes and Zacatecas. See Escudo de armas del Imperio Mexicano, Quartier General de Colima, Mexico, February 9, 1866, BLAC, Achille Bazaine Papers, G500, vol. 18.

101. Guy P. C. Thomson, *Patriotism, Politics, and Popular Liberalism in Nineteenth-Century Mexico: Juan Francisco Lucas and the Puebla Sierra* (Wilmington, DE: Scholarly Resources, 1999), 89; Florencia E. Mallon, *Peasant and Nation: The Making of Postcolonial Mexico and Peru* (Berkeley: University of California Press, 1995), 44–45.

102. For an example of Indigenous forces supporting the empire, see Brittsan, *Popular Politics*.

103. For Dupin's education, see Douglas Porch, *The French Foreign Legion: A Complete History of the Legendary Fighting Force* (New York: HarperCollins, 1991), 145.

104. Mary Virginia (Plattenburg) Edwards, ed., *Shelby's Expedition to Mexico: An Unwritten Leaf of the War* (Kansas City, MO: J. Edwards, 1889), 43.

105. *Catalogue des objets précieux . . . objets d'art et de curiosité provenant en grande partie du palais d'été de Yen-Meng-Yuen composant le musée japonais et chinois de M. le colonel Du Pin* (Paris: Renou et Maulde, 1862).

106. See letter from Jules Doazan, French Consul at Veracruz, to Minister of Foreign Affairs Drouyn de Lhuys, from Veracruz, March 2, 1863, announcing that Dupin had taken command of his forces. AMAE, Correspondance politique des consuls, 1826–1870, Mexique 3, 1863–1864, La Vera Cruz, Tampico.

107. For soldiers of fortune, see Musser, *Establishment of Maximilian's Empire*, 80.

108. See "Promesses du colonel Dupin," in Lefèvre, *Documents officiels*, 350–351.

109. "Ordre amende a 1000 piastres a Purisima," April 24, 1866, SHD, GR 7 G Expédition du Mexique, 86 Contre-guérrilla du colonel Dupin.

110. "Une proclamation du colonel Dupin," in Lefèvre, *Documents officiels*, 351–352.

111. Niox, *Expédition du Mexique*, 305–306.

112. Sebastián I. Campos, *Recuerdos históricos de la ciudad de Veracruz y Costa de Sotavento del estado durante las campañas de "tres años," "la intervención" y el "imperio," por el mayor de infantería Sebastián I. Campos* (Mexico City: Oficina tipde la Secretaría de fomento, 1895), 350–351.

113. See memorandum condemning "amends" imposed on populations, dated June 27, 1865. "The quite evident goal of [the forces of the Republic] is to place us in the role of oppressor." SHD, GR 7 G, Expédition du Mexique Contre-guérilla au Mexique, 227.

114. For the decree justifying the destruction of San Sebastián, see Lefèvre, *Documents officiels*, 119–120; see also Stevenson, *Maximilian in Mexico*, 163–164.

115. Niox, *Expédition du Mexique*, 463.

116. On Mazatlán trade and coastal shipping, see Eugène Duflot de Mofras, *Exploration du territoire de l'Orégon, des Californies et de la mer Vermeille, exécutée pendant les années 1840, 1841 et 1842* (Paris: A. Bertrand, 1844), 175–176. The foreign presence included agents representing investors; see Michael P. Costeloe, *Bonds and Bondholders: British Investors and Mexico's Foreign Debt, 1824–1888* (Westport, CT: Praeger, 2003), 117; these West Coast ports also figured in US calculations at the time of the McLane-Ocampo Treaty. See William R. Manning, ed., *Diplomatic Correspondence of the United States: Inter-American Affairs, 1831–1860.* 12 vols. (Washington, DC: Carnegie Endowment for International Peace, 1932), 9:260–264.

117. See Castagny's letter of January 31, 1865, in Lefèvre, *Documents officiels*, 116–118.

9. Volunteers and Refugees

1. José María Gutiérrez Estrada, *Le Mexique et l'archiduc Ferdinand Maximilien d'Autriche* (Paris: Garnier, 1862).

2. Andreas Cornaro, "Österreich und das mexikanische Freikorps," *Mitteilungen des Österreichischen Staatsarchivs* 14 (1961): 64; for startup funds, see Edmund Daniek, *Sie zogen nach Mexiko: Ein Denkmal für die österreichischen Freiwilligen unter Kaiser Maximilian, 1864–1867* (Vienna: Amalthea, 1964), 16; also Josef Wiedenhofer, "Die öffentliche Meinung in Österreich zum Abenteuer Kaiser Maximilians I. von Mexiko" (diss., University of Vienna, 1979), 15–16.

3. See *L'Etoile belge*, March 24, 1864.

4. "Theatrum mundi—Karroussel in der Hofreitschule," *Der Zwischen-Akt*, February 5, 1863.

5. "Das Carrousel in der k. k. Hofreitschule," *Wiener Zeitung*, March 2, 1863.

6. Carl's parents had encouraged him to join the military in the hope it would bring him discipline and purpose. Franz Müllner, "Johann Carl Fürst Khevenhüller-Metsch, ein Kampfgefährte Kaiser Maximilians von Mexiko," in *Maximilian von Mexiko. 1832–1867*, ed. Werner Kitlitschka (Vienna: Enzenhofer, 1974), 136–137.

7. Franz Müllner, "Johann Carl Fürst Khevenhüller-Metsch, ein Kampfgefährte Kaiser Maximilians von Mexiko" in Kitlitschka, *Maximilian von Mexiko*, 136, 140.

8. "Das Carrousel."

9. Carl Khevenhüller, *Con Maximiliano en México: Del diario del príncipe Carl Khevenhüller, 1864–1867*, ed. Brigitte Hamann (Mexico: Fondo de Cultura Económica, 1994), 84–85.

10. Some volunteered under assumed names to escape detection. Khevenhüller, *Con Maximiliano*, 159.

11. Khevenhüller, *Con Maximiliano*, 86–89.

12. Wiedenhofer, "Die öffentliche Meinung," 84.

13. Albert Duchesne, *L'expédition des volontaires belges au Mexique, 1864–1867*, 2 vols. (Brussels: Centre d'Histoire Militaire, 1967), 134–135; see also Gustave Léon Niox, *Expédition du Mexique, 1861–1867: Récit politique & militaire* (Paris: J. Dumaine, 1874), 362.

14. Cornaro, "Österreich," 64.

15. See "Convention zwischen Oesterreich und Mexico," *Wiener Zeitung*, April 14, 1865.

16. Egon Caesar Corti, *Maximilian and Charlotte of Mexico*, trans. Catherine Alison Phillips (New York: Knopf, 1928), 140.

17. Mack Walker, *Germany and the Emigration, 1816–1885* (Cambridge MA: Harvard University Press, 1964), 39.

18. See Walker, *Germany and the Emigration*, 83–85; see Ephraim Douglass Adams, ed., *British Diplomatic Correspondence concerning the Republic of Texas,1838–1846* (Austin: Texas State Historical Association, 1918), 367n, 494; Frederick Law Olmsted, *A Journey through Texas: Or a Saddle-Trip on the Southwestern Frontier* (Independently published, 2019), 132–136.

19. Duchesne, *L'expédition*, 140; Daniek, *Sie zogen nach Mexiko*, 40.

20. Wiedenhofer, "Die öffentliche Meinung," 74.

21. Daniek, *Sie zogen nach Mexiko*, 48.

22. On the role of Catholicism as a political marker the empire needed, see *El Monitor Republicano*, August 13, 1889, in Manuel Romero de Terreros, *Maximiliano y el imperio, segun correspondencias contemporaneas* (Mexico: Cultura, 1926), 50; on liberal Catholicism, see Francisco Bulnes, *El verdadero Juárez y la verdad sobre la intervention y el imperio* (Mexico: Editora Nacional, 1956), 101.

23. Daniek, *Sie zogen nach Mexiko*, 40.

24. Claudine Leysinger, *Collecting Images of Mexico: A Polychromatic View through the Lens of Teobert Maler, 1860–1910* (New York: Columbia University Press, 2008), 22–26; Adalbert Franz Seligmann, *Carl Leopold Müller: Ein Künstlerleben in Briefen, Bildern und Dokumenten* (Vienna: Rikola, 1922), 130; Raphael Waldburg-Zeil, *Fernando Maximiliano de Habsburgo, 1832–1867: Perfil humano de un archiduque-emperador* (Madrid: Gunter Quercus, 2013), 128–130. Ferstel had worked with Maximilian on the Votivkirch; see Wiedenhofer, "Die öffentliche Meinung," 107.

25. Khevenhüller, *Con Maximiliano*, 122.

26. See *Militär-Zeitung*, September 28, 1864, cited in Wiedenhofer, "Die öffentliche Meinung," 82n.

27. Daniek, *Sie zogen nach Mexiko*, 42.

28. For Europamüde, see Wiedenhofer, "Die öffentliche Meinung," 124.

29. Anton von Magnus, Prussian representative to Mexico, formed a poor opinion of the Austrian volunteers. See David Pruonto, "Did the Second Mexican Empire under Maximilian of Habsburg (1864–1867) Have an 'Austrian Face'?," *Austrian Studies* 20 (2012): 106.

30. See Louis Sonolet, "L'agonie de l'Empire du Mexique," *Revue de Paris* 34 (August 1927): 613–614.

31. See *Neue Freie Presse*, October 26, 1864, cited in Wiedenhofer, "Die öffentliche Meinung," 83n.

32. See *Militär-Zeitung*, September 28, 1864, and *Der Kamarad*, November 11, 1864, cited in Wiedenhofer, "Die öffentliche Meinung," 78–79.

33. Wiedenhofer numbers the Polish refugees at 509, citing *Militär-Zeitung*, February 25, 1864. See "Die öffentliche Meinung in Osterreich," 82n. For a contemporary account of the 1863 revolt, see *L'Illustration*, April 4, 1863, 210. For Polish lancers in Mexico, see Emile Vanson, *Crimee, Italie, Mexique: Lettres de campagnes, 1854–1867, precedées d'une notice biographique* (Paris: Berger-Levrault, 1905), 261.

34. See October 28, 1866, Baron de Lago in ÖSta Ministerium des Äußern, Politisches Archiv (PA) PA XXXIV Mexiko, 4 Mexico (1864–1867), 4-1 Berichte, Weisungen, Varia (1864–1866). See also Cornaro, "Österreich," 67–68.

35. Volunteers weren't limited to Europe. See Narcisse Henri Édouard Faucher de Saint-Maurice, *De Québec à Mexico: Souvenirs de Voyage, de Garnison, de Combat et de Bivouac* (Montreal: Duvernay et Dansereau, 1874), 12–13.

36. Cornaro, "Österreich," 68–69.

37. Not correct; Maximilian was the *second* emperor of Mexico. For the oath, see Khevenhüller, *Con Maximiliano*, 69.

38. Letter to his mother dated December 1, 1864, in Ernst Pitner, *Maximilian's Lieutenant: A Personal History of the Mexican Campaign, 1864–7*, trans. Gordon Etherington-Smith (Albuquerque: University of New Mexico Press, 1993), 25.

39. See "Mexique," *Écho du Parlement*, November 18, 1864.

40. Duchesne, *L'expédition*, 109.

41. Duchesne, *L'expédition*, 137; these were by no means the original European settler colonies. See Luis Weckmann, "Un gran archivo histórico mexicano en París," *Historia Mexicana* 8, no. 1 (1958): 92.

42. L. Leconte, "L'expédition belge au Mexique," *Carnet de la Fourragère* 2 (1930): 552.

43. The health risks were far from exaggerated. See Corps Belge État nominatif des hommes décédés depuis l'envoi de la dernier liste (9 décembre 1865)," AMBAE, Série B 68 I, II, III, 1861–1866, Enrôlements militaires à l'étranger; Légion Belge au Portugal, 1834.

44. Duchesne, *L'expédition*, 626; on variety of motives, see also Erika Pani, *El Segundo Imperio: Pasados de usos múltiples* (Mexico City: Centro de Investigación y Docencia Económicas, 2004), 36.

45. See "Interpellation relative à la question du Mexique," *L'Echo du Parlement*, April 8, 1865.

46. Belgian volunteers also included Americans, Canadians, and a recruit from Algeria. See Duchesne, *L'expédition*, 190.

47. Léon François Lambert Émile Timmerhans, *Voyage et opérations du corps belge au Mexique* (Liège: Carmanne, 1866), 10–11.

48. For a complete list, see Annexe in Duchesne, *L'expédition*.

49. Daniek, *Sie zogen nach Mexiko*, 45.

50. See Facture, Paris, le 27 octobre 1864, Eugene Taconet, Fournisseur de l'Armée de terre, de la Marine . . . , ÖSta KA, Archiv der Truppenkörper (AdT), 14 Mexiko Österreichisch-belgisches Freiwilligenkorps in Mexiko, 1864–1867.

51. Daniek, *Sie zogen nach Mexiko*, 45–46.

52. Undated letter, ÖSta KA, Archive der Truppenkörper, 14 Mexiko Österreichisch-belgisches Freiwilligenkorps in Mexiko, 1864–1867.

53. *L'Illustration*, April 4, 1865.

54. *Wiener Abendpost*, December 28, 1864, cited in Daniek, *Sie zogen nach Mexiko*, 53.

55. Pitner, *Maximilian's Lieutenant*, 31.

56. Duchesne, *L'expédition*, 210–213.

57. Duchesne, *L'expédition*, 219.

58. Samuel Basch, *Recollections of Mexico: The Last Ten Months of Maximilian's Empire*, ed. Fred D. Ullman (Wilmington, DE: Scholarly Resources, 2001), 216.

59. Shelby has them meeting in Mobile. See Mary Virginia (Plattenburg) Edwards, ed., *Shelby's Expedition to Mexico: An Unwritten Leaf of the War* (Kansas City, MO: J. Edwards, 1889), 101.

60. See Felix Salm-Salm, *My Diary in Mexico in 1867: Including the Last Days of the Emperor Maximilian* (London: R. Bently, 1868), 2; for New York arrival, see Ancestry.com, NY US Arriving Passenger Lists 1854, Arrival: New York, New York, USA, microfilm serial M237, 1820–1897, line 3, list number 982.

61. Salm-Salm, *My Diary*, 10.

62. For Rachael Price and Alexander Fitzgerald, see Ancestry.com, NA, US Freedmen's Bureau Records, Records of the Field Offices, M1903, reel 82.

63. Salm-Salm, *My Diary*, 2–4; Sara Yorke Stevenson, *Maximilian in Mexico: A Woman's Reminiscences of the French Intervention, 1862–1867* (New York: Century Co., 1899), 230–231.

64. Story of Captain Peralta desertion in Salm-Salm, *My Diary*, 9–10.

65. See "A Tragic Page of American History," *New Voice* (New York), April 22, 1899, clipping, BLAC, Reminiscencias históricas escritas por el general Mariano Ruiz.

66. Stevenson, *Maximilian in Mexico*, 231.

67. Stevenson, *Maximilian in Mexico*, 259.

68. Jose Antonio de Larrinaga, "L'Intervention française au Mexique vue par les principaux journaux canadiens-français du Québec, 1861–1867" (MA thesis, University of Ottawa, 1976), 140.

69. Larrinaga, "Intervention française," 55.

70. "Du Panama à la Mer Glaciale," *Journal de Québec*, June 4, 1865, cited in Larrinaga, "Intervention française," 154.

71. Larrinaga, "Intervention française," 141.
72. See Faucher de Saint-Maurice, *De Québec à Mexico,* 144.
73. "Europa y America," *La Voz de Méjico,* May 29, 1862.
74. See "El Archiduque Maximiliano," *La Voz de Méjico,* May 17, 1862.
75. See "Carta del Gen. Prim à Luis Napoleon," *La Voz de Méjico,* July 22, 1862.
76. "El Triunfo del 5 de Mayo," *La Voz de Méjico,* July 24, 1862.
77. See "Lista de donativos patrioticos," *La Voz de Méjico,* August 1, 1863.
78. See "Junta patriótica de Half Moon Bay," *La Voz de Méjico,* January 1, 1863.
79. "Junta patriótica de la union chilena," *La Voz de Méjico,* January 8, 1863.
80. For the "Junta Central Directiva," see *La Voz de Méjico,* January 1, 1863, 3. For Peruvians, Grenadians, and Chileans, see "Lista de donativos patrióticos," *La Voz de Méjico,* January 8, 1863.
81. See complaint of French consul Charles de Cazotte to the French Minister of Foreign Affairs, May 13, 1865, BLAC, Genaro García 80 B(2).
82. See report of Admiral Mazeres dated October 16, 1865, BLAC, Genaro García Documentos Relativos a la Reforma y a la Intervención Francesa en México 81 (5), Intervención Francesa, Documentos misceláneos, 1862–1867.
83. Robert Ryal Miller, "Californians against the Emperor," *California Historical Society Quarterly* 37 (1958): 204.
84. William Henry Bullock, *Across Mexico in 1864–5* (London: Macmillan, 1866), 5–6.
85. See letter from Hidalgo regarding Gwin and Sonora, in Eugène Lefèvre, *Documents officiels recueillis dans la secrétairerie privée de Maximilien: Histoire de l'intervention française au Mexique,* 2 vols. (Paris: Armand le Chevalier, 1870), 92–93; for silver mining in Mexico, see Eric Van Young, *A Life Together: Lucas Alaman and Mexico, 1792–1853* (New Haven, CT: Yale University Press, 2021), 89.
86. Harry Thayer Mahoney and Marjorie Locke Mahoney, *Mexico and the Confederacy, 1860–1867* (San Francisco: Austin and Winfield, 1998), 92.
87. Hallie M. McPherson, "The Plan of William McKendree Gwin for a Colony in North Mexico, 1863–1865," *Pacific Historical Review* 2, no. 4 (December 1933): 369.
88. See Todd W. Wahlstrom, *The Southern Exodus to Mexico: Migration across the Borderlands after the American Civil War* (Lincoln: University of Nebraska Press, 2015).
89. *Decrees for the Encouragement of Immigration and Colonization* (Mexico: Ignacio Cumplido, 1865).
90. Alfred J. Hanna and Kathryn Abbey Hanna, "The Immigration Movement of the Intervention and Empire as Seen through the Mexican Press," *Hispanic American Historical Review* 27, no. 2 (1947): 238; for the text of the letter, see Emmanuel Domenech, *Histoire du Mexique* (Paris: A. Lacroix, Verboeckhoven et Cie, 1868), 263–265.
91. These official offices are distinct from those proposed by the American and Mexican Emigrant Company, which was founded as a private enterprise on April 27, 1865. See "Prospectus," *Mexican Times,* December 2, 1865.
92. See Romero's letter dated December 18, 1865, in Luis Chávez Orozco, *Maximiliano y la restitución de la esclavitud en México, 1865–1866* (Mexico: Secretaría de Relaciones Exteriores, 1961), 104.

93. See A. W. Ferrell to Ct. M. De Noue, San Luis Potosí, September 18, 1865, BLAC, Genaro García, Documentos Relativos a la Reforma y a la Intervención Francesa en México 8ob, Intervención Francesa, Correspondencia miscelánea, 1846–1867.

94. Maury's home was "a sort of headquarters for Confederates" in Mexico City. See Alexander Watkins Terrell, *From Texas to Mexico and the Court of Maximilian in 1865* (Dallas: Book Club of Texas, 1933), 50.

95. The inaugural edition of the *Mexican Times* appeared on September 16, 1865. See also Sarah A. Dorsey, *Recollections of Henry Watkins Allen, Brigadier-General Confederate States Army, Ex-Governor of Louisiana* (New York: M. Doolady, 1866), 52, 334, 340, 360; Todd W. Wahlstrom, "The Southern Exodus to Mexico: Migration Across the Borderlands after the U.S. Civil War," PhD Dissertation, University of California at Santa Barbara, 2009, 96–97. For imperial subsidy, see William Marshall Anderson, *An American in Maximilian's Mexico, 1865–1866*, ed. Ramón Eduardo Ruiz (San Marino, CA: Huntington Library, 1959), xiv.

96. Tom Russell, "Adventures of a Cordova Colonist," *Southern Magazine* 4 (July 1872): 91. The large representation of Missourians was likely the result of the influence of General Sterling Price, former governor of Missouri. See also James Fred Rippy, *The United States and Mexico* (New York: Knopf, 1926), 249.

97. James M. McPherson, *Battle Cry of Freedom: The Civil War Era* (New York: Oxford University Press, 1988), 291–292; Robert E. Shalhope, *Sterling Price: Portrait of a Southerner* (Columbia: University of Missouri Press, 1971), 281–282; Carl Coke Rister, "Carlota, a Confederate Colony in Mexico," *Journal of Southern History* 11, no. 1 (1945): 38.

98. Alfred Jackson Hanna and Kathryn Abbey Hanna, *Napoleon III and Mexico: American Triumph over Monarchy* (Chapel Hill: University of North Carolina Press, 1971), 235.

99. Tepic was dominated by the forces of Manuel Lozada, who was sympathetic to the empire, at least initially. See Zachary Brittsan, *Popular Politics and Rebellion in Mexico: Manuel Lozada and La Reforma, 1855–1876* (Nashville, TN: Vanderbilt University Press, 2015), 81–106.

100. See "La Colonización," *El Diario del Imperio,* September 25, 1865.

101. Russell, "Adventures," 91.

102. Settlers complained of "dissident" forces, but also of Dupin's antiguerrilla units. See letter to Isham Harris, Colon de Carlota, dated November 13, 1866, BLAC, García: Intervención Francesa: Documentos miscellaneous, 1862–1867.

103. Harmon cites *New York Herald* articles dated October 17, 18, and 20 and December 29, 1865. George D. Harmon, "Confederate Migration to Mexico," *Hispanic American Historical Review* 17, no. 4 (1937): 459–460; see also Simon J. Ellison, "An Anglo-American Plan for the Colonization of Mexico," *Southwestern Social Science Quarterly* 16, no. 2 (1935): 49.

104. APRB, BE-A0546/36, Impératrice Charlotte du Mexique, 315 Strijdmacht in Mexico, Oostenrijks legioen en Belgisch Legioen, 1864–1866.

105. Recruitment of settlers would be distinct from attempts to recruit Confederate veterans to serve in Mexico as part of his exit strategy for French troops. Bazaine proposed a signing bonus as inducement. See Bazaine a M. H. de Saint Cyr, BLAC, Achille Bazaine Papers, vol. 20, Minute, April 29, 1866.

106. For the imperial decree, see *Decrees*. A league equals three miles.

107. Harmon, "Confederate Migration," 472.

108. Officers and soldiers were offered forty acres *gratis* along the "Imperial Mexican Railway" by the decree of September 5, 1865. See "Notice," *Mexican Times*, December 2, 1865.

109. Maximilian called it his "coup d'état." See Maximilian to Eloin, Chapultepec, August 9, 1865, APRB, BE-A0546/36, Archief Van Felix Eloin, 208 Brieven van keizer Maximilliaan aan Eloin, met bijlage.

110. See Charlotte to Leopold, March 27, 1865, in Charlotte, *Lettres de Charlotte à Léopold, 1850 à 1868* (Brussels: Capron, 1988), 147.

111. For immigrants stabilizing Mexican territories, see Andrew Torget, *Seeds of Empire: Cotton, Slavery, and the Transformation of the Texas Borderlands, 1800–1850* (Chapel Hill: University of North Carolina Press, 2015).

112. Hanna and Hanna, "The Immigration Movement," 220–221.

113. Georges Clemenceau, *American Reconstruction, 1865–1870: And the Impeachment of President Johnson*, ed. Fernand Bladensperger, trans. Margaret MacVeagh (New York: Dial Press, 1928), 44. On Kickapoo settlers in northern Mexico, see Todd W. Wahlstrom, "The Southern Exodus to Mexico: Migration across the Borderlands after the U.S. Civil War" (PhD diss., University of California Santa Barbara, 2009), 173.

114. Stevenson, *Maximilian in Mexico*, 176; Corti, *Maximilian and Charlotte*, 522–533; George Upton, *Maximilian in Mexico*, trans. J. Kemper (Chicago: McClurg, 1911), 35.

115. See letter from Hidalgo regarding Gwin and Sonora, in Lefèvre, *Documents officiels*, 92–93.

116. There were also efforts to bring in settlers who were not also volunteers. See AGN, Segundo Imperio, box 18, Tomás Murphy to Ministerio de Negocios Extranjeros, March 25, 1865.

117. Corti, *Maximilian and Charlotte*, 118.

118. Hanna and Hanna, "The Immigration Movement," 238.

119. William Marshall Anderson, *An American in Maximilian's Mexico, 1865–1866*, ed. Ramón Eduardo Ruiz (San Marino, CA: Huntington Library, 1959), 57; Jaquelin Ambler Caskie, *Life and Letters of Matthew Fontaine Maury* (Richmond, VA: Richmond Press, 1928), 153–154; Harry Thayer Mahoney and Marjorie Locke Mahoney, *Mexico and the Confederacy, 1860–1867* (San Francisco: Austin and Winfield, 1998), 97–98.

120. W. C. Nunn, *Escape from Reconstruction* (Westport, CT: Greenwood Press, 1974), 32–33.

121. Terrell, *From Texas to Mexico*, 25; for Hindman's role in the war, see McPherson, *Battle Cry of Freedom*, 668.

122. Wahlstrom, "Southern Exodus to Mexico," 87.

123. Alice Baumgartner, *South to Freedom: Runaway Slaves to Mexico and the Road to the Civil War* (New York: Basic Books, 2020).

124. Edwards, *Shelby's Expedition*, 8; Andrew Rolle puts the figure at "several hundred." Andrew F. Rolle, *The Lost Cause: The Confederate Exodus to Mexico* (Norman: University of Oklahoma Press, 1965), 4.

125. See imperial decree dated October 28, 1865, AGN, Segundo Imperio, Caja 02, Expediente 74, Colonización.

126. Anderson, *American in Maximilian's Mexico*, 124n; Ellison, "Anglo-American Plan," 47.

127. Loyusel to Eloin, May 29, 1865, APRB, BE-A0546/36, Archief Van Felix Eloin, 266, Brieven aan Eloin gericht door: Charles-Joseph Loysel.

128. Edwards, *Shelby's Expedition*, 31; for more on desertions, see Douglas Porch, *The French Foreign Legion: A Complete History of the Legendary Fighting Force* (New York: HarperCollins, 1991), 155–156.

129. For the Southern vision of slave states through Mexico to South America, see McPherson, *Battle Cry of Freedom*, 116.

130. See Maury to Reverend E. W. Temlett, August 8, 1865, in Caskie, *Life and Letters*, 153–154.

131. Matías Romero informed Seward of the colonization law; William Corwin followed up with analysis. See Seward to Romero, Washington, March 14, 1866, in Andrew Johnson et al., "Message of the President of the United States, and Accompanying Documents, to the Two Houses of Congress, at the Commencement of the First Session of the Thirty-Ninth Congress. Part III," no. serial set vol. no. 1246, session vol. no.1. 39th Congress, 1st sess., H.Exec.Doc. 1 pt. 1.3 (1866): 473–475; see also Brian R. Hamnett, *Juárez* (London: Longman, 1994), 159.

132. On the long history of peonage, see Andrés Reséndez, *The Other Slavery: The Uncovered Story of Indian Enslavement in America* (Boston: Houghton Mifflin Harcourt, 2016); see also Jack Autrey Dabbs, "The Indian Policy of the Second Empire," in *Essays in Mexican History*, ed. Thomas E. Cotner and Carlos E. Castañeda (Westport, CT: Greenwood Press, 1972), 113.

133. This point was also made in an anonymous analysis submitted to Napoléon III, dated 1862. Dossier anonyme, AN AB XIX-171, Papiers des Tuileries (1870).

134. For debt as an incentive to attract workers, see Alan Knight, "Mexican Peonage: What Was It and Why Was It?," *Journal of Latin American Studies* 18, no. 1 (1986): 45–46; on Sánchez Navarro family, see Andrés Reséndez, "North American Peonage," *Journal of the Civil War Era* 7, no. 4 (2017): 601–602.

135. Torget, *Seeds of Empire*, 131.

136. See "Condicion de los Estados fronterizos de Estados Unidos" (April 21, 1861), in Matías Romero, *Correspondencia de la legación mexicana en Washington durante la intervención extranjera, 1860–1868: Colección de documentos para formar la historia de la intervención* (Mexico City: Imprenta del Gobierno, 1870), 2:360–361.

137. See "Junta de Colonización," *El Diario del Imperio*, July 10, 1865, 2–3. I'm grateful to an anonymous reader for bringing this to my attention.

138. See APRB, BE-A0546/36, Archief Van Felix Eloin, 298 Minuten van brieven van de hand van Eloin, Mexico, September 21, 1865, Demande du S. Morales d'introduire comme Colons 100,000 nègres et asiatiques.

139. See *El Diario del Imperio*, December 14, 1865. For "coolies" and the global labor supply chain, see Moon-Ho Jung, *Coolies and Cane: Race, Labor, and Sugar in the Age of Emancipation* (Baltimore: Johns Hopkins University Press, 2006).

140. "Mariah Baldwin and Ellen Latimer, Two Black Workers Settle Accounts at the End of the Year," in *The Civil War and Reconstruction: A Documentary Collection*, ed. William E. Gienapp (New York: W. W. Norton, 2001), 388–389.

141. See especially Chávez Orozco, *Maximiliano*.

10. Things Fall Apart

1. For "Shepherdess of the Alps," see letter dated May 26, 1866, in Ernst Pitner, *Maximilian's Lieutenant: A Personal History of the Mexican Campaign, 1864–7*, trans. Gordon Etherington-Smith (Albuquerque: University of New Mexico Press, 1993), 121.

2. See letter to his mother dated January 28, 1865, in Pitner, *Maximilian's Lieutenant*, 47.

3. Related to his diary, not to his mother. See Pitner, *Maximilian's Lieutenant*, 67, 85.

4. See Omar S. Valerio-Jiménez, *River of Hope: Forging Identity and Nation in the Rio Grande Borderlands* (Durham, NC: Duke University Press, 2013), esp. 64–65.

5. See especially William Watson, *The Civil War Adventures of a Blockade Runner* (College Station: Texas A&M University Press, 2001), 28–29.

6. Pitner, *Maximilian's Lieutenant*, 104.

7. Robert W. Delaney, "Matamoros, Port for Texas during the Civil War," *Southwestern Historical Quarterly* 58, no. 4 (April 1, 1955): 483; see also Watson, *Civil War Adventures*; Brian R. Hamnett, "Mexican Conservatives, Clericals, and Soldiers: The 'Traitor' Tomás Mejía through Reform and Empire, 1855–1867," *Bulletin of Latin American Research* 20, no. 2 (2001): 203.

8. See "Journal rédigé par le Lieutenant Romignon de la Légion étrangère," in SHD, GR 7 G Expédition du Mexique, 87 Contre-guérilla du colonel Dupin, Historique, Siège de Mexico, 1863–1867.

9. Delaney, "Matamoros," 480.

10. Pitner, *Maximilian's Lieutenant*, 103.

11. See letter dated March 31, 1866, in Pitner, *Maximilian's Lieutenant*, 117.

12. Pitner, *Maximilian's Lieutenant*, 102.

13. Delaney, "Matamoros," 486; Alfred J. Hanna and Kathryn Abbey Hanna, *Napoléon III and Mexico: American Triumph over Monarchy* (Chapel Hill: University of North Carolina Press, 1971), 155.

14. Gustave Léon Niox, *Expédition du Mexique, 1861–1867: Récit politique & militaire* (Paris: J. Dumaine, 1874), 535.

15. Napoléon III was confident that a US war with France would also mean war with Britain. See letter from Napoléon III to Bazaine, March 1, 1865, AMBAE, Série Générale "Politique," 13916, Notes from sales catalog of the Parke Burnet Galleries.

16. Mejía was apparently popular in Matamoros with the municipal establishment, which thanked him publicly in a circular published in December 1865. See "Voto de Gracias presentado por el Ayuntamiento," BLAC, Genaro García Broadsides and Circulars Collection.

17. See letter from Mejía regarding a meeting at Point Isabel dated March 1865, BLAC, Genaro Garcia, Documentos Relativos a la Reforma y a la Intervención Francesa en México, 81 (3).

18. See W. Caleb McDaniel, "Remembering Henry: Refugeed Slaves in Civil War Texas" (Atlanta: Organization of American Historians, 2014), 1–8; W. Caleb McDaniel, *Sweet Taste of Liberty: A True Story of Slavery and Restitution in America* (New York: Oxford University Press, 2019).

19. Philip Henry Sheridan, *Personal Memoirs of P. H. Sheridan* (New York: Charles L. Webster and Co., 1888), 211–212.

20. See letter from A. W. Ferrell [confederate general] in San Luis Potosí to Ct M. de Noue, September 18, 1865, in which Ferrell offers to return to Texas to organize an attack on the rear of US forces, BLAC, Genaro Garcia, Documentos Relativos a la Reforma y a la Intervención Francesa en México, 80b (2).

21. Quoted in Robert Ryal Miller, "Lew Wallace and the French Intervention in Mexico," *Indiana Magazine of History* 59 (1963): 34.

22. Ephraim Douglass Adams, *Great Britain and the American Civil War* (New York: Longmans, Green and Co, 1925), 1272–1273; James M. McPherson, *Battle Cry of Freedom: The Civil War Era* (New York: Oxford University Press, 1988), 821–822; Matías Romero, *Mexican Lobby: Matías Romero in Washington, 1861–1867*, ed. Thomas David Schoonover (Lexington: University Press of Kentucky, 1986), 50; William C. Harris, "The Hampton Roads Peace Conference: A Final Test of Lincoln's Presidential Leadership," *Journal of the Abraham Lincoln Association* 21 (2000): 34–35.

23. See Miller, "Lew Wallace," 32; see also letter from Joseph Slaughter, Brownsville, April 12, 1865, BLAC, Genaro García, Documentos Relativos a la Reforma y a la Intervención Francesa en México, 81 (3), Intervención Francesa, Documentos misceláneos, 1862–1867.

24. See Hooricks to Rogier, AMBAE, Série B 68 I, II, III 1861–1866, Enrôlements militaires à l'ètranger; Légion Belge au Portugal, 1834.

25. Miller, "Lew Wallace," 38.

26. See Weitzel to Mejía, December 4, 1865, BLAC, García Documentos Relativos a la Reforma y a la Intervención Francesa en México, 80c (1). For Douay and Bazaine, see BLAC, García Achille Bazaine Papers, G500, vol. 17, Correspondencia de Achille François Bazaine, 1862–1867, January 24, 1866.

27. The Ayuntamiento of Matamoros distributed a "Voto de Gracias" thanking Mejía for his efforts against the "numerous band of outlaws." See BLAC, Genaro Garcia, Broadsides and Circulars Collection.

28. Pitner, *Maximilian's Lieutenant,* 106.

29. Miller says 150 "Negro" troops; see Miller, "Lew Wallace," 44. See Lucas Martínez Sánchez, *Coahuila durante la intervención francesa, 1862–1867* (Saltillo: Gobierno del Estado de Coahuila, 2008), 11.

30. For Mejía's protest, see Bazaine to Maximilian, February 9, 1866, AN, AB/XIX/171, Papiers des Tuileries (1870).

31. See Weitzel to Mejía, January 18, 1866, BLAC, García Documentos Relativos a la Reforma y a la Intervención Francesa en México, 81 (4). See also Jean-Yves Puyo, "The French Military Confront Mexico's Geography: The Expedition of 1862–67," *Journal of Latin American Geography* 9, no. 2 (2010): 151–152.

32. Georges Clemenceau, *American Reconstruction, 1865–1870, and the Impeachment of President Johnson,* trans. Margaret MacVeagh (New York: Dial Press, 1928), 64.

33. For a fuller account, see Emmanuel Domenech, *Histoire du Mexique* (Paris: A. Lacroix, Verboeckhoven et Cie, 1868), 375; see also José M. Vigil and Vicente Riva Palacio, *México a través de los siglos,* 5 vols. (Mexico City: Herrerias, 1940), 5:745-746.

34. Philip Henry Sheridan, *Personal Memoirs of P. H. Sheridan* (New York: Charles L. Webster and Co., 1888), 214-216.

35. James Frederick Elton, *With the French in Mexico* (London: Chapman and Hall, 1867), 68.

36. On imperial control of Monterrey, see Van der Smissen à Hooricks, Monterrey, April 8, 1866, AMBAE, Série B 68 III, 1866-1944.

37. Castelnau noted that up to eighty legionnaires deserted in a single day in 1865 during the occupation of Matamoros. Douglas Porch, *The French Foreign Legion: A Complete History of the Legendary Fighting Force* (New York: HarperCollins, 1991), 154-155.

38. On money and desertions, see Pitner, *Maximilian's Lieutenant,* 103.

39. For the condition of Austrians, see "Journal rédigé par le Lieutenant Romignon de la Légion étrangère," SHD, GR 7 G Expédition du Mexique, 87 Contreguérilla du colonel Dupin, Historique, Siège de Mexico, 1863-1867.

40. Signing bonuses were offered to Austrians and others willing to join the army of the Mexican republic. See Pitner, *Maximilian's Lieutenant,* 100.

41. See telegram from Austrian commander General Thün to General Neigre, dated May 20, 1866, ÖSta KA, Archiv der Truppenkörper, Karton 7.

42. Niox, *Expédition du Mexique,* 576; Mario Treviño Villarreal, *El principio del fin: La Batalla de Santa Gertrudis* (Monterrey, Mexico: Honorable Congreso del Estado de Nuevo León, 1999), 77.

43. Emilio Velasco, ed., *Documentos relativos a la batalla de Santa Gertrudis* (Matamoros: Segura y Ambros, 1866), 5.

44. Escobedo details a force of fourteen hundred, divided into five columns. See "Carta de Mariano Escobedo a Ignacio Mejía," in Masae Sugawara, ed., *Mariano Escobedo* (Mexico: Senado de la República, 1987), 174-175. Pitner put Escobedo's force at two thousand. See Pitner, *Maximilian's Lieutenant,* 134. Niox puts the figure at five thousand, including "twelve to fifteen hundred Americans." Niox, *Expédition du Mexique,* 577.

45. See Escobedo's initial report to the (republican) minister of war as well as the official tally in Velasco, *Documentos relativos,* 3, 8.

46. For prisoners, see Treviño Villarreal, *El principio del fin,* 73.

47. See Mariano Escobedo . . . á las tropas que concurrieron á la batalla de la Mesa de Santa Gertrudis, in Velasco, *Documentos relativos,* 4.

48. Pitner, *Maximilian's Lieutenant,* 134.

49. See "Dos entrevistas del Sr. Terán con el Baron de Pont in Jesús Terán," in *La Misión confidencial de Don Jesús Terán en Europa, 1863-66,* ed. Gabriel Saldívar (Mexico: Archivo Histórico Diplomático Mexicano, 1943), 31-32; see also Frank Averill Knapp, *The Life of Sebastián Lerdo de Tejada, 1823-1889: A Study of Influence and Obscurity* (Austin: University of Texas Press, 1951), 110.

50. Contemporaries saw the fight as being like that of the French in Algeria, where the insurgents could be defeated, though they never surrendered. See "Expedition dans le Michoacan du regiment belge Imperatrice Charlotte," *La Meuse,* May 16, 1865.

51. See Confidentielle, Circulaire, Mexico, March 7, 1866, SHD, GR 7 G Expédition du Mexique, 87 Contre-guérilla du colonel Dupin, Historique, Siège de Mexico, 1863–1867.

52. Report from Méndez to Bazaine, February 28, 1866, BLAC, Genaro García, Achille Bazaine Papers, G500, Correspondencia de Achille François Bazaine, 1862–1867, January 24, 1866, vol. 18. Méndez reports specifically regarding Michoacán.

53. Elton, *With the French,* 90; for Matamoros after the departure of imperial forces, see BMNAH, Imperio de Maximiliano Collection, documents 441, 442.

54. Niox, *Expédition du Mexique,* 578.

55. On frequency of desertions, see Elton, *With the French,* 87.

56. More than sixty soldiers from an Austro-Belgian unit were taken prisoner at Parras. See BLAC, Genaro García, Documentos Relativos a la Reforma y a la Intervención Francesa en México, 82a (2) Intervención Francesa, Estadística militar y económica, 1862–1867.

57. AMBAE, séries B 68 III, 1866–1944, Rapport du Legation (Hooricks) a Rogier (M. des A. E.) Mexico, June 9, 1866.

58. See remarks of Emilio Velasco, drafted just two weeks after Camargo, in Velasco, *Documentos relativos,* 2.

59. On Union veterans, see Niox, *Expédition du Mexique,* 577.

60. Basch mentions an American "Legion of Honor" with 150 US veterans fighting at Querétaro. See Samuel Basch, *Recollections of Mexico: The Last Ten Months of Maximilian's Empire.* ed. Fred D. Ullman (Wilmington, DE: Scholarly Resources, 2001), 143.

61. See letter from Anton von Magnus dated March 4, 1866, in Anton von Magnus, *Das Ende des maximilianischen Kaiserreichs in Mexico: Berichte des königlich preussischen Ministerresidenten Anton von Magnus an Bismarck, 1866–1867,* ed. Joachim Kühn (Göttingen: Musterschmidt, 1965), 87. For the Belgian perspective, see Bombelles to Eloin, March 9, 1866, APRB, BE-A0546/36, Archief Van Felix Eloin, 219 Brieven aan Eloin gericht door: graaf Charles-Albert de Bombelles; see also Albert Duchesne, *L'expédition des volontaires belges au Mexique, 1864–1867,* 2 vols. (Brussels: Centre d'Histoire Militaire, 1967), 556–557.

62. Duchesne, *L'expédition,* 666.

63. See Joinville to Charlotte, May 29, 1866, in Luis Weckmann, *Carlota de Bélgica: Correspondencia y escritos sobre México en los archivos europeos, 1861–1868* (Mexico: Porrúa, 1989), 40.

64. Niox, *Expédition du Mexique,* 580.

65. See Maximilian to Degollado, June 28, 1866, BLAC, Joaquín and Mariano Degollado Collection, folder 1, Correspondence, letters from Maximilian, Emperor of Mexico.

11. Charlotte Tries Diplomacy

1. For the place of the emperor's birthday among other holidays, see Robert H. Duncan, "Embracing a Suitable Past: Independence Celebrations under Mexico's Second Empire, 1864–6," *Journal of Latin American Studies* 30, no. 2 (1998): 260.

2. "Felicitaciones" *El Diario del Imperio,* July 7, 1866, 3.

3. Letter from Maximilian to Eloin, July 10, 1866, APRB, BE A0546 36, Archief Van Felix Eloin 208 Brieven van keizer Maximilliaan aan Eloin; also AMBAE, Série Générale "Politique," 13916, Notes from sales catalog of the Parke Burnet Galleries.

4. For Guanajuato, see "Cumpleaños del Emperador," *El Diario del Imperio,* July 13, 1866, 1; for Xalapa, see page 2.

5. See "Reservada" Del Ilustrisimo Señor Labastida Arzobispo de Mexico, July 10, 1866, ASV SS 1866, R. 251, fasc. 12 in Luis Ramos, María Guadalupe Bosch de Souza, Ana María González Luna, and Archivio vaticano, *Del Archivo secreto vaticano: La Iglesia y el estado mexicano en el siglo XIX* (Mexico, DF: Universidad Nacional Autónoma de México, 1997), 358.

6. For "burlesque," see Maximilian to Eloin, Palais de Mexico, July 10, 1866, APRB, BE-A0546/36, Archief Van Felix Eloin, 208 Brieven van keizer Maximilliaan aan Eloin.

7. See Dolores Almonte to Charlotte, July 15 and 31, 1866, in Luis Weckmann, *Carlota de Bélgica: Correspondencia y escritos sobre México en los archivos europeos, 1861–1868* (Mexico: Porrúa, 1989), 58, 61.

8. For "Almonte is loyal," see Dolores Almonte to Charlotte, July 15, 1866, APRB, BE-A0546/36, Imperatrice Charlotte du Mexique, 51 Brieven van particulieren aan de keizerin gericht: Juan Nepomuc De Almonte en zijn echtgenote Dolores.

9. See "Actualidades," *La Sociedad,* July 12, 1866, 2; see also "Estrangero," in *La Sombra: Periódico joco-serio ultra-liberal y reformista,* April 3, 1866, 4; "Cronica escandalosa," *La Sombra,* February 2, 1866, 3.

10. Eloin's summary of audience with Napoléon III, March 26, 1866, WRC, Charlotte and Maximilian Collection, box 1, folder 11.

11. Carl Khevenhüller, *Con Maximiliano en México: Del diario del príncipe Carl Khevenhüller, 1864–1867,* ed. Brigitte Hamann (Mexico: Fondo de Cultura Económica, 1994), 165, 171.

12. For her meeting with Meglia and her "restlessness," see Egon Caesar Corti, *Maximilian and Charlotte of Mexico,* trans. Catherine Alison Phillips (New York: Knopf, 1928), 456–457.

13. Gustave Léon Niox, *Expédition du Mexique, 1861–1867: Récit politique & militaire* (Paris: J. Dumaine, 1874), 584. Prince Metternich seems to have used this expression with regard to Charlotte. See Corti, *Maximilian and Charlotte,* 676; H. de Reinach-Foussemagne, *Charlotte de Belgique, impératrice du Mexique* (Paris: Plon-Nourrit, 1925), 32.

14. Leo Francis Stock, *United States Ministers to the Papal States: Instructions and Despatches, 1848–1868* (Washington, DC: Catholic University Press, 1933), xxxv.

15. See ASV SS 1866, R. 251, fasc. 9, letter from Charlotte to Gutiérrez, February 11, 1865, in Ramos et al., *Del Archivo secreto vaticano,* 203–204.

16. For the text of Charlotte's memoir, see "Mémoire remis par moi à l'Empereur Napoléon à Saint-Cloud le 11 Aout 1866," APRB, BE-A0546/36, Impératrice Charlotte du Mexique, 159 Teksten van politieke aard: mémoire remis par moi à l'Empereur Napoléon à St-Cloud le 11 août 1866, met een kopie van dit memorandum en bijlagen.

17. Charlotte to Maximilian, Rio Frio, July 8, 1866, HRC, MS-2733, 057–059.

18. On Sudanese impressions of Mexico, see "Mexico," *New York Herald*, August 17, 1866 in APRB, BE-A0546/36, Impératrice Charlotte du Mexique, 178 Reis van de keizerin naar Europa, 1867.

19. Charlotte to Maximilian, Havana, June 17, 1866, HRC, MS-2733, 060–062.

20. Raphael Waldburg-Zeil, *Fernando Maximiliano de Habsburgo, 1832–1867: Perfil humano de un archiduque-emperador* (Madrid: Gunter Quercus, 2013), 272–273.

21. Patricia Galeana, "Carlota fue Roja," in *Más nuevas del imperio: Estudios interdisciplinarios acerca de Carlota de México*, ed. Susanne Igler and Roland Spiller (Frankfurt: Vervuert, 2001), 69.

22. Concepción Lombardo de Miramón, *Memorias de Concepción Lombardo de Miramón* (Mexico: Porrúa, 1989), 617–618.

23. Josef Wiedenhofer, "Die öffentliche Meinung in Österreich zum Abenteuer Kaiser Maximilians I. von Mexiko" (diss., University of Vienna, 1979), 227.

24. Reinach-Foussemagne, *Charlotte de Belgique*, 289; see also the speculation of John Hay, US chargé d'affaires, in Eugène Lefèvre, *Documents officiels recueillis dans la secrétairerie privée de Maximilien: Histoire de l'intervention française au Mexique*, 2 vols. (Paris: Armand le Chevalier, 1870), 339–340.

25. Reinach-Foussemagne, *Charlotte de Belgique*, 290.

26. A slight duly noted in Vienna; see Wiedenhofer, "Die öffentliche Meinung," 133.

27. José M. Vigil and Vicente Riva Palacio, *México a través de los siglos*, 5 vols. (Mexico City: Herrerias, 1940), 5:770; Edmund Daniek, *Sie zogen nach Mexiko: Ein Denkmal für die österreichischen Freiwilligen unter Kaiser Maximilian, 1864–1867* (Vienna: Amalthea, 1964), 82; for the Grand Hôtel, see Helen M. Davies, *Emile and Isaac Pereire: Bankers, Socialists and Sephardic Jews in Nineteenth-Century France* (Manchester: Manchester University Press, 2014), 211.

28. Lombardo de Miramón, *Memorias*, 509–510.

29. For the text of her report, see APRB, BE-A0546/36, Impératrice Charlotte du Mexique,159 Teksten van politieke aard: Mémoire remis par moi à l'Empereur Napoléon à St-Cloud le 11 août 1866.

30. The source for this dramatic confrontation is unclear. It can be found in published form eight years after the supposed incident in Niox, *Expédition du Mexique*, 586n; it is repeated in Alfred Louis Adolphe Graves Van der Smissen, *Souvenirs du Mexique, 1864–1867, par le général baron Van der Smissen, . . .* (Brussels: J. Lebègue, 1892), 184; Auguste Charles Philippe Blanchot, *L'intervention française au Mexique: Mémoires*, 3 vols. (Paris: E. Nourry, 1911), 240–241; Vigil and Riva Palacio, *México a través de los siglos*, 5:771.

31. Attributed to Colin Powell regarding the invasion of Iraq.

32. Corti, *Maximilian and Charlotte*, 679.

33. Corti, *Maximilian and Charlotte*, 681.

34. Reinach-Foussemagne, *Charlotte de Belgique*, 301.

35. For the Indigenous "race" as foundation for the empire, see Maximilian to Eloin, August 28, 1866, APRB, BE-A0546/36,Archief Van Felix Eloin, 208 Brieven van keizer Maximilliaan aan Eloin.

36. See letter from Maximilian to Eloin, April 26, 1866, WRC, Charlotte and Maximilian Collection, box 1, folder 11.

37. Masseras argues unconvincingly that signs of mental instability presented themselves prior to her departure from Mexico. E. Masseras, *Un essai d'empire au Mexique* (Paris: Charpentier, 1879), 78–80.

38. Corti, *Maximilian and Charlotte*, 690–691.

39. Maximilian to Eloin, September 17, 1866, APRB, BE-A0546/36, Archief Van Felix Eloin, 208 Brieven van keizer Maximilliaan aan Eloin.

40. Corti, *Maximilian and Charlotte*, 699.

41. See dispatch from "La Courageuse," Légation de Belgique au Ministre des Affaires Étrangères, Rome, September 26, 1866, AMBAE, Série B 68 IV.

42. Augustín Fischer's agreement to convene Mexican bishops in order to hash out a concordat was also invoked as a reason a concordat could not be concluded directly with Charlotte. See Légation de Belgique au Ministre des Affaires Étrangères, Rome, September 29, 1866, AMBAE, Série B 68 IV.

43. Corti, *Maximilian and Charlotte*, 707.

44. Charlotte to Maximilian, Rome, September 26, 1866, HRC, MS-2733, 080–086.

45. See dispatch from Légation de Belgique au Ministre des Affaires Étrangères, Rome, September 29, 1866, AMBAE, Série B 68 IV.

46. See letter Charlotte to Pius, Rome, October 4, 1866, ASV, Archivo Particular de Pío IX, Mexico, 1866, in Ramos et al., *Del Archivo secreto vaticano*, 365–366.

47. See *l'Illustration*, October 27, 1866.

48. Corti, *Maximilian and Charlotte*, 708.

49. The assertion is repeated by Reinach-Foussemagne, *Charlotte de Belgique*, 318; for commentary on Corti's accounts, see Fernando del Paso, *News from the Empire*, trans. Alfonso González and Stella T. Clark (Champaign, IL: Dalkey Archive Press, 2009), 490–491.

50. Corti, *Maximilian and Charlotte*, 710–711.

51. Diplomats privately hoped the donation would be declined. See Légation de Belgique au Ministre des Affaires Étrangères, Rome, October 3, 1866, AMBAE, Série B 68 IV; another telegram also dated October 3, 1866, from the Belgian Legation in Rome to the Belgian Minister of Foreign Affairs.

52. See letter from Charlotte to Pius, Rome, October 4, 1866, ASV, Archivo Particular de Pío IX, Mexico, 1866, in Ramos et al., *Del Archivo secreto vaticano*, 365–366.

53. Translation: "Persistent delusion and monomania observed. Obstinate, unceasing eccentric behavior." Dispatch from Légation de Belgique au Ministre des Affaires Étrangères, Rome, October 5, 1866, AMBAE, Série B 68 IV.

54. José Luis Blasio, *Maximilian, Emperor of Mexico: Memoirs of His Private Secretary, José Luis Blasio*, trans. Robert Hammond Murray (New Haven, CT: Yale University Press, 1934), 107.

55. Blasio, *Maximilian*, 108–109.

56. See telegram to Paris from Bombelles at Miramar for Eloin, October 14 [1866], APRB, BE-A0546/36, Impératrice Charlotte du Mexique, 219 Brieven aan Eloin gericht door: graaf Charles-Albert de Bombelles, persoonlijke adviseur van keizer Maximilliaan, 1865–1868. En niet gedateerd. 1865–1868.

57. Although sources indicate that Charlotte never fully recovered her mental health, she had at least moments of lucidity. See letter from Charlotte to her aunt, Miramar, February 14, 1867, ÖSta, SB Coburg II-20, Familienkorrespondenz Sachsen-Coburg-Gotha, Korrespondenz, 1857–1881.

12. Like Pinning Butterflies

1. For Bringas, see José Luis Blasio, *Maximilian, Emperor of Mexico: Memoirs of His Private Secretary, José Luis Blasio,* trans. Robert Hammond Murray (New Haven, CT: Yale University Press, 1934), 115.

2. Concepción Lombardo de Miramón, *Memorias de Concepción Lombardo de Miramón* (Mexico: Porrúa, 1989), 519; Samuel Basch, *Recollections of Mexico: The Last Ten Months of Maximilian's Empire,* ed. Fred D. Ullman (Wilmington, DE: Scholarly Resources, 2001), 69–70.

3. Carl Khevenhüller, *Con Maximiliano en México: Del diario del príncipe Carl Khevenhüller, 1864–1867,* ed. Brigitte Hamann (Mexico: Fondo de Cultura Económica, 1994), 181.

4. See entry for October 1, 1865, in "Journal rédigé par le Lieutenant Romignon de la Légion étrangère," SHD, GR 7 G Expédition du Mexique, 87 Contre-guérilla du colonel Dupin, Historique, Siège de Mexico, 1863–1867.

5. José M. Vigil and Vicente Riva Palacio, *México a través de los siglos,* 5 vols. (Mexico City: Herrerias, 1940), 5:704–705.

6. Title to the property was clarified only in 1870. See note, July 5, 1870, BLAC, Genaro García, Documentos Relativos a la Reforma y a la Intervención Francesa en México, 81 (1), Intervención Francesa, Correspondencia miscelánea, 1846–1867; documentos relativos a Maximiliano, 1865–1867.

7. Napoléon III to Bazaine, Palais des Tuileries, January 13, 1866, BLAC, Achille Bazaine Papers G500, vol. 18.

8. Minute de dépêche, Mexico, February 9, 1866, BLAC, Achille Bazaine Papers G500, vol. 18. See also the report on projections for the trimester of December 1865 and January/February 1866, BLAC, Genaro García, Documentos Relativos a la Reforma y a la Intervención Francesa en México, 82a (2), Intervención Francesa, Estadística militar y económica, 1862–1867.

9. Report, Mexico, February 8, 1866, BLAC, Achille Bazaine Papers G500, vol. 18.

10. For their roles, see Gustave Léon Niox, *Expédition du Mexique, 1861–1867: Récit politique & militaire* (Paris: J. Dumaine, 1874), 559; Anton von Magnus, *Das Ende des maximilianischen Kaiserreichs in Mexico: Berichte des königlich preussischen Ministerresidenten Anton von Magnus an Bismarck, 1866–1867,* ed. Joachim Kühn (Göttingen: Musterschmidt, 1965), 115–116.

11. In June 1866 Bazaine expressed confidence that the empire might yet endure. See Bazaine to Napoléon III, June 9, 1866, AN, AB XIX-171, Papiers des Tuileries.

12. See Maximiliano to Joaquín Degollado, Rome, June 28, 1866, BLAC, Joaquín and Mariano Degollado Collection, folder 1, Correspondence, letters from Maximilian, Emperor of Mexico.

13. General Osmont would later explain that he and Friant had been called to Chapultepec, where Maximilian expressed his lack of confidence in Mexican generals to organize his army and assured them he had Napoléon III's support for their role in his government. See SHD, GR 7 G Expédition du Mexique, 87 Contre-guérrilla du colonel Dupin, Historique, Siège de Mexico, 1863–1867.

14. France had wanted troop withdrawal to follow an assurance from the United States that it would recognize the new regime in Mexico. The United States refused. Niox, *Expédition du Mexique,* 546; for the April promise, see 548.

15. See Minute, Napoléon à Bazaine, St. Cloud, August 29, 1866, BLAC, Achille Bazaine Papers G500, vol. 23.

16. For Maximilian's protest, see Maximilian to Bazaine, September 16, 1866, BLAC, Achille Bazaine Papers G500, Correspondencia de Achille François Bazaine, 1862–1867, vol. 23.

17. Maximilian summarizes his views as expressed to Napoléon III in a letter to Eloin, June 28, 1866, APRB, BE-A0546/36, Archief Van Felix Eloin, 208 Brieven van keizer Maximilliaan aan Eloin.

18. Basch, *Recollections*, 16–17.

19. This was the advice of Félix Eloin, then in Brussels, who argued against abdication. See letter from Eloin a Maximilian, September 17, 1866, APRB BE-A0546/36, Archief Van Felix Eloin, 208 Brieven van keizer Maximilliaan aan Eloin.

20. See "Sur les munitions laissés au pouvoir du gouvernement Mexicain au départ de l'armée française," in BLAC, Genaro García, Documentos Relativos a la Reforma y a la Intervención Francesa en México, 82a (2) Intervención Francesa, Estadística militar y económica, 1862–1867. See also Khevenhüller, *Con Maximiliano*, 221–222.

21. Charlotte made a point of this in her complaint to Napoléon III, which she presented in person. See "Mémoire remis par moi à l'Empereur Napoléon à Saint-Cloud le 11 Aout 1866," APRB BE-A0546/36, Impératrice Charlotte du Mexique, 159 Teksten van politieke aard.

22. Jose Antonio de Larrinaga, "L'Intervention française au Mexique vue par les principaux journaux canadiens-français du Québec, 1861–1867" (MA thesis, University of Ottawa, 1976), 196–197.

23. See letter of March 29, 1867, to Herzfeld in Vienna, in Basch, *Recollections*, 159–160.

24. Pedro Pruneda, *Historia de la guerra de Méjico, desde 1861 á 1867: Con todos los documentos diplomáticos justificativos* (Madrid: Elizalde y compañia, 1867), 198.

25. See especially Jorge Mario Magallón Ibarra, *Proceso y ejecución vs. Fernando Maximiliano de Habsburgo* (Mexico: Universidad Nacional Autónoma de México, 2005), 104n.

26. Maximilian informed Charlotte of the new government on August 31, 1866. See Luis Weckmann, *Carlota de Bélgica: Correspondencia y escritos sobre México en los archivos europeos, 1861–1868* (Mexico: Porrúa, 1989), 22.

27. Almonte (in Paris) to Charlotte (in Rome), September 23, 1866, APRB, BE-A0546/36, Impératrice Charlotte du Mexique, 178 Reis van de keizerin naar Europa, 1867.

28. Magnus, *Das Ende*, 160.

29. These visits were also the source of a rumor that Maximilian had a lover there. See José Luis Blasio, *Maximiliano en Cuernavaca* (Mexico: Talleres Graficos de Impresores de Morelos, 1905), 25–26.

30. See Gutiérrez Estrada to Napoléon III, letter dated June 21, 1866, AN, AB XIX-171, Papiers des Tuileries (1870).

31. For the resignation, see E. Masseras, *Un essai d'empire au Mexique* (Paris, 1879), 91; Basch, *Recollections*, 33; for more on Lares, see Erika Pani, "Dreaming of

a Mexican Empire: The Political Projects of the 'Imperialistas.'" *Hispanic American Historical Review* 82, no. 1 (2002): 12–14.

32. Magnus, *Das Ende,* 160.

33. Egon Caesar Corti, *Maximilian and Charlotte of Mexico,* trans. Catherine Alison Phillips (New York: Knopf, 1928), 738.

34. Basch, *Recollections,* 36; Corti, *Maximilian and Charlotte,* 748–749.

35. See Veracruz, November 1, 1866, AMAE, Correspondance politique des consuls, 1826–1870, Mexique, 4 1865–1866, La Vera Cruz, Tampico; also Pruneda, *Historia de la guerra,* 402.

36. See "Estranjero," *La Sociedad,* November 2, 1866.

37. See "Evangelio del día—Tinieblas," *La Sombra,* November 9, 1866.

38. See Hooricks to Rogier, November 29, 1866, AMBAE Série B 68 III 1866–1944.

39. See Anónima, New York, September 20, 1866, "Une conférence avec le General Ortega," BLAC, Genaro García, Documentos Relativos a la Reforma y a la Intervención Francesa en México, 83a (2) Intervención Francesa, Documentos misceláneos, 1867–1869.

40. The expectation was that Juárez would soon be in the capital and Sherman would meet him there. When Sherman arrived in Veracruz and learned that Maximilian had not departed, he returned to New Orleans. See Matías Romero, *Mexican Lobby: Matías Romero in Washington, 1861–1867,* ed. Thomas David Schoonover (Lexington: University Press of Kentucky, 1986), 144–146; Alfred J. Hanna and Kathryn Abbey Hanna, *Napoléon III and Mexico: American Triumph over Monarchy* (Chapel Hill: University of North Carolina Press, 1971), 286–287.

41. See Maximilian to Eloin, November 8, 1866, APRB, BE-A0546/36, Archief Van Felix Eloin, 208 Brieven van keizer Maximilliaan aan Eloin.

42. Corti, *Maximilian and Charlotte,* 656–657.

43. Dorothy Gies McGuigan, *The Habsburgs* (Garden City, NY: Doubleday, 1966), 342.

44. Magnus, *Das Ende,* 306; Josef Wiedenhofer, "Die öffentliche Meinung in Österreich zum Abenteuer Kaiser Maximilians 1. von Mexiko" (diss., University of Vienna, 1979), 160; Eloin's letter of September17 also touched on discontent with Franz Joseph. See Emmanuel Domenech, *Histoire du Mexique* (Paris: A. Lacroix, Verboeckhoven et Cie, 1868), 408.

45. Alejandro Franchi, archbishop of Thessalonica (an honorary title), wrote of Fischer's return on June 26, 1866. See BMNAH, Colección: Imperio de Maximiliano, Documento 412.

46. Maximilian believed entirely in Fischer's fiction. See his earnest letter to Labastida, August 31, 1866, BMNAH, Colección: Imperio de Maximiliano, Documento 428. Labastida pursued the matter with the Mexican episcopate. See, in the same collection, Labastida's letter to the archbishop of Guadalajara, dated September 2, 1866 (Documento 429).

47. See "Reservada" from Munguía, June 12, 1866, ASV SS 1866, R 251, fasc. 12 in Luis Ramos, María Guadalupe Bosch de Souza, Ana María González Luna, and Archivio vaticano, *Del Archivo secreto vaticano: La Iglesia y el estado mexicano en el siglo XIX* (Mexico, DF: Universidad Nacional Autónoma de México, 1997), 339–341.

48. Fischer was worried Maximilian might see him as immoral. See Basch, *Recollections*, 69–70.

49. Basch, *Recollections*, 27.

50. Salm-Salm remarks this regarding Fischer's children. See Felix Salm-Salm, *My Diary in Mexico in 1867: Including the Last Days of the Emperor Maximilian.* 2 vols. (London: R. Bently, 1868), 13.

51. Basch, *Recollections*, 44–45.

52. For the text of the letter, see Niox, *Expédition du Mexique*, 634. The original can be found in APRB, BE-A0546/36, Archief Van Felix Eloin, 208 Brieven van keizer Maximilliaan aan Eloin.

53. Pitner letter of March 31, 1865, in Ernst Pitner, *Maximilian's Lieutenant: A Personal History of the Mexican Campaign, 1864–7,* trans. Gordon Etherington-Smith (Albuquerque: University of New Mexico Press, 1993), 119.

54. Edmund Daniek, *Sie zogen nach Mexiko: Ein Denkmal für die österreichischen Freiwilligen unter Kaiser Maximilian, 1864–1867* (Vienna: Amalthea, 1964), 72.

55. Van der Smissen, among others, had threatened to resign rather than serve under Colonel Ramón Méndez. See Léon François Lambert Émile Timmerhans, *Voyage et opérations du corps belge au Mexique* (Liége: Carmanne, 1866), 201–202.

56. See letter, Van der Smissen to Minister Foreign Affairs, January 24, 1866, AMBAE, Série B 68 III 1866–1944.

57. Van der Smissen to Maximilian, September 15, 186, AMBAE, Série B 68 III 1866–1944. See also Albert Duchesne, *L'expédition des volontaires belges au Mexique, 1864–1867,* 2 vols. (Brussels: Centre d'Histoire Militaire, 1967), 555.

58. Basch, *Recollections*, 12–13.

59. Basch, *Recollections*, 56.

60. Khevenhüller, *Con Maximiliano,* 180.

61. Egon Caesar Corti, *Mensch und Herrscher: Wege und Schicksale* (Graz: Verlag Styria, 1952), 381; F. Fernando del Paso, *News from the Empire,* trans. Alfonso González and Stella T. Clark (Champaign, IL: Dalkey Archive Press, 2009), 498–499; McGuigan, *The Habsburgs,* 342.

62. Corti, *Maximilian and Charlotte,* 752.

63. Maximilian insisted that under the Treaty of Miramare, French troops stay until the end of 1868. See Lombardo de Miramón, *Memorias,* 509.

64. See "Minute," Kodolitsch, January 9, 1867, BLAC, Achille Bazaine Papers G500, Correspondencia de Achille Francois Bazaine, 1862–1867, vol. 26.

65. See Archevêque de Mexico à Bazaine, January 7, 1867, BLAC, Achille Bazaine Papers G500, Correspondencia de Achille Francois Bazaine, 1862–1867, vol. 26.

66. Basch, *Recollections,* 74–75; Blasio, *Maximilian,* 115.

67. Blasio, *Maximilian,* 116; for those involved in these discussions, see Domenech, *Histoire du Mexique,* 411.

68. Basch, *Recollections,* 75–79.

69. The text is reproduced in Auguste Charles Philippe Blanchot, *L'intervention française au Mexique: Mémoires,* 3 vols. (Paris: E. Nourry, 1911), 337.

70. For Ilarregui, see Douglas Richmond, "The Failure of Mid-Nineteenth-Century Liberalism in Yucatán, 1855–1876 (1)," *Journal of Caribbean History* 45, no. 1 (2011): 14–15; Magnus, *Das Ende,* 88; Alma J. Durán-Merk, "Identifying

Villa Carlota: German Settlements in Yucatán, México, during the Second Empire (1864–1867)" (Master's thesis, Augsburg, 2007), passim.

71. See *La Sociedad*, December 12, 1866, which reprinted the information from *Journal d'Orizava*, December 7.

72. The anti-Yankee ideals of the revived empire were echoed in Canada. See *Le Journal de Québec*, December 14 and 17, 1866, cited in Larrinaga, "Intervention française au Mexique," 198.

73. Maximilian had discussed with Matthew Maury the possibility of freeing California. See Frances Leigh Williams, *Matthew Fontaine Maury, Scientist of the Sea* (New Brunswick, NJ: Rutgers University Press, 1963), 414.

74. Maximiliano to Joaquín Degollado, Rome, June 28, 1866, BLAC, Joaquín and Mariano Degollado Collection, folder 1, Correspondence, letters from Maximilian, Emperor of Mexico.

75. The French consulate in Galveston suggested that the empire recruit Irish Catholics who had served in the Confederate army. See Vice Consulat de France à Galveston, "Glaveston" [*sic*], January 29, 1866, BLAC, Genaro García, Documentos Relativos a la Reforma y a la Intervención Francesa en México, 83a (2) Intervención Francesa, Documentos misceláneos, 1867–1869.

76. Khevenhüller, *Con Maximiliano*, 82.

77. Decree dissolving the Austro-Belgian units is reproduced in Basch, *Recollections*, 83–84.

78. Khevenhüller, *Con Maximiliano*, 165.

79. Andreas Cornaro, "Österreich und das mexikanische Freikorps," *Mitteilungen des Österreichischen Staatsarchivs* 14 (1961): 74.

80. Belgian soldiers were told they were needed at home. Salm-Salm, *My Diary*, 15.

81. Duchesne, *L'expédition des volontaires*, 620; Basch, *Recollections*, 84–85.

82. Alfred Louis Adolphe Graves Van der Smissen, *Souvenirs du Mexique, 1864–1867, par le général baron Van der Smissen*, . . . (Brussels: J. Lebègue, 1892), 222–229.

83. Charles d'Héricault, *Maximilien et le Mexique: Histoire des derniers mois de l'Empire Mexicain* (Paris: Garnier frères, 1869), 95.

84. For attendees, see Domenech, *Histoire du Mexique*, 411.

85. See Erika Pani, *Para mexicanizar el Segundo Imperio: El imaginario político de los imperialistas* (Mexico: Colegio de México, Centro de Estudios Históricos, 2001); Erika Pani, ed., *La intervención francesa en la revista Historia Mexicana* (Mexico: Colegio De Mexico, 2012).

86. The decision to remain was also bolstered by misinformation. See the memo dated February 1, 1867, AGN, Segundo Imperio, Caja 57, Expediente 49, Gabinete Militar del Emperador, ". . . informes de triunfos obtenidos por mar y tierra contra los disidentes. . . ."

87. For details, see Basch, *Recollections*, 65–66.

88. Magnus, *Das Ende*, 172.

89. For forced loans in Nuevo Léon, see letter from Van der Smissen to Hooricks, Monterey, April 8, 1866, AMBAE, Série B 68 III 1866–1944.

90. Magnus, *Das Ende*, 184.

91. Castelnau had been cautioned by Napoléon III not to force the abdication of Maximilian. See Napoléon III to Castelnau, Paris, January 10, 1867, BLAC, Genaro

García, Documentos Relativos a la Reforma y a la Intervención Francesa en México, 83a (3) Intervención Francesa, Documentos misceláneos, 1867–1869. See also Sara Yorke Stevenson, *Maximilian in Mexico: A Woman's Reminiscences of the French Intervention, 1862–1867* (New York: Century Co., 1899), 248–249.

    92. Lombardo de Miramón, *Memorias*, 532.

13. Querétaro, Capital of Empire

    1. E. Masseras, *Un essai d'empire au Mexique* (Paris, 1879), 150; see also Jack Autrey Dabbs, *The French Army in Mexico, 1861–1867: A Study in Military Government* (The Hague: Mouton, 1963); Felix Salm-Salm, *My Diary in Mexico in 1867: Including the Last Days of the Emperor Maximilian,* 2 vols. (London: R. Bently, 1868), 16.

    2. See handbill "Corps Expéditionnaire du Mexique," February 3, 1867, APRB, BE-A0546/36, Archief Van Felix Eloin, 318 Proclamaties. Pamfletten. Redevoeringen. 1865–1867.

    3. Concepción Lombardo de Miramón, *Memorias de Concepción Lombardo de Miramón* (Mexico: Porrúa, 1989), 540.

    4. Salm-Salm, *My Diary,* 17–18; Lombardo de Miramón, *Memorias,* 540; Masseras, *Un essai d'empire,*157. Blasio renders the remark as "At last we are free!" See José Luis Blasio, *Maximilian, Emperor of Mexico: Memoirs of His Private Secretary, José Luis Blasio,* trans. Robert Hammond Murray (New Haven, CT: Yale University Press, 1934), 127.

    5. Anton von Magnus, *Das Ende des maximilianischen Kaiserreichs in Mexico: Berichte des königlich preussischen Ministerresidenten Anton von Magnus an Bismarck, 1866–1867,* ed. Joachim Kühn (Göttingen: Musterschmidt, 1965), 185.

    6. Samuel Basch, *Recollections of Mexico: The Last Ten Months of Maximilian's Empire,* ed. Fred D. Ullman (Wilmington, DE: Scholarly Resources, 2001), 94–95.

    7. See Basch's notes on the meeting, in Basch, *Recollections,* 96–97.

    8. See letter from Aguascalientes, January 23, 1866, in Lombardo de Miramón, *Memorias,* 535.

    9. Lombardo de Miramón, *Memorias,* 536–537.

    10. See letter dated February 1, 1867, in Lombardo de Miramón, *Memorias,* 538.

    11. Jorge Mario Magallón Ibarra, *Proceso y ejecución vs. Fernando Maximiliano de Habsburgo* (Mexico: Universidad Nacional Autónoma de México, 2005), 288–289; Victor Daran, *Le général Miguel Miramon: Notes sur l'histoire du Mexique* (Rome: E. Perino, 1886), 174–175; Salm-Salm, *My Diary,* 38; José M. Vigil and Vicente Riva Palacio, *México a través de los siglos,* 5 vols. (Mexico City: Herrerias, 1940), 5:815.

    12. *Le Courrier,* a French-language newspaper in the capital, printed a letter of protest from ten French officers in the Imperial Army. See Basch, *Recollections,* 87.

    13. See memo for October 28, 1866, in Magnus, *Das Ende,* 169.

    14. Magallón Ibarra, *Proceso y ejecución,* 621; Brian R. Hamnett, *Juárez* (London: Longman, 1994), 186.

15. Emilio Velasco, ed., *Documentos relativos a la batalla de Santa Gertrudis* (Matamoros: Segura y Ambros, 1866), 133.

16. See Mariano Escobedo to Ignacio Méjia, June 16, 18666 in Velasco, *Documentos relativos*, 91.

17. The letter is reproduced in Vigil and Riva Palacio, *México a través de los siglos*, 5:815; see also Rogelio Orozco Farías, *Fuentes históricas: México, 1821–1867, Documentos y escritos* (Mexico: Editorial Progreso, 1965), 316.

18. Ernst von Tavera cites rumors that Fischer and Prussian ambassador Baron Magnus also promoted the move to Querétaro. See Ernst Schmit von Tavera, *Die mexikanische kaisertragödie: Die letzten sechs monate meines aufenthaltes in Mexiko im jahre 1867* (Vienna: A. Holzhausen, 1903), 13.

19. Vigil and Riva Palacio, *México a través de los siglos*, 5:816.

20. Basch, *Recollections*, 102–103; see also Salm-Salm, *My Diary*, 19–20; Jesús de León Toral, *Historia militar: La intervención francesa en México* (Mexico: Primer Congreso Nacional de Historia Para el Estudio de la Guerra de Intervención, 1962), 63. Concepción Miramón insists it was Márquez; see Lombardo de Miramón, *Memorias*, 542.

21. Basch, *Recollections*, 148–149.

22. This would be announced formally on February 17. Blasio, *Maximilian*, 134.

23. Salm-Salm, *My Diary*, 29; the Prussian representative puts the soldiers at 1,500. See Magnus, *Das Ende*, 204.

24. Duchesne estimates that nine out of ten infantry contingents were "Indians enrolled by force." See Albert Duchesne, *L'expédition des volontaires belges au Mexique, 1864–1867*, 2 vols. (Brussels: Centre d'Histoire Militaire, 1967), 571.

25. Salm-Salm, *My Diary*, 26.

26. Basch, *Recollections*, 113–114; Blasio, *Maximilian*, 134.

27. For proclamation text, see Basch, *Recollections*, 114–115.

28. Magnus, *Das Ende*, 205.

29. Salm-Salm, *My Diary*, 33.

30. See "Viaje de S. M. El Emperador," *La Sociedad*, February 26, 1867.

31. Basch, *Recollections*, 161.

32. For Miramón's accusation of misconduct against Márquez, see his letter to Maximilian in Lombardo de Miramón, *Memorias*, 541; for Márquez's speech, see Basch, *Recollections*, 117–118.

33. Miguel Miramón to Conchita, February 20, 1867, in Lombardo de Miramón, *Memorias*, 545; Theodor Kaehlig, *Geschichte der Belagerung von Querétaro* (Vienna: L.W. Seidel & Sohn, 1879), 13–15; see also Ramón Corona to Benito Juárez, February 23, 1867, and Escobedo to Juárez, February 26, 1867, in Masae Sugawara, ed., *Mariano Escobedo* (Mexico: Senado de la República, 1987), 245–246; Magallón Ibarra, *Proceso y ejecución*, 305, 316.

34. Lombardo de Miramón, *Memorias*, 541; see also Magnus, *Das Ende*, 157; the satirical newspaper *La Orquesta* published the cartoon, see Blasio, 48–49.

35. See "Carta de S. M. El Emperador," in *Boletin de Noticias*, Querétaro, February 26, 1867.

36. See letter from Maximilian to Eloin, Querétaro, February 23, 1867, AMBAE, 13916 Notes from sales catalog of the Parke Burnet Galleries.

37. See *Mexican Times* story reprinted as "La Intervencion francesa y sus resultados" in *Boletin de Noticias,* Querétaro, February 26, 1867.

38. Basch, *Recollections,* 140.

39. Basch, *Recollections,* 143; for "Legion of Honor," see Salm-Salm, *My Diary,* 102; for history of Lincoln Brigade, see Adam Hochschild, *Spain in Our Hearts: Americans in the Spanish Civil War, 1936–1939* (Boston: Houghton Mifflin Harcourt, 2016).

40. Basch, *Recollections,* 169–170.

41. For example, "Por Qué Tanta Sangre?," *El Pájaro Verde,* May 11, 1867.

42. Juárez had suspended *El pájaro verde,* which resumed under the Intervention. See Alfred J. Hanna and Kathryn Abbey Hanna, "The Immigration Movement of the Intervention and Empire as Seen through the Mexican Press," *Hispanic American Historical Review* 27, no. 2 (1947): 224.

43. Masseras, *Un essai d'empire,* 235.

44. For the complete text of Maximilian's instructions, see Basch, *Recollections,* 151–153.

45. Basch, *Recollections,* 152–153.

46. Maximilian also imagined civilians returning with Márquez. See letter from Maximilian to Eloin, March 21, 1867, APRB, BE-A0546/36, Archief Van Felix Eloin, 208 Brieven van keizer Maximilliaan aan Eloin.

47. Lombardo de Miramón, *Memorias,* 558.

48. Salm-Salm, *My Diary,* 87.

49. Reduced to about seventy-six hundred troops. Lombardo de Miramón, *Memorias,* 559.

50. Salm-Salm, *My Diary,* 108–18; Masseras, *Un essai d'empire,* 236.

51. For Márquez after Querétaro, see an undated, unsigned account in Eloin's hand, APRB, BE-A0546/36, Archief Van Felix Eloin, 298 Minuten van brieven en notas van de hand van Eloin, 1863–1867.

52. Gustave Léon Niox, *Expédition du Mexique, 1861–1867: Récit politique & militaire* (Paris: J. Dumaine, 1874), 706.

53. Salm-Salm, *My Diary,* 122.

54. Basch, *Recollections,* 185.

55. Salm-Salm, *My Diary,* 153.

56. Lombardo de Miramón, *Memorias,* 564.

57. There was considerable debate over whether Maximilian was betrayed, an issue too complex to enter into here. See Mariano Escobedo, "Informe del General de División Mariano Escobedo dirigido al Presidente de la República con fecha 8 de julio de 1888," in *Maximiliano y la toma de Querétaro: Documentos coleccionados,* ed. Enrique M. de los Rios (Mexico: Imprenta de las Escalerillas, 1889), 1–15. For the contrary view, see, inter alia, BMNAH, Colección: Imperio de Maximiliano, Documento 484 La toma de Querétaro. See also Juan de Dios Arias, *Reseña histórica de la formación y operaciones del cuerpo de Ejército del Norte durante la intervención francesa* (Mexico City: N. Chávez, 1867), 70; see also "Quién entregó Querétaro?," in Benito Juárez, *Documentos, discursos y correspondencia,* ed. Jorge L. Tamayo, 15 vols. (Mexico: Editorial Libros de México, 1972), 11:1005–1012.

58. Basch, *Recollections,* 199.

59. Blasio, *Maximilian*, 162. Niox called the gesture "un mouvement chevalr-esque"; see Niox, *Expédition du Mexique*, 708.

60. Blasio was with Maximilian in these final hours. His account is used here. See Blasio, *Maximilian*, 164.

61. See reprint of *Monitor Republicano*, August 10, 1889, in Rios, *Maximiliano*, 45; "La Caída de Querétaro, según Juan de Dios Arias," in Juárez, *Documentos, discursos y correspondencia*, 11:1004; Magallón Ibarra, *Proceso y ejecución*, 311.

14. Empire on Trial

1. Pedro Pruneda, *Historia de la guerra de Méjico, desde 1861 á 1867: Con todos los documentos diplomáticos justificativos* (Madrid: Elizalde y compañia, 1867), 428; Jorge Mario Magallón Ibarra, *Proceso y ejecución vs. Fernando Maximiliano de Habsburgo* (Mexico: Universidad Nacional Autónoma de México, 2005), 457.

2. Today it is called the Teatro de la República.

3. The diagnosis was malaria. See Samuel Basch, *Recollections of Mexico: The Last Ten Months of Maximilian's Empire*, ed. Fred D. Ullman (Wilmington, DE: Scholarly Resources, 2001), 20.

4. For the crowd and Maximilian's objections, see Martin de las Torres, *El Archiduque Maximiliano de Austria en Méjico: Historia de los acontecimientos ocurridos en el territorio de Méjico, desde que los españoles desembarcaron en Veracruz formando alianza con los franceses é ingleses, hasta la muerte del infortunado Emperador Maximiliano I* (Madrid: Librería de D.A. de San Martín, 1867), 482–483.

5. Basch, *Recollections*, 12.

6. See letter from Eloin to Maximilian, September 17, 1866, proposing a new "appeal to the people" as a response to the French attempt to organize Maximilian's abdication, APRB, BE-A0546/36, Archief Van Felix Eloin, 208 Brieven van keizer Maximilliaan aan Eloin.

7. Maximilian sent his telegram to Juárez requesting a meeting. Juárez didn't respond. See telegram dated May 26, 1867, in Benito Juárez, *Documentos, discursos y correspondencia*, ed. Jorge L. Tamayo (Mexico: Editorial Libros de México, 1972), 15:16.

8. Charlotte to Maximilian, Rome, September 26, 1866, HRC, MS-2733 080–086.

9. Brian R. Hamnett, *Juárez* (London: Longman, 1994), 177.

10. Concepción Lombardo de Miramón, *Memorias de Concepción Lombardo de Miramón* (Mexico: Porrúa, 1989), 591. Baron Magnus, the Prussian ambassador, seems to have shared this opinion; see Frank G. Weber, "Bismarck's Man in Mexico: Anton von Magnus and the End of Maximilian's Empire," *Hispanic American Historical Review* 46, no. 1 (February 1, 1966): 60.

11. Anton von Magnus, *Das Ende des maximilianischen Kaiserreichs in Mexico: Berichte des königlich preussischen Ministerresidenten Anton von Magnus an Bismarck, 1866–1867*, ed. Joachim Kühn (Göttingen: Musterschmidt, 1965), 169.

12. For the capture and execution of Méndez, see letter from Juárez to Pedro Santacilia dated May 22, 1867, in Juárez, *Documentos, discursos y correspondencia*, 679; for the story of his capture, see Angel Pola, *Los traidores pintados por si mismos* (Mexico: Eduardo Dublan, 1900), 133; Felix Salm-Salm, *My Diary in Mexico*

in 1867: Including the Last Days of the Emperor Maximilian, 2 vols. (London: R. Bently, 1868), 217; Leonardo Márquez, *Manifiestos (El Imperio y Los Imperiales)* (Mexico City: Vazquez, 1904), 219; José Luis Blasio, *Maximilian, Emperor of Mexico; Memoirs of His Private Secretary, José Luis Blasio,* trans. Robert Hammond Murray, (New Haven, CT: Yale University Press, 1934), 170–171.

13. Basch, *Recollections*, 218–219; see also Frederic Hall, *Invasion of Mexico by the French and the Reign of Maximilian I, Late Emperor of Mexico, with a Sketch of the Empress Carlota* (New York: J. Miller, 1868), 197.

14. For the text of the instructions, see Ignacio Méjia to Escobedo, May 21, 1867, in Juárez, *Documentos, discursos y correspondencia,* 15:12–14.

15. Basch, *Recollections*, 213.

16. Magallón Ibarra, *Proceso y ejecución*, 582.

17. See Juárez to Santacilia, May 22, 1867, in Juárez, *Documentos, discursos y correspondencia,* 679.

18. For Hotze, Romero, and Seward, see *Correspondencia de la legación mexicana en Washington con el Ministerio de relaciones exteriores de la república y el Departamento de estado de los Estados-Unidos, sobre la captura, juicio y ejecución de don Fernando Maximiliano de Hapsburgo* (Mexico: Imprenta del Gobierno, 1868), 1:6ff. When Seward intervened with Romero regarding the fate of Maximilian, Romero noted that he did not recall Seward expressing similar concern for Juárez when he risked capture and execution earlier in the war (p. 4.).

19. See Lozada to Corona, May 29, 1867, in Juárez, *Documentos, discursos y correspondencia,* 12:20–22; see also Richard N. Sinkin, *The Mexican Reform, 1855–1876: A Study in Liberal Nation-Building* (Austin: University of Texas, 1979), 110.

20. Lozada's letter is dated May 29, 1867. See Juárez, *Documentos, discursos y correspondencia,* 15:20–22.

21. For Garibaldi, see *Correspondencia de la legación mexicana,* 179–180; for Magnus, see Weber, "Bismarck's Man in Mexico," 65.

22. See letter from Romero to Juárez, June 8, 1867, in Juárez, *Documentos, discursos y correspondencia,* 12:31–32.

23. Lombardo de Miramón, *Memorias*, 588.

24. Magallón Ibarra, *Proceso y ejecución*, 476.

25. Mejía had been identified as an enemy of the Republic years before. See decree of June 4, 1861, in Márquez, *Manifiestos*, 25.

26. Magallón Ibarra, *Proceso y ejecución*, 479.

27. Torres, *El Archiduque Maximiliano*, 482–483.

28. Magallón Ibarra, *Proceso y ejecución*, 482.

29. On the political uses of Anáhuac, see Arturo Chang, "Restoring Anáhuac: Indigenous Genealogies and Hemispheric Republicanism in Postcolonial Mexico," *American Journal of Political Science* 67, no. 3 (July 2023): 718–731.

30. For a recent attempt to rehabilitate the Spanish Habsburgs in a manner consistent with Maximilian's vision, see Fernando Cervantes, *Conquistadores: A New History of Spanish Discovery and Conquest* (London: Penguin, 2021), esp. 371–377.

31. Magallón Ibarra, *Proceso y ejecución*, 502, empire "of six months" at 499.

32. Magallón Ibarra, *Proceso y ejecución*, 513, 518–521.

33. Basch, *Recollections*, 262.

34. On division of labor in Maximilian's defense, see Mariano Riva Palacio, *Memorandum sobre el proceso del archiduque Fernando Maximiliano de Austria* (Mexico: F. Diaz de Leon y S. White, 1867), iii.

35. Magallón Ibarra, *Proceso y ejecución*, 554.

36. Magallón Ibarra, *Proceso y ejecución*, 555.

37. Lombardo de Miramón, *Memorias*, 581.

38. Magallón Ibarra, *Proceso y ejecución*, 562-563.

39. Magallón Ibarra, *Proceso y ejecución*, 564, 565, 571. The deaths were exploited skillfully in the United States to turn public opinion against the empire. See Harford Montgomery Hyde, *Mexican Empire: The History of Maximilian and Carlota of Mexico* (London: Macmillan, 1946), 182; see also Matías Romero, *Correspondencia de la legación mexicana en Washington con el Ministerio de relacions exteriores de la república y el Departamento de estado de los Estados-Unidos, sobre la captura, juicio y ejecución de don Fernando Maximiliano de Hapsburgo* (Mexico City: Imprenta del Gobierno, 1868), 1:58, date June 22, 1867.

40. See "Maximiliano I, Emperador de Mexico," in Romero, *Correspondencia*, 164; on Confederate treatment of captured Black soldiers, see James M. McPherson, *Battle Cry of Freedom: The Civil War Era* (New York: Oxford University Press, 1988), 792-793.

41. For Wirz's boast, see Georges Clemenceau, *American Reconstruction, 1865-1870 and the Impeachment of President Johnson*, trans. Margaret MacVeagh (New York: Dial Press, 1928), 42.

42. Lombardo de Miramón, *Memorias*, 581.

43. Basch, *Recollections*, 246.

44. For efforts to rescue the prisoners, see Magnus, *Das Ende*, 265-267.

45. Benito Juárez, *Documentos, discursos y correspondencia*, 12:159.

46. Lombardo de Miramón, *Memorias*, 602.

47. Juárez, *Documentos, discursos y correspondencia*, 159-163; for Franz Joseph, see Dorothy Gies McGuigan, *The Habsburgs* (Garden City, NY: Doubleday, 1966), 343.

48. See "A Tragic Page of American History," *New Voice*, New York, April 22, 1899, clipping, BLAC, Reminiscencias históricas escritas por el general Mariano Ruiz.

49. Brian R. Hamnett, "Mexican Conservatives, Clericals, and Soldiers: The 'Traitor' Tomás Mejía through Reform and Empire, 1855-1867," *Bulletin of Latin American Research* 20, no. 2 (2001): 205.

50. Eyewitness Father Figueroa, spiritual counselor to Mejía, insists the order was Mejía, Miramón, Maximilian, their order of arrival at the place of execution. See *Semanario Literario Ilustrado* for June 17, 1901.

51. Lombardo de Miramón, *Memorias*, 943.

15. Leaving Mexico

1. For Márquez after Querétaro, see an undated, unsigned account in Eloin's hand, APRB, BE-A0546/36, Archief Van Felix Eloin, 298 Minuten van brieven en notas van de hand van Eloin: minuten van brieven en nota's van Eloin aan de keizer en aan allerlei personen of nota's die tot op memorandum gediend hebben, 1863-1867.

2. José M. Vigil and Vicente Riva Palacio, *México a través de los siglos* 5 vols. (Mexico City: Herrerias, 1940), 5:826.

3. Díaz had retaken Oaxaca in the fall, before moving on to Puebla in the spring. See Gustave Léon Niox, *Expédition du Mexique, 1861–1867: Récit politique & militaire* (Paris: J. Dumaine, 1874), 706; for Márquez's rationale, see Leonardo Márquez, *Manifiestos (El Imperio y Los Imperiales)* (Mexico City: Vazquez, 1904), 44–45; see also Juan de Dios Arias, *Reseña histórica de la formación y operaciones del cuerpo de Ejército del Norte durante la intervención francesa* (Mexico: N. Chávez, 1867), 653ff.

4. For Díaz's account of his actions, see letter of May 3, 1867, in Matías Romero, *Correspondencia de la legación mexicana en Washington con el Ministerio de relacions exteriores de la república y el Departamento de estado de los Estados-Unidos, sobre la captura, juicio y ejecución de don Fernando Maximiliano de Hapsburgo* (Mexico City: Imprenta del Gobierno, 1868), 1:87–90.

5. Felix Salm-Salm, *My Diary in Mexico in 1867: Including the Last Days of the Emperor Maximilian,* 2 vols. (London: R. Bently, 1868), 5–6; Ritter Ernst Schmit von Tavera, *Die mexikanische kaisertragödie: Die letzten sechs monate meines aufenthaltes in Mexiko im jahre 1867* (Vienna: A. Holzhausen, 1903), 42.

6. Salm-Salm, *My Diary,* 309.

7. Tavera, *Die mexikanische kaisertragödie,* 51–52.

8. See "Parte Oficial," *Diario del Imperio,* June 10, 1867.

9. Tavera, *Die mexikanische kaisertragödie,* 51.

10. See Díaz to Romero, May 26, 1867, in Benito Juárez, *Documentos, discursos y correspondencia,* ed. Jorge L. Tamayo, 15 vols. (Mexico: Editorial Libros de México, 1972), 12:45.

11. See "Querétaro," *El Pájaro Verde,* May 23, 1867, 4.

12. Manuel Ramírez de Arellano, *Ultimas horas del imperio* (Mexico City: Tipografía Mexicana, 1869), 167–171.

13. Conchita Miramón regarded Márquez as motivated by revenge here, too. Concepción Lombardo de Miramón, *Memorias de Concepción Lombardo de Miramón* (Mexico: Porrúa, 1989), 586; for fictions, see, for example, letter from Dolores Hidalgo to Angel Pola, November 10, 1891, in Márquez, *Manifiestos,* 341.

14. Salm-Salm, *My Diary,* 313. Márquez actively promoted such beliefs; see Ramírez de Arellano, *Ultimas horas del imperio,* 167–169.

15. Ramírez de Arellano, *Ultimas horas del imperio,* 173–174.

16. Salm-Salm, *My Diary,* 321–322.

17. See "El Imperio vivirá," *Diario del Imperio,* June 10, 1867.

18. See Bazaine to Comité Superieur de Matehuala, September 30, 1866, BLAC, Achille Bazaine Papers G500, Correspondencia de Achille François Bazaine, 1862–1867.

19. Pedro Pruneda, *Historia de la guerra de Méjico, desde 1861 á 1867: Con todos los documentos diplomáticos justificativos* (Madrid: Elizalde y compañia, 1867), 399.

20. *El Cronista de México* and *El Pájaro Verde* for February 11, 1867, cited in Porfirio Díaz, *Archivo del general Porfirio Díaz, memorias y documentos,* vol. 1 (Mexico: Elede, 1947), 343. On *El Pájaro Verde,* see Kristine Ibsen, *Maximilian, Mexico, and the Invention of Empire* (Nashville, TN: Vanderbilt University Press, 2010), 46.

21. Hooricks, Belgian Legation Mexico, to Charles Rogier (Minister, Brussels), Mexico, June 28, 1866, and November 29, 1866, AMBAE, Série B 68 III 1866–1944.

22. "Journal rédigé par le Lieutenant Romignon de la Légion étrangère," SHD, GR 7 G Expédition du Mexique, 87 Contre-guérilla du colonel Dupin, Historique, Siège de Mexico, 1863–1867.

23. See Ministro de Guerra, México, Orizaba, January 19, 1867, ÖStA KA, Archive der Truppenkörper, 19 Mexiko Österreichisch-belgisches Freiwilligenkorps in Mexiko, 1864–1867, 19 Exhibiten-Protocoll für geheime Correspondenz.

24. A group of one thousand volunteers was canceled after the US ambassador to Vienna threatened to break diplomatic relations if the enrollment went forward. See Egon Caesar Corti, *Maximilian and Charlotte of Mexico*, trans. Catherine Alison Phillips (New York: Knopf, 1928), 620.

25. La Tour Du Pin, *Traversées de France au Mexique et du Mexique en France* (Paris: Paul Dupont, 1868), 1.

26. For back pay, see undated memo and roster, ÖStA KA, Archive der Truppenkörper, 19 Mexiko Österreichisch-belgisches Freiwilligenkorps in Mexiko, 1864–1867, 19 Exhibiten-Protocoll für geheime Correspondenz.

27. Anton von Magnus, *Das Ende des maximilianischen Kaiserreichs in Mexico: Berichte des königlich preussischen Ministerresidenten Anton von Magnus an Bismarck, 1866–1867*, ed. Joachim Kühn (Göttingen: Musterschmidt, 1965), 211–212.

28. La Tour Du Pin, *Traversées de France*, 28–31.

29. See État nominatif des militaires francais appartenant à l'armée mexicaine faits prisonniers à Queretaro le 15 Mai 1867 et retenus encore au Mexique, SHD, GR 7 G Expédition du Mexique, 92 Troupes à laisser au gouvernement mexicain, Légion étrangère, Prisonniers mexicains, militaires autorisés à rester au Mexique, Demandes de renforts, Cadres de détachement, 1866.

30. See État rectificatif, 51eme Regiment d'infanterie de ligne, SHD, GR 7 G Expédition du Mexique, 92 Troupes à laisser au gouvernement mexicain, Légion étrangère, Prisonniers mexicains, militaires autorisés à rester au Mexique, Demandes de renforts, Cadres de détachement, 1866.

31. Carl Khevenhüller, *Con Maximiliano en México: Del diario del príncipe Carl Khevenhüller, 1864–1867*, ed. Brigitte Hamann (Mexico: Fondo de Cultura Económica, 1994), 171.

32. Edmund Daniek, *Sie zogen nach Mexiko: Ein Denkmal für die österreichischen Freiwilligen unter Kaiser Maximilian, 1864–1867* (Vienna: Amalthea, 1964), 109; see also M. le Ministre de Württemberg à Paris, May 25, 1867, SHD, GR 7 G Expédition du Mexique, 95 Contingents belges et autrichiens, Rapatriement de l'armée, 1866.

33. Andreas Cornaro, "Österreich und das mexikanische Freikorps," *Mitteilungen des Österreichischen Staatsarchivs* 14 (1961): 75; Daniek, *Sie zogen nach Mexiko*, 92.

34. Albert Duchesne, *L'expédition des volontaires belges au Mexique 1864–1867*, 2 vols. (Brussels: Centre d'Histoire Militaire, 1967), 740.

35. For Kodolitsch, see *Militär-Schematismus für 1887* (Wien: K. K. Hof- und Staatsdruckerei, 1886), 31, in Ancestry.com.

36. See Ambassade d'Autriche, Paris, September 30, 1867, SHD, GR 7 G Expédition du Mexique, 95 Contingents belges et autrichiens, Rapatriement de l'armée,

1866; for Italy, see in same box Ministre des Affaires Etrangères to Ministre de la Guerre, Paris, November 12, 1867.

37. Josef Wiedenhofer, "Die öffentliche Meinung in Österreich zum Abenteuer Kaiser Maximilians I. von Mexiko" (diss., University of Vienna, 1979), 150.

38. Wiedenhofer, "Die öffentliche Meinung," 152.

39. Cornaro, "Österreich," 77.

40. See "Kaiser Maximilian," *Neue Frei Presse*, July 1, 1867.

41. For the wordplay, see Wiedenhofer, "Die öffentliche Meinung," 152; "keiner" in Austrian dialect is pronounced "kaner," hence, "mog sie keiner." I'm grateful to Rainer Huber for help solving this riddle.

42. Wiedenhofer, "Die öffentliche Meinung," 151.

43. Wiedenhofer, "Die öffentliche Meinung," 153.

44. Duchesne, *L'expédition des volontaires*, 720.

45. Imperial Mexico had planned an exhibit at the Exposition. See "Para la exposición universal en Paris de 1867," APRB, BE-A0546/36, Impératrice Charlotte du Mexique, 159 Teksten van politieke aard: mémoire remis par moi à l'Empereur Napoléon à St-Cloud le 11 août 1866, met een kopie van dit memorandum en bijlagen. Mexico was represented unofficially. See Christiane Demeulenaere-Douyère, "Expositions internationales et image nationale: Les pays d'Amérique latine entre pittoresque 'indigène' et modernité proclamée," *Diacronie. Studi di Storia Contemporanea* 18, no. 2 (July 8, 2014): 10–12; *Exposition Universelle de 1867 Illustrée*, 1867, 46–47.

46. See SHD, GR 7 G Expédition du Mexique, 95 Contingents belges et autrichiens, Rapatriement de l'armée, 1866.

47. Harry Thayer Mahoney and Marjorie Locke Mahoney, *Mexico and the Confederacy, 1860–1867* (San Francisco: Austin and Winfield, 1998), 169.

48. See Montluc to Juárez, in Léon de Montluc, ed., *Correspondance de Juarez et de Montluc, ancien consul général du Mexique: Accompagnée de nombreuses lettres de personnages politiques, relatives à l'expédition du Mexique* (France: Charpentier, 1885), 221–222.

49. See letter from Labastida to Antonelli, Havana, March 9, 1867, in Luis Ramos, María Guadalupe Bosch de Souza, Ana María González Luna, and Archivio vaticano, *Del Archivo secreto vaticano: La Iglesia y el estado mexicano en el siglo XIX* (Mexico, DF: Universidad Nacional Autónoma de México, 1997), 459–460.

50. José Luis Blasio, *Maximilian, Emperor of Mexico: Memoirs of His Private Secretary, José Luis Blasio,* trans. Robert Hammond Murray (New Haven, CT: Yale University Press, 1934), 221.

51. Tom Russell, "Adventures of a Cordova Colonist," *Southern Magazine* 4 (August 1872): 92–98.

52. George D. Harmon, "Confederate Migration to Mexico," *Hispanic American Historical Review* 17, no. 4 (1937): 471.

53. Alexander Watkins Terrell, *From Texas to Mexico and the Court of Maximilian in 1865* (Dallas: Book Club of Texas, 1933), 29–30.

54. Mary Virginia Edwards, *Shelby's Expedition to Mexico, an Unwritten Leaf of the War* (Kansas City, MO: J. Edwards, 1889), 105.

55. W. C. Nunn, *Escape from Reconstruction* (Westport, CT: Greenwood Press, 1974), 110.

56. Wiedenhofer, "Die öffentliche Meinung," 204–205.

57. Magnus, *Das Ende*, 222n.

58. See "Princess Salm-Salm Is Here," *Iowa State Register,* May 4, 1899, BLAC, Reminiscencias históricas escritas por el general Mariano Ruiz.

59. He was peppered with requests for back pay that he could not fulfill. See letter from Eloin to Fischer, February 28, 1867, BE-A0546/36, Archief Van Felix Eloin, 247 Brieven aan Eloin gericht door: Augustin Fischer, adviseur van keizer Maximilliaan, 1866–1867.

60. Samuel Basch, *Recollections of Mexico: The Last Ten Months of Maximilian's Empire,* ed. Fred D. Ullman (Wilmington, DE: Scholarly Resources, 2001), 59.

61. Ramos et al., *Del Archivo secreto vaticano,* 531–532.

62. Magnus, *Das Ende*, 330–332.

63. In addition to Magnus, *Das Ende,* see Wiedenhofer, "Die öffentliche Meinun," 207.

Epilogue

1. Staatsarchiv Hamburg, Hamburg, Germany, Hamburger Passagierlisten, vols. 373–37 I, VIII A 1 Band 149, page 2869, microfilm no. K_1782, available on Ancestry.com.

2. *El Imparcial,* March 12, 1901, ÖSta, Ministerium des Äußerns, PA XXXIV 12-2, Liasse I: Sühnkapelle in Queretaro, 1898–1901; on his pharmacy and calle Espíritu Santo, see also Enrique M. de los Rios and Mariano Escobedo, *Maximiliano y la toma de Queretaro: Documentos coleccionados* (Mexico: Imprenta de las Escalerillas, 1889), 124.

3. Benito Reyes, *Benito Juárez: Ensayo sobre un carácter* (Madrid: Ediciones Nuestra raza, 1935), 151; Jacqueline Covo, "L'image de Juárez dans la presse française à l'époque de l'intervention au Mexique (1862–1867)," *Bulletin hispanique* 73, no. 3 (1971): 387; Brian R Hamnett, "La Ejecución del Emperador Maximiliano de Habsburgo y el Republicanismo Mexicano," in *Historia y nación (actas del Congreso en homenaje a Josefina Zoraida Vázquez)* (Mexico: Collegio de Mexico, 1998), 239; Matías Romero, *Correspondencia de la legación mexicana en Washington con el Ministerio de relacions exteriores de la república y el Departamento de estado de los Estados-Unidos, sobre la captura, juicio y ejecución de don Fernando Maximiliano de Hapsburgo* (Mexico City: Imprenta del Gobierno, 1868), 1:178; Erika Pani, *El Segundo Imperio: Pasados de usos múltiples* (Mexico: Centro de Investigación y Docencia Económicas, 2004), 55.

4. See Detail Programm, ÖSta, OMeA, NZA 32-1 Ableben von Kaiser Maximilian von Mexiko; Frederic Hall, *Invasion of Mexico by the French and the Reign of Maximilian I, Late Emperor of Mexico, with a Sketch of the Empress Carlota* (New York: J. Miller, 1868), 311–113; E. Masseras, *Un essai d'empire au Mexique* (Paris: Charpentier, 1879), 371–372.

5. Ramírez de Arellano, *Ultimas horas del imperio* (Mexico City: Tipografía Mexicana, 1869), lvii–lviii; Felix Salm-Salm, *My Diary in Mexico in 1867: Including the Last Days of the Emperor Maximilian,* 2 vols. (London: R. Bently, 1868), 2:127–128, 313; Concepción Lombardo de Miramón, *Memorias de Concepción Lombardo de*

Miramón (Mexico: Porrúa, 1989), 614; Victor Daran, *Le général Miguel Miramon: Notes sur l'histoire du Mexique* (Rome: E. Perino, 1886), 212n; Ritter Ernst Schmit von Tavera, *Die mexikanische kaisertragödie: Die letzten sechs monate meines aufenthaltes in Mexiko im jahre 1867* (Vienna: A. Holzhausen, 1903), 127–130; Benito Juárez, *Documentos, discursos y correspondencia,* ed. Jorge L. Tamayo, 15 vols. (México: Editorial Libros de México, 1972), 12:305–306.

6. See "Juzgado de Distrito. Causa instruida al Dr. Vicente Licéa," in *Derecho Periódico de Jurisprudencia y Legislacion,* vol. 4, February 19, 1870, 147–155.

7. See Fahr-Ordnung, Separat Zug, in ÖSta, OMeA, NZA 32-1 Ableben von Kaiser Maximilian von Mexiko.

8. See "Leichenfeier des Kaisers Maximilian," *Konstitutionelle Volks-Zeitung,* January 19, 1868.

9. Richard Blaas, "Die Gedächtniskapelle in Querétaro und die Wiederherstellung der diplomatischen Beziehungen zwischen Österreich-Ungarn und Mexiko," *Mitteilungen des österreichischen Staatsarchivs,* 1955, 193.

10. Anon., "Aniversario, 19 de Junio de 1867," *Semanario Literario Ilustrado,* June 17, 1901, 287.

11. Tavera, *Die mexikanische kaisertragödie,* 134.

12. For *momuxtles* and Emilia Soto, see Anon., "Aniversario," 288.

13. Josef Wiedenhofer, "Die öffentliche Meinung in Osterreich zum Abenteuer Kaiser Maximilians 1. von Mexiko" (diss., Vienna, Vienna, 1979), 209.

14. The ceremony also honored the memory of Miramón, Mejía, and Méndez. Invitations for 1906, 1911, 1913, and 1914 can be found in BLAC, Joaquín and Mariano Degollado Collection, folder 3, Correspondence, invitations, memorials, 1861–1914. In later years the service was held at the Colegio de Niñas chapel.

15. See "13 Años después," in *La Voz de México,* June 19, 1880; see also Enrique M. de los Rios, ed., *Maximiliano y la toma de Queretaro: Documentos coleccionados* (Mexico: Imprenta de las Escalerillas, 1889), 65.

16. See testimony of Mariano Lara, dated June 28, 1867, Mexico, BLAC, Genaro García, Documentos Relativos a la Reforma y a la Intervención Francesa en México, 81b Intervención Francesa, Documentos misceláneos, 1862–1867. On the debate surrounding López, see also Mariano Escobedo, "Informe del General de División Mariano Escobedo dirigido al Presidente de la República con fecha 8 de julio de 1888," in *Maximiliano y la toma de Queretaro: Documentos coleccionados,* ed. Enrique M. de los Rios (Mexico: Imprenta de las Escalerillas, 1889), 1–15; BMNAH, Colección: Imperio de Maximiliano, Documento, 484 La toma de Querétaro. See also Juan de Dios Arias, *Reseña histórica de la formación y operaciones del cuerpo de Ejército del Norte durante la intervención francesa* (Mexico City: N. Chávez, 1867), 70; see also "Quién entregó Querétaro?," in Benito Juárez, *Documentos, discursos y correspondencia,* ed. Jorge L. Tamayo, vol. 11 (México: Editorial Libros de México, 1972), 1005–1012.

17. The hunt for locks of hair and other relics began immediately. See criticism by Félix Eloin, Enseñanza, September 12, 1867, AMBAE, 13916 Notes from sales catalog of the Parke Burnet Galleries. A parallel phenomenon occurred in Europe, especially Austria. For photos, see, for example, "Interessante Neuigkeiten! Photographische Porträts: Kaiser Maximilian und Kaiserin Charlotte von Mexico," *Neue Freie Presse,* July 13, 1867, 11.

18. Kaska made his fortune as a pharmaceutical wholesaler in Mexico. See "Abschrift des Prinzen Fürstenberg an Sections-Chef Grafen Szécsen, Mexico, 23 März 1901," ÖSta, Ministerium des Äußerns, PA XXXIV Mexiko, 12-2 Liasse I: Sühnkapelle in Queretaro, 1898–1901.

19. ÖSta, Ministerium des Äußerns, PA XXXIV Mexiko, 12-2 Liasse I: Sühnkapelle in Queretaro, 1898–1901, "Dr. F. Kaska Mexico den 30 Oktober 1900."

20. Paul H. Garner, *Porfirio Díaz* (New York: Longman, 2001), 26, 220.

21. Garner, *Porfirio Díaz*, 102; Jorge Fernando Iturribarria, "La política de conciliación del general Díaz y el arzobispo Gillow," *Historia Mexicana* 14, no. 1 (1964): 81–101.

22. Blaas, "Die Gedächtniskapelle," 196.

23. Blaas, "Die Gedächtniskapelle," 198–199.

24. Kaska was accompanied by another Austrian/Mexican, Mr. Lorenz, a resident of Puebla, described as "uno de los miembros mas distinguidos de la colonia austriaca en México"; *El Imparcial*, March 12, 1901.

25. ÖSta, Ministerium des Äußerns, PA XXXIV Mexiko, 12-2, Liasse I: Sühnkapelle in Querétaro, 1898–1901.

26. Ernst Pitner, *Maximilian's Lieutenant: A Personal History of the Mexican Campaign, 1864–7*, trans. Gordon Etherington-Smith (Albuquerque: University of New Mexico Press, 1993), 186, 190, 198–199; Theodor Kaehlig, *Geschichte der Belagerung von Querétaro* (Vienna: L.W. Seidel & Sohn, 1879), 115; Charles d'Héricault, *Maximilien et le Mexique: Histoire des derniers mois de l'Empire Mexicain* (Paris: Garnier frères, 1869), 285.

27. "im Vertrauen einem Freunde wie Sie einen Wink zu geben": see Díaz to Khevenhüller October 15, 1900. ÖSta, Ministerium des Äußerns, PA XXXIV Mexiko, 12-2, Liasse I: Sühnkapelle in Querétaro, 1898–1901.

28. Fernando Núñez, Carlos Arvizu, and Ramón Abonce, *Space and Place in the Mexican Landscape: The Evolution of a Colonial City* (College Station: Texas A&M University Press, 2007), 104; Blaas, "Die Gedächtniskapelle," 200b.

29. See "Fürsten Khevenhüller ruf eine Pietà," Vienna, July 19, 1900, ÖSta, Ministerium des Äußerns, PA XXXIV Mexiko, 12-2, Liasse I: Sühnkapelle in Querétaro, 1898–1901.

30. Blaas, "Die Gedächtniskapelle," 220.

31. See "Austria Princes: Noted Foreigners Received with Every Honor," *Mexican Herald*, March 13, 1901, ÖSta, Ministerium des Äußerns, PA XXXIV Mexiko, 12-2, Liasse I: Sühnkapelle in Querétaro, 1898–1901.

32. For the ceremony and the aftermath, see Max Ahlschier, "Die Einweihung der Maximilian-Kapelle in Querétaro," April 12, 1904, ÖSta, Ministerium des Äußerns, PA XXXIV Mexiko, 12-2, Liasse I: Sühnkapelle in Querétaro, 1898–1901.

33. For the cross, see Altschier, "Die Einweihung der Maximilian-Kapelle," and Anon., "Aniversario," 288.

34. On peso/dollar conversion, see Miguel Ángel González-Quiroga, "Conflict and Cooperation in the Making of Texas- Mexico Border Society, 1840–1880," in *Bridging National Borders in North America*, ed. Benjamin Johnson and Andrew R. Graybill (Durham, NC: Duke University Press, 2010), 55.

35. See Abschrift eines Memorandums des Grafen Hohenwart aus dem Jahre 1904: Die Erinnerungs-Kapelle zu Querétaro, ÖSta, Ministerium des Äußerns, PA XXXIV Mexiko, 12-2, Liasse I: Sühnkapelle in Querétaro, 1898–1901.

36. Blaas, "Die Gedächtniskapelle," 213.

37. See letter from Giskra to Lexa von Aehrenthal, July 23, 1907, Mexico, ÖSta, Ministerium des Äußerns, PA XXXIV Mexiko, 12-2, Liasse I: Sühnkapelle in Querétaro, 1898–1901.

38. Blaas, "Die Gedächtniskapelle," 210–211.

39. Notaria Publica N. 47 y de Hacienda Lic. Manuel Borja Soriano, ÖSta, Ministerium des Äußerns, PA XXXIV Mexiko, 12-2, Liasse I: Sühnkapelle in Querétaro, 1898–1901.

40. The press certainly was full of reminders of Habsburg tragedies. See "Die Blutzeugen des Hauses Habsburg," *Illustrierter Hans Jörgel von Gumpoldskirchen (Volksschrift im Wiener Dialekte),* January 18, 1868.

Acknowledgments

Transnational history—history that transcends a single national frame, the kind of history found on these pages—can only happen thanks to hundreds of scholars and local specialists whose work provides a learned foundation. May my profound gratitude find its way to them through these pages.

Research for this book took place in Mexico, Europe, and the United States. Research requires travel and travel takes money. Startup funding from the University of Washington Royalty Research Fund got me to archives, libraries, and museums of Mexico, not only in the capital but elsewhere, too, including Veracruz, Puebla, and Querétaro. The same funding source made possible travel to archives and museums in Brussels and a visit to Seville, where Maximilian was profoundly moved walking in the footsteps of his Spanish Habsburg ancestors. A fellowship from the Botstiber Institute for Austrian-American Studies gave me time in Vienna at the Österreichisches Staatsarchiv and the Kriegsarchiv, as well as time to visit relevant museums, churches, and crypts. A stint as Andrew W. Mellon Foundation Research Fellow at the Harry Ransom Center of the University of Texas, Austin, provided access to the Maximilian and Charlotte correspondence. While resident in Austin, I was also able to work with the extraordinary materials at the Nettie Lee Benson Latin American Collection, where Michael Hironymous, José Montelongo, and Carla Alvarez provided guidance. Austin was also base of operations for forays to sites in the US/Mexico borderlands as well as to the collections of the Woodson Research Center in the Fondren Library at Rice University, where Rebecca Russell presides as archivist and librarian. Able leadership in the History Department at the University of Washington—Anand Yang and Glennys Young—meant that support for research was never lacking.

The Donald W. Wiethuechter Endowed Faculty Fellowship, the Joff Hanauer Endowed Faculty Fellowship, the Jon Bridgman Endowed Professorship, and the Howard and Frances Keller fund of the History Department of the University of Washington supported travel to Paris to work in the Archives nationales, the Archives diplomatiques, and the military archives at Vincennes.

Scholarly support also comes in the form of attentive listening and sound advice. Adam Warren and Tony Lucero, colleagues at the University of Washington, helped me to get my bearings in the history of Mexico. Lynn Thomas was an early advocate; Lynn Hunt has been a lifelong inspiration. Alem Kebede and Gonzalo Santos of California State University Bakersfield asked thoughtful questions as the project germinated. Larry Winnie, Ed Countryman, Bianca Lopez, John Chávez, Erin Hochman, Andrew Graybill, and the other members of the Stanton Sharp Symposium at Southern Methodist University offered a pleasant forum in which to try out ideas as the project matured. Yearlong membership in the Society of Scholars at the University of Washington Walter Chapin Simpson Center for the Humanities, ably directed by Kathleen Woodward and Rachel Arteaga, gave me time to write. María Elena García and the other members of the Society of Scholars seminar offered supportive readings of portions of the manuscript as a work in progress, as did the University of Washington History Colloquium, organized by Jorge Bayona and Adam Warren.

Research breakthroughs came about owing to timely expert support. Ann Rosentreter, archivist at the Jesuit Archives of the Central United States, helped me run down one of Augustín Fischer's more outrageous claims. Reading Maximilian's crabbed hand sometimes felt like an exercise in code breaking; Michael Neininger, colleague in Germanics, transcribed Maximilian's letters into legible German. Minh Phan and Henry Grandy scrubbed Belgian recruitment data, making the map of European volunteers possible. Isabelle Lewis turned my draft maps into lovely maps worthy of print. Hoang Ngo compiled a roster of relevant Mexican newspapers. Brandon Guglielmetti waded through the *New York Times* and *New York Herald* flagging key articles. Rainer Huber decoded Austrian wordplay. Julian Divine drew my attention to the importance of *La Voz de Méjico* as a vehicle for Mexican American mobilization. Mark Jonas helped me to recognize the perverse humanity of some of the characters.

Two anonymous readers for Harvard University Press produced generous and insightful commentary on the manuscript. Their suggestions informed a crucial final revision. I thank them cordially here for their critical collegiality. Finding such colleagues is the mark of a diligent and wise editor. This is my second book with Kathleen McDermott at Harvard. I cannot imagine a steadier collaborator and guide. Aaron Wistar, editorial assistant, provided timely nudges and technical support.

Most of the research for this book was completed before COVID set in and libraries and archives shut down, but there are always sources one must see in the writing stage. Theresa Mudrock of the Suzzallo Library at the University of Washington found things for me when no one else could. Deb Raftus, also of Suzzallo Library, came to the rescue with a resource I had missed. COVID shutdowns turned our home into a schoolhouse. Lucca Ravi Jonas—and morning recess—were welcome parts of the writing routine. Patricia Scarlett Jonas, Anthony and Krissy Jonas, Elizabeth Jonas and Melvin Tse, and Katherine Jonas and Daniel Strecker provided joy and companionship throughout.

Index

Page references set in *italics* refer to illustrative material, maps, and photographs.

Ludwig Victor (Archduke, brother to
Maximilian), 85, 150
Lutheranism, 125

Magnus, Anton von (Baron), 237
Magruder, John, *170*, 175–176
Mahan, Alfred Thayer, 19
Majoma, 139–140
Maler, Teobert, 153
Manchester Guardian (newspaper), 29
Manifest Destiny, 5, 10, 21
maps, *59*, *84*, *160–161*, *172*, *226*
Marie Antoinette, 270
Mariscal, Ignacio, 269
Márquez, Leonardo: as ally, 60; evacua-
tion from Mexico, 254; fragility of
forces, 71; and Maximilian, 211,
224, 228; military career, 45–46, 53,
61–62, 209, 245–247; and Querétaro,
223–224, 227–230
Marseillaise (song), 43
Martinez, Paula, 166
Martínez, Teófilo, 73
Martinez de la Torre, Rafael, 56, 239
Marx, Karl, 31
Masson, Réné, 66–67
Matamoros, 138–139, 176, 179–187, 208
Maury, Matthew Fontaine, 1–4, 96,
168–171, 175, 177
Maximilian (emperor of Mexico): capture
of, 54; death of, 243–244, 257–260,
270; and Escobedo, 231, 234–235; and
Fischer, 127, 208, 255; and Juárez, 227,
234, 236, 239; and Lares, 219–221,
228; and Latin America (vision of), 7;
laws from, 177–178; legacy, 153, 251,
257–258, 261–266, 267, 268; letters
from Pope Pius, 121–122; letters to
Degollado, 130–131; letters to Escudero,
123–124; letters to Gutiérrez, 120,
129; and Márquez, 224; marriage to
Charlotte, 76–78, 82, 84; and Maury,
3–4; as Mexican, 233–234; and military
recruitment, 155, 176–177; modern
vision of, 81–82; Napoléon III's preference for, 29; and nation building, 5;

perceptions of, 90–91, 99, 112–113,
224–225; personal characteristics,
224–225; personal life, 201, 204–205;
personal pride, 81, 87, 91, 100, 189,
211, 220, 227; political life, 87–88,
90, 92–97, 112–113, 190, 202–204,
206–211, 213–214, 216–217, 219–220,
224; political power, 124–125, 128–129;
portraits of, *94*, *233*; and Querétaro,
221–232; and refugees, 80; as royalty,
98–116, 166, 227, 239, 241; as savior,
9, 105–106; self-image of, 135; support
for, 75; travels, 147; trial of, 232–244,
243, 246–247. *See also* Maximilian
and Charlotte
Maximilian and Charlotte: and Bazaine,
131, 202; church/state relations, 123;
and clergy reform, 124–125; enemies of,
117; and Indigenous Mexicans, 133–137;
and Labastida, 120, 190; legacy of,
270; letters between, 196–197; military
recruitment, 147–148, 150–151; military
supervision, 188; and Napoléon III,
202–203; and Pope Pius, 121–122; and
populism, 204; portraits of, 135–137;
reception of, 123; relationships with
Mexican notables, 126; as royalty, 90,
94–95, 147, 192; and US, 168. *See also*
Charlotte (Empress, wife of Maximilian);
Maximilian (emperor of Mexico)
Mazatlán, 138, 143–146
McLellan, George, 110
Medellín, 45, 143
Meglia, Pedro Francisco, 120–125, 193
Mejía, Tomás: and forced loans, 214;
legacy, 265–266; and Matamoros,
181–184, 187; military career, 139;
portraits of, *133*, *233*; and Querétaro,
71, 229–231, 236–244; volunteers for,
208
memorials, 260–261. *See also* death
Méndez, Ramón, 218, 223, 229–230,
234
Mercure (French vessel), 25
mestizo peoples, 8, 20–21, 244
Mexican Americans, 166–168